Contested Transformation

Race, Gender, and Political Leadership
in 21st Century America

CAROL HARDY-FANTA
University of Massachusetts Boston

PEI-TE LIEN
University of California, Santa Barbara

DIANNE PINDERHUGHES
University of Notre Dame

CHRISTINE MARIE SIERRA
University of New Mexico

CAMBRIDGE
UNIVERSITY PRESS

CAMBRIDGE
UNIVERSITY PRESS

One Liberty Plaza, 20th Floor, New York, NY 10006, USA

Cambridge University Press is part of the University of Cambridge.

It furthers the University's mission by disseminating knowledge in the pursuit of education, learning, and research at the highest international levels of excellence.

www.cambridge.org
Information on this title: www.cambridge.org/9780521144544

© Carol Hardy-Fanta, Pei-te Lien, Dianne Pinderhughes, and Christine Marie Sierra 2016

First published 2016

Printed in the United States of America by Sheridan Books, Inc. in 2016

A catalogue record for this publication is available from the British Library.

Library of Congress Cataloging-in-Publication Data
Names: Hardy-Fanta, Carol, 1948– author.
Title: Contested transformation : race, gender, and political leadership in 21st century America / Carol Hardy-Fanta, Pei-te Lien, Dianne Pinderhughes, Christine Marie Sierra.
Description: New York: Cambridge University Press, 2016. |
Includes bibliographical references and index.
Identifiers: LCCN 2016028357| ISBN 9780521196437 (hard back) |
ISBN 9780521144544 (paper back)
Subjects: LCSH: Political participation – United States. |
Women – Political activity – United States. | Minorities – Political activity – United States. | Cultural pluralism – United States. |
United States – Politics and government. | United States – Race relations. |
United States – Social conditions.
Classification: LCC JK1764.H363 2016 | DDC 320.973–dc23
LC record available at https://lccn.loc.gov/2016028357

ISBN 978-0-521-19643-7 Hardback
ISBN 978-0-521-14454-4 Paperback

To our mothers
HELEN ARAUJO SIERRA
1919–2015
SUE M. HARDY
1913–2013
ROSA C. PINDERHUGHES
1918–2012
YU-CHENG CHANG LIEN
1928–2006

Contents

Figures

Maps

Tables

Boxes

Acknowledgments

As co-principal investigators of a research project of this scope and duration, we have numerous colleagues and friends to thank. Forgive us if this list of acknowledgments is incomplete. We have enjoyed and benefited from the advice, support, and encouragement of many people along the way, in and outside of academia.

The Gender and Multicultural Leadership (GMCL) Project would not have come to fruition without a generous grant from the Ford Foundation. We express special thanks to our program officers, not only for the funding that made this project possible, but also for their genuinely enthusiastic support. We begin by acknowledging Jacqueline Berrien, Ford Program Officer for Participation and Representation in American Politics, who passed away in 2015. We especially appreciated the warm relationship we developed with Jackie along the way; we are greatly saddened by her untimely death.

Program officers also instrumental in providing foundation support include Gertrude Fraser, Higher Education; Sara Ríos, Racial Justice and Minority Rights; and Barbara Y. Phillips, Women's Rights and Gender Equity. Initial conversations with Ford Foundation officers extend to years preceding the grant. Marcia Smith, June Zeitlin, and Srilatha Batliwala deserve thanks for encouraging us to move forward with the initial proposals.

Origins of this project are traceable to the early 1990s, when several of us as colleagues and scholars brainstormed on how to further the study of women of color in politics, within and across our respective disciplines. On the ground floor of these discussions were Adaljiza Sosa-Riddell (University of California Davis) and Paule Cruz-Takash (University of

California San Diego and Los Angeles). Folded into this mix was Linda F. Williams (University of Maryland and the Congressional Black Caucus, Inc., in Washington, DC), who encouraged a cross-racial study of Black and Latina women in national politics. With support from the Inter-University Program for Latino Research (IUPLR) and the Chicana/Latina Research Center at UC Davis, Ada and Paule invited Christine to launch the "Gendered Politics Working Group," focused on the study of Latina politics in the United States. The crystallization moment for a national study of elected officials of color came from a conference in 1994 sponsored by the Center for American Women and Politics (CAWP) at Rutgers University, where Carol Hardy-Fanta joined the group. Subsequently, Dianne Pinderhughes and later Pei-te Lien accepted invitations to join, bringing complementary expertise and talent to this research initiative. The GMCL Project team was subsequently formalized with funding from the Ford Foundation.

Early on we benefited from collaboration with Cathy Cohen, Karin Stanford, and Luis Fraga. Paige Ransford, senior research associate at the University of Massachusetts Boston, deserves special thanks: she played a central role in developing the National Database, coding and carrying out analyses, and dedicating more than nine years to the GMCL Project. Joining our team as program associates were Wartyna Davis, who assisted in the design of the survey, and Lorrie Frasure, who offered her many talents in coordinating and assisting us through the project's final phases. Sharing their own data with us were Becki Scola (on state legislators) and Carlos Cuéllar for data on Latino/a mayors. Kira Sanbonmatsu responded generously when asked for information on CAWP studies.

Equally important are our colleagues at the Joint Center for Political and Economic Studies, the National Association of Latino Elected and Appointed Officials (NALEO), and the Asian American Studies Center at UCLA for providing us with lists of Black, Latino/a, and Asian American elected officials at the start of our project and with subsequent updates. Special thanks go to David Bositis and Richard Hart formerly of the Joint Center and Rosalind Gold and Martha Recio at NALEO; they consistently responded in a timely fashion to our many requests. We also appreciate the contributions of the Asian American Studies Center at UCLA. We thank James Lai and the late Don Nakanishi from the Center for their invaluable assistance and sharing with us their directories. Thanks also to the Institute for Public Policy (IPP) at the University of New Mexico. Amelia Rouse, IPP deputy director, and Amy Sue Goodin, associate director for research, assisted in the construction of the survey and supervised its implementation in the field.

Assisting in the development of the GMCL Project were members of our advisory board, acknowledged here with their institutional affiliations at the time of their service to the project: Lawrence D. Bobo, professor of Sociology and of Afro-American Studies, Harvard University; Susan J. Carroll, professor of political science and women's and gender studies, senior scholar, Center for American Women in Politics, Rutgers University; Michael Dawson, professor of government and Afro-American studies, Harvard University; John A. Garcia, professor of political science, University of Arizona; James Jackson, professor, Department of Psychology, University of Michigan; James Jennings, professor of environmental policy and planning, Tufts University; Laughlin McDonald, director, Southern Regional ACLU; Gwendolyn Mink, professor in the Women's Studies Program, Smith College; Don Nakanishi, professor, social sciences and comparative education and director, Asian American Studies Center, University of California, Los Angeles; and Kay Lehman Schlozman, J. Joseph Moakley Professor of Political Science, Boston College.

Philippa Strum, director of the US Studies Division at the Woodrow Wilson International Center for Scholars in Washington, DC, extended support by hosting two events: the GMCL Project's National Interest Group Meeting in 2004, a forum that included a number of women's and civil rights/ethnic organizations to consult with us on the project, and the public release of the GMCL Survey in 2007. The GMCL Project team also held meetings at the University of Chicago (thank you Cathy Cohen, then director of the Center for Race, Politics and Culture) and at the national headquarters of the American Political Science Association (APSA) in Washington, DC (thank you Michael Brintnall and Rob Hauck). Thanks also to the Kroc Institute at the University of Notre Dame, led by interim director Ruth Abby, which hosted a September 2014 meeting, as well as faculty assistant Cathy Laake, and Andre Ratasepp, senior technical support consultant. Appreciations to Charles, Bob, Ellen, Rick, and Howard Pinderhughes, who accommodated our meeting on Martha's Vineyard in their wonderful house a block from the Inkwell.

We thank our affiliated institutions: the John W. McCormack Graduate School of Policy and Global Studies and Center for Women in Politics and Public Policy at the University of Massachusetts Boston, who hosted us many times; the Political Science Departments at the University of Utah and the University of California Santa Barbara; the Department of Political Science and the African American Studies Program at the University of Illinois, Urbana Champaign; the College of Arts and Letters, the Department of Political Science, and the Department of Africana Studies at the University of Notre Dame; and the Political Science Department at the University of New Mexico. Christine is also grateful to Mexican American Studies at the University of Arizona and the Center for American Women and Politics (CAWP), Eagleton Institute of Politics, Rutgers University, for hosting her as a visiting scholar during the development of this project. The University of Notre Dame, through the Institute for Scholarship in the Liberal Arts (ISLA) in the' College of Arts and Letters, provided funding for the Index.

We are extremely grateful for the research associates and assistants who worked with us over the years: besides Paige Ransford, we thank Jennifer Lambert and Jeong Park, who went through the early directory information with a meticulous eye; and Katie Swain, Jeanette Yih Harvie, Rebecca Loya, Marla Aufseeser, and Rhoanne Esteban. Thanks also to staff at the Center for Women in Politics and Public Policy at UMass Boston for their support during data collection and analysis.

Thanks to Dianne Pinderhughes' graduate students Rosalind Fielder (University of Illinois, Urbana Champaign) and Maryann Kwakwa (University of Notre Dame) and undergraduate research assistants at the University of Notre Dame: Garren Bryant, class of 2011; Sarafina Joseph, class of 2018; and Asha Barnes, class of 2018. University of New Mexico research assistants include Lisa Bryant, Angelina Gonzalez-Aller, Julia Marin Hellwege, Rongal Nikora, and Albert Palma. Special thanks also to Carol Brown and Joann Buehler, political science administrators at UNM, who assisted with the Ford Foundation grant.

Those who helped with data and technical aspects of the project include Rose Hessmiller, CEO of Ferguson Lynch, who developed and implemented the GMCL Project website: www.gmcl.org. We also thank Joan Gardner, founder and past president of Applied Geographics, Inc. (AGI), and David Merwin, PhD, associate professor and chair of geography, Framingham State University, for their generosity and skill in creating the Environmental Systems Research Institute (ESRI) maps featured in Chapter 1; and Anthony Roman of the Center for Survey Research at the University of Massachusetts Boston for his top-notch technical assistance – always provided with a smile and chocolate. Rose-Anne Coveney, of UMass Boston, was gracious and demonstrated her design talents when we turned to her for assistance in developing the book's cover.

Thank you to Cambridge editors Ed Parsons and Robert Dreesen, and the editorial team, who were a pleasure to work with, for their patience, insightful advice, and encouragement. We are also especially grateful for the anonymous reviewers for Cambridge whose feedback helped to strengthen and bring this book to fruition. Thank you to Katherine Tengco, content manager at Cambridge; as well as Theresa Kornak, copy-editor; and the team at Newgen Knowledge Works Pvt. Ltd. who provided excellent edits and comments for drafts of this manuscript.

On a more personal note, Carol would like to thank her husband Christopher and daughters Allison and Caroline, as well as friends María Luisa, Sue, Sara, and Ken and Gail, for listening and providing support during the "blood, toil and tears"[1] that produced this book. Christine gives special thanks to Ellie for her constant support from the project's start to end. Christine's only regret is that her mom is not with her to celebrate the book's publication. Dianne appreciates her sister Gayle's support and patience on this project over the years. Pei-te wants to thank her entire family for being patient and understanding of the extraordinarily long and often grueling research schedule to gather and analyze data for this project.

Finally, and most importantly, we would like to thank the many elected officials who participated in our survey. We hope we did you justice in giving voice to your experiences, hopes, and the issues you care so much about.

[1] This phrase, which originated with Winston Churchill during World War II, appeared in a *Boston Globe* article discussing the impact of computers on the quality of writing (Muro 1992): "Good writing requires blood, toil and tears."

Introduction

On a freezing day in January 2009 hundreds of thousands of people lined the mall in front of the Capitol in Washington, DC, to witness Barack Obama take the oath of office as our first African American president of the United States. The changing face of the top US elected official symbolizes a changing of the guard in US political leadership and reflects the dramatic growth and diversification of the nation's population and governing bodies over the last five decades. This change is evident on Capitol Hill where, in January 1965, Patsy Takemoto Mink of Hawaii ascended to federal office as the nation's first woman of color in Congress. She served as the sole congresswoman of color for four years until joined by Shirley Chisholm of New York in 1969. It would be another twenty years before the nation's first Latina congresswoman, Ileana Ros-Lehtinen of Florida, joined their ranks. Today, women and men of color in the US Congress number in the double digits. A similar change also happened to the nation's highest court when Sonia Sotomayor, a woman from a working class Puerto Rican family in New York City, took the oath of office in 2009 and became the first Latina Supreme Court justice, having been nominated by President Obama. More recently, statewide officials such as Nikki Haley, the daughter of immigrants from India, and governor of South Carolina, argued for the removal of the Confederate battle flag from state property.[1]

[1] As we discuss later, the impetus was the outcry over the murder of State Senator Reverend Clementa Pinckney by a White supremacist. Governor Haley, the Asian Indian American female Republican governor of South Carolina, broke ranks with South Carolina's tradition and called for the removal of the Confederate battle flag from state capitol grounds, flanked by both of the state's Black members of Congress, Rep. James Clyburn (D-SC) and US Sen. Tim Scott (R-SC) at the signing of the legislation. All twenty-nine Black state

CHANGE AND PROGRESS

New faces of diversity appear not only in the halls of the White House, US Congress, Supreme Court, and state legislatures. Across the nation and at all levels of government – federal, state, and local – the racial, ethnic, and gender profile of America's governing officials includes more people of color and women than ever before in the nation's history. Add in the growing share of the population and increased electoral participation of Latinos and Asian Americans due to changes in immigration policies and demographic patterns and it is not surprising to see that people of color have gained greater influence in US society and politics.

They are changing the contours of political leadership and governance in this country. One measure of the scope of change is that the number of Black, Latino, Asian American, and American Indian women and men holding elected office today stands at more than 12,000, compared to just a few hundred prior to the implementation of the Voting Rights Act (VRA) of 1965. We discuss the growth for each group, the impact of the VRA, and the factors causing it more fully in Chapter 1.[2]

With the majority of elected officials of color in the United States serving at the county, municipal, and school board levels, their political leadership in those positions both reflects and has the potential to effect symbolic and substantive changes in local governance and for the communities they represent. As a whole, local elected officials oversee budgets totaling a trillion dollars or more every year and make critical hiring decisions, including those of particular concern to communities of color, such as police chiefs

representatives supported legislation to take down the flag compared to 69 percent of their White colleagues. Almost nine in ten women legislators compared to fewer than three-quarters of their male counterparts voted for the ban; the vote included 81 percent of White women but just 67 percent of White men. Source: GMCL Project analysis of South Carolina House Roll Call Vote Number 912, which passed on July 9, 2015, www.scstatehouse.gov/votehistory.php?KEY=10618 (Accessed July 5, 2016). Because there is only one (White) woman in the SC Senate, we did not include analysis of the Senate votes supporting S897, which were as follows: Black (male) senators 100 percent; White male: 76 percent, www.scstatehouse.gov/votehistory.php?KEY=10430 (Accessed July 5, 2016). State Representative Jenny Horne, a White Republican woman descended from the president of the Confederate States, Jefferson Davis, offered her impassioned plea: "I cannot believe that we do not have the heart in this body ... to do something meaningful, such as take a symbol of hate off these grounds on Friday." For one example of the impact of her speech on the outcome of the legislation, see Miller (2015).

[2] The Leadership Conference on Civil Rights reported 300 Black elected officials as of 1964 (Henderson 2005). The numbers of Asian American and Latino elected officials were probably a few dozen; for a discussion of Latinos see Melissa R. Michelson (2010, esp. 166).

and school superintendents. Given that for centuries, people of color along with women of all races were deprived of their rights as equal citizens and excluded from political participation and representation, it is not an over-statement to describe recent progress made to local elective leadership and governance as transformational. It is in this historical context that we celebrate the election of Michelle Wu, a young Asian American woman who became president of the City Council of Boston in 2016; her swearing-in is featured in the cover photograph. She replaced a White man from South Boston, the epicenter of 1970s anti-busing protests, where *"It was like a war zone"* during fights over school desegregation (Gellerman 2014).

Although only time may tell if we are too optimistic, we also share the belief that positive political changes may ensue because of the changing faces of diversity in the city/town halls and elsewhere in the structure of governance. A case in point is that, with the rise of elected leadership of color in a former bastion of White southern dominance, Black elected officials were able to secure an apology from the county for the murder of Emmett Till – the African American Chicago teenager visiting Money, Mississippi, in summer 1954, who was abducted and murdered when he reportedly

FIGURE INT.1 Black officials mark Tallahatchie County's apology for Emmett Till's murder. Photograph by Clay McFerrin, *The Charleston Sun-Sentinel*, Charleston, Mississippi, 2007. Used with permission.

whistled at a White woman shop owner. Black local officials also erected a memorial (Figure Int.1) in recognition of Till and the violence perpetrated against civil rights activists and many Blacks in those days.

Despite the trend of progress since the mid-1960s, incidents of regress and racial conflict persist. Well-publicized episodes of racial violence against non-White minorities have inundated the nation's traditional and social media in recent years. We have also witnessed a seemingly endless stream of videos posted to a variety of social media of young Black men and women interacting with, and all too often being killed by, local police – moving images that may dash any hope for racial harmony and limit our ability to imagine the nation making continued progress toward a more inclusive and multicultural leadership and governance. We are haunted by the tragic and senseless deaths of Black men such as Trayvon Martin in Sanford, Florida; Michael Brown in Ferguson, Missouri; Freddie Gray in Baltimore, Maryland; Eric Garner in Staten Island, New York; Walter Scott in North Charleston, South Carolina; and the death in police custody of Sandra Bland in Waller County, Texas. Let us also not forget twelve-year-old Tamir Rice in Cleveland, Ohio, or Latinos who have suffered the same fate – and on video: Antonio Zambrano-Montes, shot by three police officers in Pasco, Washington, for throwing rocks; and Ruben Garcia Villalpando, an unarmed Mexican immigrant, shot in Grapevine, Texas, while moving toward the police car with his hands up.

What do these events say about sociopolitical progress for communities of color in America today? Some argue race relations recently have become worse in large part *because* of the election of President Obama, which inflamed racial tensions (see, e.g., Lang 2015; Skocpol and Williamson 2012). According to polls taken shortly after his first inauguration, 69 percent of Americans thought race relations were "generally good"; but polling in 2015 showed that a majority of Americans thought race relations became worse under the nation's first Black president, and just 37 percent described racial conditions as "generally good" (Ross 2015). Some might argue that one result of the violence itself, brought to light by the widespread reporting of such incidents, is generating a heightened awareness of racial problems and a reexamination of race in this country that has been long overdue; see, for example, Ta-Nehisi Coates' best-selling, award winning book *Between the World and Me* (2015).

Yet, informed by our research, we also observe that minority elected officials can play critical roles in leading investigations of these racial events, challenging or investigating the police in individual cases, requiring changes to the racialized [mis]conduct of police departments as a whole, and prosecuting (often, but not always, White) policemen charged with crimes. We note that investigations into these deaths, and responses to the public outcry in communities of color, are typically determined by elected officials at the local level (see Chapter 2). In some cases, the race of the political leaders may factor into whether the responses are quick or slow, violent or peaceful, and result in indictments. It remains an empirical question subject to future scrutiny whether changes in descriptive representation in such troubled places will result in a more just society. We note the possibly contested nature of any assessment of substantive change that results from increased descriptive representation in governance; hence, we entitle our book "contested transformation."

Another reason for questioning the pace and direction of change is that the demographic transformation that we observed in the impressive growth of the nation's elected officials of color is partial and incomplete. Although their numbers have grown dramatically, elected officials of color still make up a much smaller share of the total number of elected offices compared to their proportion of the population. When the US Census conducted a survey of popularly elected officials in 1992, there were 85,006 governments and a total of 513,200 elected officials.[3] Barack Obama was elected president in the 232nd year of the United States of America's existence. It has been only in the last decades since passage of the 1965 Voting Rights Act that people of color have gained any significant number of elected offices in the United States; these dual narratives of recent progress and continuing exclusion are an integral part of Chapters 1 and 2.

This brings us back to Governor Haley, mentioned earlier, and another image in the media: the empty chair in the South Carolina state legislature that belonged to State Senator and Minister Clementa Pinckney, who, on June 17, 2015, was murdered along with eight of his fellow parishioners at Emanuel African Methodist Episcopal Church in Charleston, one of the nation's oldest Black churches. This event reminds us that political

---

[3] The number of governments increased to 89,476 in 2007, but it is not possible to determine the total number of elected officials in the United States today. This is because, although the Census continues to issue periodic reports on the number of governments, it discontinued its survey of elected officials after 1992.

leaders of color have themselves been subject to attack, illustrating their own vulnerability in racially charged political environments.

The title of this book, *Contested Transformation*, reflects the tension between change (moving forward toward greater political representation and influence) and resistance toward that change. Such tension is typical of politics and remains uncomfortably at the heart of race and gender in American politics today: Whatever transformation of the polity that *has* been achieved has occurred on contested political terrain and can hardly be considered permanent. Such changes for the betterment of marginalized communities have not occurred without a fight, are vulnerable to setbacks, and have been bedeviled at every point and in numerous ways. Omi and Winant (2015) recognize the give-and-take of racial politics in America in their dynamic model of racial formation in the United States. They depict social change with regard to race as contested – whereby social structures and political elites define power/race relations and yet are impacted by forces pushing for change from the ground up.

The growth in the number of elected officials of color since the mid-1960s, however dramatic in terms of numbers or percentage change, has hardly resulted in permanent transformation of American politics. On the *best* day, the situation for people of color, including their elected officials, has taken on the character of "two steps forward, one step back." In this scenario, there is some momentum toward a net gain over time. But the events on the very *bad* days such as those of racialized violence previously mentioned represent a situation in which one step forward is followed by two steps back, suggesting Sisyphean efforts with little gain. One of the most recent scholarly attempts to characterize this paradoxical nature of American racial politics is made by Wilson (2015). The attention we pay in this book to the women and men of color, serving mostly in subnational politics, adds an important and critical dimension to the nation's dialogue and debate on this ever-riveting issue of progress and regress and how and why minority elected officials matter.

Why This Book

We would like to share another, more personal image: In 2004, before he was elected to the presidency, Obama was a state senator representing a

FIGURE INT.2 GMCL Project meeting, Chicago, 2004. (l to r): Carol Hardy-Fanta; (unidentified male); Wartyna Davis; Barack Obama, then candidate for US Senate; Dianne Pinderhughes; Pei-te Lien; and Christine Sierra. (Photograph courtesy of Wartyna Davis; used with permission.)

Southside district of Chicago and running for the US Senate. During one of the meetings of our research group at the University of Chicago, we happened upon him outside a barber shop late on a Saturday afternoon in Hyde Park, striding along 53rd Street near Harper Court.

After telling him about the Gender and Multicultural Leadership (GMCL) Project, he looked at us – a group of women, Black, Latina, Asian, and White (Figure Int.2) – and, with an air of considerable puzzlement, asked, *Who are you guys?* In a sense, the way we wrote this book responds to his question, not about who *we* are, as a multicultural group of women scholars, but rather about *who they are* – the women and men who make up the nation's multicultural elected leadership and govern this country: their personal, family, and political backgrounds; why they first ran for office; and their views on and experiences with political leadership, governance, and representation.

This book offers a timely study of America's multicultural elected leadership in the early part of the twenty-first century. It constitutes a first-of-its-kind, comparative study of racial and ethnic minorities, both women and men, that focuses on those holding elective offices at subnational levels of governance. It is national in geographic scope and comprehensive in the topics covered. Further, our study disaggregates analyses by race and gender (alone) and in combination and provides a baseline portrait of Black, Latino, and Asian American women and men holding elective office in national, state, and local government in the United States today. (We also include a subsample of American Indians serving in nontribal elected positions in state legislatures.)

About This Book

The words "contested" and "transformation" in the title carry multiple meanings. That the nation is undergoing a demographic transformation in its ethnoracial profile cannot be disputed. We show in this book how the leadership ranks in the nation's governing institutions increasingly, if incrementally, reflect the demographic diversity evident in the population at large. The roads leading to demographic and political change, however, have been fraught with "contestation." Focusing specifically on elected officials of color, we outline further considerations of "contested transformation" by exploring the reasons and ways they ran for their first office, their styles of leadership and governance, and their possible impacts on public policy that aim to protect and advance the interests of disadvantaged communities.

To what extent has American political leadership and governance been transformed by the growing presence of women and men of color in elective offices, especially at state and local levels of government? We do not have definitive answers but raise questions for consideration as we analyze elected officials of color along various dimensions of electoral politics and governing. In grappling with this central question, we submit that transformation implies profound and significant change in the way politics and political institutions function. Challenges to the status quo, that is, the usual ways of doing things, may be a prerequisite for, but do not necessarily involve, transformative change (a debate noted in Chapter 6 on styles of leadership). An increasing body of scholarship on the significance of elected officials of color in the American polity raises important questions regarding the impact of these officials, their connections to previously underrepresented groups (e.g., Dovi 2002; Mansbridge 1999; Philips 1995), and the institutional characteristics and structural constraints under which they govern.

As we examine elected officials of color and their ability to penetrate governing institutions that at points have been hostile to their inclusion, we draw upon the literature on political incorporation, which can take various forms with regard to how power is distributed within governing bodies (Browning, Marshall, and Tabb 1984; Schmidt, Barvosa-Carter, and Torres 2000). We draw attention to "four benchmarks of incorporation" for racial minorities as outlined in Schmidt et al. (2010, 125): "(1) full access to political participation [among all groups], (2) representation in governmental decision-making offices, (3) substantial power/influence on governmental decisions, leading to (4) adoption of ethnoracially egalitarian public policies." We discuss in the book various dimensions of political incorporation for the elected officials of color in our study (e.g., levels of office, leadership positions in Congress and state legislatures, political allies, etc.). We note here, however, scholarly critiques that point to limitations involved in governing that may *not* result in transformative change.

Dovi (2002, 736) notes that descriptive representatives may not fulfill the expectations of constituency groups who elected them; elected officials of color (like any elected officials) may "reach out to (or distance themselves from) historically disadvantaged groups." Several studies on Black electoral politics question the commitment of Black elected leaders who seek elected office out of narrow self-interest and personal ambition, as opposed to commitments to empower communities of color (Gillespie 2010; Reed 1986, 2000; Smith 1996; Walters and Smith 2007).

Beyond individual attitudes and behavior are the rules of the game in governance that impose boundaries on elected officials' decision-making processes and representational roles. Rosenthal (1998a, 16) draws attention to how leaders are constrained by institutional rules and norms: "Institutions reinforce behavior through powerful written and unwritten norms, through the selection and promotion of leaders who adopt those norms, and in daily processes, rules, and procedures." Referencing Guinier's (1994) *The Tyranny of the Majority*, Abdullah and Freer (2008, 99) suggest that the majority support rule "especially restricts the ability of Black legislators to propose more *transformative* policy solutions, since they must gain the support of a significant number of white colleagues for bills to pass" (emphasis added).

Hence, though we admit to a normative value of support for the expansion of elected leadership to underrepresented groups, which we consider expanding democratic participation, we also hold that their leadership may or may not result in transformational change in America's governing structures and political processes. Bluntly stated by Junn and Brown (2008, 71): "... more women in government – does not always mean better government for women. As long as government – replete with gendered and discriminatory institutions – remains intact rather than transformed, populating it with diversity can at best alter outcomes incrementally. Is small change better than no change? *Perhaps, but let us at least acknowledge it is small change*" (emphasis added). Thus, the notion of transformative leadership must be seen as contested, from above, below, and within institutional structures.

Finally, by placing elected officials of color – especially women of color – at the center of our work and consistently incorporating an inter-sectional lens in our analysis, we are challenging assumptions, practices, and findings of mainstream political science literature regarding elected leadership and governance. Studies of women and gender in American politics posit that women exercise leadership differently from men. Indeed, some scholars argue that women practice a transformative type of leadership that challenges, if not changes, American political processes and institutions in important and fundamental ways. We advance the argument that changes in America's elected leadership are under way, which is a more complex phenomenon than simply its demographic diversity and descriptive characteristics. The transformation rests in the descriptive and the substantive dimensions of the participation brought by this new cohort of elected officials.

In this book, we also argue that, if we are to understand fully who the elected political leaders of this country are, we must include a de-tailed portrait of the Black, Latino, Asian American, and American Indian women and men holding office today. Women of color constitute an espe-cially important part of the demographic change among the nation's po-litical leadership. As we demonstrate in Chapters 1 and 2, their numbers have increased over time steadily and at a comparatively more rapid pace vis-à-vis their male coethnics and White women, especially in particular offices. Yet women of color and their politics remain understudied in the field of political science. To be sure, a developing literature on women of color is emerging, largely associated with studies of women in American politics or of racial and ethnic minorities in the United States. Yet even these literatures, with their emphasis on the study of White women and/ or racial groups (each considered "minorities") often ignore or overlook the case of women of color or the politics of gender in their analyses.

The central findings of this book show commonalities and contrasts between, within, and among the different groups by gender and race: in other words, between Blacks, Latinos, and Asian American elected offi-cials; by gender within each racial group (e.g., between Latina women and Latino men); and among women by race (i.e., Asian American, Black and Latina women of color compared to their male counterparts). In this scenario, we present results for three races, two genders, and six groups by race and gender combined. Moreover, we include American Indians, who are mostly state legislators in our sample, when analyses of that level of office or policies are of particular relevance to them. There is of course the full intersectional approach, which compares each combination by race and gender alone or in interaction on multiple socioeconomic and political dimensions included in this comprehensive study.

Black, Asian American, and Latina men and women of color have a lot to add not only about patterns and sources of growth in numbers over recent decades and the struggles that they have faced and those they face today (Chapter 1); but also about how they serve mostly at the local level and what that is like for them (Chapter 2); what resources they bring with them from their personal and family backgrounds (Chapter 3); why they ran for office (Chapter 4); how they navigated the campaign trail (Chapter 5); and how they view their leadership and governance styles and their representational roles (Chapters 6 and 7). We also hear their voices when we report what they said – in their own words – when asked in our GMCL Survey, *"Why did you run for office the very first time?"* and *"What do you think are the most important policy issues facing your constituents?"*

By the end of the book, we anticipate readers will have a better grasp of the nature of the tensions and struggles – as well as accomplishments – of the nation's men and women of color elected officials. We also project that the reader can answer affirmatively the question: Do minority elected officials, especially women of color, matter in contemporary American politics? By accounting for the voices of diversity among these officials, we wish to provide a clearer answer to the "so what" question of whether their election and public service have advanced America toward a more inclusive democracy in the early twenty-first century and onward.

FILLING A VOID IN PRIOR RESEARCH

Despite their importance for the current state and future of democracy in this country, there has been remarkably little research on elected officials of color that is comprehensive and comparative in scope, includes a national sample, and disaggregates findings by race and gender. Political science has produced voluminous amounts of research on elected officials, but race was largely ignored or discussed in the context of White ethnic politics and assimilation. Overall, the default norm for elected leadership was White men.[4]

---

[4] It truly would be impossible to list even a partial list of scholarship demonstrating the hegemony of White men in the field as scholars or subjects. Dahl (1961) and Banfield and Wilson (1963) are two examples.

Once the field began studying race, it followed the larger American tradition of seeing race solely in terms of "black" and "white"[5]; gender was either studied separately or seen as another "minority" (i.e., results reported for "minorities and women"). Black women, as they assumed greater roles in women's studies and feminist scholarship, decried the fact that *All the Women Are White, All the Blacks Are Men* (Hull, Scott, and Smith 1982). Subsequent scholarship drew attention to the politics of "women of color," yet in cases obscured the differences there might be between women of different races.

Finally came intersectionality scholars (e.g., Brewer 1993, 1999; Cohen 1999; Cohen, Jones, and Tronto 1997; Crenshaw et al. 1995; Githens and Prestage 1977; Hancock 2007; Hill Collins 1990; Jordan-Zachery 2009; King 1988; Smooth 2006; Williams 2001, 2003; Baca Zinn and Dill 1994; see also works in Hardy-Fanta et al. 2006). These scholars argue that "the distinguishing categories within a society, such as race/ethnicity, gender, religion, sexual orientation, class, and other markers of identity and difference, do not function independently but, rather, act in tandem as interlocking or intersectional phenomena" (Manuel 2006, 175).

As we discuss and test in Chapter 3, intersectionality theory coexists with and contributes to a substantial scholarship on whether Black women, in particular, are "doubly disadvantaged" (Gay and Tate 1998) socioeconomically and politically by their sex and race compared to Black men and/or White women (see, e.g., Darcy and Hadley 1988) or are, like some argue for Latinas (Fraga et al. 2008; Navarro 2008), advantaged in some way (Bejarano 2013). And, as we discuss in Chapter 8, according to a number of theoretical and empirical studies (Dawson 2001; Fraga and Navarro 2007; García et al. 2008; and Simien 2006), intersectionality in identity of women of color may lead to the development of a bridging function, which can create opportunities for coalitions across race and gender.

Our book serves to change long-term traditions in research in political science, gender/women's studies, and ethnic studies that privilege White men, White women, and men of color, respectively. We are putting women of color at the center of our analysis and conceptualization, documenting with empirical research the unique experiences they bring to

---

[5] Below we discuss why we generally capitalize Black and White throughout this volume; in this case we have deliberately used lowercase to reflect the tradition in earlier years to designate race as a color, not as ethnoracial political groups in the same way Latinos are.

the political arena. There is nothing to be contested in this regard, despite their working in a political terrain that often challenges or opposes their equal rights to political participation and representation. Inspired by the title of Cohen, Jones, and Tronto (1997), our book discusses how women of color elected officials are transforming American politics from the bottom up.

AN INTERSECTIONAL APPROACH: FRAMING THE ANALYSIS BY RACE, GENDER, AND RACE*GENDER

The landscape of our democracy becomes even more complex when examined through the lens of intersectionality. Throughout this book we often speak of using an "intersectional lens" to examine the backgrounds, trajectories to office, and views on leadership, governance, representation, and policy positions of elected officials by race alone, gender alone, and gender and race in interaction – for which we have coined the term "race*gender." What do we mean by the "lens of intersectionality"? And why henceforth do we use "race*gender" rather than just "race and gender"?

We argue that race and gender, whether alone or in interaction, are not simply demographic classifications or identity markers, but rather factors that interact in dynamic ways with historical and structural political conditions. Being Black, alone, brings with it experience and struggles we discussed briefly earlier. Add in gender (as well as class, life experiences, whether easy or hard, and the historical context of the racial group), the *whole* (combination) becomes much more than the sum of its parts. Most models treat race and gender in an additive way, and may lead to situations in which being a Black woman, reduced to a demographic category, may lead one to see her as indistinguishable from any other woman (see a critical review in Hancock 2007). King (1988, 7) characterizes this issue as follows: "Unfortunately, most applications of the concept of double and triple jeopardy have been overly simplistic in assuming that the relationships among the various discriminations are merely additive. These relations are interpreted as equivalent to the mathematical equation, racism plus sexism plus classism equals triple jeopardy .... Such assertions ignore the fact that racism, sexism, and classism constitute three, interdependent control systems. An interactive model, which I have termed multiple jeopardy, better captures those processes."

We use race*gender to make it clear that race and gender have multiplicative effects, and we consider the effects of the histories, disadvantages and/or advantages, conveyed to them as individuals who bring a host of personal, familial, societal, economic, and political resources as well as "baggage" with them. Thus, besides being shorthand for the analysis at the intersection of race and gender, the asterisk in race*gender affirms the multiplicative nature of sociopolitical life for women and men of color.

ORGANIZATION OF THE BOOK: WHAT WE GAIN FROM STUDYING ELECTED OFFICIALS OF COLOR

This book is organized into four parts. Part I, Transforming the American Political Landscape, addresses the question: To what extent and in what ways has the American political landscape been transformed by the increasing numbers of elected officials and populations of color? In Chapter 1, we address this question by providing the historical context for any discussion of political representation for Blacks, Latinos, Asians, and American Indians in this country, a context that is one of exclusion and continuing struggle. We also analyze factors that have infused their continuing growth as well as perpetuated their underrepresentation in the post-1965 era. We draw attention to two federal policies that greatly increased access to the political system (and nation) for people of color: the Voting Rights Act (1965) and the Immigration and Nationality Act of 1965.

Chapter 2 responds to the question asked in *Who Governs?* by Robert Dahl (1961) by providing an in-depth look at the women and men of color who govern America's cities, towns, counties, and school boards. Among the key findings of this chapter is the fact that, in contrast to prior research with its limited focus on large cities, the majority of city/town councilors and mayors of color serve in smaller cities/towns and counties – as do elected officials in general. It is in these smaller localities where key decisions that directly impact the livelihood of the nation's racial minority communities are made.

We identify women of color as key to the phenomenal growth in local elective governance by people of color. Yet, any recorded growth that has occurred in local governance has not reached anything close to representational parity. They also typically preside over smaller jurisdictions than their male counterparts. Furthermore, our analysis challenges the prevailing, somewhat archaic, view that local government is not gendered because, supposedly, the decisions made at that level are of a more practical nature and focus on physical infrastructure.[6] On the contrary, the

---

[6] For a review of this literature, see, for example, DeSena (2008).

women and men of color who responded to our survey and hold elective offices at the local level help move the nation closer to the ideal of a more inclusive and multicultural democracy.

Chapter 3 provides a baseline portrait of elected officials with regard to their personal, political, and family backgrounds. We analyze the qualifications, experiences, and resources they bring with them in their trajectories to political office as well as the barriers that may exist for them on the campaign trail. Contrary to the "double disadvantage" thesis that posits that political women of color would be disadvantaged by the intersection of their racial and gender identities, we find that, at least among those we surveyed: "the winners," that is, those who succeed in their campaigns and are elected to public office, Black and Latina women are significantly *less* likely to be disadvantaged in education and occupation, compared both to women in general and to their male counterparts. In the end, our portrait of advantages and disadvantages in the *backgrounds* of elected officials – that is, the personal and family resources they bring with them to their campaigns – is a mixed one, and certainly one that cannot be easily captured by the received wisdom of the double disadvantage thesis for women of color in general when Black and Latino men are often found to be the least advantaged.

A central question considered by the two chapters in Part II, Paths to Political Office, is, in what ways do race and gender shape the paths to political office for elected officials of color? Chapter 4 explores the trajectories to elective office for women and men of color. We suggest that the pipeline theory may be limited in its utility to explain the electoral experiences of women and men of color, and we provide a more nuanced understanding of why and how these women and men enter the world of electoral politics. Using qualitative and quantitative analyses of survey respondents' comments, we uncover the commonalities as well as differences between women and men of color in why they first ran for office. As prescribed in the literature for "authentic" descriptive representatives of minority populations, the elected officials in our survey reveal in their own words multiple connections to community as they give expression to why they ran for office the first time. Overall, we find that no single reason (such as personal ambition) explains their motivation in seeking office. The chapter also uncovers how these elected officials are not newcomers to politics but rather were elected quite a number of years ago to the office they currently hold. We also find mixed evidence regarding their recruitment by parties and others to elective office.

Chapter 5 continues our challenge to the notion that personal ambition underlies paths to public office. Although political ambition carries a different meaning for racial minorities than for Whites, several key elements in the electoral structure examined in our survey show similar effects on the electoral fates of both White women and women of color. Personal ambition was far from the primary motivation for women and men of color to launch their first campaign for public office. Instead, we find strong evidence of minority elected officials' leveraging community-based resources as social and political capital to help launch their political careers. Among the race*gender groups, Black women are particularly active in civic engagement.

Included in the analysis are institutional factors that influence elections (such as types of electoral systems, term limits, etc.) and perceived campaign disadvantages identified by survey respondents. Minority elected officials in our survey were elected more from single-member districts than from at-large or multimember districts. We find some evidence of legislative term limits having a positive impact on cracking open the opportunity structure for minority women. On perceived campaign disadvantages, men of color and especially Black men reported the highest incidence of feeling marginalized and discriminated against on the campaign trail because of their race. Women of color who perceived themselves as being disadvantaged on the campaign trail compared to other candidates tended to attribute their mistreatment to both their race and gender. We suggest that women of color's greater awareness of structural intersectionality may put them in a better position to support and champion political causes that require them to play a transformative role in bridging differences and building coalitions for social and/or political change.

The two chapters in Part III, Leadership, Governance, and Representation, provide an intersectional analysis of leadership styles, governance and representation, returning to the notion of "transformation." We begin the chapter by identifying various definitions and meanings of leadership – focusing especially on debates informed by feminist, womanist, and other critiques of traditional theories within the field of political science. We then pursue a key question that emerges from the literature: given the increase in their numbers as positional leaders, to what extent does – or will – the presence of women of color in government lead to a "politics of difference" – that is, significant change, even transformational change – in how government operates? We draw on our survey to provide answers to that question. We find that elected officials of color, both women and men, think that women (and by implication women of color) – work harder, are better at building consensus, avoid the limelight to get the job done, and are more persuasive and more transparent when developing public policy. This provides a parallel to findings in the literature on women in general (i.e., studies of White women). Hence, our study supports the notion that gender does matter in how elected officials engage in the policymaking process within their governing bodies.

This chapter also evaluates aspects of political incorporation, that is, the degree of success with which elected officials of color have penetrated governmental institutions and exercised leadership within them. Data on leadership positions held by elected officials of color in Congress and at the state legislative level show some progress over time, but institutional constraints such as party control of legislative bodies limit their opportunities for advancement At the same time, the elected officials of color in our study – overwhelmingly local officeholders – report they belong to voting majorities, for the most part, in their governing bodies, suggesting a level of effectiveness as substantive representatives for various constituencies.

In Chapter 7 we describe how well elected officials of color "match" their constituents on key dimensions of descriptive and symbolic representation: race, class, ideology, and partisanship. We then explore the links between these dimensions of representation for elected officials situated at the intersection of race and gender serving in state and local offices. Are those who "match" their constituents more likely to support legislation that protects minority rights? The degrees to which they "look alike" and "think alike" differ across race and gender groups and by level of office. The extent of perceived partisan and ideological congruence between minority officials and their constituents differs with the directions of partisanship and ideology. Providing empirical support to the concept of descriptive representation, the majority of non-White officials in our study perceived their jurisdictions as made up largely of constituents who shared their racial background and partisan affiliation, but not necessarily ideological outlook.

Our respondents were remarkably accurate in their estimation of the constituent makeup by immigration generation. And the majority of them also correctly identified the majority class status (by household income) of their constituents. Their reported degrees of responsiveness to issues related to disadvantaged constituents are found to be positively associated with the degrees of congruence in race and partisanship with their constituents. Their support for minority-targeted legislation appears to be influenced more by the degree of congruence in partisanship than in racial identity or ideology.

The vast majority of our elected officials, especially those holding higher levels of office, reported a great deal of contacts with their constituents, but gender differences did appear. There are few racial or gender differences, however, among minority elected officials in their perceptions regarding policy issues of concern for their constituents – suggesting minorities have a more unified policy outlook than found among Whites.

Part IV, Advancing Democracy in the United States, examines the prospects for advancing democracy in a country that is increasing its demographic diversity. Chapter 8 compares the positions of each group of elected officials of color on a number of public policy debates, including immigration, voting rights, welfare reform, and women's rights. We evaluate the implications of these findings for the prospects of advancing political representation and coalition-building abilities of women and men of color. In the conclusion to Chapter 8, we return to the discussion of "contested transformation," and share our thoughts on the possibilities for advancing democracy.

A NOTE ON DATA AND RESEARCH METHODOLOGY

The research for this book draws heavily from two primary sources constructed for the GMCL Project: a national database of minority elected officials from the selected populations mentioned earlier and a telephone survey of a national sample of those elected officials serving in state legislative and local office from 2006–2007. (See Box Int.1 for who was included in the database and survey. For more on the data and methodology, see Appendix A; the Survey Questionnaire may be found in Appendix B.) Although the data from these sources are from 2006–2007, we contend that they offer an important – and still unique – baseline portrait of elected officials of color at the beginning of the twenty-first century, and one that includes women and men of four ethnoracial groups; is national in coverage; and provides the opportunity to study not only members of Congress and state legislators, but also the vast majority of officials who serve on elected county, municipal, and local school boards.

We decided to update certain aspects of the National Database in 2012–2014 to include members of the 113th Congress; we then gathered data on the occupations, prior offices held, religion, marital status,

---

**Box Int.1. Who's Included in the GMCL
National Database? In the Survey?**

In the Database:

- Members of Congress
- Statewide officials who hold the position of governor, lieutenant governor, secretary of state, attorney general, state treasurer, or state auditor/controller
- State legislators
- Members of county commissions and boards of supervisors
- Mayors and members of city governing bodies (i.e., city/town councils and boards of aldermen/ selectmen)
- Members of school boards (including county-wide, unified-district and local, but excluding college/university boards of trustees)

In the GMCL Survey?

- State legislators
- Members of county commissions and boards of supervisors
- Mayors and members of city governing bodies (i.e., city/town councils and boards of aldermen/ selectmen)
- Members of school boards (including county-wide, unified-district, and local boards, but excluding state boards of education and college/university boards of trustees)

---

and other characteristics of congressional members of color in the original database.[7] We also updated the database for the state legislators of color in 2012–2013 and gathered data on whether the state legislators who were surveyed in 2006–2007 had subsequently run for higher offices. We gathered comparable information on a sample of local officials in 2014. And, finally, we gathered information on leadership positions and committee assignments for members of color in the 113th Congress.

---

[7] Members of Congress exclude delegates except for the delegate from the District of Columbia.

CHALLENGES IN UNDERSTANDING
RACE/ETHNIC IDENTITY

As we began to work on the GMCL project, we found ourselves challenged by several issues. How would we define race? We could approach the question (1) *theoretically*, drawing from the fields of political science, sociology, anthropology, racial and ethnic studies; (2) *historically*, considering how definitions have been defined in changing fashion over the centuries[8]; (3) *legally*, as defined by American law (or by the law of other nations in the Americas); or (4) *administratively*, as used by the US Census Bureau (which circles back to the analysis of historical change). The definitions used by the Census have shifted and evolved over time; since the 2000 census, individuals have had the option of self-identifying with more than one race.[9] Above all, (5) *structurally:* we need to heed the postmodern tendency suggesting that racial distinctions are products of "social construction." (See Hardy-Fanta et al. 2013.)

Whatever the definitional possibilities, and this short list by no means exhausts the range, our team assumed that racial categories would be clearly delimited as we began our research; that is, an official (or any other person) could be classified into a racially singular category. One would be Black, *or* White, *or* Asian, *or* Latino, and the officials would fit, with few exceptions, into racially discrete categories, rather than overlap, be racially mixed, or offer some combination of them. We based our assumption in part on the fact that, on combining the directories/rosters of Black, Latino, and Asian American/Pacific Islander elected officials to construct the GMCL National Database, there was almost no overlap between them. We had expected that the Joint Center and National Association of Latino Elected and Appointed Officials (NALEO), in particular, might include individuals of multiracial backgrounds, given

---

[8] See, for example, Nobles (2000) and Cox (1948).
[9] Source: US Census (2011; CB11-CN.125). By 1995, the Census Bureau's About Race reported: "The data on race were derived from answers to the question on race that was asked of individuals in the United States. The Census Bureau collects racial data in accordance with guidelines provided by the U.S. Office of Management and Budget (OMB), and these data are based on self-identification. The racial categories included in the census questionnaire generally reflect a social definition of race recognized in this country and not an attempt to define race biologically, anthropologically, or genetically. In addition, it is recognized that the categories of the race item include racial and national origin or sociocultural groups. People may choose to report more than one race to indicate their racial mixture, such as "American Indian" and "White." People who identify their origin as Hispanic, Latino, or Spanish may be of any race. OMB requires five minimum categories: White, Black or African American, American Indian or Alaska Native, Asian, and Native Hawaiian or Other Pacific Islander." www.census.gov/topics/population/race/about.html (Accessed March 4, 2016).

that, on the East Coast especially, Dominicans and Puerto Ricans typically include those who are racially Black. As it turned out, of the more
than 10,000 elected officials in the database, there were very few who
appeared in more than one of the four groups.[10]

Confounding our assumptions and political science practice more broadly,
we found that, when asked to describe their racial/ethnic backgrounds, the
officials surveyed provided a diverse and complex picture. Thus, to the five
ways to define race described earlier, we must add a sixth: *methodologically*.[11]

---

[10] One of the few was Adam Clayton Powell IV, who is both Black and Latino (and the
grandson/great grandson of the late Congressman of the same name); to confound matters further in this case, there are two Adam Clayton Powell IVs, one who was born in
Puerto Rico. Another involved a Latino state legislator who was – it turned out – mistak-
enly included in the Black directory, most likely because he was a member of the Black
Legislative Caucus in his state's legislature. And Alberto Torrico, who served on both the
Hispanic and Asian Pacific Island Caucuses in the California State Assembly from 2004
to 2010, was listed in the NALEO and Asian Institute directories because his father is
from Bolivia and his mother is Japanese. www.smartvoter.org/2010/06/08/ca/state/vote/
torrico_a/bio.html (Accessed January 22, 2016).

[11] We found seven local officials, for example, whose ascriptive identity was Black (based
on the original Joint Center roster) but, when asked how they would describe their racial
identity, gave answers that could only be coded as American Indian (e.g., "Amerindian,"
"American Indian," "Native," etc.). Given the small number, the fact that American
Indians in our sampling frame (the GMCL Database) were all state legislators, and the
history of Black American Indians in this country, it would render their inclusion as
American Indian local officials meaningless; we therefore returned them to the "Black"
category for analytical purposes. In other cases in which the elected official was publicly
known to be of two races, we coded him or her within the group with the smaller number
in the database. To an important extent, our research had begun with an assumption of
the importance of the categorical, and that we could and should assign each official to
a specific box. Given the rapid growth in the overall racial and ethnic population, our
failure to think through definitions of race, whether static or changing, or at least to
think about the fact that this would be an important element in our analysis, led us into
difficult methodological issues. What should we do with officials who did not respond
compliantly with our categories? What did it mean that some proportion, but by no
means all of the officials offered mixed, multiracial, or other challenging responses that
did not fit the survey? Nevertheless, even if we had addressed these issues earlier, and
even after taking these methodological issues into account, race is a complex issue that
has had and continues to generate many different configurations. Our efforts to "force"
our elected officials into specific, discrete racial categories is one that offers a fascinating
challenge: our theoretical expectation that there be specific categories for each official
and into which each official should fit, is necessarily challenged by the reality that the
rapid increase in "new" racial/ethnic groups since 1965 would lead to population interaction, intermarriage, and change. The presence of Blacks and Latinos in cities such
as Los Angeles, Chicago, New York, and Miami and of Asians, Latinos, and Blacks in
Houston and Los Angeles, would lead within some reasonable period of time to changes
in the racial boundaries of some portion of the population. For a number of reasons,
we did not include a sample of White elected officials. First, we debated the relative importance of centering the research on people of color – in other words, not privileging
the White "norm" versus the scientific demands for a White sample. Second, practical

At a very basic level, how do scholars carry out research with race/ethnicity as a key variable if it is not possible to "fit" the research subjects into mutually exclusive categories?

What might seem to be the simplest of analytical tasks – the distribution by race/ethnicity – therefore turned out to be more complex than expected. First of all, simply selecting what terms to use in discussing each group was complicated and based in the political struggles detailed in Chapter 1. For the sake of consistency, we use Black (rather than black or African American); Latino/a rather than Hispanic; and Asian American, which includes native Hawaiians and other Pacific Islanders. We use the term American Indian rather than Native American, and this category also includes Alaskan Natives.

Second, each decision related to terminology reflected oft–irresolvable tensions associated with racial identity and relations: Are they, as a collective, "minorities"? Should they be called "non–White?" Who is Black, who is Asian, who is Hispanic/Latino, and who is American Indian? For reference to all non-White groups in our study, we sometimes use the term "elected officials of color." We are aware of the scholarly argument that "White" is itself a "color" in a social and political sense. We respect the differences in scholarly opinion on this issue, but for our purposes, references to people of color do not include non-Hispanic Whites. In addition, the discussion of racial and ethnic identity – whether ascriptive, self-selected, or what Márquez (2003) calls asserted – is important theoretically, as the tendency in the early phases of comparative racial and ethnic group social science research was to elide the differences among Blacks, Latinos, Asian Americans, and American Indians in an effort to aggregate political coalitions beyond minority status in relationship to the majority White population. The common group identity names we use were settled on after considerable discussion. We've settled on "multicultural" for the four groups as a collective, but readily acknowledge that tensions remain.

Third, we have chosen to capitalize Black (and White) when the words refer to racial groups of people for a number of reasons. These include the fact that, otherwise, Blacks would be visually diminished compared to Latinos/as, Asians, or American Indians, who, by virtue of their nationalities, are capitalized. Tharps (2014, A25) makes "The Case for Black

considerations (including the daunting task of generating comparable samples of Whites) influenced our decision. Finally, we concluded that there was sufficient information on White elected officials in the literature to allow for meaningful comparative analysis.

with a Capital B. Again" because "Black refers to people of the African diaspora. Lowercase black is simply a color." The third reason is political: Clark (2015), for example, locates her argument with publishers' style editors in current events: "As media coverage of networked activism in the *#BlackLivesMatter* movement revives discussions of how media talk about race, the question persists: Why won't mainstream news outlets capitalize the b in Black?" She responds: "It's a question of social and political will ... If you put it up – capital B – you are really trying to call attention to a very political identity, very much a communal activity, as 'Black'."

Illustrating Complexities of Race in the GMCL Project

Elected officials in the GMCL Survey were first asked: *How would you best describe your* primary *racial or ethnic background?* Almost nine in ten (88 percent) gave a response to this question that was a singular racial/ethnic category: 45 percent Black/African American; 34 percent Hispanic/Latino; 7 percent Asian/Pacific Islander; and 2 percent American Indian (see Figure Int.3). Seven percent gave responses that diverted attention away from race or ethnicity, essentially providing nonracial responses: one of the most common was a statement such as "good," "very good," "excellent," or "super." There were also 4 percent

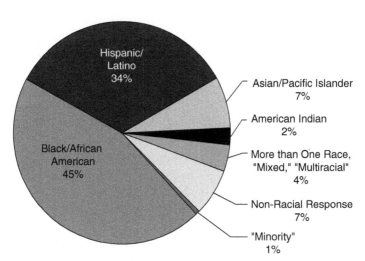

FIGURE INT.3 Primary racial/ethnic background, elected officials of color.
Note: Percentages are those reported by elected officials of color when asked, *What is your primary racial or ethnic background?*
Source: GMCL National Survey, N = 1,170.

who said their *primary* racial or ethnic background included more than one race (with an Hispanic/Latino group included as analogous to Black, Asian, or American Indian) or said "mixed" or "multiracial."

Simply asking for a primary racial/ethnic background fails, however, to capture the full picture on how the elected officials see their racial and/or ethnic backgrounds. When asked in an open-ended question, *How would you describe your ancestry or ethnic origin?* the officials in our survey provided considerable detail. Combining the responses from both questions, we find that more than a quarter of elected officials of color claim a racial identity that is not exclusive or singular – and this varied significantly by group.

"Latino" and Race

Finally, we fully recognize that "Latino/Hispanic" is not a race as in the conventional usage of Black, Asian, American Indian, or White.[12] For simultaneously theoretical, historical, and methodological reasons (although not, according to the current US Census, administratively), there are times when they should be included in analysis as one of their more traditionally racial counterparts. There is some justification for this. Schmidt, Barvosa-Carter, and Torres (2000, 564), for example, describe the racialization of Mexican Americans and Puerto Ricans that occurred following these groups' "violent incorporation" into the United States. Hochschild and Weaver (2010, 748), in their study of multiracialism, discuss the logic of "including Hispanic as a 'race' analogous to Black, White, Asian, and American Indian." Comparing Hispanics/Latinos to Blacks, Asian Americans, and Whites is also common practice in public opinion polls (see, for example, the *Race and Ethnicity in 2001: Attitudes, Perceptions and Experiences Survey* [Kaiser Family Foundation 2001]).

This decision to treat Latinos as a racial group is not dissimilar to Masuoka's (2008, 258) study of a nationally representative sample (N = 1,709) of the general population: she found that 18.5 percent responded Yes to the question, *"Do you consider yourself to be of mixed race, that is, belonging to more than one racial group?"* Furthermore, drawing on the data she used,[13] we found that the percentage of Blacks

---

[12] For a more theoretical discussion of race, see, for example, Omi and Winant (2015), *Racial Formation in the United States*; Nobles (2000), *Shades of Citizenship*; and Stokes-Brown (2012), *The Politics of Race in Latino Communities: Walking the Color Line*.

[13] We would like to thank Natalie Masuoka for generously sharing her data from the *Kaiser Family Foundation/Washington Post/Harvard University 2001 Race and Ethnicity Poll* (Kaiser Family Foundation 2001); Masuoka's and our analysis of the data were based

in the general population reporting a multiracial identity (31.1 percent) was virtually identical to that among elected officials in our survey (31.8 percent).

The percentage of Asian Americans in the general population reporting a mixed/multiracial identity (16.6 percent) was higher than that among elected officials of that group (5.7 percent), as was that for Latinos (36.5 percent in general population compared to 24.1 percent in the GMCL Survey).

Gender and Multiracial Identities

But what does a "multiracial identity" mean? The answer to this question is that it differs significantly for each group – and these differences reflect the theoretical, historical, legal, socially constructed, and administrative challenges discussed above. We also found that women officials (at 33.7 percent) were significantly more likely than their male counterparts (at 21.2 percent) to claim a background that included more than one group.

RACE, GENDER, AND DESCRIPTIVE REPRESENTATION IN AMERICA IN THE TWENTY-FIRST CENTURY

Political theorists generally consider there to be four types of political representation: descriptive, symbolic, substantive, and formalistic.[14] Though we discuss the meaning of each type in Chapter 7, here we describe the ways race and gender interplay when it comes to *descriptive* representation for Blacks, Asian Americans, and Latinos in America at the start of the twenty-first century. We consider as well some aspects of the *symbolic* dimension for elected political leaders of color and their constituents.

What is descriptive representation? John Adams, one of the framers of the US Constitution and the nation's second president, said it best: a

---

only on the survey of 1,709 people conducted March 8 to April 22, 2001. See documentation in her report for more details.

[14] According to Hannah Pitkin's (1967, 209) "dimensions of political representation," which we discuss and use in the analysis in Chapter 7, descriptive dimension refers to the extent to which the social characteristics of the representatives "look alike" or resemble in important ways the characteristics of the represented. The symbolic dimension refers to the extent that representatives "think alike" or "stand for" the values of the represented through the taking of a certain stance or making a certain speech that may earn the constituents' trust and confidence. In the substantive dimension, the representatives are expected to be "acting in the interests of the represented, in a manner responsive to them." The formalistic dimension refers to the institutional arrangements that regulate the selection and removal of representatives such as through the electoral mechanism.

representative body "should be in miniature, an exact portrait of the people at large" (Adams 1776). In its most basic and normative sense, achieving descriptive representation for people of color in this country would mean that the racial and gender composition of America's governing bodies from Congress, State Houses, city/town halls, to county and school boards would be, as a national average, about half women and about 40 percent people of color. This number would vary, naturally: all should still be 50 percent women, but the racial makeup could fluctuate from close to 0 to 100 percent depending on the demographic makeup of the jurisdiction.

What we find, instead, is that despite the remarkable growth overall, each group – whether by race, gender, or race*gender – is severely underrepresented in Congress, statewide offices, state legislatures, and local governing bodies. In Chapter 1 we demonstrate that White men are considerably overrepresented, and the Black women in Congress do as well as White women, although both rank well below where they should be by at least 50 percent. If government reflected proportional percentages, women, with more than half of the population, should hold at least 50 US Senate seats (instead of 20) and 218 House seats (instead of 82). Neither women in general, White women, nor women of color do better in other levels of office. And, as of mid-2016, no woman has ever been elected president of the United States.

In sum, we posit that, rather than assuming the growth in political representation and influence of minorities and women to be the result of a natural progression in a country that has become more diverse demographically, the United States has not become a "postracial" nation but one in which reforms move in the direction of racial change, but are constantly contested. Setbacks may be fully expected, given our institutional structures, and they have been an intrinsic part of our nation's history (Shaw, DeSipio, Pinderhughes, and Travis 2015). Getting elected to public office may just be the first step toward a more inclusive nation and exerting influence may take more than descriptive representation. We wish to contribute to a better understanding of what happens on the ground in American politics by accounting for evidence and possibilities of progress, however slow in coming or small in impact, by elected officials of color serving in state and local level offices. In fact, we argue in Chapter 1 that there may be two competing narratives in the post-1965 era: one is of important change or the promise of it, while the other is a continuing story of struggle as new dimensions of resistance to racial marginalization reveal themselves.

PART I

TRANSFORMING THE AMERICAN POLITICAL LANDSCAPE

I

Dual Narratives

Dramatic Growth and Continuing Underrepresentation

As the twenty-first century unfolds, two dominant narratives regarding race and gender in US politics emerge. On the one hand, American democracy has produced dramatic increases in the number of women and people of color who serve as elected officials at the local, state, and federal levels. Given the increasingly diverse racial and ethnic composition of the American electorate, the presence and influence of minorities – female and male – in America's governing structures promises further increase. On the other hand, our analyses suggest that patterns of underrepresentation at all levels are likely to persist for these populations as well.

In this chapter, we first provide the historical contexts for the changing political status of Blacks, Latinos, Asian Americans, and American Indians in the United States. Their histories, while having some parallels that may best be understood as narratives of exclusion, are still distinctive for each group and go far in driving growth in political representation as well as explaining their continued underrepresentation. Second, we describe the growth in descriptive representation achieved by elected officials of color. Third, we lay out the convergence of factors and structural changes that have occurred in the past fifty years leading to the growth in descriptive representation for people of color. Next, we provide an intersectional analysis that demonstrates the central role women of color have played in this growth. Finally we demonstrate the patterns of geographical distribution for each racial group, that is, the *geographical* landscape in which they function politically.

THE HISTORICAL CONTEXT

How do we make sense of both the growth in the numbers of elected officials of color and, at the same time, their continuing underrepresentation?
Throughout this book we argue that the gains in descriptive representation by people of color are neither markers for nor a natural progression
toward an increasingly tolerant postracial society, but rather the result of
political struggles by individuals and communities of color, struggles that
were contested at the time and continue to be contested today. Rather,
they must be understood within the gendered and racialized American
political context. Key to understanding this paradox is to acknowledge
that efforts by Blacks, Latinos, Asian Americans, and American Indians
to gain political representation and influence have faced resistance at
every step of reform and in numerous ways.

Narratives of Exclusion

The legal frameworks, economic institutions, constitutional recognition of citizenship, and different purposes for which African Americans,
Latinos, Asian Americans, and American Indians became part of the
Americas helped create important and varying patterns of political
life for each group. They have distinctive histories and experiences,
but they share what we have chosen to characterize as *narratives of
exclusion.*

Blacks were brought here from Africa by force and enslaved for
centuries.[1] The other groups represented by the elected officials in our
study arrived in the country from nations with complex diplomatic relations with the United States (e.g., Japanese and Chinese Americans);
were made part of the United States through postwar negotiations (e.g.,
Mexican, Puerto Rican, and Filipino Americans); or had been conquered
by population expansion and competition for land and natural resources
(e.g., American Indians, Native Alaskans).

The African American Experience

Generally more than 90 percent of the Black population was enslaved
for most of the period between the founding of the American Republic
and the abolition of slavery in 1865 at the end of the American Civil

---

[1] Portions of this section draw from and/or appeared in somewhat modified form in earlier
works (Lien 2006; Lien et al. 2007; Pinderhughes et al. 2009, esp. 5–7).

War. Freed from slavery and granted citizenship, Blacks nevertheless faced a long period of de jure segregation, which, accompanied by violence and the inattention of national government, strengthened by the decade (Payne 1995). The creation of sharecropping kept most Blacks outside of the cash economy and unable to acquire land or property (Du Bois 1999; Oliver and Shapiro 2006). In summary, slavery became deeply embedded in our nation from its inception, as European nations sought to create a labor force in the Americas capable of the work European settlers avoided if at all possible (Lowndes, Novkov, and Warren 2008).

After Blacks began to migrate to the North early in the twentieth century and entered the industrial economy, it might have been expected that they would gain access to better education and more stable employment, but racial discrimination in the North limited their participation in these sectors and region as well. Simultaneously, social policies created during the Franklin D. Roosevelt era deliberately eliminated protection for Blacks, including in the areas of social security, unemployment, and other supports that were routinely extended to Whites under the New Deal. This had the impact of undermining socioeconomic protection for the first and second generations of African Americans who migrated north early in the twentieth century. In the post–World War II period, a few Blacks began to take advantage of certain federal programs for education, including, for example, the GI Bill (Mettler 2005; Parker 2009; Payne 1995). While protecting civil rights, prohibiting employment discrimination, and promoting affirmative action in higher education ostensibly became national policy in the 1960s, these issues were only modestly addressed at the time (Hamilton and Hamilton 1997; Katznelson 2005; Oliver and Shapiro 2006; Williams 2003).

The centuries of slavery and racial subordination from the earliest years of colonial America helped generate what Dawson (2001) calls "linked fate," in which Blacks see their individual experiences related to the status of the group as a whole (see also Pinderhughes 1987; Williams 2003). For Blacks, this pattern of exclusion, the shared history, and experiences of discrimination, without added African immigration until recent times, produced a more consistent attitude, "linked fate," toward the American state and its relationship to the status of Blacks than has been the case with any other of the groups we study (Kluger 1975; Nelson 2000; Perry and Parent 1995; Tichenor 2002).

Latino Experiences

The Latino experience, in particular around issues of American citizenship, has differed for the various national groups. Lien (2006, 130–131) explains:

> Like American Indians, Mexicans were indigenous to the ten-state region known today as the American Southwest and West. Those living in this region gained U.S. citizenship at the end of the Mexican-American War (1846–1848) by means of the Treaty of Guadalupe Hidalgo of 1848.

She continues,

> Residents of the island of Puerto Rico received quasi-citizenship as U.S. nationals through the Jones Act of 1917. Puerto Rico is officially a commonwealth associated with the United States. Puerto Ricans may not vote in U.S. general elections, but they may carry U.S. passports for foreign travel and migrate to the U.S. mainland without immigration restrictions.... Mexican nationals as well as other legal Latino immigrants from South and Central America and the Caribbean who came in increasingly larger numbers in recent decades may become citizens through naturalization.
>
> Chicanos in the southwestern United States were gradually incorporated into the national polity, but were rapidly subordinated to the new "White" Anglo-Americans who settled and displaced the indigenous populations (see, e.g., Hero 1992).

The Cuban immigrant experience is equally complex (Masud-Piloto 1996). The United States gained control of Cuba as a consequence of the Spanish-American War in 1898. Although Cuba gained formal independence in 1902, many decades of internal strife, instability, efforts at reform, dictatorships, and continued US dominance followed. Fulgencio Batista won election in 1940, seized control in a bloodless coup in 1952, and remained in power under a repressive dictatorship until overthrown in 1959 in the Cuban Revolution led by Fidel and Raúl Castro (see Gott 2005, esp. 71–189).

Although initially supportive of the demise of the Batista regime, upper- and middle-class Cubans were quickly disenchanted by the Cuban Revolution and began immigrating to the United States Others entered the United States via Operation *Pedro Pan*, which at the time (1960–1962) was the largest exodus of unaccompanied minors to the United States in this country's history (Conde 1999; Torres 2003); Freedom Flights (1965–1973); and the Mariel Boatlift of 1980 (Silver et al. 1985). The United States has also provided considerable political and financial support for Cuban immigrants. The current "wet-foot, dry-foot" policy, under which "unless they cite fears of persecution, Cubans intercepted at sea are returned to Cuba, where the Cuban government, per signed accords, cannot retaliate against them, while those who reach the United States are generally permitted to stay and may adjust to permanent resident status after one year" (Rusin, Zong, and Batalova 2015, 1). The US policy toward Cuba entered a new phase in July 2015 with the restoration of full diplomatic relations between the two countries.

Asian American Experiences

Asian Americans were long isolated after the Chinese Exclusion Act of 1882 and other legislation barring immigration or citizenship. During World War II, about 120,000 Japanese Americans, of whom two-thirds were citizens, were sent to internment camps and had their property confiscated (Figure 1.1). President Franklin D. Roosevelt's Executive Order 9066 mandating these actions was upheld in *Korematsu v. United States* – a 1944 Supreme Court decision that has not, to this day, been officially rescinded (Lien 2006).

Japanese immigrants were eligible to become citizens in the 1950s, after the post–World War II legislation, when racial restrictions "set forth in the Nationality Act of 1790 were rescinded, [and] all Asian American groups were able to petition for naturalization" (Lien 2006, 131). However, small numbers of Asians, primarily of Japanese, Chinese, and Filipino origins, were still isolated from their families and denied citizenship or the comfort of new immigrant cohorts from their homelands prior to 1965 (Hing 1993). Now Asians of many different nationalities have access to the United States, and, except for certain refugee communities, tend toward a much more highly educated and high-income population than either Latino/as or African Americans (Saito 1998, 21–22).

Acceptance of the political incorporation of immigrants in this country seems to wax and wane. Burnham (1965, 9), for example, notes that in a number of western states, eager for settlers during the late nineteenth century, "aliens who had merely declared their intention to become citizens were permitted to vote." Despite bipartisan support for immigration reform during the second term of George W. Bush's presidency and again in 2013, for example, when the US Senate passed a sweeping immigration bill, many on the Right today would deny any path to citizenship for the 12 million or more immigrants who entered the country without legal documents.[2]

---

[2] Even today, many on both the Right and the Left seek to ensure ongoing access to a willing, cheap, and compliant work force because "despite its faults, illegal immigration has

FIGURE 1.1 People of Japanese descent awaiting transport to an internment camp 1942, with US troops at right.
Source: Associated Press, used with permission.

The American Indian Experience

The indigenous American Indian population, having been reduced by genocide from the time of the earliest European settlers, saw their rights further circumscribed by efforts to control, even destroy, the character and strength of tribal cultural life. For this group, "[u]nconditional federal citizenship arrived with the American Indian Citizenship Act of 1924, but many states continued to deny these Americans voting rights in as late as 1956" (Lien 2006, 130; see also, Wolfley 1991). For example, "The courts did not affirm the right of reservation Indians in

been hugely beneficial to many US [sic] employers" (Hanson 2009, 1). The candidates competing for the Republican Party presidential nomination have not only turned away from the idea of reform with a path to legalization, let alone citizenship, but they have also embraced ever-more-stringent anti-immigrant sentiments and policies, including building a wall on the border with Mexico, deporting all illegal immigrants, and banning all Muslims from entering (or reentering) the country. The outcome remains to be seen and depends greatly on the result of the 2016 presidential election.

Arizona and New Mexico to vote until 1948" (Blades 2016). World War II brought a need for more soldiers, leading to the Nationality Act of 1940, which affirmed the citizenship of American Indians. When the American Indians returned from war, they found that they still were not allowed to vote, however. And, once American Indians and Asian Americans were granted the right of naturalization following the enactment of the Immigration and Nationality Act in 1952, "[t]he Bureau of Indian Affairs beg[an] selling 1.6 million acres of Native American land to developers."[3]

According to Blades (2016), while lawmakers have curtailed the Indian vote in many states, "no state has been as bad as South Dakota." It was not until 1951 that South Dakota repealed its

1903 law requiring a culture test for Indians to prove they had abandoned their identity as Indians, their culture, their language and their homeland in order to vote or hold office. As late as 1975, authorities prohibited Indians from voting in elections in Todd, Shannon (now Ogala Lakota), and Washabaugh counties, whose residents were overwhelmingly Indian...[and] prohibited residents of these counties from holding county office until as recently as 1980 (Blades 2016).

The South Dakota attorney general, when prosecuting activists of the American Indian Movement (AIM) in the 1970s, told reporters, "The only way to deal with these AIM leaders is to put a bullet in their heads" (ACLU 2009, 28).

The concept of citizenship and voting rights for American Indians has been complicated by their triple citizenship – tribal, state, and federal – as well as by the tribal nations' unique sovereign governmental status and land-owning rights. Despite the potential conflicts between participation in tribal and nontribal elections, American Indians have registered, voted, and campaigned in nontribal elections in unprecedented numbers in recent years in order to preserve or protect their sovereignty, lands, treaty rights, and gaming interests (Lien 2006, 130).

At the beginning of the twentieth century, all four of the groups were legally constrained, but in sharply different ways. By its end, civil rights reform had significantly reframed the political status of Blacks, Latinos, Asian Americans, and American Indians, and had begun remaking the character of the American polity. The civil rights movement in the American South, the protests and challenges of Chicanos and Latinos in the American West and Southwest, the American Indian rejection of federal Indian policy, and Asian American legal campaigns and protests gradually opened the American political system to these groups (Carmichael and Hamilton 1967; Deloria 1985; Wei 1993).

[3] Source: "Brief History of American Response to Immigration." *Immigration News Daily*, www.idexer.com/articles/immigration_response.htm (Accessed June 27, 2016).

GAINING THE RIGHT TO VOTE PAVES THE WAY
TO INCREASED REPRESENTATION

Passage of the Voting Rights Act (VRA) of 1965 was a milestone in these efforts. With its subsequent amendments and renewals, citizenship, voting, and representation – long denied to Blacks and certain immigrant groups – had become largely available to all of the groups by the last decades of the twentieth century (Browning, Marshall, and Tabb 1990; Hero 1992; Shaw et al. 2015; Sonenshein 1993).

Voting Rights and the American State

Although, as of 2007, there were more than 14,000 elected officials of color,[4] securing the right to vote required complicated, lengthy efforts using the full federal system (Barker 1994). Linear progress from the creation of citizenship and voting rights to the rapid election of officials of color does not characterize this history. The racial/ethnic groups in this study had limited or no access to voting prior to the enactment of the 1965 Voting Rights Act. Voting first came into existence during Reconstruction through a series of amendments to the US Constitution, which provided for citizenship (Fourteenth Amendment) and voting (Fifteenth Amendment) to previously enslaved (Thirteenth Amendment) African Americans. These amendments created a constitutional foundation for citizenship and political participation for African Americans, yet still failed to sustain their political status for much longer than a decade or two. After the 1880s, southern states revised their state constitutions to evade the protections for the new class of citizens; the updates created poll taxes, grandfather clauses, literacy tests, multiple ballot boxes, and complex voter registration procedures (Shaw et al. 2015). And within two decades of the Civil War, Congress had erected further barriers to Chinese immigrants' access, as citizenship and other constitutional protections applied only to African Americans (Lien 2001; Tichenor 2002).

Enactment of the Voting Rights Act

Civil rights legislation of the mid-twentieth century (e.g., the 1957 and 1960 Civil Rights Acts) was followed by the 1964 Civil Rights and 1965 Voting Rights Acts (Keyssar 2009; Sullivan 2010). Box 1.1

---

[4] GMCL Project, 2007. See "National Database of Non-White Elected Officials: A Note on the Numbers," www.gmcl.org/database.htm

provides a helpful summary of legislation, extensions, and key provisions. The 1965 Voting Rights legislation shifted policy from case-by-case individual lawsuits claiming discrimination into a distinctive new framework that gave the national government power to govern state and county governments' behavior regarding the voting of African Americans.

Box 1.1. The Voting Rights Act: Key Provisions

General Provisions – 1965

Section 2: Reaffirms the Fifteenth Amendment. Prohibits state and local government from imposing any voting law that results in discrimination against racial minorities, including literacy tests, poll taxes, intimidation, and so forth.

Section 4: "Identifies jurisdictions using tests to discourage voters and where less than 50 percent of eligible citizens were registered/voted in 1964."

Section 5: (Preclearance provision): Prohibits jurisdictions from implementing any changes that affect voting without gaining preapproval from the US Attorney General or US District Court for the District of Columbia, to ensure that the proposed change does not discriminate against Blacks.

Provisions Based on the 1975 Extension

Section 203: Protects speakers of minority languages, for example, Spanish and/or Asian, and Native American languages, in areas where certain criteria are met; requires jurisdictions with large language-minority populations to provide ballots and other election materials in languages other than English.

Provisions Based on the 1982 Extension

Section 2 Violations may be proved by the effect of changes rather than the legislators' intent.

Section 4 Covered jurisdictions could "bail out" from (terminate) coverage.

(continued)

Provisions Based on the 2006 Extension

In 2006 Congress extended Sections 4, 5, and 203 for twenty-five years, but opponents brought a case (*Shelby County v. Holder*, 2013) to the Supreme Court, which struck down Section 4.

Sources: Shaw et al. (2015, esp. Figure 7.2, 216). See also "The Voting Rights Act of 1965" and "The 1970 and 1975 Amendments," available on the US Department of Justice website, www.justice.gov/crt/history-federal-voting-rights-laws (Accessed January 9, 2016).

The legislation included several provisions: Section 2 explicitly reaffirmed the post–Civil War Fifteenth Amendment, but greater power was also incorporated. Most significantly, Sections 4 and 5 created a new framework for denoting southern state and county jurisdictions, as *"covered,"* within which voting processes could be carefully monitored by federal officials. Jurisdictions were designated as deserving *coverage* if they used tests or devices to restrain voting and where less than 50 percent of the voting age population was registered to vote as of November 1964. *Covered* jurisdictions were required to seek preclearance for any new voting legislation; these new voting rights ordinances could be objected to and stopped at the federal level (Berman 2015; Davidson and Grofman 1994; Wirt 2008).

Renewals

The legislation required renewals at five-year or longer intervals (1970, 1975, 1982, 2006), which, although unintended, resulted in continuous innovation and expansion of Voting Rights policy. Two examples follow:

(1) **Language Minorities and Nationwide Framework.** Mexican Americans lobbied successfully for coverage when the Act was renewed in 1975 and their focus on protections from discrimination against Spanish-language speakers grew into language protections across a wide array of population groups, now termed "language minorities." (See, e.g., Flores 2015.) Coverage grew beyond the states of the Old Confederacy and evolved into a national rather than regional framework. See Lien, Pinderhughes, Hardy-Fanta, and Sierra (2007) for a brief discussion of this

change. The language provisions were extended again in 1982, 1992, and in 2006. American Indians were unique in their simultaneous extrafederal tribal (or *collective* status) sovereignty and their status as *individual citizens* under state laws. They obtained coverage under the VRA through language protections.

(2) **Voting and District Systems.** Southern states, such as Mississippi, set out to constrain the effects of civil and voting rights reforms; even after Blacks could and did vote, the introduction of at-large voting systems and various redistricting efforts limited their impact (Parker 1990). After the 1982 Voting Rights Extension, the Supreme Court's (1986) *Thornburg v. Gingles* decision upheld majority–minority districts as a strategy for providing an opportunity for Black, Latinos, Asians, and language minority voters to elect "representatives of their choice." In addition to minority vote dilution, majority–minority districts, single-member districts, and a complicated array of options associated with legislative redistricting were implemented.

With the historical context in mind, let us turn now to the changing face of political leadership in America at the beginning of the twenty-first century.

DRAMATIC GROWTH IN DESCRIPTIVE REPRESENTATION WITHIN A CONTESTED POLITICAL LANDSCAPE

The impact of the VRA on the growth of elected officials of color cannot be overstated. In our previous analysis (Lien et al. 2007, 491), we find that the vast majority of members of color in the US House of Representatives, as well as elected officials of color in general, were elected from districts covered by one or more provisions of the VRA.

Within just five years after passage of the Voting Rights Act in 1965, the number of Black elected officials rose by 425 percent, increasing sevenfold since 1970); and now stands at more than 10,500 (Bositis 2003a, 2012). The impact of the VRA was not limited to Blacks: "In fact, every single Latino member in the House was elected from a congressional district covered by the VRA, particularly under Section 203. Furthermore, a higher share of Latino than Black representatives was elected from districts with Section 5 coverage. Although a very small number, an equal proportion of Asian officials were elected from covered districts" (Lien et al. 2007, 491).

A similar pattern holds true at the state legislative and local levels. We found that the preponderance of the nation's elected officials of color (except for Asians at the county level) was elected from counties (or equivalent jurisdictions) that were protected by the VRA statutes. As is the case for state legislative district levels, Section 203 (the language provisions) had a significant effect on the election of Asian and Latino local officials, whereas, for the most part, Section 5 (preclearance) was most important for the election of Black local officials.

Data for Latino elected officials have been harder to come by for some years and methodologies changed, making exact comparability difficult, but the change over time has been similarly impressive: with the 1975 extension of the VRA revised to include language minorities, Latino officials rose by 363 percent over 1970 (see Figure 1.2). The number of Asian American elected officials, like the population, is smaller in overall number, but we have also seen a 273 percent increase for Asian Americans since the first data were gathered in 1978 (Lai, Cho, Kim, and Takeda 2001, 613; see Figure 1.3).[5]

Nevertheless, as a number of scholars have noted, "The emergence of Latino and Asian American elected officials is transforming racial and ethnic politics in numerous local and state political arenas" (Geron and Lai 2002, 42). From the perspective of descriptive representation, the growth in Black, Asian American, and Latino elected officials has, by its sheer size, had a major impact on the political landscape of this country.

CONVERGENCE OF FACTORS LEAD TO GROWTH

Barack Obama's historic victory was made possible by two great converging forces that began near the middle of the last century: the civil rights revolution and the changes engendered by the Immigration Act of 1965. The civil rights movement led to the rapid dismantling of Jim Crow and the inclusion of black Americans in politics, the military, the middle class and popular culture. The 1965 immigration act set in motion vast demographic and social changes that have altered the nation's ethno-racial landscape.

Orlando Patterson (2009, 23)

Impact of the Voting Rights Act

The huge gains for Blacks in registering to vote and the rise in the number of Black elected officials clearly derive from one of the historic bills

---

[5] It should be noted that the number of Asian American elected officials is likely considerably higher because, in contrast to the tabulations for Blacks and Latinos, data sources for Asian American elected officials in many years did not include either school board members or elected judges, in contrast to the sources for Blacks and Latinos.

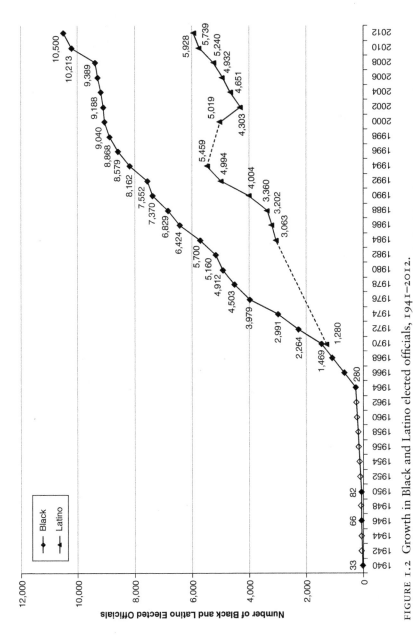

FIGURE I.2 Growth in Black and Latino elected officials, 1941–2012.

Note: The 1970 data point for Latinos is from Lemus (1973). The dashed line between 1995 and 2000 represents a period in which the methodology for counting school board members changed. Between 1992 and 1994,

Note continued in next page

passed in 1965: the Voting Rights Act. A modest increase in Black voter registration rates followed World War II, and then a sharp rise following passage of the VRA.

As Terchek (1980, 35) notes, "That registration by blacks increased following the Voting Rights Act is not surprising. What is surprising is the magnitude and distribution of the rise in registration within the space of three years"; he points out that "Registration among blacks in the Deep South increased from 21 percent in 1962 to 62 percent in 1967" (25–26). The impact in certain states was remarkable: "Mississippi, the state with the lowest median income, education, and previous registration of blacks, and with the highest proportion of blacks in its population, jumped from a registration of 6.9 percent of blacks in 1964 to 59.8 percent three years later" (Terchek 1980, 28). The literature on the impact of the Voting Rights Act is justifiably vast; for a summary of key elements of the law and its impact on Black registration in the South, see, for example, McCrary (2003); for the impact on Latino registration and voting of the 1970 and 1975 extensions to non–English-speaking minorities see, for example, Garcia (1986).

Equally striking is the increase in the number of Black elected officials since the VRA was enacted. The numbers were minuscule between 1940 and 1965. As a result of continued efforts, Blacks began a steady increase after passage of the VRA, which has continued without tapering off since then: rising from 33 in 1940 to more than 10,500 in 2012 (Figure 1.4). As we discuss later and in Chapter 2, some caution is appropriate: however dramatic the growth for Blacks, in particular, at that point in time their share of all elected positions in the United States was still only about 2 percent.

Note to Figure 1.2

the National Association of Latino Elected and Appointed Officials (NALEO) included all school-based Local School Councilmembers (LSCs) in Chicago; the apparent decrease between 1994 and 2000 is due to the fact that, for purposes of comparability, NALEO discontinued that practice. For more on this issue, see NALEO (2012, p. v). For ease of reading, not all data points are labeled; markers with no fill indicate extrapolations due to lack of data for those years. *Sources*: Data for Black elected officials are from the *National Rosters of Black Elected Officials*, prepared by the Joint Center for Political and Economic Studies, Washington, DC. For 1970–2000, see Bositis (2002); for 2009, the number is an estimate from Richard Hart, Joint Center for Political and Economic Studies. Latino data for 1984–2008 are from US Census (2012, 262) and NALEO (2012).

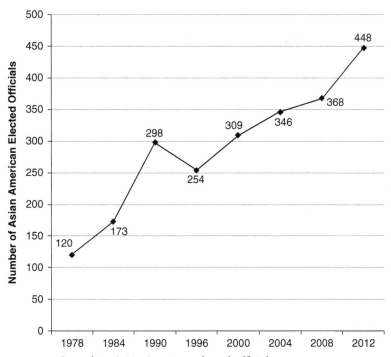

FIGURE 1.3 Growth in Asian American elected officials, 1978–2012.
Note: 2012 total includes school board member; other years may be inconsistent.
None of the totals include judges/judicial officials.
Sources: For 1978–2008, data are from *The National Asian Pacific American Political Almanac*, 1st to 13th editions, courtesy of Pei-te Lien, November 6, 2013. For 1996, data are from Lai et al. (2001, 613) and, for 2012, from *Political Database of the Asian Pacific American Institute for Congressional Studies*, http:// apaics.org/resources/political-database/ (Accessed November 5, 2013).

The Immigration Act of 1965: Demographic Changes and Shifting Political Influences

At the same time as the struggles to overcome centuries of oppression paid off with the Civil Rights Act of 1964 and the Voting Rights Act of 1965, other groups challenged the existing policy of highly restrictive country-of-origin quotas. According to Chin (1996, 273), the Immigration and Nationality Act of 1965 (also known as the Hart–Cellar Act) may prove to be one of the most consequential of the civil rights initiatives of the 1960s.

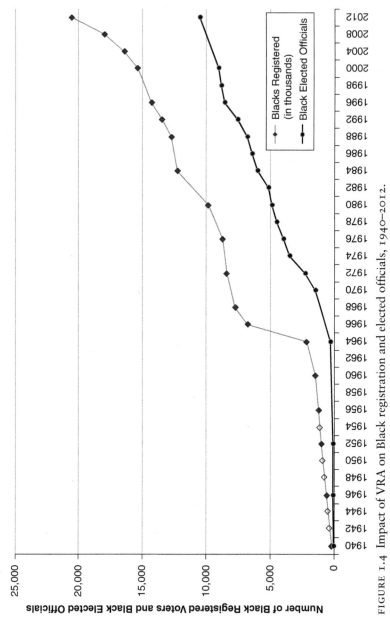

FIGURE 1.4 Impact of VRA on Black registration and elected officials, 1940–2012.

Note: Data are not available for all years, as indicated by data point markers that are either missing or have no fill.

Sources continued in next page

This legislation removed a preference for Anglo Whites that had been a central feature of American immigration and nationality law since 1790. As Carolyn Wong (2006, 44) writes, "[T]he new law brought an end to racist policies that had underpinned immigration law for many decades." Instead of country quotas, Hart–Cellar changed the admissions criteria; abolished quotas that had given preference to immigrants from Northern European countries; and took education, occupation, refugee status, and family reunification into account. Immigrants entering the country increasingly came from Latin America, Asia, and Africa, instead of select Northern European countries.[6]

In the fifty years since the passage of the Immigration and Nationality Act, the demographic landscape in this country has shifted dramatically (see Figure 1.5). In 1960 about nine out of every ten US residents were classified by the Census as White, and one in ten was Black. Latinos/as were counted in a variety of ways, but estimates suggest that in 1960 about 4 percent of the US population was "Hispanic origin."

By 2006, Latinos and Asians had grown to about 15 percent and 5 percent, respectively. By 2012, Latinos, Blacks, and Asian Americans made up "37% of the population, and they cast a record 28% of the votes in the 2012 presidential election, according to the election exit polls" (Taylor and Cohn 2012, 1). Furthermore, the US Census projects the nation will become majority–minority by 2050; non-Hispanic Whites are projected to fall to less than half; and Latinos will become close to a

---

Sources to Figure 1.4

Sources: Walton, Puckett and Deskins (2012, Table 23.1, 488) and Jaynes and Williams (1989). Data on registration rates prior to 1968 are for southern states only; data for 1968–2012 are from US Census Voting and Registration, *Reported Registration Rates in Presidential Election Years, by Selected Characteristics: November 1968 to 2012, Historical Time Series Tables*, www2.census.gov/programs-surveys/cps/tables/time-series/voting-historical-time-series/a10.xls (Accessed June 27, 2016). Data on Black elected officials through 2000 are from Bositis (2002); for 2012, the estimate is from the Joint Center for Political and Economic Studies, *National Roster of Black Elected Officials Fact Sheet 2012.*

---

[6] We recognize that this is a very short description of the Immigration and Nationality Act of 1965, and one that does not come close to covering its history, the struggles of many groups to change laws, policies, and practices, nor its differential impact on certain groups over time. There is a considerable literature on the subject, including, for example, Lien et al. (2007) and Tichenor (2002).

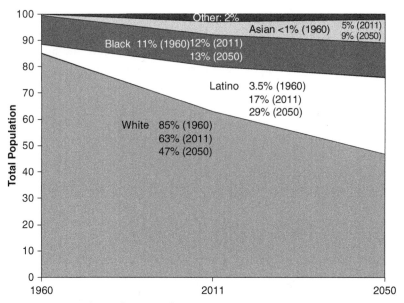

FIGURE 1.5 Population by race/ethnicity, 1960, 2010, and (projected) 2050. *Sources*: US Census data and the Pew Research Center (2012).

third of the US population. Blacks are likely to hold steady at 13 percent and Asian Americans to rise to 9 percent.

Demography Is Not Destiny: Influence beyond Population Growth

Parallel to the demographic shift comes a simultaneous shifting of political influence, with Latinos becoming a more powerful political force. During the 2008 and 2012 presidential elections, media and academics alike focused on the "Latino vote" – a practice that heated up in the 2016 race. At the same time, demography is not destiny. For example, despite the fact that the Black vote overwhelmingly supported Obama, and had a significant impact on his victory, Black population does not explain either the election of President Obama or the rise in Black political participation and influence, as the share of the population that is Black has increased only slightly over the past half century. Black leadership, not rising population numbers, made the difference. The title of Taylor's (2012) analysis of Black voter turnout, "The Growing Electoral Clout of Blacks Is Driven by Turnout, Not Demographics," makes his point. The outcome of the 2012 election was also a product of participation by a coalition of groups, including Asians, Latinos, and women of diverse races[7]; weariness with the party of George W. Bush; and the fact that it is rare for a candidate from the outgoing party to win.

GENDER AND GROWTH OF ELECTED OFFICIALS OF COLOR: LOOKING THROUGH AN INTERSECTIONAL LENS

The landscape of our democracy becomes even more complex when examined through the lens of intersectionality, with race, ethnicity, and gender not simply demographic classifications or identity markers, but rather factors that interact in dynamic ways with historical and structural political conditions. In other words, we would argue that the nation's *gendered* as well as ethnoracial landscape has also shifted substantially – and, according to a number of researchers, the growing clout of Blacks, Latinos, Asian Americans, and American Indians as elected officials is also driven by the contributions of women of color (see, e.g., Bositis 2003a, 2003b; Hardy-Fanta et al. 2005, 2006; Smooth 2006).

Analysis of the Gender and Multicultural Leadership (GMCL) National Database shows that, as a group, women of color currently make up about a third of all elected officials of color (Figure 1.6). The growth of female elected officials of color must be understood within the context of the gains and struggles discussed earlier. We must acknowledge similar trends but also different timelines for different groups. Figure 1.7, for example, shows that there were virtually no Black women elected officials until after the Voting Rights Act was passed in 1965; their numbers picked up in the 1970s, and took off in the 1990s. It is evident that the gains in Black female officeholders have outpaced those of Black males to the extent that Black women holding office now make up 37 percent of all Black officials, compared to just 11 percent in 1970.

In fact, since 1970, the number of Black female elected officials "increased twenty-fold, while the number of their male counterparts increased only four-fold" (Hardy-Fanta et al. 2006, 11). According to Bositis (2003a, 3), in the early 1970s, about 82 percent of new Black elected officials (BEOs) were men; by "the post-1995 period, 85 percent of the growth in the number of black elected officials was from black women being elected to office." In recent years, "all of the gains in the

---

[7] Teixeira and Halpin (2012, 4), for example, report, "President Obama achieved victory by carrying 93 percent of African American voters, 71 percent of Latino voters, [and] 73 percent of Asian American voters..."

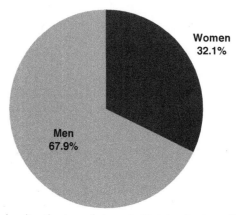

FIGURE 1.6 Gender distribution of elected officials of color, all levels.
Sources: GMCL National Database, 2006–2007; N = 10,159.

number of BEOs are attributable to gains in the number of black women holding office."

Data on trends for Latina women elected officials are not available for each year but they also show a similar pattern. First, according to the National Association of Latino Elected and Appointed Officials (NALEO), "The level of representation of Latinas ... in the United States is greater than the level for all female officeholders" (NALEO 2007, 2). Second, the pattern is similar to that of African Americans, with the number of Latina elected officials growing faster than that of their male counterparts: Latinas made up 12 percent of Latino officeholders in 1984; by 1988 their share rose to 19.7 percent (Hardy-Fanta et al. 2006, 11). "Between 1996 and 2010, the number of Latina elected officials grew faster than the number of male Latino officials; the number of Latinas increased by 105%, compared to 37% for male Latinos. As a result, the Latina share of all Latino elected officials grew from 24% in 1996 to 32% in 2010" (NALEO 2011, 2) – and to "nearly 35 percent of the total number of Latino elected officials nationwide" in 2014 (NALEO 2014, 1).

Carroll and Sanbonmatsu (2013, 98–99) note that the rise of female elected officials of color in general – with the vast majority Democrats – has contributed significantly to the overall growth in Democratic women in office – "a rise that is one of the most notable changes in women's office holding since the early 1980s." Bejarano (2013, 6) shows Latinas have made significant strides at attaining political office in the last ten years: "Latinas' political success has surpassed expectations and

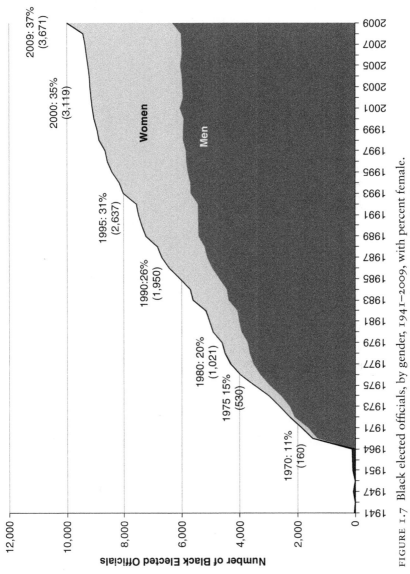

FIGURE 1.7 Black elected officials, by gender, 1941–2009, with percent female.

Note: Entries are year, percent female, and, in parentheses, number female.

Sources: Data for 1941–2000 are from Bositis (2002); data post-2000 are from Hart (2009).

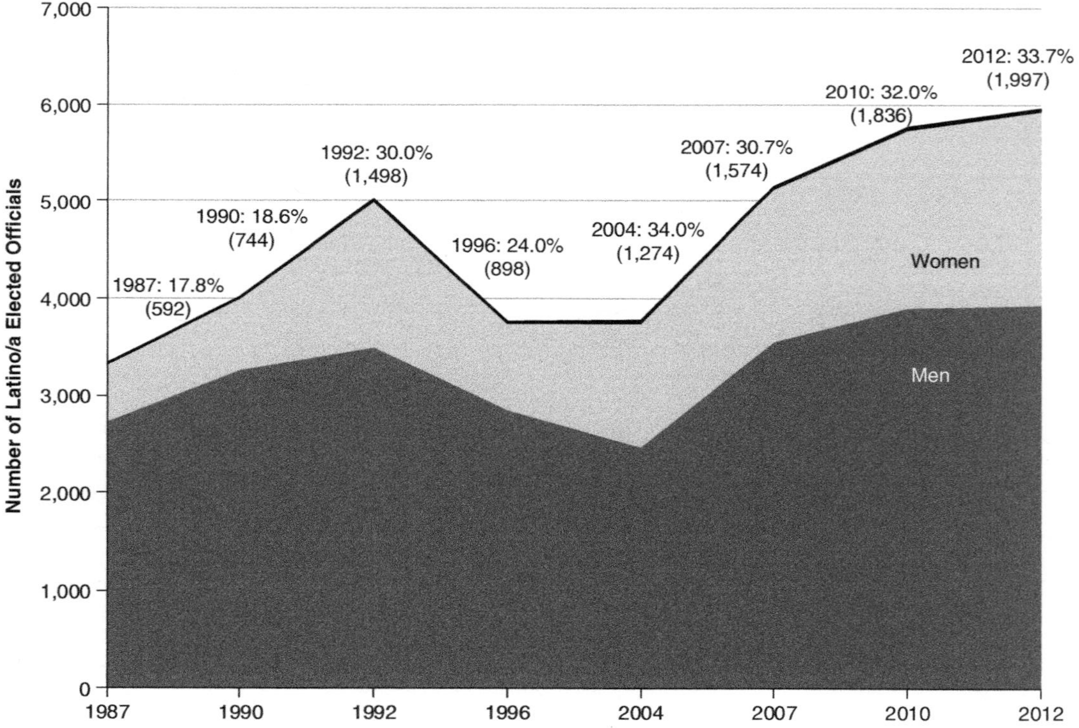

FIGURE 1.8 Latino/a elected officials, 1984–2012, with percent female (selected years).

Note: Entries are year, percent female, and, in parentheses, number female. Because data on the number of Latinas holding office are very limited, the chart shows only years for which these

Note continued in next page

explanations." She attributes these gains to "increased candidate quality" and advantages in terms of "attitudinal support" which, according to Bejarano, "results from the softening of perceived racial threat."

As Hardy-Fanta et al. (2006, 11) note, "Systematic long-term data and analysis of the office-holding patterns of Asian American women are also missing from the literature" (see also Lien 2001; Ong 2003). Our tabulations of data from various sources by gender for Asian American officeholders do suggest that, like other women of color, Asian American women appear to share a similar trend of dramatic growth over time (Figure 1.9).

In 2012 Asian American women made up 32 percent of all Asian American elected officials, up from just 12 percent in 1978. And, despite certain data limitations,[8] it is clear that, not only are women making up a larger percentage of Asian American elected officials over time, but also that their share of officials from this group is also increasing, in a pattern similar to that of the Black and Latino/a groups.

Comparing Growth of Women of Color and Non-Hispanic White Female Elected Officials

Women of color's share of all officeholders of color (32.1 percent; Figure 1.6) is significantly higher than the approximately 20 percent for

---

Note to Figure 1.8

data are available. See note in Figure 1.2 for explanation of apparent decrease in both Latino and Latina officials between 1994 and 2000.

Sources: See note for Figure 1.2 for data sources for 1984–2008; data for 1987 are from Sierra and Sosa-Riddell (1994); otherwise, the breakdown by gender is from NALEO directories for the relevant years.

[8] A cautionary note: data collection methods for Asian American elected officials differ by source and year. The data presented in Figure 1.9 likely underestimate the number of Asian American elected officials overall and the percentage of women in particular. For example, in contrast with the numbers reported earlier for Blacks and Latinos/as, those for Asian American women do not include judges; furthermore, in many years the rosters of the officials from which these data are drawn do not include (or vastly underreport) elected school board members and yet the number of school board members is often somewhat larger than that of all other levels combined, even when judges are excluded from the tabulation. In one of the years that did include school board members (2007–2008), for example, there were 278 listed whereas officeholders from all other (nonjudicial) positions combined totaled just 263. Given that women do make up a relatively large number of elected officials at the school board level, not having consistent access to this level in other years means that the percentage of Asian American women is not fully represented.

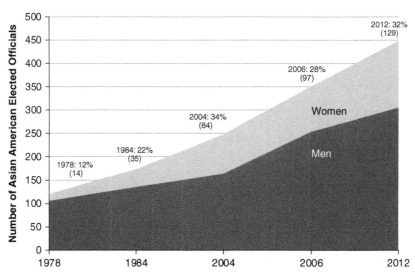

FIGURE 1.9 Asian American elected officials, 1978–2012, by gender with percent female (selected years).

Note: Entries are year, percent female, and, in parentheses, number female. The total for 2012 includes school board members. None of the totals include judges/judicial officials. The years shown are those for which gender was able to be determined.

Source: For 1978–2008: *The National Asian Pacific American Political Rosters/ Almanac*, 1st to 13th editions, courtesy of James Lai and Pei-te Lien, November 6, 2013. For 1996: Lai et al. (2001, 613); for 2006, the GMCL National Database; for 2012: Political Database of the Asian Pacific American Institute for Congressional Studies, http://apaics.org/resources/political-database/ (Accessed November 5, 2013) and the 2011–2012 *National Asian Pacific American Political Almanac*.

non-Hispanic White women.[9] For the past decade or more, researchers have noted that, especially since the early 1990s, women of color have been driving the growth in elected officials of color in a way that has surpassed that of non-Hispanic White women. Several scholars have confirmed our finding that female legislators of color have not achieved a level of representation proportionate to their share of the population, yet they do hold more seats than White women as a proportion of their

---

[9] Data on non-Hispanic White women are difficult to come by at lower levels of office. A recent report by *Who Leads US?* (2014) indicates that they make up 25 percent of all 42,000 elected officials in their database; a review of their data suggests, however, that their numbers are overstated and prone to errors. For example, 81 percent of officials in their dataset apparently serve at the county level and less than 1 percent at the municipal level; adjusting for these errors, we estimate their percentage to be closer to our own: 20 percent.

respective racial/ethnic group (Darcy and Hadley 1988; Fraga et al. 2003; Fraga and Navarro 2007; Hardy-Fanta et al. 2005, 2006; Pachon and DeSipio 1992; Scola 2006, 2014; Tate 2004).

Growth in Congress, by Race and Gender

Much has been made of the fact that the proportion of women in the 113th Congress reached 18.5 percent. Figure 1.10 shows that the share of women in Congress who are women of color has continued to increase (from 1.1 percent in 1991 to 5.6 percent in 2013), whereas, since 2005, the share of their non-Hispanic White counterparts has, at best, plateaued at 12.9 percent.

Furthermore, even the decade following the so-called "Year of the Woman" (1992) produced distinctive patterns of growth: over this period, the rate of change may have doubled for non-Hispanic White women in Congress, but it tripled for women of color.

Growth in State Legislatures, by Race and Gender

The number of women in state legislatures has increased as well (Figure 1.11). What has received less attention is the significant variation by race in this growth, and how women of color have driven the growth in a way that parallels their contribution to that of their respective racial groups, discussed earlier. In 1983, when data first began to be collected, Black women made up just 7 percent of female state legislators. Their numbers doubled between 1983 and 1991, from 59 to 124, and doubled again to 243 by 2013; their share is now 20.5 percent.

The slope of the line for Latinas in Figure 1.11 looks more gradual because of the differences in total size among groups, but, in fact, their numbers quintupled within two decades: from just 15 in 1991 to 79 in 2013 (Carroll and Sanbonmatsu 2013, 101–102). Our analysis of data from 1983 indicates that their numbers have increased tenfold since that point in time. Of particular note is the fact that, as seen in the graphic in Figure 1.12, Latinas are the group among all female state legislators that has grown the most since 1991, followed by Asian American and Black women, whose numbers have doubled in the past two decades.

The importance of taking an intersectional look at the growth of female elected officials is demonstrated by the fact that the percent change in the numbers of women of color greatly overshadows that of women as a whole, who grew by just 31 percent – and even more of non-Hispanic White women, whose numbers increased by just 17 percent since 1991, whereas women of color more than doubled during the same time period

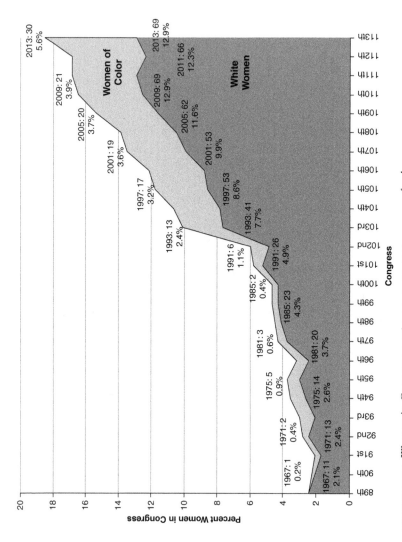

FIGURE 1.10 Women in Congress, 1965–2013, percent women of color.

Note: Entries are year, number, and percent in Congress for women of color and (non-Hispanic) White women; the top line shows the percent of all women.

Sources continued in next page

(see shaded area in Figure 1.11). Figure 1.12 also shows that American Indian women made gains during this period, doubling their numbers; starting at just six female state legislators in 1991, their percent change should be viewed with some caution, as it reflects the power of small numbers.[10]

FACTORS CONTRIBUTING TO GROWTH IN DESCRIPTIVE REPRESENTATION OF WOMEN OF COLOR

How do we account for the gains in descriptive representation by Black, Latina, and Asian American women? As mentioned earlier, passage of the Voting Rights Act of 1965 was a key factor in accounting for the dramatic growth of elected officials of color in recent decades. Focusing on Black women, a number of scholars suggest that the modest but significant rise in the number of Black women elected officials of color was due to opportunities created by the Voting Rights Act, in particular, redistricting that created Black-majority districts. Darcy and Hadley (1988, 633), for example, suggest that redistricting under the VRA "created an opportunity for black women." Black women's activism within the Civil Rights Movement, including their reaction to marginalization because of their sex within the movement, was also an important factor.

Sources to Figure 1.10

Sources: "History of Women in the U.S. Congress," www.cawp.rutgers.edu/history-women-us-congress (Accessed June 27, 2016); 1998–2013 data are from individual fact sheets, by year, from the Center for American Women and Politics (Accessed November 14, 2013). For women of color, data are also from "Women of Color in Congress," www.history.house.gov/Exhibitions-and-Publications/WIC/Historical-Data/Women-of-Color-in-Congress/ (Accessed June 27, 2016). See also Manning and Brudnick (2014).

[10] Furthermore, tabulating the numbers of women (or men) who are in state legislatures is also subject to some debate for certain groups. The National Caucus of Native American State Legislators (NCNASL), for example, reports seventy-two American Indian state legislators (of which 36.1 percent are women), but there is some overlap with Asian Americans in Hawaii. Gender analysis even for this relatively small and well-documented list is further complicated, with the Center for American Women and Politics (CAWP) suggesting that there are just thirteen female Native American legislators, whereas our analysis of data by the NCNASL (Daffron 2013) reveals twice that many. For the sake of consistency across all groups, we are using CAWP data, but invite more research on American Indian legislators by gender.

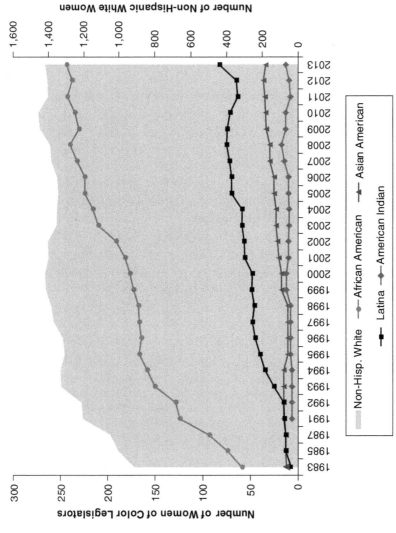

FIGURE 1.11 Women of color state legislators, by race, 1983–2013.

Note: This figure was constructed by the GMCL Project, 2014, building on one in Carroll and Sanbonmatsu (2013, 102); our chart adds data from additional years (1983–1990) and, in the shaded area with their numbers in a second scale on the right, for non-Hispanic White women state legislators.

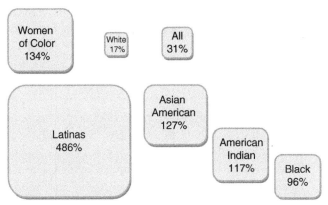

FIGURE 1.12 Women state legislators, percent change, 1991–2013, all women and by racial group and non-Hispanic White women.
Note: Squares are approximately proportional to the degree of percent change.
Source: Data for this figure were compiled by the GMCL Project, 2014, from the archived and current fact sheets of the Center for American Women in Politics.

Impact of Majority–Minority Districts

Darcy and Hadley's (1988) investigation of state and local politics finds that the initial creation of majority–minority districts produced an increase in the number of open seats, which may have proved beneficial for the election of Black women. Moncrief, Thompson, and Schumann (1991) seek to answer the question of why Black women made more gains at the state level of elective office than their White female colleagues did. After examining 1,500 legislators from eleven states, the authors eventually conclude that factors such as political ambition and level of education were unsatisfactory explanations of Black women's electoral gains. They instead point to the initial creation of new majority-Black districts, which essentially created open seats in which Black women could contest an election without challenging a male incumbent, as a key factor that may have helped Black female legislators relative to White female legislators. (See also Hardy-Fanta et al. 2006; Lien 2006; Lien et al. 2007; and Tate 2003).

The Anita Hill–Clarence Thomas Hearings: Impact of the "Year of the Woman"?

In 1991, President George H. W. Bush nominated Clarence Thomas to fill the US Supreme Court seat vacated by the retirement of the first

Black Supreme Court Justice and legendary NAACP civil rights lawyer, Thurgood Marshall. Thomas, a Black man with conservative credentials, was the former head of the Equal Employment Opportunity Commission (EEOC) and served on the United States Court of Appeals for the District of Columbia Circuit. His nomination generated intense debate within the racial and liberal interest communities over his suitability as to descriptive or substantive representation, given the more liberal ideology and Democratic Party affiliation of Blacks in this country. (See discussion in the Introduction and Chapter 7 of this volume.)

Then Anita Hill's allegations of sexual harassment against Thomas generated racial versus gender conflict across partisan, racial, *and* gender dimensions. Thomas's Senate confirmation hearings, televised on C-Span and on the national networks gripped the nation as many watched law professor Anita Hill being grilled by an all-White-male Senate committee (Pinderhughes 1992; 1995). Stimulated, to a great extent, by these proceedings, "a record 119 women stood for election as major party candidates for the House and Senate and 53 of them were victorious" (Dolan 1998, 272). And, according to Bositis (2012, 18), like women in general, the number of Black women candidates for Congress almost doubled (from 8 to 14) between 1990 and 1992; they made up 12 percent of all female candidates that year.

We should point out that Black women and White women responded to the hearings in different ways and for different reasons. Mansbridge and Tate (1992), for example, seemed to conclude that "race trumped gender" when African Americans were faced with the conundrum of "choosing" between supporting Clarence Thomas or Anita Hill. Indeed, public opinion polls at the time suggested that Blacks did see the racism as a greater threat to progress than the sexism Anita Hill confronted. Nevertheless, Figure 1.13 shows clearly that a significantly larger percentage of women of color (74 percent) than men of color (66.6 percent) ran for office the first time in the post-1992 era.

The literature also suggests that, once women of color candidates – especially Black women – run for office, the effects of the VRA kick in: "[T]he single most important fact that explains the higher percentage of Black women serving in the U.S. Congress is the new opportunities created by the Voting Rights Act in providing new majority-Black districts from which to run" (Tate 2003, 64–65). Tate continues: "The largest surge in the numbers of women occurred in 1992 when thirteen new Black lawmakers were added to the House, all because of the new Black districts that had been created" – and five of the thirteen (38.5 percent) were women.

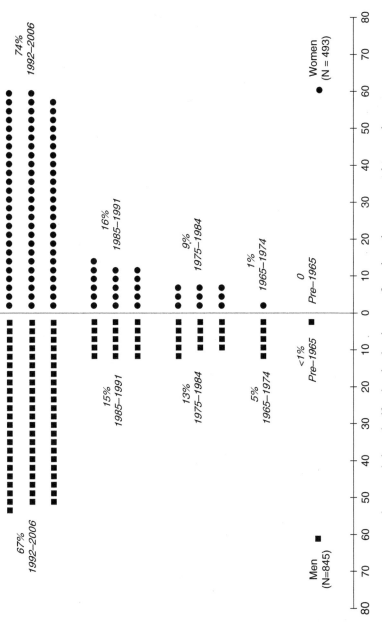

FIGURE 1.13 Distribution of elected officials of color, by year first elected, percent within gender.
Source: GMCL National Survey, 2006–2007.

59

Other factors may also contribute to a surge in numbers, especially for women of other racial/ethnic groups. A "perfect alignment" of factors, for example, propelled Asian American women to historic gains in Congress in 2012. Three were incumbents (Doris Matsui, Judy Chu, and Colleen Hanabusa), and three of the four new women were running for an open seat (Mazie Hirono, Tulsi Gabbard, and Grace Meng), which has been well documented as helping women candidates (Burrell 1992).

Three of the four Asian American women who ran as challengers had held national, state, and/or local offices prior to running, including Mazie Hirono, who moved up from the House to the Senate, and two (Tammy Duckworth and Tulsi Gabbard) were veterans of the Iraq War. Six of the seven were from Hawaii or California, where Asian Americans make up large percentages of the state and local populations. All were Democrats who ran with an incumbent Democratic President Barack Obama, a childhood resident of the state of Hawaii. It remains to be seen whether such a dramatic increase during one election cycle – and in one level of office – represents a rising trend for Asian American political representation or a one-time occurrence.

We must return now to the other narrative of this chapter – and, indeed, the book – the apparent paradox of growth coinciding with continued underrepresentation.

CONTINUED UNDERREPRESENTATION BY GENDER IN A CONTESTED POLITICAL TERRAIN

The growth in descriptive representation laid out in the preceding text has not come easily and coexists with continuing underrepresentation. Furthermore, the instruments of growth – that is, passage of the 1965 Voting Rights Act and subsequent amendments, immigration policy reform, and the role and contributions of women of color – have not been sufficient to yield descriptive representation for communities of color proportional to their shares in the population.

Furthermore, women make up more than half of the American population (and more than half of all voters), but these facts have not translated into proportional representation for women of color or White women at any level of government.[11]

---

[11] Some scholars (see, e.g., Hancock 2009) argue that, while Obama certainly faced racism and Hillary Clinton sexism in 2008, a subtle dynamic may have been that he benefited from being male and she from being White.

Indeed, elected officials of color – male or female – and women in general have not achieved political parity, that is, representation proportionate to their shares of the population. Political parity is achieved when the share in each level of office is equal to the group's share of the population; in such cases the parity index would be 1.

Race and Gender Parity in Congress

What we find is that non-Hispanic Whites are overrepresented in Congress as a share of their population, with a parity ratio of 1.32 (Table 1.1), although White men are at 2.25 compared to White women's .39. With the Black population in the United States at about 14 percent and their share of seats in the US Congress at 7.9 percent, Blacks's ratio of 0.56 is a bit more than half of where it should be. Parity ratios for Latinos and Asian Americans are just 0.34 and 0.31 respectively. American Indians, with just two members of Congress, fare the worst.

Parity by race and gender together presents a mixed picture, with Black men coming closest to parity, and Black and Latina women faring worse than their male counterparts within each racial group; among women, Black and Asian American women's congressional parity ratios equal those of non-Hispanic White women (see Table 1.1). In contrast, the parity ratio for Latina women is quite low, just 0.21; the parity ratio for Asian American women is the only one that is higher than that of their male counterparts and it remains to be seen whether this growth is sustained or was a single-election occurrence. No American Indian women serve in Congress.

Small comfort is the fact that, with Non-Hispanic White men so *over*-represented (at 2.25), one could argue that women of that group have farther to go to achieve parity with White men – or men have farther to fall.

Race and Gender Parity in State Legislatures

How do state legislators of color fare in proportion to their respective shares of the population? We find that Blacks do somewhat better at this level than in Congress, with a parity ratio of 0.63, and Latinos do worse (0.22), with less than a quarter of the seats they should have, and Asian Americans at 0.30 (Table 1.2). The differences in parity ratios by gender*race are stark, with White men at 2.10 in state legislators compared to 0.45 for Black women and just 0.14 for Latina and Asian American women; among men of color state legislators, only Black men approach parity (0.78).

TABLE 1.1. *Parity Ratios by Race and Gender, 113th Congress, 2013–2014*

	Black			Latino/a			Asian American			American Indian			Non-Hispanic White		
	All	Women	Men	All	Women	Men	All	Women	Men	All	Women	Men	All	Women	Men
N =541	42	16	27	30	9	19	10	7	3	2	0	2	451	68	382
% among Congress	7.9	3.0	5.0	5.6	1.7	3.7	1.9	1.3	0.9	0.4	0.0	0.4	84.3	12.8	70.6
% among US population	14.0	7.3	6.7	16.3	8.1	8.3	6.0	3.2	3.0	1.7	1.0	1.0	63.7	32.5	31.4
Parity ratio	0.56	0.41	0.74	0.34	0.21	0.45	0.31	0.40	0.31	0.24	0.00	0.37	1.32	0.39	2.25

Note: The *N* includes nonvoting delegates; for precedent, see Manning, Shogan, and Brudnick (2013). The parity ratio is calculated as the percentage share of all legislators divided by the percentage share of the national population for each group of women and men according to US Census estimates of the US population by "race alone or in combination"; the population estimates are based on the 2010 Census (see Humes, Jones, and Ramirez 2011).

Sources: GMCL Project, 2014; Annual Estimates of the Resident Population by Sex, Race, and Hispanic Origin for the United States: April 1, 2010 to July 1, 2012." US Census Bureau, Population Division. Release Date: June 2013.

TABLE 1.2. *Parity Ratios by Race and Gender, State Legislators, 2012*

	Black			Latino/a			Asian American			American Indian			Non-Hispanic White		
	All	Women	Men	All	Women	Men	All	Women	Men	All	Women	Men	All	Women	Men
N (Total N=7,382)	664	243	387	221	81	186	73	33	100	72	26	46	6,349	1,422	4,880
% among state legislators	8.53	3.3	5.2	3.62	1.1	2.5	1.80	0.5	1.4	0.97	0.4	0.5	86.0	19.3	66.1
% among US population (2010)	13.6	7.3	6.7	16.3	8.1	8.3	6.0	3.2	3.0	1.7	1.0	1.0	63.7	32.5	31.4
Parity ratio	0.63	0.45	0.78	0.22	0.14	0.30	0.30	0.14	0.45	0.57	0.35	0.50	1.35	0.59	2.10

Note: The parity ratio is calculated as the percentage share of all legislators divided by the percentage share of the national population for each group of women and men according to US Census estimates of the US population by "race alone or in combination"; the population estimates are based on the 2010 Census (see Humes, Jones, and Ramirez 2011).

Sources: GMCL Project, 2013. The total number of state legislators is from the National Conference of State Legislatures (NCSL) for each racial group and is the product of percents provided by NCSL times the total,www.ncsl.org/research/about-state-legislatures/number-of-legislators-and-length-of-terms.aspx (Accessed November 5, 2013). Population data are from Annual Estimates of the Resident Population by Sex, Race, and Hispanic Origin for the United States: April 1, 2000 to July 1, 2009. (NC-EST2009-03). U.S. Census Bureau, Population Division. Release date: June 2010. Data for Black and Latino men in office during 2012 are courtesy of the Joint Center for Political and Economic Studies and National Association of Latino Elected and Appointed Officials; data for Asian Americans are from the 2011–2012 *National Asian Pacific American Political Almanac*, courtesy of James Lai, Santa Clara University; White women and men in office in 2010 are courtesy of Becki Scola. The number of American Indian women in office are from "Women of Color in Elective Office 2013" (CAWP 2013a). Data on American Indian state legislators are from the National Caucus of Native American State Legislatures, courtesy of Irene Kawanabe, plus research reported by Daffron (2013); the N for all adds up to more than the total of 7,382 state legislators because the American Indian count (N = 72) includes officials who may also be counted in another group, especially Asian American, particularly those in Hawaii and Alaska. See text for explanation. Note also that the category "American Indians" includes a number of state legislators also counted in the Asian American group because Native Hawaiians are counted as both Native American and Asian.

Despite continuing underrepresentation, the growth discussed in this chapter has transformed the American political landscape. One of the most concrete ways to visualize how the political landscape has been changed by the election of greater numbers of Black, Latino/a, Asian American, and American Indian officials is to examine where these officials are located geographically. Using data from the GMCL National Database, we mapped the geographical distribution of elected officials of color from each racial group by state.

Mapping the Geographical Landscape for Elected Officials of Color

Map 1.1 shows that, at the time the GMCL National Database was constructed (in 2006), Black elected officials were quite concentrated in one region – with seven out of ten located in the South. At the same time, Black elected officials tend to be more dispersed than the other ethnoracial groups: there were no states with a share of Black elected officials greater than 9 percent of the total, but there were also just three states where there were no Black elected officials (Montana, North Dakota, and South Dakota). These findings are consistent with Bositis (2003b) and Kaba and Ward (2009, 42).

In contrast, about half (47.4 percent) of Latinos holding elective office were concentrated in the West, with another four in ten elected in southern states (see Map 1.2). Although much has been made of the growing migration of Latinos even to "deep South" states such as Louisiana (especially post-Katrina: see, for example, Smith and Furuseth 2006; Winders 2005) and North Carolina, the real reason for the high percentage in the South is that Texas (which 40 percent of Latino/a elected officials call home) is considered to be in the South (at least by US Census designation), despite its historical connection to the American Southwest or its iconic western cowboy image in American popular culture. (Some might also argue that Texas' political character resembles the South more than the political cultures often associated with the West (such as libertarian or even liberal values.)

A quarter of Latino/a elected officials were in California; thus, more than 60 percent of all Latino elected officials lived in just these two states. About one in ten were found in Arizona and New Mexico. Differently from the distribution of Blacks, there were many more states in 2006 with no Latino/a elected officials: Alabama, Alaska, Arkansas, Kentucky,

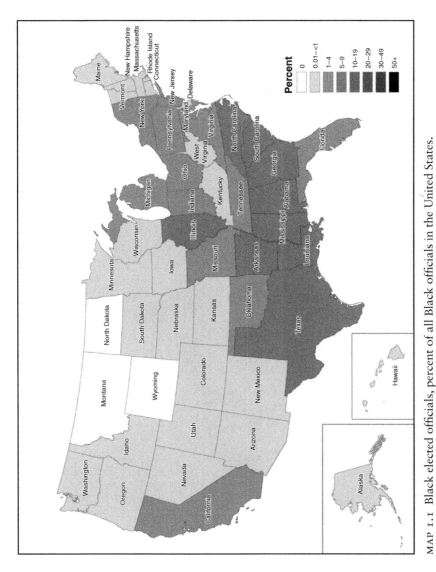

MAP 1.1 Black elected officials, percent of all Black officials in the United States.
Note: The shading indicates the percentage of all Black elected officials in the state as a percent of all
Black elected officials nationally (N = 6,020) in 2006–2007.
Sources: GMCL Project, 2011, and ESRI, Inc.

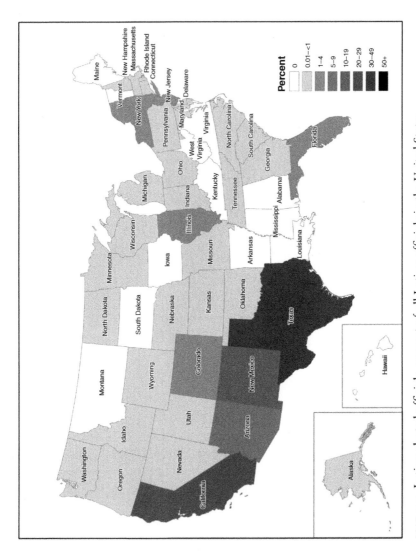

MAP 1.2 Latino elected officials, percent of all Latino officials in the United States.
Note: The shading indicates the percentage of all Latino elected officials in the state as a
percentage of all Latino elected officials nationally (*N* = 3,737) in 2006–2007.
Sources: GMCL Project, 2011, and ESRI, Inc.

Maine, Mississippi, Montana, Oklahoma, South Carolina, South Dakota, Vermont, and West Virginia.

The geographical landscape is even more dramatically concentrated for Asian American elected officials, with three-quarters in just two states: California and Hawaii (Map 1.3). At the time of the construction of the GMCL National Database in 2006, there were no Asian American elected officials in almost half (23) of the states.

State Rankings: Another Perspective on Geographical Distributions

Another way of looking at the distribution of elected officials of color is through their state rankings. Table 1.3 shows the distribution and state rankings of elected officials by race for the "top 20" states ranked on their number and share of all elected officials for each racial/ethnic group. For each group, the table also displays their respective shares of the total US population living in the state and the percent the group made up of each state's population at the time we constructed the GMCL National Database. For example, Mississippi ranked first for Blacks: the 531 Black officials in that state (column 2) means that close to one in ten (8.8 percent) of all Black elected officials in the United States held office in Mississippi (column 3). At that time, 2.8 percent of the Black population in the United States lived in Mississippi (column 4), where they made up 37 percent of the state population (column 5).[12]

Of particular note are the following. First, as seen in the maps and Table 1.3, the geography of Black representation is markedly different than that of Latinos and Asian Americans. The Latino top-ranked state (Texas) included 40 percent of all Latino elected officials in the county, with 19 percent of the Latino population in the United States, with Latinos making up 37.6 percent of the state's population. The picture for Asian American officials is even more striking: the top state was California, with more than half of all Asian officials in the United States; almost a third of all Asians in the United States resided in California, although they only made up 13.4 percent of the state's population. One in five of all Asian American elected officials was found in the second-highest ranked state

[12] It is not possible to determine the percent of elected officials of color in a given state because there is no way to determine how many local elected positions there are (i.e., a denominator) to use in the calculation.

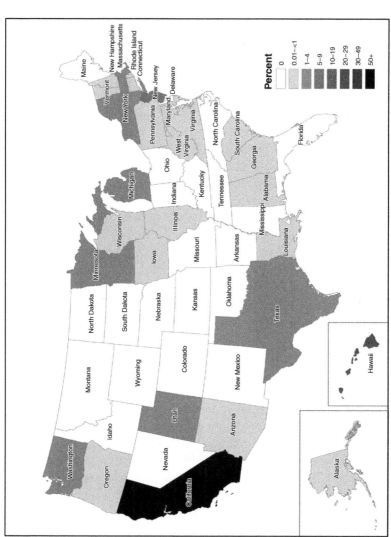

MAP 1.3 Asian American elected officials, percent of all Asian American officials in the United States. *Note:* The shading indicates the percentage of all Asian American elected officials in the state as a percentage of all Asian American elected officials nationally (*N* = 351) in 2006–2007. *Sources:* GMCL Project, 2011, and ESRI, Inc.

of Hawaii. Although Asians made up almost half of the state's population, owing to the relative size differentials of the states, these represent just 4.4 percent of the total Asian population in the country. In comparison, none of the highest ranking states for Black elected officials reached even 10 percent: in fact, almost one in ten of Black officials served in a state beyond the "top 20" (see "All other states" row in Table 1.3).

Second, population density does not necessarily determine rank for Black political leadership. Although the state rankings on representation for Latinos in Texas and California and for Asian Americans in California and Hawaii may seem logical because of their respective shares of the population, there are a number of states with large Black populations that rank very low in terms of the number and share of Black elected officials. Maryland is a case in point: Blacks made up 29.4 percent of the state population, but with just 96 Black officials (1.6 percent of all in the United States), it ranked last, even below California, which had a Black population of just 6.2 percent.

Distribution of American Indian Elected Officials

As discussed in the Introduction, American Indians are one of the least studied racial/ethnic groups in American politics. Whereas there is a body of literature on tribal politics, very little data have been collected on nontribal elected officials who are American Indian/Native American. Despite the fact that, for this group, the GMCL National Database includes only American Indian state legislators, the geographical analysis by state is interesting for several reasons. For example, more than one in five (21.2 percent) American Indian state legislators may be found in the top-ranked state of Oklahoma, whereas that state's share of the total American Indian population in the United States was about 10 percent, and at the time of data collection made up 8.6 percent of the state's population (see Table 1.4).

Furthermore, their representation (as state legislators) is limited to just 16 states, and there are no state legislators representing this group in California, despite the fact that it is the state with the largest share (12.6 percent) of American Indians in the country. At the same time, given the state's size, this group's share of California's population (final column in Table 1.4) is just 1 percent. Also of interest is that, with American Indians making up 14.8 percent of the population in Alaska, their proportional share of state legislators should be higher than that of

TABLE 1.3. *Distribution of Elected Officials by Race: State Rankings, Top 20 States*

Black Elected Officials in State		Black Population			Latino Elected Officials in State	
State Ranking	N	As Percent of *All* Black Elected Officials	Share of US Black Population in State	Percent of State Population	State Ranking	N
Mississippi	531	8.8	2.8	37.0	Texas	1493
Alabama	498	8.3	3.2	26.2	California	851
Louisiana	466	7.7	3.7	32.0	New Mexico	464
Georgia	457	7.6	7.6	30.5	Arizona	298
South Carolina	425	7.1	3.3	27.9	Colorado	117
North Carolina	402	6.7	5.2	21.5	New Jersey	107
Arkansas	387	6.4	1.1	15.4	Florida	93
Illinois	379	6.3	4.7	14.5	Illinois	67
Texas	311	5.2	7.8	11.8	New York	53
Florida	225	3.7	7.8	16.0	Connecticut	31
New Jersey	208	3.5	3.1	13.7	Massachusetts	20
Michigan	194	3.2	3.5	14.2	Washington	15
Ohio	183	3.0	3.6	12.2	Pennsylvania	14
Virginia	178	3.0	4.0	19.4	Michigan	12
New York	139	2.3	7.9	15.9	Kansas	11
Tennessee	139	2.3	2.7	16.7	Oregon	11
Missouri	129	2.1	1.8	11.6	Indiana	9
Pennsylvania	116	1.9	3.5	10.8	Maryland	9
California	102	1.7	6.0	6.2	Wisconsin	8
Maryland	96	1.6	4.4	29.4	Nevada	6
All Other States	455	7.6	12.3	5.9 (mean)	All Other States	48
Total (US)	6,020	100	100	12.6	Total (US)	3,737

Note: The GMCL National Database includes all levels, including Congress and statewide, as well as state legislative, county commissioners/supervisors, and municipal and school board members; it does not, however include judicial, or law enforcement or other county positions.

Sources: GMCL National Database, 2006–2007; population data are from US Census Bureau, 2006 American Community Survey, B02010: Black, Latino, or Asian American/Pacific Islander alone or in combination with one or more other races.

Oklahoma (with 8.6 percent) and Montana (with 6.3 percent), but such is not the case.

Gender and Geographical Patterns of Representation

Analysis of the geographical distribution of elected officials by gender as well as race reveals that 66 percent of all Black women elected officials are located in the South; this is similar to the 61.4 percent described by

Latino Population			Asian American Elected Officials in State		Asian American Population		
As Percent of *All* Latino Elected Officials	Share of US Latino Population in State	Percent of State Population	State Ranking	N	As Percent of *All* Asian Elected Officials	Share of US Asian Population in State	Percent of State Population
40.0	19.0	37.6	California	181	51.6	33.0	13.4
22.8	27.7	37.6	Hawaii	79	22.5	4.4	48.6
12.4	1.9	46.3	New Jersey	15	4.3	4.8	8.3
8.0	3.8	29.6	Washington	13	3.7	3.5	7.8
3.1	2.1	20.7	New York	12	3.4	9.3	7.3
2.9	3.0	17.7	Texas	6	1.7	6.6	3.9
2.5	8.4	22.5	Michigan	5	1.4	1.5	2.4
1.8	3.9	15.8	Minnesota	5	1.4	1.4	4.0
1.4	6.7	17.6	Massachusetts	4	1.1	2.3	5.3
0.8	0.9	13.4	Utah	4	1.1	0.5	2.9
0.5	1.2	9.6	Connecticut	3	0.9	0.9	3.8
0.4	1.5	11.2	Oregon	3	0.9	1.0	4.0
0.4	1.4	5.7	Alaska	2	0.6	0.3	6.4
0.3	0.8	4.4	Iowa	2	0.6	0.4	1.8
0.3	0.6	10.5	Louisiana	2	0.6	0.4	1.5
0.3	0.9	11.7	Maryland	2	0.6	2.1	5.6
0.2	0.8	6.0	New Hampshire	2	0.6	0.2	2.2
0.2	0.9	8.2	Alabama	1	0.3	0.3	1.1
0.2	0.0	5.9	Arizona	1	0.3	1.3	3.0
0.2	1.4	26.5	Georgia	1	0.3	2.1	3.3
1.3	12.9	5.9 (mean)	All Other States	8	2.3	23.7	2.2 (mean)
100	100	16.4	Total (US)	351	100	100	4.9

Kaba and Ward (2009) for Black women. We find, however, that Black women are less concentrated in the South than their male counterparts – whether because of greater opportunities elsewhere or a longer political history for Black males in the South. The same pattern holds true for Asian American women, who show patterns of greater dispersion than their male counterparts; Latinos/as are mixed, with more than half of Latina officials located in the West compared to 45 percent of Latino men.

What can we conclude from this discussion of the geographical distribution of elected officials of color by race and gender? Certainly population numbers and density matter, but are not, in and of themselves, determinative. Equally important are structural features of state political systems, a group's political history, and political cohesion and

TABLE 1.4. *Distribution of American Indian State Legislators:
State Rankings*

State	N	Percent of all American Indian State Legislators	Share of US American Indian Population in State	American Indians as Percent of State Population
Oklahoma	11	21.2	10.9	8.6
Alaska	7	13.5	3.6	14.8
Montana	7	13.5	2.1	6.3
New Mexico	5	9.6	6.5	9.4
South Dakota	4	7.7	2.4	8.8
Washington	3	5.8	3.4	1.5
Arizona	2	3.8	10.0	4.6
Colorado	2	3.8	1.9	1.1
Louisiana	2	3.8	1.1	0.7
North Carolina	2	3.8	4.2	1.3
North Dakota	2	3.8	1.3	5.4
Maryland	1	1.9	0.8	0.4
New Jersey	1	1.9	0.9	0.3
South Carolina	1	1.9	0.6	0.4
Texas	1	1.9	6.1	0.7
Wyoming	1	1.9	0.5	2.4
California	0	0	12.6	1.0
All other states	0	0	31.1	0.6 (mean)
Total (U.S.)	52	100	100	0.96

Sources: GMCL National Database, 2006–2007; population data are from U.S. Census Bureau, 2006–2010 American Community Survey, B02010: American Indian and Alaska Native alone or in combination with one or more other races.

mobilization, among other factors. The high proportion of Latino elected officials who come from Texas, for example, may indeed reflect the fact that one in five of all Latinos in this country live in that state – and they make up almost four in ten of the state's population. It is, however, also the result of the very large number of elective positions in Texas, which opens up greater opportunities for electoral success at the local level – especially in South Texas, where there are the heaviest concentrations of Latinos. Moreover, as noted earlier, a group's political history, cohesion, and mobilization also frame contemporary politics. In this regard, Mexican Americans in the US Southwest (formerly part of Mexico prior to the mid-nineteenth century) draw upon a rich history to defend their rights and advocate for full political inclusion in the US body politic (see, e.g., Acuña 2011; Montejano 1987; and Sierra 1993).

Furthermore, the relatively high number of Asian American elected officials who serve in western states such as California (where a third of all Asians in the United States reside) and in Hawaii (where they make up half of the state's population) reflects not only the effects of population share, but also the long and unique political culture and history of Asian Americans in these states. And, for groups such as American Indian state legislators, whose remarkably high share of elected office in Oklahoma, for example, despite a relatively smaller share of the population, suggests that their historical struggles for survival trump demography.

It is precisely these histories and struggles that shape the second narrative of this chapter: at the same time as the increasing numbers of elected officials of color may be transforming the American political landscape, Black, Latino, Asian American, and American Indian communities have faced – and still face – long odds in their struggles for representation.

EXCLUSION AND STRUGGLES TODAY

As we discussed earlier, increased access to the vote paved the way for increased political representation for previously excluded groups. On the one hand, the Voting Rights Act received remarkable bipartisan support during its reauthorization as recently as 2006 – passing in the Senate 98-0 and in the House 390-33 and being signed into law by President George W. Bush. At the same time, we should also not forget that the VRA has been challenged on constitutional grounds many times in its history, including almost immediately after the 2006 vote.

Persily (2007, 180) points out that the relative ease of passage in 2006 was because Republicans saw it as a "relatively costless step toward thawing relationships with African Americans and maintaining gains among Hispanic supporters"…, and "freezing in place districts that capture large and compact minority populations benefits Republicans" (238). Despite being renewed for twenty-five more years, challenges began immediately and gained momentum. Since 2006, 294 bills were proposed[13] – and half the states passed a total of forty pieces of legislation – to curtail voter access (Bentele and O'Brien 2013). These include, for example, requiring photo identification cards and proof of citizenship; reducing or

---

[13] According to Erin E. O'Brien, email message to Hardy-Fanta, January 17, 2014, the N of 294 does not include (or double count) resubmissions of the same legislation in multiple years, but rather counts discrete pieces of legislation.

repealing early registration and voting; imposing greater scrutiny over voter registration drives; and more. Research by Bentele and O'Brien (2013, 1088) confirms that the proposal and passage of these types of legislation "are highly partisan, strategic, and racialized affairs. The findings are consistent with a scenario in which the targeted demobilization of minority voters and African Americans is a central driver of recent legislative developments." These efforts culminated most recently with the 2013 Supreme Court decision overturning Section 4 of the VRA in *Shelby County v. Holder*, which also neutralizes Section 5 (see Box 1.1). States such as Texas and North Carolina began implementing voter ID laws, and a variety of other policies that had previously been constrained by Section 5 (Lopez 2014).

Rather than a simple narrative of "progressive extension of the franchise," Bentele and O'Brien (2013, 1,088) make it clear that "electoral reforms have worked to both expand *and* restrict the franchise for particular categories of voters over time" (emphasis in original; see also Keyssar 2009; Wang 2012). The restrictions and challenges to minority voters in particular increased dramatically since the 1990s and early 2000s, when many states adopted measures to increase access to the franchise. The year with the most pieces of legislation striving to restrict voting access (or, alternatively, to "prevent fraud") was 2011, "when the GOP picked up 11 governorships and gained control of 57 state legislative chambers.... Of the 41 adopted voter restrictions ..., 34 restrictive changes (83 percent) passed in Republican-controlled state legislatures" (Bentele and O'Brien 2013, 1099).

Another contentious arena of political life since the time we began the GMCL Project has been the presidency of Barack Obama. He won election in 2008 with a clear majority of the popular vote (52.9 percent) and of the Electoral College (67.8 percent) and took office in January 2009 (Figure 1.14). There have, nevertheless, been direct challenges to the very legitimacy of his presidency in ways that few other presidents have encountered (Skowronek 2003).

Although Obama won election and was reelected in 2012, his time in office has been marked by strongly negative responses to his policy proposals, by efforts to stigmatize and racialize his presidency, and even by challenges to his right to hold office and to exercise routine presidential power (see, e.g., Kennedy 2011; Pinderhughes 2011; Press 2012; Rucker 2013; and Skocpol and Williamson 2012).

Critics have called him a "socialist"; a "neo-Marxist; fascist dictator"; a "magic negro," who, according to Rush Limbaugh, would not

FIGURE 1.14 Barack Obama and family at 2009 inauguration. Photograph by
Chuck Kennedy/Corbis, used with permission.

have gotten elected if he were White; a Muslim; a terrorist; a Nazi; and
a foreigner who was not born in the United States (Press 2012, esp. 76–
90). The "birther" movement,[14] specifically, with its flames fanned by
Donald Trump and Maricopa County sheriff Joe Arpaio, coupled with
Senator Mitch McConnell's vow in 2008 to "make Obama a one-term
president"[15] often seemed to occupy much of the 2008–2012 period.
Most recently, Obama's decision to join Twitter in 2015, for example,
generated a large volume of racist comments, which included visual
symbols of lynching and many other types of attacks (Badash 2015;
Capehart 2015).

Johnson (2012, 383) states, "The claim that President Obama is con-
stitutionally ineligible for the Presidency has placed into question, in
the minds of a vocal minority of Americans, the legitimacy of his entire

[14] See, for example, Crawford and Bhatia (2012); D'Souza (2010); McGee (2011).
[15] For a discussion of Sen. McConnell and this goal, see, for example, Rucker (2013, esp. 53).

administration. The birther controversy highlights the intersection of race and citizenship. It demonstrates how people of color – even the duly elected president of the United States – whether legal citizens or not, must struggle for full membership in US society, thus belying the notion that the election of President Obama demonstrates that we now live in a post-racial America."

CONCLUSION

To conclude this chapter, we must address the question: To what extent has the American political landscape been transformed by the increasing numbers of elected officials and populations of color? Demographically, the answer is a definitive yes, as we move toward becoming a majority–minority country. In terms of descriptive representation, the answer is more tentative, but women of color have been driving growth for each racial group, and for women in general.

The numbers still fall far short of being proportionate to their shares of the population because, as described earlier, change has been contested every step of the way. There have been breakthroughs with the modern Black civil rights movement, the Hart–Celler Immigration and Nationality Act of 1965, and the Voting Rights Act in 1965 and subsequent amendments, although they are still being challenged. Also, the nation elected the nation's first Black president; despite that improbable event, racialized challenges to his legitimacy began early in his candidacy and have continued throughout his presidency.

The challenges to increased representation by people of color are not limited, of course, to race-based challenges to Obama's presidency or to restrictive policies on immigration and voting rights. Furthermore, many policies affect people of color – male and female – and not only on the national stage and in state capitals. Most research on elected officials focuses on those holding federal and state-level positions, but elected officials of color are key players in local-level policy decisions. In Chapter 2, we explore who are our elected officials of color, examine the levels of office in which they serve, and consider the various ways the interaction of gender and race give us a better understanding of descriptive representation in the American political system.

2

Who Governs at the Local Level?

Local politics has long been integral to the field of political science. Nevertheless, the discipline currently pays pitifully little attention to those serving on governing bodies in county, municipal, and school board positions, as compared to those serving in state or national level offices. According to a recent review of the field of local politics by Marschall, Shah, and Ruhil (2011, 97), "Not only is the literature rather small and not particularly cohesive, but the data collection and methods of analysis are also somewhat primitive, particularly compared to research on state and federal elections."

A search we conducted of the top political science journals covering 2006 to mid-2015 yielded just 12 articles with "local elected officials" as the search term and 95 when queried for specific local offices, in comparison to 369 for members of Congress, 419 for governors, and 478 for state legislators.[1] Even less attention has been paid to women and men of color holding elective positions on local governing bodies. Such research that exists is limited in scope, focuses almost exclusively on large cities, and fails to apply an intersectional lens.

---

[1] The search was conducted on April 20, 2015, of the following journals using JSTOR (using the "full text" parameter and English as the language): *American Political Science Review; PS: Political Science and Politics; Journal of Politics; Political Science Quarterly; Perspectives on Politics;* and *American Journal of Politics.* Search terms for specific local officials included "mayors," "city councilors," "county supervisors," "county commissioners," and "school board members"; "members of Congress" included "US Representative(s)" or "US Senator(s)"; "governor" included "governors"; and the specific terms for state legislators were "state legislator(s)," "state representative(s)," or "state senator(s)." A search of the same journals over the same time period using the term "local government" yielded just 177 articles, whereas the term "Congress" yielded 2,073.

AN IN-DEPTH LOOK AT LOCAL ELECTED
OFFICIALS OF COLOR

In this chapter we provide an in-depth look at elected officials of color serving on the governing boards of America's cities and towns – from the largest to the smallest – as well as its counties and local school districts. We maintain that political leadership at the local level is different from that at the state or national level. For one, the electoral structure is different (e.g., elections that typically are nonpartisan). For another, some argue that women participate less in local politics – including as candidates for elective office – because of a "widespread lack of faith in municipal governments" and that "municipal government is seen to focus primarily on physical infrastructure rather than social services" (DeSena 2008, 255). In some views, local government is not gendered because the decisions made at that level are of a more practical nature. DeSena disagrees, however, pointing instead to women's justifiable perception that local government operates "[w]ithin a gender regime that favors male-dominated business elites" (257); and, citing a chapter by Parker (2008), she notes that these regimes in cities are not only gendered but also racialized, "It is white, heterosexual, economically privileged men who have the most access to power…" (DeSena 2008, 5).

Furthermore, Dolan (2008, 112) writes, "How much of what we know about women … [elected officials] is a function of the data we have, which tends [*sic*] to focus on congressional elections and state legislatures … [W]e should take care in assuming that our understanding of how sex and gender shape elections involving women candidates for [and elected officials in] Congress or statewide office translates to those seeking office of other types and at other levels."

In this chapter, we begin by asking: Why do local-level elected officials receive so much less research attention than those in state legislatures, statewide offices, and the halls of Congress? We then consider another question: Why is it important to study local officials? We submit that there are a number of reasons that warrant greater attention to officials at the local level. First, elected officials of color – like elected officials in general – serve, by and large, at the local level, on city/town councils, as mayors, as county supervisors/commissioners, and as members of locally elected school boards. Second, demographic change by race in the nation's leadership structure described in Chapter 1 has been driven by growth in numbers at the local level, especially, again, by women of color. Third, there is a need to study officials serving in smaller cities and towns: whereas most of the literature on city or town councilors, for example, draws on data from large cities, the vast majority of municipal officials of color – again, like all municipal officials – serve in places with populations of fewer than 25,000 residents. Fourth, growth in descriptive representation at the local level has both symbolic and substantive impact when race and gender are included in the analysis. Fifth, decisions made at the local level impact the well-being of communities of color, and it is there that critical decisions to the local community are made – including expenditures that can go as high as a trillion dollars per year. Above all, we argue that political leadership at the local level is different in nature from state- or higher-level offices, and political science does a disservice to the field by ignoring the impact of race and gender on local governance.

LACK OF ATTENTION TO LOCAL ELECTED OFFICIALS

Why have elected officials serving at the local level of government received so much less research attention than their colleagues in other levels of office? One reason is the ubiquity and decentralized nature of local governments: the most recent U.S. Census of Governments reports that that there are "3,031 counties, 19,519 municipalities,...16,360 townships" and "12,880 independent school districts" in this country (Hogue 2013, 1). Of the more than 500,000 elected officials in the United States, *96 percent serve at the local level* (Marschall et al. 2011, 97). This fact alone makes a strong case that, by their sheer size, the elected political leaders serving on county, municipal, and school boards deserve much greater academic scrutiny.

Decentralization means there is also considerable variation in sizes and forms of local government. And, in contrast to the uniform directories of members of Congress and state legislatures, there are no comparable national (or even state) rosters of local elected officials (Assendelft 2014, 200). The totality of the sheer size and diversity of the population, the "context-specific" nature of local politics, and the wide range of institutional arrangements such as election dates and election systems across the spectrum of local jurisdictions make it difficult to identify who these individuals are and how to contact them. "[A]s such, researchers interested in ... [local] politics must engage in intensive data-collection efforts" (Kaufmann and Rodriguez 2011, 101). The reliance on conventional conceptualizations of elected officials as de-raced and de-gendered further contributes to the marginalization and invisibility of research on locally elected women and men of color.

If studying local politics has, according to some authors (e.g., Kauffman and Rodriguez 2011; Trounstine 2009), lost some of its cachet since the publication in 1961 of Robert Dahl's *Who Governs?*, the demographic changes and dramatic growth of elected officials of color discussed in Chapter 1 suggest that greater attention must be paid to municipalities, counties, and school districts as they have become ever more diverse.

Until now, there have been no studies of local-level officials with representative data on Blacks, Latinos, and Asian Americans for all states – let alone any that also include a gender focus. A recent dataset by *Who Leads US?* (2014), purporting to provide an "exploration of the race and gender composition of more than 42,000 American elected officials," counts only federal, state, state legislative, and county officials – excluding the much larger numbers of those who serve on municipal governing bodies, as mayors, or as locally elected school board members.[2] Other studies are small in scale and limited in scope (see, e.g., Assendelft 2014). Svara's (2003) study of city councilors does include findings on race and gender, but separately, not with an intersectional lens. The special journal section on local elections in the April 2015 volume of *Politics, Groups, and Identities* (see, e.g., Marschall and Shah 2015; Shah 2015) helps fill the research vacuum, but the data are limited to the states of California and Louisiana.

WHY STUDY LOCAL OFFICIALS?

We turn now to answer the question: In exploring the political leadership of people of color by race and gender, why study local officials? Like Willie Sutton, who supposedly said that he robbed banks "because that's where the money is," we respond, "because that's where the vast majority of elected officials serve."

Vast Majority Serve at the Local Level

For the purposes of this chapter and throughout this book, we consider local officials as those serving on the governing bodies of America's

[2] In fact, a close examination of the data by the GMCL Project reveals that more than 38,000 of the individuals in their dataset are at the county level of government and just 386 are classified as "municipal"; we also uncovered a number of errors, including 308 city councilors who were misclassified as "county."

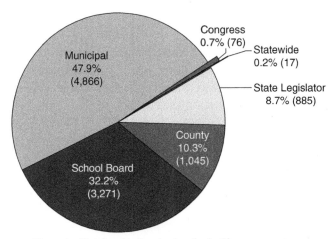

FIGURE 2.1 Elected officials of color, by level of office.
Note: Entries are percents. Statewide officials include governors, lieutenant governors, attorneys general, secretaries of state, treasurers, controllers, and auditors; county officials are elected county commissioners/supervisors only; and municipal officials include mayors, city/town/village councilors, city/town commissioners, and members of boards of selectmen/aldermen. School board includes elected board members of public school systems and does not include trustees or members of boards of higher education. The database does not include those elected to special districts, judicial and/or law enforcement officials, or other types of county positions.
Source: GMCL National Database, 2006–2007; $N = 10{,}160$.

counties, cities and towns, and local school districts. As shown in Figure 2.1, nine in ten of all elected officials of color serve at the local level: 47.9 percent as municipal officials (e.g., city or town councilors and aldermen/selectmen); 32.2 percent are members of locally elected school boards; and another 10.3 percent are county supervisors/commissioners.[3]

These percentages are in keeping with prior findings which suggest that about six in ten local officials in general serve in municipal or town government, one in ten in county government, and two in ten on school boards (Lawless 2012, 33).[4] Their percentages for municipal and

---

[3] As there is so much state-by-state variation, ultimately we agreed to include county officials but only very specific types: those who hold are elected, serve on a governing board, and are consistent throughout the states, in other words, county supervisors/commissioners and members of county councils. For cities and towns councils, we also include those elected to village boards and mayors. For more information about who is in the GMCL National Database, see note to Figure 2.1 and Appendix A.

[4] These numbers were computed from Table 3.1 in Lawless (2012, 33) and do not include the one in ten holding "special district" positions.

school board officials might be different from those in the Gender and Multicultural Leadership (GMCL) National Database because some tallies of local officials include additional elective positions. Nir (2015), for example, writes that counting those serving on local governing bodies "*still* scarcely covers it, though, because that doesn't include things like judges, ... water boards, mosquito control boards (!) – hell, even coroner is an elected position in some places. And in Duxbury, Vermont, they actually elect, yes, *the dog catcher*" (emphasis in original).

Growing Importance of Local Governance

Because of the decentralized political system in the United States, a significant proportion of the nation's political activities occurs at the state and local levels (Trounstine 2009). This means that most campaigns and elections are local affairs, and that, with the trend of devolution, local decisions account for a large and growing share of governing activities. Officials in cities and towns, which may have strong or weak mayoral systems, set policy, approve the budget, determine the tax rates, and have responsibility for hiring and firing department heads, including, in most cases, police chiefs and other key administrators who have direct impact on communities of color.

Local school boards, meanwhile, are involved in all aspects of school policymaking such as the hiring and firing of superintendents, the setting of curricula and spending priorities, and the adoption of reform plans (Leal, Martinez-Ebers, and Meier 2004). School boards also play a prominent role in articulating local issues and concerns. In doing so, local school boards serve as an important liaison between professional educators and the public (Allen and Plank 2005). While school boards tend to rely on a professional superintendent for management, they also provide for democratic representation to citizens through typically nonpartisan at-large, ward- or district-based elections or have city councilors appoint members of the local school board (Stewart, England, and Meier 1989; Land 2002).

Counties, traditionally viewed as administrative arms of the state, are also witnessing an increase in their discretionary authority. In many counties, elected officials such as county supervisors and commissioners[5]

---

[5] Allow us to take a brief tangent to acknowledge some of the other designations for members of these governing bodies; some are quite unique to the states and not obvious: Board of Chosen Freeholders (New Jersey), Board of Selectmen for the County of Nantucket (Massachusetts),

are central actors in the local government network, major collaborators in contracts and agreements, and direct providers of area-wide services (Berman and Salant 1996). Traditional county services, once restricted to welfare, health and hospitals, roads and transportation, police and corrections, and tax assessment and collections, are today increasingly expanding to include the provision of services that have been the customary purview of municipal governments (Benton 2005). More likely than not, counties are now joining municipal governments as key players in fire protection, utilities, libraries, education, planning and zoning, housing and urban development, natural resource conservation, and sewage and solid waste disposal.

The broad political functions that counties, cities, and school boards engage in indicate that a large and growing amount of policymaking and political activity occurs at the local level. The variations in forms of government and election systems found among local political institutions provide a diverse set of opportunity structures and shape the context under which racial minorities are elected into these offices. As the numbers of elected officials of color have grown at the local level, there has been a corresponding increase in governing decisions made by women and men of color in cities, towns, counties, and school districts across America.

More Growth Than Meets the Eye?

Another reason to study local-level officials of color is because of the potentially transformative effect they may have on the American political

Borough Assembly (Alaska), and County Legislature (New York). There are also counties where the term "county judge" is *not* a judicial position, but rather one akin to county supervisor or councilmember: County Judge of the Commissioners' Court (Texas), County Judge of the Quorum Court (Arkansas), County Judge (selected counties in Oregon), and Justice of the Peace and County Judge (Kentucky). (There are county judges in other states, however, who *are* judicial officials.) Police jurors in Louisiana are equivalent to county commissioners – *not* law enforcement – and parish council members (also in Louisiana) are *not* parts of religious bodies but rather are equivalent to county commissioners/supervisors. County trustees (Tennessee) serve as treasurers and are not members of the county governing body; boroughs, which are often municipal government bodies in most of the country, are county equivalents for the City of New York: for example, Queens and also Kings County (Brooklyn). It takes a rigorously detailed endeavor to keep track of these offices and, given their ubiquity and complexity, a great deal of effort to determine race and even gender at a given point in time let alone over time in a consistent way. Many studies of county officials do not distinguish between members of these governing bodies and the even larger number of other elective positions, such as treasurers, assessors, clerks, county/prosecuting/state's attorneys, members of the various commissions, sheriffs, and coroners/medical examiners, to name a few.

landscape. Given the small numbers at federal and state levels (Figure 2.1), the growth documented in 1 clearly has been driven by increases on the governing bodies of cities and towns, counties, and school boards – not in the halls of Congress or state houses around the country.

Following passage of the Voting Rights Act of 1965 and subsequent amendments, Black representation in municipal office rose from 623 in 1970 to more than 4,477 in 2001, including 3,538 on municipal governing bodies (Bositis 2003a, 13–15; see also Grofman and Handley 1989). The number of Blacks on county governing boards also rose: from 68 to 809 between 1970 and 2000; on local school district boards, Black representation grew from just 95 in 1970 to 2,142 in 1992 (US Census Bureau 1995, 23–26).

According to Lai et al. (2001, 613), the number of Asian Americans holding key elective positions at the local level has also increased: from 52 in 1978 to 248 in 2000. We observe similar patterns of growth in local offices for Latinos (Table 2.1): the number of Latinos holding any type of local office grew by 82 percent over the past 30 years: from 2,545 in

TABLE 2.1. *Growth in Latino Local Officials, by Types of Office and Sources, 1984–2012*

	All Types of Local Office				Local Governing Boards		
	1984	1990	2007	2014	1991–1992	2006–2007	2012
County	292	351	512	547	106	270	311
Municipal officials	1,041	1,290	1,640	1,766	1,605	1,589	1,687
School board	1,212	1,458	1,847	2,322	1,717	1,620	2,119
Total local	2,545	3,099	3,999	4,635	3,541	3,479	4,117

Note: Here and in all subsequent tables, "Municipal" includes city/town councilors, commissioners, supervisors, and mayors; "County" includes county councilors, supervisors, and commissioners; "School board" includes those elected to local school district boards, not college or state boards. American Indian officials are not included because all were state legislators (see Introduction for explanation). For our analysis of municipal officials, governing boards include mayors. The 1992 Census "Municipal Official" category includes both city and town officials; the GMCL National Databases for 2004 and 2006–2007 and our analysis of 2012 National Association of Latino Elected and Appointed Officials (NALEO) data also include both, but it is not possible to determine whether other sources do or do not.
Sources for "All Types": 1984: Vigil (1987, 88); 1990–1992: Pachon and DeSipio (1992, 214) and 1992 Census of Governments (US Census Bureau 1995); 2007: NALEO (2007, 1); 2014: GMCL Project analysis of data provided by NALEO (2014). Sources for local governing bodies: 2006–2007 and 2012 data are from GMCL National Database 2006–2007, and GMCL Project analysis of data provided by NALEO.

1984[6] (Vigil 1987, 88) to 4,635 in 2014 (NALEO 2014, 5). Growth is also evident in the numbers of Latinos on governing boards at each level.[7]

Challenges in Calculating Growth on Local Governing Bodies

The effort to track the growth of local officials of color across race, type of office, and year reveals a number of discrepancies, depending on the source of the data and operational definitions applied. For example, the 1992 Census of Governments reports that, in 1990, there were 4,511 Black municipal elected officials (and another 363 in elected town positions) whereas the Joint Center for Political and Economic Studies (JCPES) reported that the total number of municipal and town officials at that time was 3,671(Bositis 2002, 17).[8] The same problem exists for Latinos: whereas National Association of Latino Elected and Appointed Officials (NALEO) reported 3,099 local officials in 1990, the 1992 Census of Governments, which surveyed all units of government and collected racial and gender data for almost 400,000 local elected officials, identified 5,298 Latinos in these positions.[9] Furthermore, after Pachon and DeSipio (1992, 215) reported that the number of Latino elected officials in general grew 25 percent

---

[6] He excludes those holding law enforcement/judicial seats; see Table VIII in Vigil (1987, 88).

[7] Data are not available for this specific of type of office before 1991 and show considerable variability on school boards, owing to changes in how National Association of Latino Elected and Appointed Officials (NALEO) counted officials in different years. We provide these numbers as the "best estimate" but are aware that NALEO (2014, i) itself acknowledges that data in the 2014 *"Directory* should not be used to make statistical comparisons with the data in previous *Rosters"* (italics in original); for more on other changes in their methodology, including regarding Chicago local school-based council members, see also p. iv.

[8] The 1992 Census of Governments survey was in the field for six months, beginning October 1991; the Joint Center for Political and Economic Studies (JCPES) data are for 1990.

[9] The numbers are GMCL Project analysis of data from Tables 20 to 23 of the 1992 Census of Governments survey of Popularly Elected Officials (US Census Bureau 1995, 23–26). We should also point out that NALEO initially drew on the 1992 Census of Governments efforts and results to develop their own data collection methods (see Pachon and DeSipio 1992, note 3, 216). The first and perhaps only comprehensive report on race and gender in local government is the 1992 Census of Governments, produced by the US Census Bureau (1995, xii), which was a survey "conducted by mail over a 6-month period beginning in October 1991" which had a response rate of 88.2 percent. It succeeded in gathering race on 92.9 percent of the more than 58,000 county officials at that time, including those serving on county governing boards (17,724), as well as 88.8 percent of municipal and 89.2 percent of school district officials (xiii). Although it is true that the 1992 Census of Governments is the only comprehensive survey of elected officials, it has limitations (see xii); scholars have cautioned that the Census data might have inflated the number of possible elected positions and the database itself could use some scrutiny.

between the first enumeration in 1984 and their analysis in 1990, they raised several important questions such as, "Why have these numbers increased so rapidly? Is it, for example, simply a function of Latino population growth? Or, on the other hand, have the numbers of elective offices been increasing equally rapidly? A third possibility is that these factors – an increasing Latino electorate and increasing numbers of offices – supplement post–Voting Rights Act reapportionments that reduce the effect of past efforts to dilute the minority vote." They conclude, however, "Unfortunately, there is [*sic*] little data on which to evaluate these competing claims."[10]

Discrepancies such as these make it difficult to track with certainty the precise number of Blacks and Latinos in specific local offices over time. Reasons for the inconsistencies include differences in data collection methods by various groups; lack of clarity on who is included in what categories when findings are reported in the academic literature, online, and in other reports; and variation in counts for the same years from different sources. For example, much of the literature on the numbers of Black elected officials relies on rosters/directories produced by the Joint Center for Political and Economic Studies (JCPES) and, for Latinos, by the National Association of Latino Elected and Appointed Officials (NALEO). Sources do not always specify whether "municipal" officials include those representing towns, or just cities (and of what sizes), which makes it difficult to compute the percentages of Blacks and Latinos in the make-up of all municipal elected officials.

---

[10] A close analysis of county-level officials provides further evidence of the problematic state of affairs for accurately tracking the growth of local officials of color by ethnoracial group. The 1990 National Roster of Black Elected Officials (BEOs) reports, for example, that the number of BEOs elected to all types of county offices "has grown nearly nine fold: in 1970 it was 92, last year it was 793, and by 1990 it was 810" (Joint Center for Political and Economic Studies [JCPES] 1991, 3). The 1992 Census of Governments, however, reports that, in 1990–1991, there were a total of 1,707 Black county officials (US Census Bureau 1995, 23). For those on county governing bodies (a subset of all county officials), we see dramatic growth – from 68 in 1970 (Grofman and Handley 1989, 267) to 809 in 2000 (Bositis 2002, 17). That number was, however, *lower* than the 867 the 1992 Census of Governments reported for a *decade earlier*. Furthermore, when we drew on data provided by the JCPES for inclusion in 2006 for inclusion in the GMCL National Database, the number of Black members of county governing boards was still lower: 757. We doubt the numbers have actually gone down, but rather that, as the Joint Center was undergoing some reorganization, fewer Black officials were identified in those years.

For Asian Americans, the few studies that exist report on the broader category of "local officials," that is, do not separate out municipal from county or school board offices (see, e.g., Lai et al. 2001). Going through the hard copy rosters to tally each office by year and locality is time consuming (and prone to error). Finally, most reports do not separate out officials serving on governing boards from other types of offices, which is problematic because the rolls of elected municipal or county legislators (such as city or county councilors) are very different from those serving, for example, as "administrative officials (auditors, clerks, treasurers, etc.)" (US Census 1995, vii).

For American Indians/Alaskan Natives, there simply are no data to be found on nontribal local elected officials over time.[11] The only tally is the 1992 Census of Governments, which reported a total of 862 American Indian municipal (including town) elected officials, of which 655 served on the governing boards. They made up less than 1 percent of all at this level of office. Table 2.2 shows that there were also 147 county officials, including 66 on county governing boards, and 564 elected school officials, of which 558 served on school boards (US Census Bureau 1995, 23–26). Although these data are old, they are, to our knowledge, the only ones available.

Estimating Political Parity at the Local Level

In Chapter 1 we provided indexes of political parity for elected officials of color at congressional and state legislative levels to demonstrate that, despite the growth in numbers, Blacks, Latinos, and Asian Americans have not reached a degree of representation proportionate to their respective shares of the population at these levels. Although we are handicapped by the lack of comparable data, we wondered if a similar issue exists at the local level.

If one includes *all* local offices, that is, not just those in the nation's cities and towns, but also its counties, school boards, and even special districts, the 1992 Census of Governments, which was the last comprehensive tally by race and gender – and which disaggregated data by race in interaction with gender on almost 500,000 individuals – reported that

---

[11] Wilkins and Stark (2011) include no reference to elected officials in the index of their book, *American Indian Politics and the American Political System*; their Table 4.2, however, lists American Indians who have served in the US Congress, showing tribe, state, and service years (89), and Table 7.6 provides a list of American Indian and Alaska Native state legislators in 2009, with tribe, party, and first year in office (181–182).

TABLE 2.2. *American Indian Local Officials, by Type of Office, 1992*

	All	Governing Boards
School	564	558
Municipal	862	655
County	147	66

Source: 1992 Census of Governments (U.S. Census Bureau 1995, 23–26).

there were 14,000 Black, Asian, and American Indians in these positions. That number, nevertheless, added up to only 3.3 percent of the more than 400,000 in total; Latinos (who may be of any race, and who were counted separately) made up another 1.4 percent (US Bureau of the Census 1995, Tables 18 and 19). Together, it means that in the early 1990s no more than 5 percent of the local offices were held by people of color, in a nation where at that time minorities made up one-fourth of the population. The percentages vary considerably, however. Svara (2003, 1), for example, writes, "The share of people of color serving on the governing bodies of America's cities and towns doubled from 1979 to 2001" – from 7 percent in 1979 to 13 percent in 2001 (see also National League of Cities 2013a).[12] This remarkable growth in local political leadership was still far from parity, given that non-Whites accounted for 31 percent of the US population in 2000.

These numbers suggest that any recorded growth that has occurred in local governance has not reached anything close to representational parity. Furthermore, such growth was not evenly distributed by ethnoracial group:

African-American representationx [on city councils] remained essentially the same between 1989 and 2001 (10 percent and 8 percent, respectively), maintaining gains made in the decade after 1979, when 5 percent of council members were African American. Between 1989 and 2001, Hispanic council membership increased substantially in medium and large cities, jumping from zero to 6 percent and 1 to 11 percent, respectively. During the same period, the proportion of Asian Americans serving on councils declined somewhat, from 3 percent to 1 percent. The percentage of White council members decreased from 92 percent in 1979 to 87 percent in 2001 (National League of Cities 2013a).[13]

---

[12] Among the limitations in research on local officials is the fact that most do not cover municipalities below a certain size; in this case, the cities in question are all 25,000 or larger (for an explanation, see Svara 2003, 2).

[13] We note certain discrepancies in these data: a table accompanying this statement shows the share of city council seats for Hispanics as 1 percent in 1979 and 3 percent in 2001.

Still, we note that the current state of data collection for local officials is problematic, making it extremely challenging to calculate rates of growth over time for each ethnoracial group.[14] Different researchers use different methods to count and/or report different types of offices (e.g., all municipal elected offices versus those on governing bodies; cities and/ or towns), and the methods for determining race and gender are neither always clear nor consistent. These limitations make it difficult to decide the precise extent to which growth at the local level has occurred and for which groups. Moreover, although the overall percentages provided by groups such as the National League of Cities (2013a) showing growth at the municipal level seem clear cut, it is impossible to tell from their reports how they arrived at their calculations. In fact, in response to a recent inquiry, the director of research at the NLC said that the information "will be deleted since it cannot be properly defended in terms of its substance" (Brooks 2015).

Methodological issues aside, we conclude that in general the numbers of local elected Blacks, Latinos, and Asian Americans officials have increased over time. The lack of parity proportionate to their shares of the population nevertheless also makes clear that the dual narrative of significant growth accompanied by continuing underrepresentation discussed in Chapter 1 still applies here at the local level. Nowhere is this more true than when we turn from a focus only on race to one that includes gender.

GENDER AND LOCAL OFFICE HOLDING

Key to expanding the knowledge base of the nation's increasingly diverse political leadership is to use an intersectional lens and center the analysis on women of color. Because those serving at the local level make up more than 90 percent of all Blacks, Latinos, and Asian American elected officeholders, the overall growth in descriptive representation by these groups

---

[14] What is quite remarkable about the study of local officials, including tracking growth in municipal officials, is how problematic the data are. If the 1992 Census of Governments is the largest scale study of local officials, including county, that includes data on race, gender, and type of position, there are others that make it possible to estimate growth over time. Most academic papers on Black and Latino county officials rely on national rosters produced by the JCPES and NALEO. The National Center for the Study of Counties (NCSC) has conducted a study every year or so since 2004 (Clark 2004), but, although their surveys are stratified by size of county, there is no attempt to oversample by race, and, given that the total N is just 500 and race/gender is based on self-reporting, the validity of their results may be called into question.

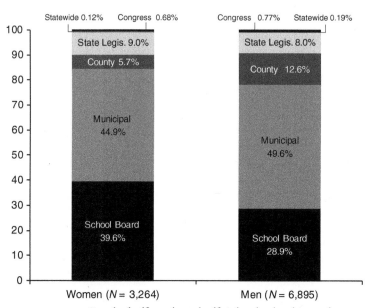

FIGURE 2.2 Level of office, elected officials of color, by gender.
Note: Entries are percents within gender.
Source: GMCL National Database, 2006–2007.

is clearly driven by increases on the governing bodies of cities and town, counties, and school boards. And, since, as demonstrated in Chapter 1, women have driven the overall growth for elected officials of color, logic would suggest that women of color are also driving the growth at the local level. We begin by laying out a baseline of local office holding by women of color as a group, and then with race and gender in interaction.

Female and male elected officials of color are equally likely – at 90 percent each – to serve in local offices, as opposed to state legislatures, Congress, or statewide (see Figure 2.2[15]). This is in keeping with earlier studies, which show that "[m]ost women who hold public office in the United States do so at the local level" (Darcy, Welch, and Clark 1994, 30).

Of those serving at the local level, we see some gender differences among elected officials of color. About half of male elected officials of color are in municipal offices compared to 44.9 percent of their female counterparts. There is a 10-point spread by gender for those serving on

---

[15] We did not include American Indians because, for reasons discussed earlier, in our database almost all are state legislators; their inclusion might have thrown off the findings.

school boards, and men are more likely than women (12.6 percent compared to 5.7 percent) to hold positions on county governing boards.

At the same time, however, the percentage of female officials who are state legislators is larger (9.0 percent) than that of males (8.0 percent); while the difference is small, it is significant because the GMCL National Database is the universe, not a sample, of all elected officials of color. Whereas political science devotes a great deal of attention to statewide and federal office holders in part because of the substantial policy impacts officials have at these levels, and also perhaps because they are easier to study, it is evident that, at less than 1 percent each, these offices are a minuscule proportion of elected officials of color of either gender – as they are of elected officials in general.

Three questions related to gender and race come to mind. First, how does the share of women of color compare to that of their male counterparts in positions governing America's cities, towns, counties, and school districts? Second, what variation is there when race and gender are studied intersectionally? Finally, has the growth in local officials of color at the level of city/town councilors, county supervisors/commissioners, and school board members – as hard as it may be to document consistently over time – been driven by women of color?

WOMEN OF COLOR GOVERNING AMERICA'S CITIES, TOWNS, COUNTIES, AND SCHOOL DISTRICTS

In the early years of the twenty-first century, Robert Dahl's question, *Who Governs?* requires an answer that reflects the country's greater racial diversity and attention to gender equality in politics. It also requires disaggregating not only by race and gender but also by distinguishing between different types of local office. The roles of elected local *legislators* (such as city or county councilors, members of local school boards, etc.) and mayors are also very different from those serving, for example, in more administrative or regulatory, albeit elected, positions (such as clerks, water boards, and, as remarked on earlier in the quote from Nir, the proverbial dog catcher). To address these issues we must establish the number of women and men of color in each type of office compared to nonlocal positions.

What Local Offices Do They Hold? Comparing Men and Women of Color – and Women in General

Women of color are somewhat more likely than their male counterparts to serve on school boards and, correspondingly, less likely to hold municipal

TABLE 2.3. *Type of Office: Local Elected Officials of Color, by Gender*

Gender	Local Officials			
	All	Municipal	County	School Board
Women	32.0	30.1	17.6	39.4
	(2,936)	(1,463)	(184)	(1,289)
Men	68.0	69.9	82.4	60.6
	(6,246)	(3,403)	(861)	(1,982)
All	100	100	100	100
	(9,182)	(4,866)	(1,045)	(3,271)

Note: Entries are percents, with N in parentheses; all findings are significant because the GMCL National Database is the universe, not a sample, of elected officials of color.
Source: GMCL National Database, 2006–2007, N = 10,160.

office (Figure 2.2). We find that three in ten municipal officials of color are women (Table 2.3), which is about the same as reported for "women in general," who are predominantly White in most studies. At 39.4 percent of all school board members of color, they also match the 40 percent for women in general in these positions (Assendelft 2014, 200).

They are least likely to serve as county supervisors/commissioners: just 5.7 percent of all female officials of color serve at the county level, a pattern noted by MacManus (1996, 66), who writes, "Studies show that the proportion of women serving on county governing boards is smaller than for any type of elective office other than the U.S. Congress." When viewed as a proportion of county officials of color, however, women make up 17.6 percent (Table 2.3), a percentage again not dissimilar from that found by other researchers – and their numbers and share have risen over time. According to MacManus et al. (2006, 121), among others, the numbers of women on county commissions increased from 3 percent in 1975 to 25 percent in 2001.

Disaggregating "Local": Gender, Race, and the Importance of Governing Boards

There is more complexity in local governance than the terms "local" or even "municipal" would suggest. Why should we study those on governing boards rather than use broader categories (e.g., "local" or "municipal") as units of analysis? One reason, as stated elsewhere, is that the governance roles of municipal, county, and school district board members are primarily legislative, not administrative. Another is that, by

---

Box 2.1. Women on City Councils

Among women of color = 32%
Among women in general = 28%

Note: "Among women of color" is percent female of the 4,009 officials of color holding nonmayoral municipal positions.

Sources: Data on women of color are from the GMCL National Database, 2006–2007; percentage for women in general is from Assendelft (2014, 200, citing MacManus 2006).

---

doing so, we find that women of color actually make up a slightly higher percentage than women in general of those holding positions on city/town councils or boards of aldermen/selectmen: 32 percent compared to 28 percent (Box 2.1).

Looking specifically at elected officials of color serving in these types of positions, we see distinctive patterns by race, and by race in interaction with gender, as well as by type of office. More than half of Black local officials, for example, serve in municipal positions compared to four in ten of Latinos and just a third of Asians. Latinos/as are most likely to be school board members compared to 25 percent of Blacks and again about a third of Asian Americans.

Another significant difference is that 12.6 percent of Black elected officials are elected county commissioners/supervisors, compared to 7.2 percent of Latinos and 5.1 percent of Asians. Whereas nine in ten of all elected officials of color hold positions on the governing bodies of cities, towns, counties, and school districts – as do the vast majority of Asian Americans, their 74 percent is considerably lower than the 90-plus percent for Blacks and Latinos.[16]

---

[16] The distinctive patterns of Asian American elected officials can be attributed in part to contextual factors: more than half of Asian American elected officials hold offices in the state of Hawaii, which has no elected local school board members. There is only one school board in Hawaii, whose members are appointed by the governor (National Center for Education Statistics 2011–2012; Hawaii Board of Education, 2014). We thank Don Nakanishi for pointing out this issue to us early on. And, according to Jennifer Higaki of the Hawaii State Department of Education, "Hawaii is a single-district state, which means that the Hawaii State Department of Education serves as both the state educational agency (SEA) and local educational agency (LEA); thus, we do not have local school boards (personal communication via email with Carol Hardy-Fanta, September 26, 2014).

Furthermore, while there are definite differences in representation by gender*race and type of local office, the differences are greatest among Asian Americans than the other groups – especially when it comes to municipal and school board members (Table 2.4). Whereas Black and Latina women are less likely than their male counterparts to serve on municipal boards, the size of the gender gap is less than 3 points for Blacks and about 9 points for Latinas, compared to the 14-percentage-point deficit for Asian women.

Tracking Growth in Women of Color at the Local Level: The Case of Latinas

A number of researchers suggest that women's share of local-level offices should rise for a number of reasons: the sheer number of available positions means greater opportunities for women; furthermore, "many local races are nonpartisan, the media may be less invasive, campaigns can be less expensive, the job is often part-time, and local officials do not have to relocate their families" (Assendelft 2014, 199). Nevertheless, despite the fact that local elections require less time and fewer resources at the local level, "women remain vastly underrepresented, and in some cases their numbers have stalled or even declined over the last decade" (199). The 28 percent share on city councils for women in general is no greater than it was in 2001; in fact, Svara (2003, 1) found that "there was no more gender diversity among council members in 2001 than in 1979."

We address the issue of estimating growth in diversity among local officials over time by, as an example, taking a close look at Latinas who, according to a number of sources, have increased their shares of school boards and municipal offices, while gaining little ground as county officials. Figure 2.3 shows data from three points in time: 1990, demonstrating that Latinas made up just 18 percent of all Latino municipal officials at that point in time and 25 percent of Latino school board positions. By 2006–2007, their share of seats on municipal governing bodies (city/town councils, etc.) rose to 24.9 percent, and by 2012 they made up 30.4 of Latino council members. (Latinas also made up 28.8 percent of those in the GMCL National Database with titles of "Mayors" and 20.5 percent of Deputy/Vice Mayors/Mayors ProTempore, a topic we examine later in this chapter.) Their share of school district seats rose significantly as well, to almost half.

TABLE 2.4. *Type of Office: Local Elected Officials of Color, by Gender and Race*

	All	Asian		Black		Latino/a		Total	
		Women	Men	Women	Men	Women	Men	Women	Men
Municipal	53.0	35.2	48.9	56.2	58.9	39.1	48.4	49.8	54.5
	(4,860)	(25)	(92)	(1,039)	(2,115)	(396)	(1,193)	(1,460)	(3,400)
School board	35.6	60.6	43.1	36.3	23.8	56.7	42.4	43.9	31.7
	(3,270)	(43)	(81)	(671)	(855)	(575)	(1,045)	(1,289)	(1,981)
County	11.4	4.2	8.0	7.5	17.2	4.2	9.2	6.3	13.8
	(1,045)	(3)	(15)	(138)	(619)	(43)	(227)	(184)	(861)
% Local (of All)	90.8	73.2	74.0	89.6	90.7	92.9	93.2	90.2	91.0
N (All local)	(9,175)	(71)	(188)	(1,848)	(3,589)	(1,014)	(2,465)	(2,933)	(6,242)
N (All)*	(10,108)	(97)	(254)	(2,063)	(3,957)	(1,092)	(2,645)	(3,252)	(6,856)

Note: Entries are percents, with N in parentheses. American Indians were not included in this analysis because virtually all were state legislators, the N for this analysis is therefore 10,108.

Source: GMCL National Database, 2006–2007.

95

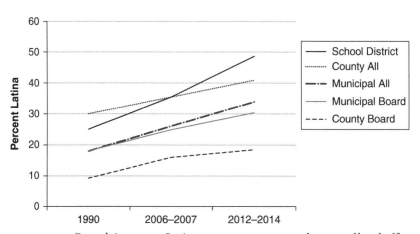

FIGURE 2.3 Growth in percent Latina women, 1990–2014, by type of local office.
Note: School District includes elected school boards only for 2006–2007; the other years may include other school district elective positions.
Sources: Pachon and DeSipio (1992, 215); US Census Bureau (1995); GMCL National Database (2006–2007, 2012); NALEO (2014); data for "County Board" in 2012–2014 are from a GMCL Project 2015 analysis of data from *Who Leads US?* (2015).

The Latina share of all types of Latino county officials[17] has increased by a third over the past twenty-five years: in 1990, Latinas made up 30 percent of all county officials (Pachon and DeSipio 1992, 215); by 2014, Latinas made up 40.6 percent (NALEO 2014). The proportion of Latinas on county governing boards doubled over roughly the same period of time (from 9.1 percent according to the 1992 Census to 18.1 percent in 2012). Of particular note is that, in America's counties, seven in ten of Latino non-board county elected officials are Latinas, compared to just two in ten serving as county commissioners, supervisors, or council members. These data point to the urgency of developing consistent classification and reporting of elected officials of color at all levels because otherwise it is difficult to measure growth over time accurately.[18] To compensate for these problems, we employed multiple sources to help estimate growth of minority women in local offices.

[17] "All types" of county officials include not only those on governing boards and but also those holding administrative positions such as District Clerk, Property Appraiser, Register of Deeds, Supervisor of Elections, Tax Assessor/Collector, to name just a few.
[18] In 2014, NALEO reported 222 of all 547 Latino county officials are women, a percentage (40.6) very close to the 37.1 percent from our analysis of data from *Who Leads US?* (2015). NALEO does not report the percentage of county officials who serve on county governing boards (i.e., county councilors, supervisors or commissioners) in 2014, but our analysis of *Who Leads US?* data shows the percentage Latina drops to 18.4 percent.

A CLOSER LOOK AT MAYORS OF COLOR

Mayors are local chief executive officers who, with a few prominent exceptions, are among the least known and often overlooked group of elected officials. Have the percentages of mayors of color – including women – grown over time? Trend data are hard to come by. According to the Center for American Women and Politics at Rutgers University (CAWP 2002, 2007, 2015), in cities with populations higher than 30,000 residents, women made up 20.8 percent in 2002, before falling to 16.2 percent in 2007, and rose slightly to 18.4 percent in 2015. However, an earlier study that tracked the number of Black elected officials between 1970 and 1989 shows a dramatic growth rate of 523 percent among Black mayors (Chambliss 1992). In addition, the number of Black women mayors rose from just 12 in 1975 to 95 in 1996 (a 692 percent growth rate), and were observed to do better than White women in terms of their proportion among mayors during roughly the same period (Williams 2001, 308).

Tracking growth by gender and race for Latino/a mayors and Asian American mayors is harder. We were able to uncover data showing that, between 1984 and 2009, the number of Latino mayors (male and female) increased by 78 percent, from around 139 in 1984 to 247 Latino mayors in 2009 (Cuéllar 2013, 6). A gender analysis by the GMCL Project of Cuéllar's original data[19] shows that in 1985 there were 17 Latina mayors (12.1 percent) out of all 141 Latino/a mayors. Our analysis of data from NALEO shows that, by 2012, the number of Latina mayors had reached 51 (20.4 percent) of the 248 Latinos serving in those positions, suggesting that the numbers of Latinas serving as mayors of US cities and towns *tripled* between 1985 and 2012.[20]

Using data provided by the UCLA Asian American Studies Center,[21] we see that the number of Asian American mayors has grown from fourteen

[19] We thank Carlos Cuéllar for graciously providing his dataset, which allowed us to conduct the gender analysis.

[20] It is not always clear from various data sources who is being counted as a "mayor"; in the preceding analysis, we have followed the path taken by the earlier researchers and excluded those whose titles were Vice or Deputy Mayor or Mayor Pro Tempore. According to our analysis of data provided by NALEO to the GMCL Project in 2012, there were 44 Latinas and 109 Latino men in these types of positions. We thank Martha Recio at NALEO for sharing these data.

[21] We thank Don T. Nakanishi and James Lai of the Asian American Studies Center at UCLA for providing hard and/or electronic copies of the Center's National Asian-American Political Rosters/Directories from 1978 through 2012, which made this analysis possible. See also Nakanishi and Lai (2003, esp. Part III; 2015) and Lai et al. (2001). For a gender perspective, see Ong (2003).

in 1984 to fifty-three in 2012.[22] Whereas, in 1984, there were no Asian American women mayors; by 2011–2012, there were eighteen (34 percent) out of 53. Recently, Asian Americans have served as mayors of major cities, including Edwin Lee, mayor of the City and County of San Francisco (elected in 2012), Jean Quan, mayor of neighboring Oakland (2011–2015), and Marilyn Strickland of Tacoma, Washington (elected in 2010). Asian Americans also served as mayors of key counties in Hawaii, including Charmaine Tavares, who was the mayor of Maui from 2007 to 2011.

Almost one in ten (8.4 percent) of elected officials of color in the 2006–2007 GMCL National Database held the positions of mayor, vice/deputy mayor, or the equivalent. Of these 857 individuals, 621 (72.4 percent) were identified as Mayor, another 147 (17.1 percent) as Mayor Pro Tempore, with the rest (10.5 percent) being identified as Councilmember/Mayor or Deputy/Vice Mayor. Of the seventy-one mayors interviewed in the GMCL National Survey, more than half (53.5 percent) indicated they were listed on the ballot as a candidate for mayor and popularly elected; equal percentages (22.5 each) were popularly elected to the municipal governing body and served as mayor either through rotation or selection by colleagues or by being the top vote getter in a municipal election.

Studying the population of mayors of color in 2006–2007, we find striking gender differences, with men of color making up more than three-quarters (77.9 percent) of this group.[23] An intersectional perspective shows another layer of difference: whereas a quarter of Black mayors are female, this drops to 17.4 percent for Latinas, and it goes further south among Asians. Of the 28 Asian American mayors, 89.3 percent are male, compared to just 10.7 percent female. In fact, at the time the GMCL National Database was constructed in 2006, eleven of the twelve Black mayors who lead the largest cities (200,000 plus) were men, as were all of the Latino mayors at that city size. In contrast, for the smallest municipalities, a quarter of Black mayors were women, as were 14.9 percent of Latino mayors.

Women of color in our database serve as elected mayors at about the same rate as women in general reported elsewhere. For cities 30,000 or larger, 17 percent of mayors of color are women of color, which is virtually identical to the 17.4 percent for women in general reported by Assendelft

---

[22] This number includes one vice mayor in 1984 and 18 vice/deputy mayors in 2011–2012.

[23] In this analysis, "mayor" includes those in the database whose title was "Mayor," "Vice/Deputy Mayor" "Mayor Pro Tempore." Eight in ten of those whose title was just "Mayor" were men.

(2014) or the 16.2 percent reported in CAWP (2007).[24] However, the share of women among mayors of color increases to 19.7 percent when we consider municipalities of all sizes, big and small. It is important to not pay attention only to big city mayors, for up to three in five women of color and more than half of men of color mayors in our database presided over cities with populations of fewer than 5,000 residents in each. Women of color mayors also tend to be elected from cities that are significantly smaller in size than their male counterparts of each race. This pattern is consistent with prior research that finds women likely to occupy offices that are considered less desirable in the power structure (Lien and Swain 2013; Smith, Riengold, and Owens 2012).

MUNICIPAL FINANCING: A TRILLION DOLLARS AT STAKE

Despite the fact that local officials are often considered to be at the tail end of the power "food chain," the fourth reason to delve deeply into local government is that decisions made at this level can have a major impact on the well-being of communities of color, and it is there that critical decisions are made – from the hiring of city managers, school superintendents, and police chiefs to overseeing budgets involving a great deal of money. "The nation's municipalities spend more than a trillion dollars a year, and city councils have much say in how that is spent" (Fausset 2014, A12).

Public policies on municipal financing have life-and-death consequences tied to the issue of race: after the 2014 shooting of Michael Brown, a Black teenager, by a White police officer in Ferguson, Missouri, many noted that 20 percent of that city's operating budget comes from traffic stops and "skyrocketing court fines" (Maciag 2014), which are levied disproportionately on Blacks (Guilford 2014; Harvey et al. 2014). At that time, in a city where Blacks made up more than two-thirds of the population, Black voting rates were very low. Also, five of the six city council members and the mayor were White – as was the vast majority of the police force. However, in the first local election since the shooting, the Black voting rate more than doubled, and the number of Blacks on the city council tripled (Salter and Suhr 2015). Blacks now hold half of the seats on the city council and now have power to select a new city manager and

---

[24] We should acknowledge that the numbers may not be precisely comparable, in that Assendelft's data are for 2012, whereas the GMCL National Database covers those in office in 2006–2007.

police chief; in May 2016, Ferguson swore in its first Black police chief. This case illustrates the positive role exposing racial grievances can play in stimulating minority political participation and representation (Hardy-Fanta 1993, esp. 137–138; Manuel 2006).

As discussed at length in the last chapter and throughout this book, changes such as this do not reflect a natural progression of diversity and democracy, but a struggle for minority inclusion that is ongoing: at the same time that Ferguson elected more Black city councilors, in Parma, another Missouri town, five of the six members of the local police force resigned immediately after the town's first Black female mayor officially took office, citing "safety concerns" (Kutner 2015).[25] Parma's city attorney, city clerk, and water treatment supervisor also resigned.

In many ways, local-level offices are laboratories of American democracy, and we have seen devolution of many responsibilities from the federal to state and local levels. This devolution has come, however, "often without corresponding fiscal capacity or authority" (Krane, Ebdon, and Bartle 2004, 515; for a discussion of race, devolution, and social control, see Soss, Fording, and Schram 2008) – or for that matter, without a corresponding uptick in political science investigation.

FOCUS NEEDED ON SMALLER LOCALITIES

A further reason to study local officials is that, although people of color now hold offices at the highest levels – in the White House, the halls of Congress, gold-domed state houses, and city halls that are imposing edifices (such as City Hall in Atlanta, Georgia, Figure 2.4) – most represent smaller municipalities, including locations such as Duncan, Mississippi (population 578), where resources and power are limited (see Figure 2.5).

Drawing on data from the GMCL National Database, we see that city/town councilors of color, like their peers in general, serve in smaller cities and towns: seven in ten serve in municipalities with populations of fewer than 25,000 residents – including four in ten in cities/towns with a population of fewer than 5,000 (Table 2.5).[26]

---

[25] The announcement was made after Mayor-elect Tyrus Byrd was sworn in by outgoing mayor Randall Ramsey, who was defeated after thirty-seven years in office; the *New York Times* (Eligon 2015) reported later that it was four, not five officers who resigned.

[26] Source: GMCL National Database, 2006–2007. We identified the "Census Designated Place" for each elected official in the database; for local officials this location was his or her home/office address; for state legislators or above, it was the location of their main district office (as opposed to the state capital or, for those in Congress, Washington, DC. A "place"

FIGURE 2.4 Atlanta City Hall, Atlanta, Georgia. (Photograph courtesy of Library of Congress, Prints and Photograph Division, Historic American Buildings Survey HABS, GA, 61-ATLA, 7-1.)

is "a concentration of population either legally bounded as an incorporated place, or identified as a Census Designated Place (CDP)....Incorporated places have legal descriptions of borough (except in Alaska and New York), city, town (except in New England, New York, and Wisconsin), or village" (Source: "Glossary," U.S. Census 2000, www.census.gov/main/www/cen2000.html [Accessed July 15, 2006]). We then linked demographic data on race/ethnicity, nativity, education, poverty, and other demographic characteristics for each place to each official who completed the telephone survey. These data are from US Census 2000, Summary File 1 (SF1) and Summary File 3 (SF3); we would like to thank Anthony Roman

FIGURE 2.5 Town Hall, Duncan, Mississippi. (Photograph by P. J. Chmiel, October 18, 2004. Modified to grayscale; used with permission of the artist.)

As noted earlier in this chapter, research on local office holders has traditionally relied almost exclusively on either single-state or small-scale case studies – and cities with populations of 25,000 or more. Data on women in municipal office, for example, typically are limited to those greater than 30,000 (CAWP 2015) or even greater than 100,000 (Smith, Reingold, and Owens 2012). And yet, according to the National League of Cities (2013b), "The vast majority (over 90%) of municipal governments in the U.S. have populations under 25,000" and 76.8 percent have populations under 5,000.[27]

RACE *GENDER AND SIZE OF MUNICIPAL GOVERNMENT

In the GMCL database, women of color are found to be more likely than their male counterparts (50 percent to 44 percent, respectively) to hold offices

of the Center for Survey Research at the University of Massachusetts Boston and Roy Williams and John Gaviglio of the Economic and Public Policy Research Unit, UMass Donahue Institute, UMass President's Office, for their assistance.

[27] The percent for under 5,000 is calculated from the table "Subcounty Municipal Governments by Population-Size Group and State: 2007" in National League of Cities (2013b).

TABLE 2.5. *Municipal Officials of Color,
by Size of Municipality*

Population	Percent (N)
Fewer than 5,000	43.8 (2,120)
5,000 to 25,000	26.0 (1,258)
25,000 to 69,999	13.7 (664)
70,000 to 199,999	9.4 (455)
200,000 or more	7.0 (341)
Total	100.0 (4,838)

Note: Entries are percents, with N in parentheses.
Source: GMCL National Database, 2006–2007.

in municipalities with a population under 5,000. Because very little prior research exists at this level, so much about who these folks are is unknown, clearly demonstrating a need to go deeper than the study of large cities alone.

As shown in the distribution by size of municipalities (Table 2.6), there are large gender differences within and between certain race*gender groups. First, half of all Black female municipal officials represent municipalities with populations with fewer than 5,000 residents, compared to just 8 percent of their Asian American counterparts. Second, such differences are lost unless gender and race are studied in interaction, because, as we see from the final two columns, the gender differences alone are relatively small. Third, race alone is determinative as well: just 8.5 percent of Asian American municipal officials represent places that are smaller than 5,000 in population, compared to almost half of Blacks (48.9 percent) and more than a third of Latinos (36.5 percent).

On the flip side, the share of Asian Americans at this level of office representing the largest cities (population of 200,000 or more) is twice that of Blacks and three times that of Latinos (17.1 percent, 7.5 percent, and 5.4 percent, respectively). The exceptional pattern of Asian Americans may be attributed, in part, to their higher tendency to congregate in urban/suburban areas located in western states than other groups, but is still intriguing and deserving of further research.

TABLE 2.6. *Municipal Officials of Color, by Size of Municipality, Race, and Gender*

Population	Black		Latino/a		Asian		All	
	Women	Men	Women	Men	Women	Men	Women	Men
Less than 5,000	51.8	47.4	42.0	34.6	8.0	8.7	48.4	41.8
5,000–24,999	19.8	23.9	31.4	33.4	24.0	25.0	23.0	27.3
25,000–69,999	11.3	13.1	11.9	15.6	36.0	31.5	11.9	14.5
70,000–199,999	8.3	8.7	9.6	10.8	12.0	18.5	8.7	9.7
200,000+	8.7	6.9	5.1	5.5	20.0	16.3	7.9	6.7
N	2,063	3,957	1,092	2,645	97	254	1,454	3,384

Note: Entries are percents by size of municipality. Categories for 25,000+ are based on Svara (2003).
Source: GMCL National Database, 2006–2007.

This discussion of size of city and the distribution by race and gender of municipal officials of color is more than an academic exercise. MacManus et al. (2006, 120) assert that "[t]he typical American cares more about property taxes, potholes, traffic congestion, and local schools than about U.S. efforts at nation building…, the space program, or fast track authority for the president" and that "[m]ore voters now realize that *local* offices impact their lives more directly than do the higher profile decisions rendered in Congress or the state legislature." One might make the case that, if, as they also say, "[c]itizens regard local officials as more approachable and better capable of resolving problems that matter to the average person in the street" then the most approachable local officials are those in the smaller cities and towns that constitute the bulk of municipal government in this country. We also wish to suggest that because women of color make up larger shares of municipal elected officials in cities and towns with populations under 25,000, they are holding the keys to more responsive leadership and governing.

Compensation, Race, and Gender: Impact of Size of Municipality

Overall, eight in ten municipal officials in the GMCL National Survey reported receiving a salary, including more than nine in ten Asian Americans, eight in ten Blacks, and seven in ten Latinos ($p < .001$). Women of color are less likely than their male counterparts to receive a salary for their service as a local elected official, but the difference is quite modest (74.9 percent, 82.7 percent, respectively). The most significant gender difference by race was for Blacks, with three-quarters of Black women compared to about nine in ten Black men at this level of office reporting receiving a salary ($p < .05$).

Size of city affects whether an elected representative receives a salary in a variety of ways. First, the 95 percent of city councilors receiving a salary as reported by Svara (2003) is larger than the 79.9 percent reported by municipal respondents in the GMCL National Survey, until we recall that his study was of cities with a population of 25,000 or larger. Once we replicated his analysis, while controlling for city size, the number of officials receiving a salary increased to nine in ten of all municipal officials of color serving in cities of that size.

Second, Svara acknowledges that "increasing city size affects salaries" (10); and almost all elected officials of color – women and men alike – in the largest cities (200,000-plus in population) reported receiving a salary. For what are generally referred to as "small cities" (25,000 to 69,999), the racial differences are modest, but Latinas (at 42.9 percent) are significantly less likely than their male counterparts (at 82.1 percent) to report they received a salary ($p < .05$).

It is in the smallest municipalities (population of fewer than 5,000 residents) that are rarely studied, but where the majority of all municipal officials serve, where we see considerable variation across the board: Black officials in places of this size are much more likely than Latinos to report a salary (75.2 percent to 53.8 percent), with noteworthy race*gender differences: Black women are 20 percentage points less likely than Black men ($p < .05$); for Latinas, the spread is ten percentage points. With few serving in these smallest municipalities, such analysis is not possible for Asian American officials.

We also ask, besides *whether* women and men of color receive a salary as municipal representatives, what impact does city size have on *how much* they earn? Women in the smallest municipalities clearly make considerably less than their male counterparts (Table 2.7), somewhat more in cities that are somewhat larger, and about the same in "small cities" and "medium cities." None of these differences are statistically significant, however; although women also make more in the largest cities, the numbers at that size are quite small and should be approached with caution.

There are few differences in salaries by race alone for cities of different sizes. Asian American municipal officials representing cities of 5,000 to 24,999 in population report, on average, larger salaries ($17, 062), compared to Blacks ($6,610) and Latinos ($5,334), and this difference

TABLE 2.7. *Salaries of Municipal Officials of Color, by Gender and Size of City*

Population:	Less than 5,000		5,000 to 24,999		25,000 to 69,999		70,000 to 199,999		200,000 or more	
	Female	Male	Female	Male	Female	Male	Female	Male	Female	Male
Mean	$3,881	$5,097	$8,593	$5,978	$10,933	$10,233	$12,196	$13,221	$27,583	$20,489
Standard error	(613)	(810)	(2,313)	(456)	(1,055)	(920)	(1,740)	(1,188)	(4,192)	(5,269)
N	42	63	43	89	25	64	14	34	6	9

Note: Entries are means (s.e.). The analysis includes municipal officials for whom we had size of municipality and who responded to the question whether they received a salary (N = 546) and then provided that salary in a subsequent question (N = 389).

Source: GMCL National Survey and Database, 2006–2007.

is significant at $p < .005$; they also receive somewhat higher salaries in medium-size cities ($p < .1$).[28]

At the county level, almost all county officials of color (90.7 percent) report they receive a salary, and although Blacks are least likely to respond that they do, differences by race are not statistically significant – nor are there any differences by gender. There are also few race*gender differences (see Box 2.2).

Box 2.2. County Salaries and Size of County

- Nine in ten county officials of color report receiving a salary.
- Size of county affects salaries: $23,200 for the largest counties compared to about $13,500 on average for smaller counties.
- Black women serving in mid-size counties (150,000 to 400,000) receive significantly smaller salaries, on average, than Black men: $10,062 compared to $18,500 ($p < .05$).

Source: GMCL National Survey and Database, 2006–2007; County $N = 123$.

COUNTY SIZE AND THE DISTRIBUTION OF OFFICIALS OF COLOR, BY GENDER AND RACE

Size may also affect governing – and policy outcomes – at the county level. A number of scholars have studied the relationship of county size with health outcomes (see Franzini, Ribble, and Spears 2001). Others focus on its relationship to demographic change and land use (Cho, Wu, and Boggess 2003; Vesterby and Heimlich 1991); "hostility of society toward the poor" and those receiving public assistance (Day 1979, esp. 106); or on arrest data (Barth et al. 2010). With this in mind, it is important to examine the distribution of elected officials of color by size of counties as well. We find that the majority (55.6 percent) of the 1,045 county officials of color in the GMCL National Database serve in smaller counties, those with populations under 50,000. This finding is in line with counties of that size in general, which, according to the National Association of Counties (NACo), "accounted for about 70 percent of all county governments in 2009" (NACo 2015).

---

[28] Values in parentheses are means. They also receive much higher salaries in the largest cities ($32,400) compared to about $17,000 each for Blacks and Latinos, but these differences are not significant and the numbers are small.

MacManus et al. (2006, 121–122) reports that, at the time of a 1993 survey of the "nation's largest counties" – defined as 423,000 or more in population – women made up 27.5 percent of governing board members[29] – perhaps because there may be more resources and support for women – and more women willing to run within urban areas in large counties. We find that governmental size does increase the share of women of color on county governing boards: more than a third (35.6 percent) of the 174 county officials of color in the largest counties (400,000 or more in population) and almost the same (31.3 percent of 112) in the next largest (150,000 to 400,000) are women. Keep in mind, however, that more than half of all county officials of color serve on governing boards in counties with populations of fewer than 50,000 residents, and it is in these smaller counties where women of color make up less than 10 percent. Furthermore, when looked at intersectionally, we see that Latina women hold just 6.1 percent of 164 county board seats held by Latinos in counties under 50,000; and Black women just 10.1 percent of the 417 seats held by Black county board members ($p < .1$).

What else may we take away from this discussion of size of counties? One might notice we have not discussed much about gender differences among Asian American county officials in either the smallest or largest counties, where we see differences for Blacks and Latinas/os. Table 2.8 shows why: in contrast to the other racial groups, the vast majority (72.2 percent) of Asian Americans serve on the governing boards of moderate-sized counties (50,000 to fewer than 150,000 in population); it is also possible that small numbers might skew the results, but, because the database is the universe of officials, not a sample, all differences are statistically significant.

SYMBOLIC AND SUBSTANTIVE IMPACT AT THE LOCAL LEVEL

Thus far in this chapter, we have trained an intersectional lens on the growth of local officials of color, exploring the distribution by race, gender, and jurisdiction size of those serving on municipal and county boards as well as providing a concise look at mayors of color. We also believe that another reason to study local officials is that growth in descriptive representation at the local level has both symbolic and substantive impact. As

---

[29] What constitutes a "large," as opposed to "small" or "medium" sized county? Barth et al. (2010, 109–110) classified counties with more than 2 percent of the state population as large, counties with 1 to 2 percent as medium, and those with less than 1 percent of the state population as small. Others measure populations in 50,000 increments; the "largest" counties, according to MacManus et al. (2006, 121–122), are those with 423,000 or more.

TABLE 2.8. *Distribution of County Officials, by Size of County and Race*

County Population	Asian American	Black	Latino	All
Fewer than 50,000	0.0	55.1	60.7	55.6
	(0)	(417)	(164)	(581)
50,000–149,500	72.2	18.1	10.4	17.0
	(13)	(137)	(28)	(178)
150,000–399,999	5.6	11.4	9.3	10.7
	(1)	(86)	(25)	(112)
400,000+	22.2	15.5	19.6	16.7
	(4)	(117)	(53)	(174)
NTotal	(18)	(757)	(270)	(1,045)
	100.0	100.0	100.0	100.0

Note: Entries are percents, with N in parentheses.
Source: GMCL National Database, 2006–2007. Because the database is the universe of county officials, not a sample, all differences are statistically significant.

noted in the Introduction, not only are there more Black elected officials in Tallahatchie County, Mississippi, but they also have pushed for and succeeded in bringing about change.

One might argue that such action is symbolic only and has little value in terms of substantive change, but it also brings to mind the struggles people of color went through in the history of this country in the past – the lynchings and perpetrators of murder who were never were brought to justice – struggles that are not necessarily behind us. A recent piece in the *Boston Globe* (Associated Press 2014, A2), for example, highlights the limitations of symbolic representation and increased descriptive representation for effecting substantive change: "There has been only one prosecution under the Emmett Till Act,…The government has closed the books on all but 20 of the 126 deaths it investigated under the law…[a]nd Congress has not appropriated millions of dollars in grant money that was meant to help states fund their own investigations." Furthermore, "[t]he law expires in 2017 unless Congress extends it." At this point in time such an extension seems unlikely, hindering efforts to achieve change at the local or state level. As we write, the current manifestation of these ongoing struggles at the local level is the number of police shootings of (virtually always unarmed and young) Black men. Such incidents have not only roiled Black communities but also increasingly raised the consciousness of the nation as a whole with movements such as "Black Lives Matter," among others. (For early academic analysis of the Ferguson and related cases, see, for example, Hooper 2015; Miller 2014; Rogers 2014;

for a perspective informed by gender as well as race, see Falcón 2015; Schiffer 2014; see also Barthélémy, Martin, and Piggins 2014).

At the same time, reparations – including the apology by Tallahatchie County, quick and large, multimillion dollar settlements by cities such as Baltimore and Chicago, among many others, over police misconduct leading to deaths of Black men – would not happen without the increased presence and influence of elected leaders of color. Svara (2003, 17), in his study of city councilors, suggests that

African-American, Hispanic, and other minority council members are more sensitive to a wider variety of groups than are white council members. The differences are greatest in attitudes toward representing racial and ethnic groups, whose representation is far more commonly seen to be very important among minority than white council members. There is also more concern for representing the [*sic*] women, municipal employees, neighborhoods, and political parties among African-Americans, other minorities, and Hispanics ... Representatives from minority groups, who may have faced more exclusion from politics, may feel a greater need to be inclusive in their attitudes toward representing other groups and to have a broader base of support. Female council members in comparison to males are much more likely to view the representation of women and racial minorities as being very important.

The impact of minority representation on local public policy making is also evident in American school districts. A study by Stewart, England, and Meier (1989, 295), for example, provides clear evidence that, school "[d]istricts with a higher percentage of black school board members are more likely to employ a larger percentage of black school administrators" opening up opportunities for black teachers; they conclude: "In terms of representation, therefore, a developmental sequence exists where black school board representation leads to black administrative representation which in turn leads to greater representation for black teachers" (300).[30] In the chapters that follow we draw on data from the GMCL Survey to provide details about the personal and family backgrounds, political experiences, and perspectives on leadership and governing of Black, Latino, and Asian American officials serving on local elected school boards.

Finally, evidence from the GMCL National Survey clearly supports the idea and previous research that having more elected officials of color in

---

[30] Other factors are also important, such as district elections, which promote more black representation; region also matters: "[B]lacks are less well represented on Southern school boards....Representation for black teachers is determined by Southern region, black administrators, and black population" (Stewart, England, and Meier 1989, 300).

office makes a difference in policy. We asked Black, Latino/a, and Asian American elected officials serving at the local level, *Would you say that minority elected officials have made a difference in terms of helping pass policy initiatives to benefit racial or ethnic groups?* They responded overwhelmingly in the affirmative: 49.3 percent of county officials said a lot of difference and another 43.3 percent said some; the percentages were similar for municipal (a lot: 41.7 percent; some: 48.3 percent) and for school board members (a lot: 35.2 percent; some: 50.9 percent), with no significant differences by race or gender. Judging whether having more elected officials of color make a substantive difference at the local level requires more research, but the Black, Latino/a, and Asian American respondents to the GMCL National Survey clearly believe it does.

CONCLUSION

The findings presented here create a baseline of knowledge about Black, Latino, and Asian American women and men who serve as America's city/town councilors, mayors, school board members, and county supervisors/commissioners. The import of our work extends beyond Blacks, Latinos, and Asian Americans, however: it also highlights the realities of those serving in U.S. government in general because local elected officials make up the vast majority of *all* office holders, whether Black, Latina/ o, Asian American, or, for that matter, Anglo (i.e., non-Hispanic White).

The majority of local elected officials of color serve in smaller cities/ towns and counties, again, like the majority of elected officials in the United States; 90 percent of municipal governments are in cities with populations under 25,000 (and three-quarters are under 5,000). Although city and town councilors and mayors of larger cities may have a larger voice in the media and academic studies, they are actually the numerical minority of elected leaders in municipal government.

We also think it essential to employ an intersectional lens of both gender and race when studying who governs the cities and towns of today's America. The growth in the numbers of elected officials overall has clearly been driven by growth at the local level – and by women of color – and this growth has both symbolic and substantive impact when race and gender are included in the analysis. Decisions made at the local level impact the well-being of communities of color, including overseeing expenditures of a trillion dollars a year overall, hiring police chiefs, school superintendents, and other key policymakers, and more. Above all, we argue that political leadership at the local level is different in nature from state- or higher-level offices, and political science does a disservice to the field by ignoring the impact of race and gender on local governance.

Based on our findings, we conclude that elected officials of color holding elected positions on the governing bodies of America's cities, towns, counties, and school districts have much to contribute to the larger discourse on *Who Governs?* It matters who represents and makes decisions affecting the residents of the vast majority of America's cities, towns, counties, and school systems.

We also conclude with a number of recommendations for further research needed to build on and expand the work described here. First, we recommend reinstating the "popularly elected officials" reports that had been part of the regular Census of Governments; the last one with breakdowns by race and gender for the governing boards of cities, towns, counties, and school districts was in 1992. Despite their flaws, they formed the original foundation of much of the data initially collected by the JCPES, NALEO, and the Asian American Studies Center at UCLA. We support a comprehensive data-gathering initiative done in such a way that supports the efforts of organizations such as these that have deep roots, expertise, and experience in locating and identifying the elected officials of color, especially at the local level, in their respective communities of color. Improvements should include, however, greater consistency on what information is included for each official; clarity about who is included; standardization of what is coded for each individual (e.g., categories such as those of the 1992 Census of Governments) so as to be able to distinguish between those on governing boards, versus more general categories of "county," "municipal," "special district," etc.); and resolution of issues of racial identity. Such issues include: Is race self-reported and/or ascribed by an organization, as is the practice of the organizations that have traditionally developed and maintained the "rosters" (i.e., JCPES, NALEO, UCLA) and the National League of Cities? Or is it gathered and reported by cities/towns, counties and school boards (with all the attendant potential for errors and inconsistencies) to a central data collection group, such as was the case with the US Census in 1992? A critical addition to these efforts is to institute a system for identifying local representatives who are American Indian/Native American and/or Alaskan Native – as there is not even a rudimentary database on these individuals.

As Palus (2011, 114) concludes, "Local governments are among the most under-studied areas in political science, which is a terrible oversight, considering the diversity of their populations, elected leadership, political institutions, and metropolitan contexts. ...The construction of a local elections data repository that will stand the test of time is critical. Such an archive would afford the discipline of political science a unique opportunity to collect data that otherwise might be lost or underused and, in doing so, to inform policy and the processes of democratic governance and representation."

Nowhere is this more important than in the study of the women and men representing communities of color whose populations will make up the majority of this country within our lifetimes. In Chapter 3, we turn to learning about their personal and professional backgrounds and using this knowledge to provide a detailed portrait of Black, Latino, Asian American, and American Indian women and men holding positions of public leadership in America at the turn of the new millennium.

3

A Portrait of Elected Officials of Color

Who are our elected officials of color? What are their personal and family backgrounds? What qualifications and resources do they bring to their election campaigns? In what ways do race and gender shape the paths to political office for elected officials of color? In this chapter we answer these questions and provide a baseline portrait of the backgrounds of elected officials of color – what they carry with them on their trajectories to political office.

Keenly aware of the importance of group histories and experiences as the context for understanding their paths to political office, we also address issues of marginalization and disenfranchisement by tackling the notion of "double disadvantage." According to intersectionality theory, women of color are "doubly burdened by the obstacles" they face because of both their race and their gender (Clayton and Stallings 2000, 578). At the same time, prior research also suggests that there may be a "Black female advantage." Darcy and Hadley (1988, 642), for example, suggest that candidates' background characteristics and political ambition are important in explaining their success. They write that Black women's greater electoral success may be attributed to "their greater political ambition derived from their having more politically relevant backgrounds such as participation in the long civil rights struggle." Others also see a "Latina advantage" (Bejarano 2013), one that Fraga et al. (2005, 1) call a "multiple identity advantage."[1] Unfortunately, these studies draw

---

[1] Fraga et al. (2005, 7) suggest that "[a]s ethnic women, their multiple identities better position [Latinas] to build cross-group coalitions that are more likely to attain threshold levels of legislative support"; and hypothesize that "the intersection of gender and ethnicity might position Latina legislators to have a richer set of strategic options, relative to Latino male legislators."

only from samples of state legislators and fail to include more than one racial group.

Because, as discussed in the previous chapters, their share of elective offices within each of their respective racial groups is higher for Black and Latina women than that for White women, one might conclude that they are not doubly disadvantaged. Keep in mind, however, that none of the race*gender groups approaches parity in representation and that perceptions of the greater political success of women of color than their White female counterparts may in fact reflect even greater disadvantages experienced by men of color (e.g., disproportionate rates of unemployment and incarceration, lack of professional advancement, or barriers they face in running for elected office) than their White male counterparts.

Furthermore, research on Black and Latina women suggests that certain groups of women must demonstrate a higher level of educational and occupational attainment than White women and men to succeed in politics (Moncrief and Thompson 1992). Under this scenario, a larger share of Black women political activists are college educated and active in civic and interest groups compared to their White and male counterparts, perhaps positioning them for greater electoral success.[2] What about the political fortunes and personal resources of male elected officials of color – a missing population in much of the prior research on gender, race, and political trajectories? Using the intersectional lens, this chapter seeks to reveal the commonalities and differences in personal and family backgrounds and resources of both women *and* men of color on their paths to political office.

PATHS TO OFFICE: RACIALLY GENDERED ASSUMPTIONS IN TRADITIONAL POLITICAL THEORY

In many ways the received wisdom is that becoming an elected official is a linear process in which parents (especially the father) play a key role in socializing an individual to be politically informed; parents, peers, and schools are among the most important socialization agents that contribute to an individual's political ambition, even at a relatively young age (Fox and Lawless 2014). The popular media also affect children's views of their potential political roles, thus influencing their aspirations for

---

[2] We would like to thank Rebecca Loya, PhD, for her contribution to this section.

political office – or lack thereof (for the impact of media on girls' views, see, e.g., Hooghe and Stolle 2004).

Individual ambition supposedly leads to well-thought-out preparation to develop one's qualifications ("human capital") including higher education, the "practical knowledge, acquired skills and learned abilities of an individual that ... equip him or her to earn income in exchange for labor" (Johnson 2013; see also Klomp and deHaan 2013; Woodhall 1987); establish personal and family connections (i.e., "social capital"); serve in appointed or other civic positions that provide name recognition and votes, and working within and being recruited by a political party (which build "political capital"). Of course, according to Flora and Flora (2015, 110), human capital includes not only "those attributes of individuals that contribute to their ability to earn a living," but also those that "strengthen community, and otherwise contribute to community organizations, their families, and self-improvement." Furthermore, "interpersonal skills, values, and leadership capacity of individuals" are also key (Stofferahn 2009, 154). Besides these markers along a conventional path to elected office, there is "monetary capital": having enough money to finance a competitive election campaign.

When scholars began to study women's paths to political office, they tended to focus on the same individual, demographic characteristics that had been used in decades of research on (White) men. In this tradition, women's lack of political representation was due to their lower levels of education and occupational attainment, family responsibilities, and a lesser degree of political ambition; once these barriers were removed, women's representation levels would rise in due course (Bledsoe and Herring 1990; Burt-Way and Kelly 1992, 11–12; Carroll and Sanbonmatsu 2013, esp. 18–41). Studies of political behavior hold that women need to develop key political attitudes (e.g., ambition), attain high levels of education, and pursue certain types of "feeder occupations" (i.e., business, education, activism, and the law) that more closely match those of their male counterparts. Women with the requisite set of characteristics and attitudinal predispositions crafted to match or parallel those of (White) men are considered to comprise a social and political "eligibility pool" from which candidates are drawn to elective office (Carroll and Sanbonmatsu 2013; Darcy, Welch, and Clark 1994; Fox and Lawless 2004; Lawless and Fox 2005, 2010, 2012; Sanbonmatsu 2002, 2003). The implicit (and often explicit) goal is to recruit such women as candidates, who then succeed in winning elective office.

EDUCATIONAL ACHIEVEMENT, OCCUPATIONAL ATTAINMENT, AND MARITAL STATUS: A CONTESTED DYNAMIC

Traditional analyses treat education, occupation, marital status, and family background, for example, as fixed or *static* characteristics rooted in the individual. We assert, instead, that characteristics typically viewed as measures of an individual's "qualifications" (such as educational attainment) or those viewed as "personal choices" (such as occupation and marital status), however much they affect electoral success, are, for people of color, *dynamic*, not static, and rooted in group efforts within a contested political arena rather than in the individual alone. Increased levels of education and occupational attainment, for example, would not have been possible without the work of many in the Civil Rights and women's movements; and, as discussed in Chapter 1, scholars attribute the rising numbers of women of color elected officeholders (especially Black women) to "the political opportunities resulting from the Voting Rights Act of 1965 and subsequent judicial challenges which led to the creation of black majority political districts" (Darcy and Hadley 1988, 642). Conventional political theory and research are so bound to an individualistic orientation – even when expanded by increased attention to gender – that their applicability to women and men of color is problematic, unless we interrogate their assumptions and conduct analyses using fully intersectional methods.

Turning our attention to a baseline portrait of elected officials of color in the early twenty-first century, what do we know about their backgrounds?[3] What personal and family resources did they bring to their campaigns and elective positions? How do we understand their trajectories to public office in the context of the structured discrimination they have faced and continue to face today? To what extent do our data shed light on the "double disadvantage" theory of women of color in elected office? We begin by examining the educational achievements of elected officials of color, as education typically prepares one for an occupation, which together are often considered important measures of an individual's "qualifications" to hold elected office.

---

[3] Some of the demographic characteristics presented in this chapter appeared in a modified form in a paper presented at the Annual Meeting of the American Political Science Association, Chicago, Illinois, August 30–September 2, 2007 (Hardy-Fanta et al. 2007).

ELECTED OFFICIALS OF COLOR: A HIGHLY
EDUCATED GROUP

Data from the Gender and Multicultural Leadership (GMCL) National Survey reveal that elected officials of color are highly educated, with 65 percent having a college degree or higher. This is double that for the general population, which in 2008 was just 29.4 percent for those twenty-five years of age and older.[4] Like the general population (with just 13.3 percent with college degrees or higher for Latinos/as, 19.8 percent for Blacks, but 52 percent for Asians and 32.5 percent for non-Hispanic Whites[5]), there is considerable variation among elected officials by gender and race.

Overall, women of color elected officials are more likely to have a college degree or higher than their male counterparts (70.2 percent compared to 61.8 percent, respectively; see Figure 3.1). Asian American women and men are the most likely to have at least a college degree, and Latinos/as the least. In fact, almost all Asian American male elected officials (and nine in ten of their female counterparts) have college degrees, compared to 66.7 percent of Black men and 49.2 percent of Latino men. At the same time, Black and Latina women (at 77.4 percent and 53.8 percent, respectively) are more likely to be college educated than their male counterparts; the reverse is true for Asian Americans.[6] Latino elected officials – male and female alike – are close to 40 percentage points *less likely* to have a college degree than Asian Americans.[7]

The apparent gender differences, nevertheless, pale in comparison to those by race: 94.4 percent of Asian American officials have a college degree or higher, compared to 71.2 percent of Blacks and 50.7 percent of Latinos/as.

We also find that female elected officials of color are at least as well educated as women in general, who, according to prior research, tend to be more highly educated than men (Dolan, Deckman, and Swers

---

[4] Source: Table 1. Educational Attainment of the Population 18 Years and Over, by Age, Sex, Race, and Hispanic Origin: 2008 (All Races), www.census.gov/hhes/socdemo/education/data/cps/2008/tables.html (Accessed January 20, 2016).

[5] Source: Table A.2. Percent of People 25 Years and Over Who Have Completed High School or College, by Race, Hispanic Origin and Sex: Selected Years 1940 to 2013, www.census.gov/hhes/socdemo/education/data/cps/historical/index.html (Accessed June 27, 2016).

[6] As shown in Figure 3.1, the differences by gender for All and for Black officials are significant at $p < .01$; other gender differences are not statistically significant.

[7] The gender differences for these two groups, though not small, are not statistically significant.

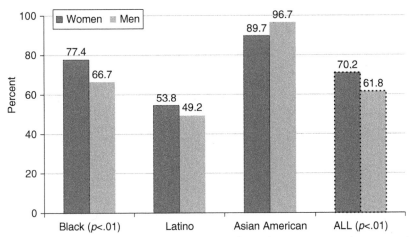

FIGURE 3.1 Elected officials of color with college degree or more, by race and gender.
Source: GMCL National Survey, 2006–2007; $N = 1{,}210$.

2007). Because so many of these studies draw on state legislator data, for comparative purposes we must disaggregate our data by level of office. We find that state legislators of color are as highly educated as legislators in general, with eight in ten holding college degrees or higher (Table 3.1). In fact, in keeping with numerous other studies (Barrett 1995; Carroll and Sanbonmatsu 2013; Moncrief, Thompson, and Schuhmann 1991; Takash 1993), the percentage of women of color with master's degrees is greater than that of men of color and about the same as women in general. It is also evident that, while women of color holding this level of office are, like women in general, less likely than their male counterparts to have a JD (Juris Doctor), higher percentages of women of color state legislators hold a law degree than women *and* men in general, and the percentage of *male* state legislators of color attaining that degree (20.3 percent) is triple that of male legislators in general (7.3 percent).

With 90 percent or more serving at the local level, the percentage of officials of color with at least a college degree is less than that among state legislators, 62.9 percent, although that is still considerably higher than that of the nation as a whole – and very similar to the figure for local officials in general. Svara (2003, 8) finds, for example, that 27.7 percent of city councilors in municipalities with populations of 25,000 or more report having a four-year college degree. Percentages for local officials of

TABLE 3.1. *Educational Attainment, by Gender and Level of Office*

	State Legislators in General		Elected Officials of Color			
			State Legislators		Local	
	Female	Male	Female*	Male	Female*	Male
High school	3.7	5.7	4.3	1.3	7.4	11.7
Some college	16.3	14.5	15.2	12.7	23.1	29.4
College graduate	31.6	35.2	26.1	29.1	38.3	29.7
Master's degree	33.4**	21.4	32.6	27.8	23.1	22.7
JD	4.8*	7.2	8.7	20.3	1.5	1.8
MD/PhD/ED	9.8	15.9	4.3	8.9	3.9	2.8
Advanced studies (not specified)	0.3	0.0	8.7	0.0	2.7	1.9
College degree or higher	79.9	79.8	80.4	86.1	69.5	58.9
	N = 670	N = 509	N = 46	N = 79	N = 407	N = 677

Note: Entries are percents; *$p < .05$; **$p < .01$.

Sources: GMCL National Survey, 2006–2007; data for state legislators in general by gender are from a 2008 survey conducted by the Center for American Women and Politics (Carroll and Sanbonmatsu 2013, 27); we computed numbers for state senators and representatives and then the percentage for state legislators in general.

color with master's degrees are not dissimilar from those for city councilors in general, which, for cities 25,000 or larger, is 26.8 percent. Not surprisingly, the percentage of local officials who hold law degrees drops dramatically,[8] but, overall, elected officials of color are a very educated group, with seven in ten women and six in ten men reporting having at least a college degree.

So to answer the question, Do women of color bring higher educational qualifications to their political office?, we respond: *It depends on the racial group.* And, the explanation for these differences lies in the distinctive "narratives of exclusion" discussed in Chapter 1, which have affected access to education in dramatic ways for each group.

---

[8] Svara (2003) for example, writes that 9 percent of his city councilors report JD or equivalent. His data are not exactly comparable because "Local" in our Table 3.1 includes not only city councilors, but also school board members as well as county officials in jurisdictions ranging in size from the smallest to largest, whereas his study reports on city councilors only in cities of 25,000+ in size.

EDUCATIONAL ACCESS AND ATTAINMENT:
THE HISTORICAL CONTEXT

For Blacks, Latinos, Asian Americans, and American Indians, one's educational level is not just a personal choice or the result of individual effort. Rather, it also reflects historical patterns of discrimination, political fights, and collective action. Issues blocking education and economic opportunities typically go hand in hand and also affect one's eventual occupation.

Numerous studies document that one's level of education correlates with parental education and socioeconomic assets, and these vary significantly by race. Patterns of discrimination in education and occupation as well as persistent differentials in earnings and assets serve as barriers to economic advancement. Together with the barriers experienced by parents, grandparents, and earlier generations, these form what is for many an insurmountable barricade traceable back to the era when the vast majority of the non-White population was either enslaved, colonized, or otherwise excluded from sociopolitical incorporation.

Protecting civil rights, prohibiting employment discrimination, and promoting affirmative action in higher education and employment became major policy initiatives in the 1960s; the issues were, however, only modestly addressed at the time (Hamilton and Hamilton 1997; Katznelson 2005; Oliver and Shapiro 2006; Williams 2003). While outlawing racial discrimination was the primary focus of Title VII of the Civil Rights Act of 1964, a prohibition against sex discrimination was, according to some historians, added only to derail it (see Freeman 2008). In many ways, however, women turned out to be primary beneficiaries. Holzer and Neumark (2000) suggest that the overall economic gains by Black women were even greater than those by White women, and were substantially more for both than for Black men. Kalev, Kelly, and Dobbin (2006) examined corporate affirmative action and concluded that White women benefited most, followed by Black women; Black men benefited least.[9]

Of course, access to higher education and subsequent occupational attainment depends on equal rights to education at the K–12 level as well – rights that have been illusory for communities of color. School segregation and educational inequality for Blacks did not end in 1954,

---

[9] See also Randall Kennedy (1986).

for example, with *Brown v. Board of Education*. A long-standing racial gap in school quality and educational outcomes continues today (Jencks and Phillips 1998; Kane 1998). American Indians continue to suffer the painful consequences of the US policy of sending children to boarding schools, which had the explicit goal of removing their "Indianness," and may be viewed, as Adams (1995) does, as "education for extinction." Extinction was, for this group, not only metaphorical: the genocide that started with the landing of the first White Europeans continued into recent years. During the three-year siege at Wounded Knee by the American Indian Movement (AIM) in 1975, "Williman Janklow, who was running for state attorney general, told a newspaper during his campaign, 'The only way to deal with the Indian problem in South Dakota is to put a gun to AIM leaders' heads and pull the trigger' " (Konigsberg 2014, MM34).

Latinos and Asians have faced considerable discrimination and barriers to entry in US public schools. According to Darder, Torres, and Gutiérrez (1997, xiii), for a long time Latino "parents presented their children for enrollment, but often found that their children were either not accepted or segregated and provided an inferior education." Then came what appeared to be a watershed moment: in 1973, a case was filed on behalf of 2,856 Chinese American students in the San Francisco public schools arguing that, although the school system provided some language assistance to Latinos with limited English, none was available to the vast majority of Chinese-speaking students. With *Lau v. Nichols*, the US Supreme Court held in 1974 that "public schools had to provide an education comprehensible to limited-English-proficient (LEP) students" (Lucas, Henze, and Donato 1997, 371).[10] States rapidly mandated bilingual education for "language minority" students and it seemed destined to become settled policy. As Moran (2005, 4) writes, however, "Since *Lau* was handed down ... its legal underpinnings have been under siege in the federal courts," and bilingual education became a locus of political struggle in this country, especially for Latinos and Asians, even if the two groups hold different attitudes toward the bilingual education issue.

The efforts of Ron Unz, a "Silicon Valley millionaire," achieved passage of Proposition 227 in California, which banned bilingual education;

---

[10] *Lau v. Nichols*: 414 U.S. 563 (1974); 42 U.S.C. § 2000d to d-7; see also letter issued by the US Department of Justice, Civil Rights Division, and US Department of Education, Office for Civil Rights, www2.ed.gov/about/offices/list/ocr/letters/colleague-el-201501.pdf (Accessed June 28, 2016).

his movement spread to other states (e.g., Arizona, Massachusetts, and Colorado) with similar results (Ryan 2002, 487). His goal was to dismantle bilingual programs in the United States. As a result, student dropout rates in California and Massachusetts increased significantly, as did referrals for special education placement and services.[11]

With the "English-only"[12] movement on the upswing; Proposition 187 in California (which, if it had survived appeals, would have denied social services, medical care, and public schooling to undocumented immigrants); and the Unz initiatives in a variety of states aiming at doing away with bilingual education, education policy shifted from increasing access for English Language Learners (ELL) students to English immersion, No Child Left Behind, and Common Core State Standards, with an emphasis on high-stakes testing. Although the Supreme Court "acknowledged that nearly every ELL student ... was either Hispanic or Asian/Pacific Islander...," it determined that such cases were "not about race but about education" – leaving language minority students struggling within a "highly contested system of standards-based accountability" (Salomone 2010, 156–158).

The picture is especially complicated for Asian Americans, who stand out for their academic achievements and high educational mobility (Sue and Okazaki 1990). High levels of education come, nevertheless, in the face of de facto or explicit racial quotas at Ivy League and other colleges, with some likening it to earlier restrictions against Jews (Reynolds 2014; Riley 2015; Zimmerman 2012). Walker-Moffat (1995, xiv–xv) reminds us that there is considerable diversity in the Asian educational experience in America, points to the "danger of racism and inaccuracy in the Asian American success story," and urges a look at the "other side of Asian American academic success." Furthermore, she locates the Asian American experience within a larger socioeconomic and political context – one that has broad and pervasive implications for all communities of color in this country:

It is in the vested interests of those who want to avoid the costs of educational reform to maintain the "success" of Asian Americans as evidence that ethnic minorities can succeed in the existing schools without affirmative action, in-service teacher education, or special program support. Particularly in times of economic recession, the costs and benefits of educating distinct groups, and immigrants in particular, become a political issue (Walker-Moffat, 5).

---

[11] Source: María Luisa Wilson-Portuondo, past president of the Massachusetts Association for Bilingual Education (MABE); interview with Carol Hardy-Fanta, June 15, 2014.

[12] For a timeline on "Official English," see, for example, Draper and Jiménez (1992).

According to Perea (1992, 280), these are "only the latest in a long history of nativist attempts to exclude certain unpopular Americans from the definition of what is American" – with Latinos and Asians being the most recent targets.

RACE, GENDER, AND OCCUPATIONAL ATTAINMENT

Turning to occupational attainment, we examine the top seven occupations for Black, Latino, and Asian American elected officials. More than a third work in education, followed by one in five in business (either as self-employed/small-business owners or in financial operations); and 13.0 percent in community programs/activism, social services, and/ or non-profits. Of the top occupations for elected officials of color, law (at 6.9 percent) is second to last.

There is also considerable variation by race and gender. Although education is the top occupation for male as well as female elected officials of color, the percentage for women is significantly higher than for men (42.4 to 29.0 percent; see Table 3.2). And the differences by race and gender together are even greater: almost half of Black women and 39.4 percent of Latina women, but only 10 percent of Asian women work in education, compared to 35.1 percent, 24.6 percent, and 16.2 percent, respectively, for their male counterparts. The figures for the next highest occupation – business and financial operations – range from a low of 11.3 percent for Black women to a high of 33.9 percent for Latino men. The next sector is community/ social services and nonprofits. Of the four supposed "feeder occupations" (law, business, education, and community activism), law (at 5.2 percent) ranks last for women of color (and second to last for men) – with dramatic differences by race and gender: 10.0 percent of Asian American women and 21.6 percent of Asian American men gave law as their occupations. The top occupation for Asian American women, in contrast, is in the nonprofit sector: 30 percent compared to 5.3 percent for men – a difference that is large, but not statistically significant. Asian American officials reported working in education at significantly lower rates than the other groups: just 10 percent for Asian women and 16.2 percent for Asian men.

Variation by Level of Office

To enrich our understanding of occupational attainment among elected officials, we compare the GMCL respondents who are state legislators to state legislators in general – and to those in local offices (Table 3.3).

TABLE 3.2. Top Occupations, by Race and Gender, All Levels of Office

Occupation	All	All***		Black†		Latino/a*		Asian American†	
		Female	Male	Female	Male	Female	Male	Female	Male
Education	34.6	42.4	29.0	48.2	35.1	39.4	24.6	10.0	16.2
Business & financial operations	20.4	15.3	24.1	11.3	13.8	20.2	33.9	25.0	29.7
Community/social services/nonprofit	13.0	15.3	11.4	14.9	16.0	13.8	7.6	30.0	5.4
Sales	9.8	7.6	11.4	6.5	12.2	8.5	12.3	15.0	5.4
Government/civil service	9.4	6.6	11.4	7.1	9.6	7.4	13.5	0	13.5
Law	6.9	5.2	8.2	4.8	9.0	4.3	4.1	10.0	21.6
Health care	5.8	7.6	4.5	7.1	4.3	6.4	4.1	10.0	8.1
N	1,309	228	403	168	188	94	171	20	37

Note: Entries are percents, which may not add up to 100 because of rounding. "Law" includes not only forty-four attorneys, but also four who responded, "paralegal," "legal technician," "legal assistant."

†p < .1; * p < .05; *** p < .0001.

Source: Data are from the GMCL National Survey, 2006–2007, and include those who responded that they were employed outside of the home; N = 691; their responses were coded using the Standard Occupational Classification (SOC) categories used by the US Department of Labor, Bureau of Labor Statistics.

TABLE 3.3. *Occupations of State Legislators of Color and in General, and Local Officials of Color, by Gender*

Occupation	State Legislators in General		Elected Officials of Color			
			State Legislators		Local	
	Female	Male	Female	Male	Female	Male
All education	25.4	15.6	31.5	16.9	32.5	19.1
Elem./secondary teacher	18.1**	10.1	22.9	13.8	23.2	12.5
College prof.	3.5	2.5	0.0	3.1	2.7	2.2
Educ. admin.	2.0	2.7	2.9	0.0	3.3	2.4
Educ.: Other	1.8	0.4	5.7	0.0	3.3	2.0
Lawyer	9.5	14.6	17.1	24.6	1.8	3.0
Nonprofit/community program/activist	5.0**	0.7	8.6	0.0	4.8	3.3
Nurse/other health worker	8.2**	0.7	0.0	1.5	6.3	1.8
Phys./dentist	2.2	0.6	0.0	1.5	0.0	0.4
Other health	0.7	2.3	n/a	n/a	n/a	n/a
SW/counselor	2.2	1.0	5.7	1.5	4.8	0.9
Self-employed/business owner	7.3	8.8	5.7	10.8	6.3	8.3
Other business	7.0	13.0	2.9	1.5	3.0	5.4
Real estate/insurance	2.7	4.3	5.7	7.7	3.6	4.6
Farmer/rancher	2.3**	6.2	2.9	1.5	0.6	2.6
Editor/reporter	2.2	0.9	0.0	0.0	0.3	0.6
Minister	n/a	n/a	0.0	4.6	0.6	2.0
Government	0.0	0.0	2.9	1.5	5.4	5.5
Homemaker	3.8**	26.2	0.0	0.0	5.1	0.2
All other	21.2**	5.2	17.1	26.2	24.7	42.3
	N = 673	N = 535	N = 35	N = 65	N = 332	N = 542
	p < .05, **p* < .01		n.s.			*p* <.0001

Note: Entries are percents, which may not add up to 100 because of rounding.

The "all other" category for male local-level officials is particularly large because, by following the CAWP protocol for the sake of comparability, it captures a broad range of occupations – from laborer and mechanic to engineer.

Sources: GMCL National Survey, 2006–2007; data for state legislators in general were computed from a 2008 survey by the Center for American Women and Politics (CAWP) Carroll and Sanbonmatsu (2013, Tables 2.1–2.4), which does not include the categories of "minister" or "government."

Education continues as the no. 1 occupation for both women of color state legislators (at 31.5 percent) and women legislators in general, who are mostly White (at 25.4 percent),[13] with most of these reporting being elementary or secondary teachers; the figures for male state legislators of color, at 16.9 percent, resemble those for men in general. The predominance of an occupation in education for women of color elected officials is only true for African Americans and Latinas. Only one in ten Asian American women, compared to a third of African American and a quarter of Latina women, hold occupations in that field, whereas their share in business resembles that of their male counterparts – and also Latino men. They also are more likely than the other race/gender groups to work in nonprofit organizations.

The no. 2 occupation for state legislators of color, especially men, is the law – a point we discuss later – but this is not true for local officials. Of additional interest is the fact that 8.6 percent of female state legislators of color reported coming from the community activism/nonprofit world compared to none of the men of color and only 5 percent of women state legislators in general; at the same time nursing or health care seems more prevalent for women state legislators in general (and for women of color in local offices) than for their female counterparts of color.

What is missing in traditional reporting on occupations by women in politics scholars may be hinted at by the 42.3 percent of male local officials of color who do not fall into one of the standard categories used by the Center for American Women and Politics (CAWP). One reason for this is likely to be a gender bias in the categories: when using CAWP categories, occupations as diverse as engineers, architects, and systems analysts; blue collar workers, barbers, and funeral home directors; and mail carriers, firefighters, police officers, and retired or active military – fields that are more "male" – fall into an "all other" category, a gender bias especially pronounced for local-level elected officials of color.

The Profession of Law: Impact of Level of Office, Gender, and Race

A major flaw in the study of occupations among elected officials is that most of the research is done at the congressional and state legislative

---

[13] State "legislators in general" are those who responded to the 2008 CAWP Recruitment Survey (see Sources in Table 3.3).

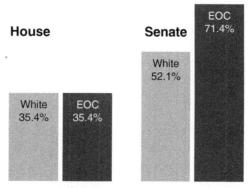

FIGURE 3.2 Lawyers in 113th Congress.
Note: Percents shown are for members of the US House and Senate who are (non-Hispanic) White or EOCs (i.e., elected officials of color) serving as US senators or representatives.
Sources: For members of color in Congress, the source is the GMCL Project, 2014; N = 87. For other members of Congress, the source is Manning (2014, 2–4).

levels, whereas, as discussed in Chapter 2, the vast majority of all elected officials serves at the local level, as city/town councilors, county commissioners/supervisors, and on local school boards. Much of the literature also is segmented either by a singular focus on men and women (who are mostly White) or on Blacks and Latinos (who are mostly male). Largely missing from the literature on occupational attainment is a systematic understanding of elected officials of different races situated at the intersection of race and gender; Githens and Prestage (1977) is a rare exception.

Although the well-documented view of law as one of the top occupations for elected officials may be an artifact of researchers' almost exclusive focus on members of Congress and state legislators, the GMCL data do provide some support for findings from prior research that suggest women of color have to be even more qualified than women in general (Moncrief et al. 1991), including attaining an occupation in the law. Almost one in five (17.1 percent) of women state legislators of color, for example, reported "attorney" or "lawyer" as their occupation – close to double that of women state legislators in general. But, with law as the occupation of one-quarter of male state legislators of color, compared to 14.6 percent of male legislators in general, one must also conclude that for men holding this level of office, they, like their female counterparts, must present credentials that go beyond their nonminority colleagues. The importance of disaggregating by level of office is evident in that, for local officials, law drops 15 percentage points for women of color to 1.8 percent for local officials – and by more than 20 points for men (from 24.6 percent to 3.0 percent).

At the same time, our analysis of the elected officials of color (EOCs) in the 113th Congress reveals that about a third (35.4 percent) of US representatives of color in the 113th Congress were lawyers[14] – a percentage that is identical to that of non-Hispanic White members (Figure 3.2). And five (71.4 percent) of the six US senators of color in the 113th Congress were lawyers, a share that is substantially higher than the 52.1 percent of non-Hispanic White senators.

AT THE HEART OF PIPELINE THEORY: A CRITIQUE OF "FEEDER OCCUPATIONS" AND THE "ELIGIBILITY POOL"

The continued underrepresentation of women in elective positions has puzzled scholars for several decades. Is it simply that, as Lawless and Fox (2005) and Lawless (2010) suggest, not enough women run? Or is it that women suffer defeat when they seek elected office because they are not as qualified as men? According to a review by Mariani (2008, 291), "All things being equal, candidates with occupational backgrounds that facilitate and complement their accumulation of both financial and political resources will have an advantage over those from occupations that provide fewer resources and less politically relevant experience." He notes that in the 1970s and 1980s, "a number of studies found that women were at a disadvantage relative to men in terms of their professional backgrounds and education"; women were also "more likely than men to serve in lower-paid professions and to have lower personal incomes in comparison to men..." But as discussed earlier, many of these patterns no longer hold true.

Gendered-, Class-, and Raced-Based "Feeder Occupations"?

Research also suggests that women have made gains in the "feeder occupations" – law, business, education, and activism – which, according to a number of scholars, fills the "eligibility pool" of potential candidates (Fox and Lawless 2004, 2005; Lawless 2012; Lawless and Fox 2005,

---

[14] The percentage includes Eleanor Holmes-Norton (D-DC), the nonvoting delegate from the District of Columbia; she is an attorney.

2010; Sanbonmatsu 2002). We remind the reader that, by studying candidates, not elected officials, their findings are not precisely comparable to the GMCL National Survey respondents. Nevertheless, we find that the vast majority of elected officials of color *do* work in one of the supposed "feeder occupations" and may have emerged from an "eligibility pool" of candidates when they won their election. Two-thirds (64.9 percent) of women of color in the GMCL National Survey compared to 48.6 percent of their male counterparts report an occupation in one of these fields ($p < .0001$). Because of their strong presence in the field of education, Black women (at 71.4 percent) take the lead, compared to 66.5 percent of Latinas and 60.7 percent of Asian American women holding office; each of these is higher than those of their male peers (Black men at 53.0 percent; Latino men at 49.9 percent; and Asian American men at 45.1 percent).

The notion of feeder occupations and eligibility pools has been challenged in a number of ways, however, including by the fact that the experiences of Black, Latino, and Asian American women and men are more complex than what these numbers suggest, for several reasons. First, although women in general have been making steady gains in such occupations over the last four decades, there has not been a corresponding gain in their share of elective office-holding in recent years (see Reingold 2008a; and Chapter 1 in this volume). Second, most studies of elected officials' occupations that include attention to gender draw only on data from state legislators and leave out officeholders of color (Carroll and Sanbonmatsu 2013; Moncrief et al. 1991). Williams (2001) studied the occupations of elected officials of color but her study compared only Black and White state legislators. Carroll and Sanbonmatsu (2013, 103–106) devote just four pages within a chapter on the rise of Democratic women state legislators to "the pathways of Democratic women of color" and do not provide the detailed analysis on the background characteristics of these women as they do for women in general[15] – likely because the number of women of color in their samples is too small for meaningful analysis.[16]

Second, theories that assume there is an eligibility pool also subscribe to the idea that that pool flows easily into a "pipeline" to office, wherein

[15] They do spend another five pages (pp. 98–103) on the growth of women of color state legislators and the obstacles they face.

[16] According to a personal communication with Sanbonmatsu (email, March 21, 2013), the CAWP study included responses from eighty-one women of color state legislators who were serving in 2008; these made up 10 percent of the total sample.

potential officeholders are personally ambitious and strive to gain a set of individual qualifications (including employment in one of these feeder occupations). These theories fail to pay attention to a host of institutional factors that are also found to explain the numbers of women candidates and elected officials (Schroedel and Godwin 2005). For example, as discussed in Chapter 1 and earlier in this chapter, the activism that led to the Voting Rights Act of 1965 and the resulting creation of Black majority districts play an equally – and perhaps even more – important role in increasing political representation for people of color, especially Black women.

With education being the top occupation for both the women and the men in our survey, merely treating it as one of the four "feeder occupations" may disguise the different meanings for women and men. Prior research suggests that women officials hold occupations in women-dominated, nonexecutive professions, especially in teaching (K–12) and social work: 45 percent of the Latinas in Takash's 1993 survey of Latina elected officials in California worked in educational settings. This is higher than the percentages among women in the US Congress: García Bedolla, Tate, and Wong (2005, 166) report that, when one includes educational positions at the postsecondary and college administration levels, 28 percent of White and minority women work in educational fields, "and among black women it increases to 31 percent." They conclude that "one-quarter to nearly one-third of the women worked as teachers or in education prior to winning office to the US House of Representatives [and] is a key difference in the occupational backgrounds of men and women serving in Congress."

Finally, of those working outside of the home, women of color (at 24.3 percent) are twice as likely as their male counterparts (at 12.7 percent) to report being an elementary or secondary school teacher, as are Latinas (20.7 percent), compared to Latino men (9.5 percent). The same is true for Black women (28.9 percent) compared to Black men (16.3 percent) but not for Asian American officials, who, as a group, are significantly less likely (at just 6.8 percent) to report this occupation. It also turns out that Asian women (at just 4.5 percent) are significantly less likely than their male counterparts (at 7.8 percent) to work as a K–12 teacher.[17]

---

[17] Significance by gender is $p < .0001$, as it is by gender for Blacks; for Asian Americans it is $p < .05$, and for Latinos, the difference between women and men, though large, is not statistically significant.

AN INTERSECTIONAL PERSPECTIVE ON
OCCUPATIONAL PRESTIGE

Occupation is, of course, not just a demographic marker; it also provides one with human capital (qualifications, confidence) and social capital (connections through one's work), thus increasing one's stature within the community, district, or voter base. The majority of elected officials of color come from one of the four occupations that supposedly "feed" the eligibility pool, but their predominance in education (as classroom teachers for Black and Latina women) and in social/community service (for Asian American women) raises questions about the nature of occupational prestige.

The Sociopolitical Context of Occupational "Choices"

The question whether professions held by elected officials of color provide status and prestige useful in winning elected office must be analyzed with some consideration of the meaning of education and certain types of occupations for communities of color. Past and ongoing discrimination faced by women of color means that Black, Latina, and Asian women may rank differently (and/or be blocked from accessing) certain occupations. Those who have secured a college degree and go on to work in traditionally "female" occupations, such as elementary or high school teacher or nurse, for example, see themselves and are seen as successful within their communities – thus eminently qualified for elective office – even if such occupations are not ranked among the high-prestige professions for political office.

With so many of the respondents of the GMCL National Survey serving at the local level, where being an attorney is both less likely and less important, we find that male officials of color typically report occupations often not counted in studies on women in politics. The challenge to conventional wisdom becomes even more complicated when one looks at the sources of the data used in Lawless and Fox (2005, 2010) and others (e.g., Carroll and Sanbonmatsu 2013) to construct occupational categories.

First, whereas "law" and "education" are comparable (although, as discussed previously, the meaning of being a teacher may be racialized and gendered for communities of color), the "business" category as presented in prior research is very much biased by class. Lawless and Fox (2005, 157), for example, "randomly selected 1,800 business leaders from *Dun and Bradstreet's Million Dollar Directory*, ...which lists the top executive officers of more than 160,000 public and private companies in the United States" (italics in original). Respondents in the GMCL Survey who work, for example, as accountants, barbers, funeral home director, caterers, and even bankers would certainly not rise to inclusion in a "million dollar" directory, and therefore would not have been invited to respond to surveys such as theirs. Their findings, therefore, reflect neither an adequate sample of people of color, nor a full range of business occupations sufficient to capture the diverse occupations of these populations – and may explain why so many male local officials in our survey were relegated to the "All other" category, which was developed based on prior studies.

Second, what experiences lie behind "Vice President of Ortega Stores"; an elected official who runs a "vault business," or who is the "owner of a funeral home"? Consider also an African American female school board member from a small town in Mississippi (HS graduate) who responded, "I worked in the school system until I became disabled, and before that I worked in a plant that made lingerie, and I owned my own business." The concept of "feeder occupations" may not work for understanding elected officials of color, especially at the local level.

Measuring Occupational Prestige for Multicultural Political Leaders

Existing measures of occupational status and prestige, including the General Social Survey (GSS) by the National Opinion Research Center (NORC), which uses categories going back to the 1940s (see Hauser and Warren 1997), demonstrate considerable gender bias and reveal a number of occupational lacunae. Many studies, nevertheless, use the GSS categories, including an analysis of the occupations of Black and White state legislators (Williams 2001). Each occupation is given a Prestige Score, which ranges from 16.78 for "Miscellaneous Food Preparation Workers" to a high of 86.05 for "Physicians."[18]

According to the typology used by Williams (2001), high-prestige occupations include not only attorneys but also physicians, engineers, college professors, and other professionals.[19] Williams finds that a higher percentage of Black women state legislators hold jobs deemed "high

---

[18] Other high-prestige scores include 74.77 for attorneys; 73.70 for computer systems analysts and scientists; and 73.51 for college professors. Low-prestige scores include, for example, 29.25 for child care workers; generally, blue-color occupations range from the low 20s to mid-30s. Managers, administrators, and mid-range professionals such as nurses, and skilled technicians, as well as most business occupations, receive scores in the 40s–60s and are considered moderate-prestige occupations.

[19] We noticed a discrepancy: in her typology, Williams (2001) points to gender bias with an example of how "housewife" is considered a low-prestige occupation. We find, however, that the GSS NORC codes do not include one for Housewife.

prestige" compared to Black men, White men, and White women. A study (of women only) by Moncrief et al. (1991, 482–483) finds that "Black female state legislators are far more likely than their white counterparts to hold high prestige occupations, and far less likely to hold low prestige occupations," even if the racial gaps are not statistically significant.

To explore the occupational prestige of today's multicultural political leadership, we coded the occupations reported by the GMCL respondents using the most recent Prestige Scores from the GSS (NORC 2013, 2,993–3,000; see also Davis et al. 1991). Examining mean prestige scores by gender, race, and race*gender, we find some similarities but also significant distinctions. Female elected officials of color overall had a higher mean prestige score (56.5) than that of their male counterparts (54.4), providing some support for the notion that women bring higher levels of human capital to their offices; the difference, although significant at $p <$ .01, was not large, however. Furthermore, the average prestige score for Asian American elected officials (60.7) was significantly larger than those for Blacks (55.8) and Latinos/as (53.2).

The picture is more complicated when looked at through an intersectional lens. Figure 3.3 demonstrates that, while Asian American male officials' mean prestige score (62.57) is the highest of all race*gender groups, the "take away" of this analysis is how close Black, Latina, and Asian American women resemble each other, and to a lesser extent, Black men, in terms of occupational prestige.

Furthermore, whereas occupational prestige for Asian American female elected officials is *lower* on average than for their male counterparts, those of Black and Latina women are significantly higher; we should point out that the gender difference among Blacks is very small, and other than for among Latinos/as, only moderately significant.

A number of insights may be drawn from these findings. First, we can confirm prior research that, with the exception of Asian Americans, female elected officials of color do, indeed, have higher levels of occupational prestige overall compared to their male counterparts. Second, we must not lump all women and men of color together, as the experiences of male and female Asian Americans are different than those of Blacks and Latinos/as. Third, among Black women and Latinas, who may be the first in their families to attend college, we may need also to reassess whether traditionally female occupations (such as nurse or school teacher) merit classification into a higher-prestige category, at least for these communities. Finally, Black and Latino men may face challenges not covered by the women in politics literature – a point we discuss later in this chapter.

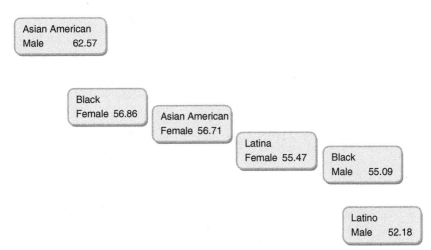

FIGURE 3.3 Occupational prestige, by race and gender.

Note: Entries are mean prestige scores for those who reported occupations and worked outside of the home. Significance by race alone: $p < .0001$; by gender within race: Asian $p < .1$; Black $p < .1$; Latino/a $p < .005$; by gender alone: $p < .01$. *Source*: GMCL National Survey, 2006–2007. Occupational prestige scores calculated using codes from the General Social Survey, 1972–2012 Cumulative Codebook (NORC 2013, 2,993–3,000).

PERSONAL CHOICES – OR POLITICAL RESOURCES? ENTERING THE "DOUBLY DISADVANTAGED" DEBATE

Just as higher levels of educational attainment and occupational status may enhance voters' perceptions of the qualifications of a candidate or elected official, for elected officials of color, even background characteristics that at first blush appear to be personal choices may in fact reflect group circumstances and show different patterns by gender and race. Marital status and the age at which one decides to run for office, for example, are not only choices made by an *individual*, but also may be constrained or eased by one's race and/or gender because of political forces and/or racialized governmental policies.

Money (just plain "capital") – whether personal or household income, family assets, or campaign contributions – is a concrete, tangible resource that can affect how voters view a candidate and determine the success of a campaign. Financial capital within an official's district can either provide resources (i.e., campaign contributions) if it is abundant, or be a drain, if poverty rates are high Finally, one's family background can open doors to education, jobs, and sociopolitical connections – or present obstacles to overcome from childhood on.

With this section of the chapter, we enter the debate over the extent to which female elected officeholders of color are advantaged or disadvantaged compared to their male counterparts when it comes to personal resources they can or cannot bring with them to their campaigns and offices. We begin with marital status and age and then move on to those derived from an official's financial resources and family background.

Marriage as a "Personal Choice" or a Racially Gendered Disadvantage?

In general, marital status for elected officials is considered to be a demographic characteristic based on a personal choice: one decides to marry or not. There is some evidence that marriage affects voter preferences somewhat, in that being married is thought to be an advantage for male candidates.[20] Political women point to "no-win" responses to their marital status: In the words of Senator Barbara Mikulski, "If you're married, you're neglecting him; if you're single, you couldn't get him; if you're divorced, you couldn't keep him; and if you're widowed, you killed him" (Lester 2003, 245; Robson 2000; Schenken 1999, 438).[21]

Missing in these traditional viewpoints is that marital status for women of color is, more often than not, fraught with complications. Intersectionality theory suggests that racially gendered government policies are at the heart of the disadvantages facing women of color, including, for example, the push to "reform" (i.e., restrict) welfare for poor women (Reingold and Smith 2012), which lowers benefits if a husband is present. Other racialized policies also affect marriage opportunities: policies ostensibly for "public safety" have led to more Black and Latino men of a certain age being incarcerated than in college. The number of adults under correctional supervision increased, for example, by 275 percent between 1980 and 2003 (Sourcebook of Criminal Justice Statistics 2011). The Justice Policy Institute (Butterfield 2002) reports that, in 1980 there were almost 500,000 Black men in college compared to about 143,000 in jail or prison. By 2000, 791,600 Black men were incarcerated compared

---

[20] Fowler and Lawless (2009, 523) find that women candidates for governor "received 64 percent of coverage regarding appearance, mannerisms, personality, and marital and parental status."

[21] Adrienne Kimmell, executive director of the Barbara Lee Family Foundation (personal communication with Carol Hardy-Fanta, June 18, 2015), among others, attribute the phrase to Gov. Ann Richards. The sentiment is expressed with slightly different phrasing and in numerous settings; it is difficult to determine who first coined the phrase.

to "603,032 enrolled in colleges or universities." Western, Schiraldi, and Ziedenberg (2003, 4) find that "from 1977 to 1999, total state and local expenditures on corrections increased by 946% – about 2.5 times the rate of increase on all levels of education (370%)." Pettit and Western (2004, 151) state that "among men born between 1965 and 1969, 3 percent of whites and 20 percent of blacks had served time in prison by their early thirties."

The impact of this "new life course" on marriage rates could not be clearer. According to Wolfers, Leonhardt, and Quealy (2015), "For every 100 Black women not in jail, there are only 83 black men. The remaining men – 1.5 million of them – are, in a sense, *missing*" (emphasis in original). Whereas almost three-quarters of the non-college White men in their study were married, a little more than half of Black men of this group were married. Welfare and mass-incarceration policies thus affect opportunities for higher education, later occupational status, and marital status of Blacks and Latinos, especially – and these are clearly stratified by race, gender, and class (Smith 1999; Tucker and Mitchell-Kernan 1995). In conclusion, even the very individualistic "marital status" may be racialized and gendered, and, in a word, marriage may not be as accessible a "personal choice" for Black (and Latina) women as for White women.

Marriage as a Sociopolitical Resource? Findings from the GMCL National Survey

Although almost seven in ten elected officials of color in the GMCL National Survey reported being married (see *All* in Table 3.4), the "marriage gap" by gender is very large and highly significant. Just over half (53.4 percent) of women of color holding office are married compared to eight in ten of their male counterparts ($p < .0001$). Table 3.4 also shows the breakdown by race and gender, with Black women 29 percentage points less likely to be married than Black men, and Asian American women and Latinas about 20 points lower than their male counterparts. Asian American officials are significantly more likely to be married (82 percent) than Latinos (76.6 percent) and Blacks (62.7 percent).

As most research leaves out local-level officials, it is not possible to know with precision the marriage gap for elected officials in general (i.e., including White women and men). However, by our calculations, women of color are also significantly less likely to be married than women officials in general, at least when serving as state legislators. According to a 2001 study (CAWP 2001, 4), 69 percent of women state legislators (presumably

TABLE 3.4. *Personal Resources, by Race and Gender*

Resource	All	Black		Latino/a		Asian American	
		Female	Male	Female	Male	Female	Male
Married (N = 1,209) percent	69.7	45.9***	74.9	62.8***	83.1	69.0*	88.3
Age in years (N = 1,190) mean	56.1	59.3	58.6	53.2	52.8	54.4	52.6
Age in years first elected (N = 1,175) mean	43.4	46.7***	43.2	43.9**	40.9	44.0	43.5
Household income <$50,000 (N = 1,156) percent	26.3	34.0***	24.9	30.1***	23.1	14.8†	7.1
Household income ($) mean	$87,012	$71,880***	$88,605	$82,769	$89,279	$115,926	$131,111
Financial Resources in District							
County (mean % poverty in county)	19.4	15.7**	19.2	18.0†	23.3	12.2	11.0
Municipal (mean % poverty in census place)	21.8	22.8	23.6	21.8	20.6	9.2	9.4
State legislators (mean % poverty in district)	20.5	23.0*	23.8	18.2	18.2	13.9	8.5
School board (mean per capita income in district)	$15,576	$18,015	$16,550	$14,697	$14,347	$19,226	$17,028

Note: Mean household income was computed using an income scale in twenty-one categories, ranging from less than $10K to $200K and over; because of difficulties gathering poverty rates for school board districts comparable to those at the other levels, we offer mean per capita income in district for school board members.

†$p < .1$; *$p < .05$; **$p < .01$; ***$p < .001$.

Source: GMCL National Survey, 2006–2007.

mostly White) compared to 87 percent of their male colleagues are married. Results for legislators of color in the GMCL Survey show a similar pattern: 56.5 percent of women of color state legislators reported being married compared to 72.2 percent of their male peers. Whether the gaps are due to race-based government policies that decrease the marriage pool for certain groups of women of color, or whether there is a gendered bias overall to the institution of marriage for women in politics is not clear: having a wife may benefit a male candidate,[22] including elected officials seeking reelection, whereas, as we discussed earlier, the absence (or, for that matter, presence) of a husband may disadvantage women.

Marriage often (although, of course, not always) brings a variety of resources to a relationship besides, in the modern era, the hoped-for love and companionship. Marriage may also provide financial support and enhance social connections. Being married to a public official may add resources for an elected official (although charges of nepotism and the potential for scandals may offset any benefits). We find that, overall, most elected officials do not report having a public official as a spouse, but, of those who do, Latina and Black women elected officials are more likely (at 17.6 percent and 12.9 percent, respectively) to be married to a public official than their male counterparts (at 2.7 percent and 8.3 percent, respectively).[23] The same is true for the American Indian state legislators in our study – with even greater margins (28.6 percent of the women, and none of the men).

Another related avenue of inquiry that has emerged in the study of elected officials of color but not in studies of White men and women is the issue of race of a spouse or partner. Fraga et al. (2006) suggest that the race of a spouse is another demographic distinction for women of color elected officials, with a significantly larger percentage of Latina women state legislators being married to non-Latino Whites than Latino men are to White women. They tentatively posited that Latina women married to White men might draw certain advantages, such as coming from more affluent households or having spouses better connected professionally. Among the respondents in the GMCL National Survey, there was a large gender difference for Asian Americans for the percentage of officials

[22] Unless, as discussed in Kallenberger (2015), the wife is seen as too ambitious, independent, or a political interloper.
[23] Significance for Latinas/os (and overall by gender) is $p < .0001$; and American Indians is $p < .1$; the difference for Blacks was not significant and there was no difference for Asian Americans, at about 10 percent each. Note, also, that the percentages reported are of those who responded to the questions on marital status and race.

who were married to a White spouse (35.0 percent of women, compared to 18.9 percent of men), but, compared to the findings by Fraga et al. (2006), none for Latinas/os. Perhaps the more important finding is by race alone: compared to just 3 percent of Black officials, 23.3 percent of Asian Americans and 18.4 percent of Latinos/as in our study reported being married to someone who was White.

We have no evidence that "marrying White" provides, as Fraga et al. (2006) suggest, a form of social or political capital for the elected officials of color we studied. As we pointed out in the discussion in Chapter 1, for example, it is Black women – for whom marriage with Whites is much less likely – who are the closest to reaching parity in descriptive representation.

Age at First Election: Personal Choice, Political Resource, or Gendered Barrier for Women?

In general, studies of women in politics have found that women "are older than men when they first consider running for office" (Lawless and Fox 2010, 167). Researchers debate the reasons, disadvantages, and potential benefits for apparent gender differences in age at which women and men first run for office. On the one hand, being older may convey greater maturity and a certain "gravitas"; at the same time, the literature suggests that family responsibilities, among other factors, lead women to enter politics later than men. In the latter view, women make a choice to forgo a political career until later in life, for personal or family reasons.

Scholars suggest that a decision to postpone entry hinders women's political progress. Running for office at a younger age has certain benefits: "Younger men and women may have more energy to enter politics, endure the rigors of a campaign, and engage in the activities necessary for networking and fundraising" (Fox and Lawless 2005, 647). For women, age at entering politics may not be a personal decision based on one's "stage of life," however, but may reflect larger societal pressures and expectations including gender roles in the home: women often feel they cannot run till their children are older.[24] According to Fox and Lawless (2005, 647), "The all-consuming nature of running for office ... may mean that age and family arrangements exert a different type of effect on potential candidates' initial decisions to run for office."

---

[24] The GMCL National Survey does not include whether the respondents had children.

Running for the first time at a more advanced age may also block advancement to higher levels of office: Witness Speaker of the House Nancy Pelosi, whose first foray into elected office was at the age of forty-seven; when asked if she might set her sights on the presidency, she replied that she was too old (Dittmar 2013). And, of course, Hillary Clinton had her own career as a lawyer and activist, but put them on hold during her husband's terms as president and did not run for office for the first time until 2000, when she was fifty-three; she initially faced considerable scrutiny over her age during her 2016 presidential race.

The question of whether women are older than men when they first run for office is still, however, open to some debate: A study conducted twenty-five years ago by the Center for American Women and Politics (CAWP) finds no significant difference in median age by gender at any level of office (Carroll and Strimling 1983, 14). And Fox and Lawless (2004, 271) suggest that, "The traditional barriers to women's entry into the political sphere, therefore, no longer appear to impede their likelihood of thinking about a political candidacy."

Most studies that include attention to age tend to ignore race alone or in interaction with gender. The few that exist suggest that age in office (or at first election) varies with race/ethnicity. The 1983 survey by Carroll and Strimling (1983, 145) finds that Black women were somewhat younger than women candidates in general. Hardy-Fanta's (1997, 16) study of all Latino/a candidates who ran for office in Massachusetts between 1968 and 1994, which included mostly local officials, shows that Latinas were about ten years older than Latino men when they first ran for office.

Gender, Race, and Age of Elected Officials of Color

Respondents to the GMCL National Survey provide some support for the contention that women elected officials are, on average, significantly older than their male counterparts (45.5 for women, 42.3 for men, $p < .0001$). Within each racial group, women of color are slightly older than their male counterparts, but these differences are not statistically significant (see Table 3.4). The larger difference is by race: Black officials overall are older (58.9 years), followed by Asian Americans (53.2 years) and Latinos/as (52.9 years) ($p < .0001$).

Of course, the key question is not how old they are *now*, but whether women are older than men when they enter the political fray and run for office the first time. We find that the mean age of the women we surveyed (45.5 years) when they first took office was significantly higher than that of men (42.3 years) ($p < .0001$), but it was most pronounced for Blacks, with Black women reporting that they were 46.7 years old compared to 43.2 years for Black men (see Table 3.4). The pattern was the same for Latinas, who were 43.9 years when they first took office compared to 40.9 years for their male counterparts.

Prior research also has shown that men in general are much more likely to run for the first time at a significantly younger age than women; Mandel and Kleeman (2004, 8; see also note 5, p. 28) find, for example, that 85 percent of elected officials younger than the age of thirty-five are men, and that this is true for all levels of office. We find that, for the most part, the pattern holds for GMCL respondents, but it is slightly less "imbalanced"[25]: the breakdown for elected officials of color who report being younger than thirty-five years of age when they were first elected to office is 78 percent male and 22 percent female ($p < .01$).

Does Level of Office Make a Difference?

The age at which women and men run for office depends on level of office: In the 113th Congress, "women's average age of entering the House is 50.2 years old and men average 46.7 years old" (Dittmar 2013). Of course, we do not know from this study the ages they ran for their first, lower-level office, but scholars find that at the school board level, women candidates tend to be younger than their male competitors (Deckman 2006, 96; Dolan et al. 2007, 146).

We find that the average age of women of color serving on local elected school boards (45.5 years) when they first took office matches the age of the (mostly White) female candidates surveyed by Dolan et al. (2007, 146), which was 45.7 years. However, male school board members of color in our sample were younger (42.2 years), whereas males were somewhat older (47.7 years) in that study.[26] In Deckman (2006), the comparable figures among the mostly White respondents are 45.5 years for women and 42.2 years for men.[27] Among those serving in municipal offices, a higher proportion of Asian American women (at 25 percent) are more likely than Asian men (at 16 percent) to report that they were younger than thirty-five when they were first elected.

---

[25] As the report says, "The ratio of men to women among young people in office ... is at once surprising and unsurprising – surprisingly imbalanced" by gender" (Mandel and Kleeman 2004, 8).

[26] We acknowledge that reporting ages of officeholders in the GMCL Survey is not precisely comparable to studies of candidates; keep in mind, however, that we ask their age at the time they first ran for office, in other words, were candidates.

[27] This difference was not statistically significant.

The pattern reverses for Black and Latino municipal officials, one in ten for each group of women, compared to a quarter of Black men and a third of Latino men, were in that age group. Among state legislators of color, the percentage male younger than thirty-five drops slightly to 76.6 percent, with some dramatic variation among women who make up 42.9 percent of American Indian state legislators younger than 35, compared to 31.3 percent of Blacks and 28.6 percent of Asian Americans.[28]

FINANCIAL RESOURCES: DISADVANTAGES BY RACE*GENDER

To the extent possible, political leaders tap into a variety of financial resources, including income and campaign contributions. One's income is a concrete, tangible resource that covers essential living expenses, can determine the ability to launch an election or reelection campaign, and may affect how voters view a candidate, especially when combined with occupational prestige. The relative wealth or poverty of one's district affects the degree to which constituents are able to contribute cash or time. In this section of the chapter, we explore the extent to which access to financial resources is racially gendered. Intersectionality theories lead us to hypothesize that, among elected officials of color, Black and Latina women would be financially disadvantaged compared to their male counterparts and Asian Americans of either gender.

In the preceding discussion we saw that, although female elected officials of color may gain certain advantages by their educational attainment and occupational status, they are disadvantaged by the marriage gap in terms of potential material resources, with the largest being for Black women. Table 3.4 clearly demonstrates that women of each racial group are also disadvantaged in terms of personal financial resources, that is, household income. Black women, in particular, stand out, with the highest percentage (34.0 percent) of officeholders reporting household income below $50,000 compared to Latinas (30.1 percent) and Asian American women (14.8 percent); their male counterparts are, on average, less likely to report household income below $50,000 (24.9 percent of Black men; 30.1 percent of Latino men; and just 7.1 percent of Asian men). Black women's mean household income is also the lowest for all

---

[28] The N's in our survey for state legislators are quite small, and should be taken with caution, especially for American Indian; we do not report the percentage Latina for this reason.

TABLE 3.5. *Household Income by Marital Status, Race, and Gender*

	Black		Latino/a		Asian American	
	Female	Male	Female	Male	Female	Male
Married	$87,965	$97,640	$95,769	$92,698	$132,222	$135,319
Not married	$58,613	$62,644	$63,269	$73,019	$83,333	$102,857
N	250	337	130	305	27	54
	$p < .0001$	$p < .0001$	$p < .0001$	$p < .01$	$p < .1$	n.s.

Note: Entries are mean incomes.
Source: GMCL National Survey, 2006–2007.

race*gender combinations; that of Black women is almost $20,000 less than that of Black men.[29]

The "Marriage Gap" and Household Income

What explains the disadvantaged financial situation for Black and Latina women given that their educational and occupational levels were higher than that of their male peers? Circle back to the "marriage gap," discussed earlier: given the historical patterns of discrimination and governmental policies that help explain the lower marriage rates for women in these racial groups, it is not unexpected that, without a spouse, women would report lower household income. In Table 3.5 we report mean household income by marital status for each group and find significant differences for all groups except Asian American male officeholders.

Being married adds, on average, about $30,000 to the household income of Black male and female officials as well as for Latinas. The "bonus" for Asian American women in office is almost $50,000 (perhaps, in part, due to a greater share having a White spouse?). The amount is smaller but still significant for Latino men and about the same for Asian men, although, for the latter group, the difference is not significant.

Impact of Poor versus Wealthy Jurisdictions

Elected officials draw on financial resources besides their own income. Constituents, local businesses, and interest groups within an official's

---

[29] Significance of differences by gender is $p < .0001$ for Blacks and Latinos, and $p < .1$ for Asian Americans.

district can either provide resources (e.g., campaign contributions) if it is a well-to-do community, or be a drain if poverty rates are high and per capita income is low. We find Latino and Black male county officials are significantly more disadvantaged on a measure of financial resources in their counties: county poverty rates are higher for Black and Latino males serving as county supervisors or commissioners (23.3 percent and 19.2 percent, respectively) than those of their female counterparts (18.0 percent for Latinas and 15.7 percent for Black women).[30] In the case of Black state legislators, the difference, although statistically significant, is very small (see Table 3.4). There is no significant difference in jurisdictional poverty levels among Asian Americans on any of these measures, nor for municipal officials or school board officials of any race.

In a similar pattern, although using a different measure, men of color school board officials represent school districts with fewer financial resources, that is, lower mean per capita income; the differences are not, however, statistically significant. We should point out, of course, that the greatest differences in resources are between Asian American officials at any level of office and those of Black and Latino/a officials – although the differences even here are surprisingly modest.

FAMILY BACKGROUNDS AS RESOURCES – OR DISADVANTAGES TO OVERCOME?

Besides demonstrating that the social, economic, and political obstacles and struggles shaped the educational attainment and occupational "choices" of elected officials of color, we must also recognize that resources made available to them by their parents impact not only their political socialization (e.g., growing up in a political family) but also one's political successes. It is well documented that the socioeconomic status of one's parents increases access and opportunities for certain types of education and jobs. Those who come from families with less education, were raised "on welfare," and whose parents were foreign born have fewer resources at their disposal when seeking educational, occupational, and political successes of their own.

---

[30] According to MacManus et al. (2006, 122): "Few studies have focused on the backgrounds of women [county] commissioners. The first, and perhaps most, extensive study (*in the 1970s*) found that women commissioners were most likely to be 40–59 years of age (68%), with some college (75%), and in professional or technical occupations (50%) [Johnson and Carroll 1978]. A high proportion belonged to a political organization (65%) while over half (53%) had held a political party position at one time or another" (emphasis added).

As seen in the preceding discussion, the picture of advantages/disadvantages by gender and race is mixed on the officials' own personal resources – with women of color generally having higher degrees of educational and occupational attainment, but lower marriage rates and less household income. Here, we show that Black and Latino *male* elected officials come from the most disadvantaged family backgrounds. In other words, not only do men of these racial groups report lower levels of educational and occupational attainment than their female counterparts, but they also are more likely to report having parents who did not graduate from high school; to have been raised with government assistance; and, in the case of Latino officials, to have parents who are foreign born.

Disadvantaged by Lack of Parental Education

As shown in the column marked "All" in Table 3.6, as a group, almost six in ten elected officials of color reported that their fathers had less than a high school diploma, and half reported the same for their mothers. In fact, the parents of eight in ten had no more than a high school education. Relatively few – two in ten – reported they were raised in families that received government assistance, with the highest percentage reported by Latino men and the lowest by Asian men. And 15.9 percent had parents who were foreign born.

The experiences of Asian American officials do not follow this pattern, with women of this group being slightly less advantaged on socioeconomic measures than their male counterparts. However, the gender differences for this group are not statistically significant, and Asian Americans, irrespective of gender, are considerably less disadvantaged than Black and Latino/a officials. Just 6.8 percent of Asian American men, for example, versus 20.0 percent of Black and 23.8 percent of Latino men were raised with government assistance.

Looking more closely at parental education, it is not surprising (given the discussion above) to find that Asian Americans come into office with more educational resources in their backgrounds: half had parents with bachelor's degrees or more compared with 11.2 percent of Latinos/as and 18.2 percent of Blacks (table not shown). The gender difference between Black women and Black men on parental education – with two-thirds of Black men compared to just under half of Black women reporting their father had less than a high school education – is noteworthy. The significant variations by race and gender affirm our earlier contention of the need to consider political context and family history in understanding

TABLE 3.6. *Family Background as a Resource, by Race and Gender*

Resource	All	Black		Latino/a		Asian American	
		Female	Male	Female	Male	Female	Male
Parents' education							
Father <HS (N = 1,138)	56.2	49.0	63.7***	57.5	63.8†	25.9	22.4
Mother <HS (N = 1,172)	50.2	44.2	48.2	58.6	63.1	25.0	23.7
Economic resources							
Raised with government assistance	18.1	12.9	20.0*	15.5	23.8*	7.1	6.8
Sociopolitical Resources							
Parents foreign born	15.9	0.4	1.4	28.5	38.6*	52.9	50.0
Raised in a political family	33.5	39.5*	31.6	42.8**	29.7	24.1	16.7
N	1,152	265	359	140	301	28	59

Note: Entries are percents. †$p < .1$; *$p < .05$; **$p < .01$; ***$p < .001$.
Source: GMCL National Survey, 2006–2007.

the nature of the political advantages and disadvantages experienced by women and men of color.

Political Family: An Underexamined Resource

Before one jumps to a conclusion about the seeming advantages in the socioeconomic backgrounds of Asian American elected officials, we wish to highlight in this section their relative *disadvantages* in political socialization, due to being more likely to have foreign-born parents and less likely to have been raised in a political family.

The last two rows in Table 3.6 show that more than half of Asian American women serving in elected office, compared to fewer than three in ten of Latina women and nearly none of Black women, have foreign-born parents. Also, just a quarter of Asian American women compared to four in ten Latinas and Black women said they were raised in a political family. Among men of color, we observe a narrower nativity gap than among women of color, except that Asian men are equally likely as their female peers to have been raised in families with foreign-born parents. In terms of being raised in a political family, we notice that, as a group, Asian American men are the most disadvantaged of all: only about one in six report having such an opportunity – a figure even lower than that of Asian American women.

When seeking to interpret these patterns, we find that there has been limited research on elected officials and their family's background in politics. The literature that is available is old and tends to focus on decision making and learning pro-political behavior rather than access to a "political pipeline." These studies are limited by level of office and region of investigation, produce mixed results, and demonstrate the paucity of analysis by race and gender. Clubok, Wilenky, and Berghorn (1969), for example, find that only 5 percent of the men serving in Congress in 1960 had close relatives who had also served in Congress. In comparison, Kurtz (1989) suggests that the family environment in which the officials grew up imbues them with the knowledge, social capital, and interpersonal skills that provide them with a political advantage. He finds that of the roughly 800 political offices in the state of Louisiana, about 25 percent of the offices were held by officials with at least two family members having served in office.

Focusing on women, Darcy, Welch, and Clark (1994) suggest that belonging to a political family is a facilitating factor for women in attaining public office. For Ransford and Thomson (2011), "political family" includes relatives serving in an elected office, parental/familial engagement in the political process such as working for political campaigns and volunteering with campaigns. They find that, of thirteen female New England mayors, eight identified as having come from a political family. They also suggest that, although some elected officials grow up in an environment that socializes them to political culture, other factors outside of one's own family may be involved in helping individuals gaining access to resources that facilitate their election.

The literature that exists on the role of political families as a possible resource to elected officials of color is quite limited. A 2005 news report on Hawaiian politics reported that "one of eight in the [l]egislature has a relative who served" (Borreca 2005). Studies of Mexican American political mobilization also point to the importance of family in the political activism of this community.[31] Tirado (1970) maintains that the involvement of families contributed to the longevity and vitality of Mexican American political organizations over time. Baca Zinn (1975) suggests that strong family ties assisted Mexican Americans to survive in the face of oppression. Strong family ties also produced "political familism," the involvement of families in political activity. Given that the overarching narrative of this book is about the potential for transformation within a contested political arena, Baca Zinn's observation that women's involvement in the Chicano movement challenged both female and male traditional roles seems particularly relevant: "The dynamics of political familism are such that while it enables Chicano groups to maintain familial ties, it also provides conditions for the *transformation of traditional sex roles*" (Baca Zinn, 19; emphasis added).

Accounts of political activism among Chicanas and Latinas often point to family members as supporters and even co-participants in their political endeavors. For example, studies of Latina working class women show how these women engage in politics by involving their spouses and especially their children in their various activities (Coyle, Hershatter, and Honig 1980; see also Hardy-Fanta 1993, esp. 138–140). Extending the theme of political familism to the contemporary period, new scholarship based on biographies of Mexican American political women show the importance of family to their political socialization experiences and their pursuit of political power (Gutiérrez, Meléndez, and Noyola 2007). Although only 14.4 percent of the California Latina elected officials in Takash's (1993) study indicated they came from political families, as

---

[31] In the section on family, we draw on our prior work (see Hardy-Fanta et al. 2007, esp. 5).

high as 42.8 percent of Latinas and 39.5 percent of Black women in the GMCL National Survey did so. As seen in Table 3.6, for each racial group, women of color are significantly more likely to have the benefit of saying they were raised in a political family. We are not aware of other research that deals with the political socialization of Asian American candidates or elected officials in the United States. Our finding of their family backgrounds being a source of relative *disadvantage* compared to other minority groups is new and worth heeding.

PERSONAL AND FAMILY RESOURCES: EXAMINING THE "DOUBLE DISADVANTAGE" THEORY

Within the framework of intersectionality theory, women of color's multiple sources of oppression would lead us to hypothesize that they would be more likely than other women (and their male counterparts) to come from marginalized backgrounds. Carroll and Sanbonmatsu (2013, 100) assert that "recent scholarship has continued to recognize the distinctive situation of women of color but has moved away from the additive models of the 1970s and 1980s in favor of an intersectionality approach." They point to research by Black feminists and other women of color[32] who "have argued that inequalities are interlocking and mutually constitutive and that the effects of race and gender oppression are not separable." Our research confirms that scholars have also woefully omitted the structural oppression faced by men of color and notes that not all women and men of color are equal in terms of the opportunities they have access to or obstacles they face. Different from conventional wisdom, not only are political women of color not necessarily doubly disadvantaged in post-1965 US politics, but also their male counterparts are often the most disadvantaged in a political order that, with few obvious exceptions, continues to be dominated by White men.

Setting aside the issue of structural oppression faced by both women and men of color, perhaps it is as Linda Williams (2001, 309) concludes, in writing about the "puzzle of black women's political success": "[D]espite being disadvantaged by not only gender but race (and for most, class), black women have been able to overcome political disadvantage." Darcy and Hadley (1988) and others suggest that Black women specifically, and perhaps women of color in general, who seek and achieve elected office

---

[32] They cite, specifically, Crenshaw (1989); Giddings (1984); Hancock (2007); Hill Collins (1990); King (1988); Mohanty (1984); and Smooth (2001, 2006).

are those who "super prepare" themselves, building qualifications and confidence that overcome prejudices among voters. The other explanation could be that women of color have greater ability to build bridges and gain support from voters than their male counterparts.

Perceptions versus Measures of Disadvantage for Elected Officials of Color

Thus far we have shown that, contrary to the "double disadvantage" theory – and at least among "the winners" (i.e., those who succeed in their campaigns and are elected to public office) – Black and Latina women are significantly *less* likely to be disadvantaged in education and occupational attainment than women in general or their male counterparts. Furthermore, although all women of color are more disadvantaged in terms of *current* income than men of color in our study, we must conclude that they are *less disadvantaged* in terms of *family resources*, including being raised in a political family. (For ease of comparison, Tables 3.7 and 3.8 provide a summary snapshot of the personal, family, and district resources discussed previously.)

With these mixed results in mind, we note that female elected officials of color are, nevertheless, consistently more likely to report that women in this country are professionally and politically disadvantaged compared to men (see Table 3.9). The sense of disadvantage was stronger when asked to compare disadvantages faced by women versus men than when comparing minority women to minority men. The gender differences for perceived professional and political disadvantages are, for the most part, larger and more highly significant among Latina than Black women. There are few gender differences among Asian Americans, except that more Asian American women believe it to be harder for women than men to get a job suitable to their education and training. Importantly, although none of our minority elected officials perceive significant gender difference in the assessment of *minority women's* chance to get ahead in elective offices than that of minority men, both Black and Latina women perceive greater difficulty than their male counterparts regarding the chance for *women* in general to get ahead in elective office than men.

In summary, we see a mixed and somewhat confusing portrait of both relative advantages and disadvantages for elected officials of color, which vary significantly by race, by gender, and at the intersection of race and gender. The findings make clear, however, how important it is to examine not only the personal resources that elected officials themselves bring to

TABLE 3.7. *Snapshot of Personal, Family, and District Resources:*
Women of Color

Resources	Black Women	Latinas	Asian American Women
Age	59.3 years	53.2 years	54.4 years
Married	45.9%	62.8%	69%
Education			
Holds college degree	77.4%	53.8%	89.7%
Father: Less than HS diploma	49.0%	57.5%	25.9%
Mother: Less than HS diploma	44.2%	58.6%	25.0%
Household Income			
Less than $50,000	34.0%	30.1%	14.8%
Mean	$71,880	$82,769	$115,926
Mean (married)	$87,965	$95,769	$132,222
Mean (not married)	$58,613	$63,269	$83,333
Family Resources			
Raised with government assistance	12.9%	15.5%	7.1%
Parents foreign born	0.4%	28.5%	52.9%
Raised in a political family	39.5%	42.8%	24.1%
Occupation			
Occupational prestige score	56.86	55.47	56.71
Education	48.2%	39.4%	10.0%
Business	11.3%	20.2%	25.0%
Activism	14.9%	13.8%	30.0%
Health	7.1%	6.4%	10.0%
Sales	6.5%	8.5%	15.0%
Government	7.1%	7.4%	0%
Law	4.8%	4.3%	10.0%
In "feeder occupation"	66.5%	60.7%	71.4%
District Resources			
Poverty rate in district (state legislators)	23.0%	18.2%	13.9%
Poverty rate in county (county officials)	15.7%	18%	12.2%
Poverty rate in census place (municipal officials)	22.8%	21.8%	9.2%
Per capita income in district (school board members)	$18,015	$14,697	$19,226

Source: GMCL National Survey, 2006–2007.

TABLE 3.8. *Snapshot of Personal, Family, and District Resources: Men of Color*

Resources	Black Men	Latino Men	Asian American Men
Age	58.6 years	52.8 years	52.6 years
Married	74.9%	83.1%	88.3%
Education			
Holds college degree	66.7%	49.2%	96.7%
Father: Less than HS diploma	63.7%	63.8%	22.4%
Mother: Less than HS diploma	48.2%	63.1%	23.7%
Household Income			
Less than $50,000	24.9%	23.1%	7.1%
Mean	$88,605	$89,729	$131,111
Mean (married)	$97,640	$92,698	$135,319
Mean (not married)	$62,644	$73,019	$102,857
Family Resources			
Raised with government assistance	20.0%	23.8%	6.8%
Parents foreign born	1.4%	28.6%	50.0%
Raised in a political family	31.6%	29.7%	16.7%
Occupation			
Occupational prestige score	55.09	52.18	62.57
Education	35.1%	24.6%	16.2%
Business	13.8%	33.9%	29.7%
Activism	16%	7.6%	5.4%
Health	4.3%	4.1%	8.1%
Sales	12.2%	12.3%	5.4%
Government	9.6%	13.5%	13.5%
Law	9%	4.1%	21.6%
In "feeder occupation"	49.9%	45.1%	53%
District Resources			
Poverty rate in district (state legislators)	23.8%	18.2%	8.5%
Poverty rate in county (county officials)	19.2%	23.3%	11%
Poverty rate in census place (municipal officials)	23.6%	20.6%	9.4%
Per capita income in district (school board members)	$16,550	$14,347	$17,028

Source: GMCL National Survey, 2006–2007.

TABLE 3.9. *Perceived Professional and Political Disadvantages for Women and Minority Women, by Race*Gender*

Respondents Who Reported That It Is Harder for:	Black		Latino\a		Asian American	
	Female (N = 287)	Male (N = 396)	Female (N = 147)	Male (N = 325)	Female (N = 28)	Male (N = 60)
Women than for *Men* to get a job suitable to their education and training	2.68***	2.27	2.81***	2.47	2.89*	2.48
Minority Women than for *Minority Men* to get a job suitable to their education and training	2.20*	2.00	2.68	2.57	2.50	2.38
Women than for *Men* to be accepted as a member of a profession	2.66***	2.43	2.69***	2.34	2.61	2.42
Minority Women than for *Minority Men* to be accepted as a member of a profession	2.39*	2.21	2.65**	2.40	2.44	2.42
Women than *Men* to be Appointed to Public Office	2.73**	2.54	2.76***	2.44	2.46	2.37
Minority Women than *Minority Men* to be Appointed to Public Office	2.44**	2.26	2.63*	2.46	2.31	2.26
Women than *Men* to Get Ahead in Elective Office	2.82***	2.61	2.85***	2.53	2.59†	2.28
Minority Women than *Minority Men* to Get Ahead in Elective Office	2.45	2.37	2.59	2.52	2.39	2.27

Note: Entries are means; response options for each question: 1 – easier; 2 – about the same; 3 –harder.
†$p < .1$; *$p < .05$; **$p < .01$; ***$p < .0001$.
Source: GMCL National Survey, 2006–2007.

office, that is, education, occupational prestige, income, and so forth, but also the resources they bring from their families.

Who Are the "Doubly Disadvantaged"?
Testing Hypotheses

We now draw on multivariate analysis to test the contributions of race and gender, and family and personal resources on the elected officials' perceptions of professional and political disadvantages. The dependent variable is a Perceived Professional and Political Disadvantages Index.[33] Model I in Table 3.10 tests the interactive effects of race and gender; Black Female is the reference category since the bulk of political science literature posits she would be the most disadvantaged of all gendered and racialized groups.

Model II (Family Resources) adds parental education, welfare status growing up, and whether the parents were immigrants. Finally, the full Model III adds personal resources of the elected officials themselves: educational attainment, occupational prestige, household income, and marital status.

What we find is striking convergence among women of color respondents that, all things considered, they perceive women facing greater professional and political disadvantages than men. We also see that, controlling for other factors and across all three models, being a Black, Latino, or Asian American male elected official makes him significantly less likely than Black women to agree that it's harder for women than men to get a job suitable to their education and training, to be accepted as a member of a profession, and to be appointed or elected to public office.

Based on the sizes of the regression coefficients, measures of the intersection of race and gender also contribute significantly more than measures for family or individual resources themselves. In addition, everything being equal, it is the average Asian American male who perceives the least amount of gender-based disadvantages than other groups of non-White women and men. Having parents with higher education makes a modest contribution, but only in Model II; it drops out in the full resources model. In Model III, we find that, other than indicators of race*gender, the only significant variable is Occupational Prestige – meaning that, controlling for other factors, having attained a higher-prestige occupation

---

[33] The measure "Perceived Professional and Political Disadvantages" was computed by summing responses to each of the questions, with a range of 1 to 3; see Table 3.9 and Appendix B for question wording.

TABLE 3.10. *OLS Estimations of Perceived Professional and Political Disadvantages: Impact of Race*Gender and Family and Personal Resources*

	I. Race*Gender Model		II. Family of Origin Resources Model		III. Personal Resources Model	
	B	(s.e.)	b	(s.e)	b	(s.e.)
Race*Gender						
(ref. Black Woman)						
Latina woman	.021	(.073)	.045	(.078)	.031	(.079)
Asian American woman	−.151	(.144)	−.155	(.154)	−.144	(.154)
American Indian woman	.111	(.256)	.100	(.258)	.068	(.260)
Black man	−.284***	(.058)	−.276***	(.058)	−.263***	(.060)
Latino man	−.269***	(.058)	−.236***	(.066)	−.232**	(.070)
Asian American man	−.379***	(.106)	−.387**	(.122)	−.394**	(.124)
American Indian man	.104	(.204)	.110	(.205)	.103	(.205)
Family Resources						
Parents' education			.030†	(.067)	.015	(.018)
Raised on government assistance			−.033	(.052)	−.037	(.053)
Immigrant family			−.013	(.027)	−.020	(.027)
Personal Resources						
Income (household)					.004	(.005)
Occupational prestige					.005*	(.002)
Educational attainment					−.005	(.020)
Age					−.003	(.002)
Married					−.041	(.049)
(Constant)	2.739***	(.044)	2.727***	(.058)	2.639***	(.168)
Adj. R^2	.052		.054		.057	
F-score	7.054		5.344		3.820	
N	766		766		766	

Notes: *b* = unstandardized slope coefficient, s.e. = standard errors. Explanation of variables: Immigrant family is a scale 1–4, with 4 being the official is foreign born, 1 = fourth generation or more, including US born; Income (household) is a scale of twenty-one income categories, ranging from LT \$10K to GE \$200K; Parents' education is the highest level achieved by either parent, ranging from 0 = LT HS to 5 = doctorate; Educational attainment is 0 = LT HS to 6 = doctorate; Occupational prestige is explained in the preceding text. Findings for American Indians should be viewed with caution, as the individuals are few in number and mostly state legislators.

†$p < .1$; *$p < .05$; **$p < .01$; ***$p < .0001$.

Source: GMCL National Survey, 2006–2007.

contributes significantly to a perception that women are more disadvantaged professionally and politically ($p < .05$).

CONCLUSION

In this chapter we argue that educational and occupational attainment as well as marital status – rather than be seen as individual *characteristics* – must be considered in light of the (1) historical context, (2) dynamic rather than static experiences for the different racial groups, and (3) political economy of education, work, and marriage, which is biased toward upper-class married Whites. Given the changing demographics and diversity profiles of the US population in the early twenty-first century, we believe the meanings of these terms will be subject to ongoing debate. Evidence of the continuing significance of structural oppression of men of color also suggests the need to incorporate their situation into any discussion of marginalization and disadvantages.

What we find is that not all groups of female elected officials of color face the same challenges and possess the same resources when they first take office. Furthermore, contrary to the "double disadvantage" thesis that posits that political women of color would be disadvantaged by the intersection of their racial and gender identities, we find that, at least among "the winners" (i.e., those who succeed in their campaigns and are elected to public office), Black and Latina women are significantly *less* likely to be disadvantaged in education and occupation, both compared to women in general and to their male counterparts. Although all groups of women of color are more disadvantaged in terms of household income, which is related in part to their lower rates of being married, both Black and Latina women enjoy higher occupational prestige and greater family resources, including having been raised in a political family, than their male counterparts. Although Asian American women are found to have higher occupational prestige, income status, and rate of marriage than other women of color, they are not as advantaged as Asian American men in these categories of resources. Yet, the situation is reversed concerning family socialization when fewer of them grew up in political family than Black and Latina women, but the rate is still higher than for Asian American men. In the end, our portrait of advantages and disadvantages in the paths for elective office among elected officials across race and gender is a mixed one, and certainly one that cannot be easily captured by the received wisdom of the double disadvantage thesis for women of color in general when Black and Latino men are often found to be the least advantaged.

We now turn from personal and family backgrounds to the next step in exploring the trajectories to office for elected officials of color by focusing on the decision to run and patterns of office holding.

PART II

PATHS TO POLITICAL OFFICE

4

The Decision to Run and Patterns of Office Holding

In Chapter 3 we explored the personal, political, and family backgrounds of elected officials of color, that is, the qualifications and experiences they brought to their political endeavors, and revealed a very complex response to the question whether Black, Latina, and Asian women – or men – serving as elected officeholders are "doubly disadvantaged" by race and gender. Our task now is to move beyond their individual characteristics, however important they may be. In this chapter we provide benchmark data of the initial decisions to enter the electoral arena and patterns of office holding for elected officials of color in America at the start of the twenty-first century.

Traditional theories of the decision to run for office tend to be characterized by assumptions that individuals emerge from an "eligibility pool," made up of men and women from the "top tier of professional accomplishment ... [and] highly political environments," with exposure to politics early in life (Lawless 2012, 11–12). According to Lawless (2012, 15), successful candidates are also those with "high levels of political activism interest, and proximity to the political arena" who have been encouraged to run. Of course, with their focus on personal, what Lawless calls "nascent," ambition and candidates, findings from studies on the decision to run may be less generalizable to the motivations of those who *did* run and won, including elected officials such as those in the Gender and Multicultural Leadership (GMCL) National Survey.

In this chapter we analyze what Black, Latino/a, Asian American, and American Indian women and men actually say when asked, *Why did you run for office the very first time?* Our approach treats what the elected officials of color said, in their own words, as the core content of our analysis and shifts the study of political motivations away from theoretical blinders of "personal ambition" so prevalent in the women in politics literature as the precursor to entry into a political life. And though strategic considerations do play a role, as we see in the text that follows, and a favorable opportunity structure is certainly important, we also challenge the "rational choice paradigm" of mainstream (White male) theories.[1] We hope to provide a more nuanced interpretation of why and how these women and men enter the world of electoral politics – an understanding grounded in their own perspectives and one that may offer an alternative to the more conventional, individual-centered theories dominating the political science literature today.

After exploring the motivations to run of Black, Latina, Asian American, and American Indian women and men serving at various levels of subnational office, we then provide a detailed analysis of what offices they held prior to their current elected position. In this way, we address questions such as: Does the "pipeline theory," together with the need to "build a farm team," so prevalent in the women in politics literature, "hold water" for elected officials of color? Furthermore, is the assumption of a "career ladder" – whereby an individual begins at a local-level office and "moves up" to a higher level – a valid narrative for the political trajectories of elected officials of color? The chapter concludes with a discussion of how, rather than following a "career ladder," race and gender interact to create varied, multiple, and complex paths to office for women and men of color.

IS THE PIPELINE THEORY RELEVANT FOR THE POLITICAL REPRESENTATION OF WOMEN OF COLOR?

In addition to supposedly providing an opening for those seeking an entry to political life, the pipeline theory has been used to explain the paucity of women in elective offices in the United States. Findings from Lawless (2012, 11), for example, "provide powerful evidence of a gender gap in political ambition and suggest that prospects for ... political representation are far more precarious than scholars often assert." Her intersectional analysis also "highlights the fact that *women*, regardless of race or ethnicity, are less likely than men to consider running for office."

---

[1] See Schlesinger (1966) for a discussion of the rational choice paradigm of the decision to run for office.

Despite these reservations, scholars suggest that the pipeline theory is the way to political progress for women: according to its proponents, "growth in the number of women in the preparatory professions [e.g., "feeder occupations," discussed in Chapter 3] will eventually cause growth in the number of women running for state and local offices, which will eventually cause growth in the number of women running for Congress" (Palmer and Simon 2008, 226; see also, MacManus et al. 2006; Mariani 2008). Others tout the importance of building a "farm team of quality candidates [at the local level] who can eventually run for higher office" (Crowder-Meyer 2011, 8) and the role of "career ladders" (see, e.g., Sanbonmatsu 2006a, 2006b). According to Dolan, Deckman, and Swers (2007, 148), for example, "women will run for higher office only after they have achieved success lower down the food chain and have built up the confidence that comes with serving in elected office." The theory, with its heavy reliance on individual ambition as a motivating force, may be limited, however, in its utility to explain the electoral experiences of women and men of color.

In fact, the idea of being *individually* ambitious is not plausible for most Black, Latina/o, Asian Americans, and American Indians because society did not permit the exercise of individual political action for most of the history of this country. There were (and still are) barriers to participation, not just at the individual level but also structurally. The whole concept of a pipe that anyone can move into and flow through is not a reality for these groups. There has been no "pipeline" for Black people or Latinos or Asians. These are groups that have had to, first of all, break down barriers to entry, construct some *capacity* to act, and figure out how to base their campaigns on networks of people. They had to *construct* something collective to enter – and that "something" is not a pipeline, because we have also seen how rapidly and how continuously the courts, the legal system, and the conservative foundations have been able to reconstruct objections and to refocus on individual activities as a legal foundation for how (White) politics should operate. Any notion of individual ambition needs to be seen within the context of a society that is very discriminatory. Using the pipeline theory as the path to political office has a presumption built into it of easy access – and that is not the reality for elected officials of color.

Additional considerations, both methodological and theoretical, arise to challenge the validity or broader applicability of the pipeline theory. Though researchers have begun to include women and men of color in studies of political trajectories, these are still quite limited and tend to focus on gender and/or race separately,[2] and/or do not include local-level officials. Furthermore, by focusing on an individual's development of a specific set of qualifications, the theory does not pay sufficient attention to a host of attitudinal, sociocultural, and institutional factors that are also found to explain the lack of women candidates and elected officials (Schroedel and Godwin 2005). It "implies a relatively steady and sequential pattern," neglecting opportunity factors such as "structure of elections, electoral context, and partisanship" (Palmer and Simon 2008, 226). The theory also ignores the impact of district-level characteristics and redistricting on the election of elected officials of color – and Black women, in particular – after passage of the Voting Rights Act, discussed at some length in Chapter 1 of this volume.

Finally, it turns out that much of the received wisdom (i.e., what "everyone knows") about why women and men run for office may be based more on anecdote and "gut feeling" than on hard data. One of the most pervasive, oft-quoted, and – we find, perhaps, most dubious – is the role of encouragement in women's decisions to run for office.

THE INITIAL DECISION TO RUN FOR OFFICE: "WOMEN NEED TO BE ASKED"

Researchers have documented a wide range of reasons individuals give for wanting to run for elected office. The literature on the routes to political office for women has focused extensively on personal recruitment: "Because of the masculine nature of mainstream politics and women's history of marginalization in the electoral arena, one might well expect women to be less likely than men to view elective office holding as an appropriate career choice or even a realistic aspiration. As a result, women more often than men might need encouragement to toss their hats into the ring and run for office" (Carroll and Sanbonmatsu 2013, 48; see also Lawless 2012). A plethora of organizations and initiatives, in fact, have sprung up to provide a structure for encouraging more women to run for elected office and typically include a phrase such as

---

[2] Lawless (2012, 11), for example, concludes, "The intersectional analysis ... highlights the fact that women, regardless of race or ethnicity, are less likely than men to consider running for office." As valuable as her work is, she falls prey to presenting findings broken down by "Man, Woman, White, Black, Latino/a" (Lawless, Figure 4.3–4.4, 65–67); she does include results by race*gender in her Table 4.2 and some of the multivariate analyses, but other than a chapter on sex and race, results in the rest of the book look at gender alone.

"*A woman needs to be asked three* [or four or more] *times before she decides to run.*" They then conclude, as did a speaker at the New England Women's Political Summit in 2003, with: "Consider yourselves asked!" (Hardy-Fanta 2003).

At times the number used in this pitch has been subject to a dynamic akin to "grade inflation." Esgar (2013) states, for example, "It's been said that women need to be asked at least *three* times to run for an elected office before they decide to make a go at it" (emphasis added). Philanthropist/ activist Barbara Lee (2012), who has supported many research studies on women in politics, writes, "Our research tells us women need to be asked between three and seven times to run for office. Men don't wait to be asked." Organizations such as EmergeAmerica and Emily's List not only increase the number but also suggest a scientific authority to these numbers by referring to unspecified research. According to Emily's List president Stephanie Schriock (Pieper 2013), for example, "a survey showed women need to be asked *up to seven times* before they agree to run for public office" (emphasis added). EmergeAmerica graduate Emiley [*sic*] Lockhart (2013) writes, "We have heard that a woman needs to be asked to run *4, 5, or 6 times* before she will actually file the papers and do it" (emphasis added). And, finally, Emerge Nevada executive director Erin Bilbray-Kohn (O'Lear 2012) is quoted as saying, "[O]n average, a woman has to be asked *eight* times before she'll run" (emphasis added).

Where do these numbers come from? There is an extensive literature on the role of personal ambition (or the lack thereof) among women that supposedly hinders them from being "self-starters," (Carroll 1994, 28–29, 45; Carroll and Sanbonmatsu 2013, 44–62; Moncrief, Squire, and Jewell 2001). "Self-starters" supposedly make an independent decision to run, rather than running as a result of being urged (e.g., by family, friends, colleagues, business or community leaders) or recruited (e.g. by a political party). Women, according to this literature, require more encouragement before "throwing their hat into the ring."

It turns out that the evidence for the numbers is anecdotal at best – and likely biased by the fact that it is based most likely only on White women. Let us begin with the evidence that women are less likely to be "self-starters" than men. Lawless and Fox (2005, 85) state clearly, for example, that "women are less likely than men to receive the suggestion to run for office for each type of electoral gatekeeper.[3] The gender

---

[3] Note from authors: Electoral gatekeepers include, for example, party officials, other elected officials, and nonelected activists who can facilitate (i.e., open doors for potential candidates) but also block entry.

gap in political recruitment varies across profession, but overall, men are 34 percent more likely than women to have been recruited to run for office from at least one of these political actors... [e.g., party officials, elected officials, nonelected political activists]."

Nevertheless, according to Jennifer Lawless, an expert on candidate recruitment, "There's no 'number.' Women's groups have read that into our data. All we say is that women are less likely to be asked and that the anecdotal evidence suggests that women may need to be asked more often if the encouragement is to resonate."[4] And Kimmell (2014) confirmed that there has been no research on how often women need to be asked to run nor on the effectiveness of being asked. It is somewhat simplistic, therefore, to assert, as activists associated with many women's political organizations seem to do repeatedly, that merely asking more often will propel more women to run. We must look more deeply to find out why women elected officials decide to run for office in the first place.

Exploring the motivations of elected officials at the intersection of race and gender may shed light not only on why they ran for office, but also on what appears to be a conflation of three distinct processes: (1) *recruitment* by a political actor or party; (2) the idea that women *need* more encouragement than men before deciding to run for office the first time (i.e., not being "self starters"); and (3) the view that *women are less likely to receive such encouragement* than men. The conflation is clear when we examine the extent to which women and men of color say they ran because they were encouraged – or recruited directly – by a political party.

ENCOURAGED, BUT LITTLE EVIDENCE OF PARTY RECRUITMENT

The vast majority (83.5 percent) of elected officials of color in the Gender and Multicultural Leadership (GMCL) National Survey did *not* report being asked or encouraged to run, but women were somewhat more likely than their male counterparts to report being asked or encouraged: 18.8 percent compared to 15.1 percent.[5] This was particularly true among state legislators, with 22.6 percent of female but just 8.8 percent of male state legislators reporting having received encouragement ($p < .05$).

---

[4] Personal email communication with Carol Hardy-Fanta, January 29, 2014.
[5] We should point out that this difference is very small and only modestly statistically significant ($p < .1$).

We find also that the agents of encouragement were *not* political parties, but rather community members, family, and friends. In fact, despite the centrality in the literature of party recruitment to advance the political prospects of minority and women officials, when asked why they ran the first time, *just two* of the officials of color in our survey mentioned being recruited by a political party. This would appear very different, indeed, from figures reported by Sanbonmatsu, Carroll, and Walsh (2009, 12), who find that more than half of female state representatives (55 percent) and state senators (57 percent) serving in 2008 were asked to run for their current office by party – and these percentages are even greater than those of their male counterparts (50 percent and 43 percent, respectively).

The literature on the importance of political parties in the advancement of women in politics is extensive but, as with so much in the field, ambiguous. On the one hand, Sanbonmatsu et al. (2009, 11) begin with the premise that "women tend to run for office as a result of recruitment." Because parties can either "encourage candidates to run, discourage candidates from running, and may even endorse candidates in primaries" they find parties to be among the most influential agents of recruitment. This point is reinforced by Baer and Hartmann (2014), who state that parties can help facilitate candidacy by providing resources, such as money and party label recognition. Among the women interviewed for their research who have considered running for office, Baer and Hartmann find they identify parties as most helpful in fundraising. Furthermore, party recruitment may be particularly helpful to women because, as candidates, they supposedly need more encouragement to run (Fox, Lawless, and Feeley 2001; Moncrief et al. 2001).

At the same time, Sanbonmatsu et al. (2009, 12) reveal doubts: "Some have suggested that political parties are the main *obstacle* to increasing women's representation…" (emphasis added). Lawless and Fox (2010), as noted already, suggest that women are less likely to be recruited than men. And Baer and Hartmann (2014), using interviews with experienced candidates, officeholders, and congressional staff, find political parties to be nearly absent in the recruitment of women.

In addition, though party organizations may play a role in women's recruitment, recruiting women candidates has rarely been used as an explicit strategy to increase the number of women in elected office (Burrell 2010). Qualitative interview data show that the party support that women received is usually through informal networks by individuals or former elected officials (Baer and Hartmann 2014). Furthermore, strong party organizations typically have a negative effect on women's presence in state legislatures (Nelson 1991; Sanbonmatsu 2002). Most locally elected women in Niven's (1998) study of four states report that party leaders discouraged potential women candidates from running for office. Other research finds that women are often slated to run as sacrificial lambs in difficult races (Baer and Hartman 2014; Carroll 1994; Carroll and Strimling 1983).

Encouraged to Run? Women and Men of Color Elected Officials – in Their Own Words

If one in five women of color officials are somewhat more likely than their male counterparts to say they ran, at least in part, because they were encouraged or asked to do so, but were not recruited by a political party, what was the nature of this encouragement? Who asked them? The words used by Black, Latino, Asian American, and American Indian elected officials – *male and female alike* – make it clear the encouragement they received was not a formal, organized effort, but one that drew on more personal relationships.

A Black female municipal official from South Carolina, for example, responded first with "*A friend's request.*" A Latino male city councilor from Texas said: "*People came to me and asked me to run.*" As is typical, officials often gave responses that fit into multiple categories. An example of one that included being encouraged to run was voiced by a Latina city councilor from Texas, who said, "*I felt that there were not enough Hispanic leaders. A group of people came to me and asked me if I would run. I ran for the school board first, and missed the run-off by one vote.*" She later ran for the city council and won. A Latina school board member from Texas gave as a reason, "*I was asked to represent the parents and children who could not voice their concerns.*" An Asian male county official from Hawaii responded: "*I was asked by the community to place my name as to give the community an alternative choice. Basically, the present government was not reflecting the desires of the community at large. The reputation of the government was that it represented more special groups rather than the interest of the community at large.*" His response illustrates the not-uncommon melding of "encouraged" and "community" motivations, discussed more later in this chapter.

Blacks were significantly more likely to say they were encouraged or recruited to run for office (20.2 percent) than Latinos/as (12.6 percent), and both more than Asian Americans (9.6 percent) ($p < .001$). There were large differences when race and gender were considered intersectionally on this variable: Black women (at 21.7 percent) were three times as likely as Asian American men (at 6.3 percent) to say they were encouraged to run for their first elective office ($p < .01$). Level of office made a difference as well, with 26.6 percent of female state legislators of color, but just 8.8 percent of their male peers reporting running for office because they received encouragement ($p < .05$).[6]

What do we make of these findings? First, as indicated by some scholars (see, e.g., Garcia et al. 2008; Pinderhughes 2003, 189–190), it may be that elected officials of color are much less likely to have been recruited by political parties than non-Hispanic Whites. Second, most of the officials in our survey serve at the local level, where elections tend to be nonpartisan and party recruitment plays a less important role. Third, we must acknowledge that we are to some extent inferring that the elected officials of color in our survey were not recruited by a party because they did not mention political parties at all when asked what motivated them to run; results might have been different if we had explicitly ask whether party leaders had actively recruited them.[7]

The Decision to Run: Traditional Perspectives

In addition to the encouragement of others, the political science literature points to a number of influences on the initial decision to run; besides "nascent" ambition, these include strategic considerations and ideological motivations. Strategic considerations include whether the potential candidate believes she or he is qualified; estimates of personal attributes and feelings of efficacy (Fox and Lawless 2005, 644); and likelihood of winning (Fox and Lawless 2011, 446). High on the list of ideological motivations, according to Fox and Lawless (2005, 645ff), are issue passion and a general interest in politics. Unfortunately, their attention to race and gender is limited to the relationship between constituent characteristics, group identification, and political ambition.

Bledsoe and Herring (1990, 213) suggest that women's success in pursuing elected office "is more closely tied to the circumstances they find themselves in than is the success of men." Their study only looks, however,

---

[6] Differences by level of office alone were not, however, statistically significant.
[7] The CAWP survey (Carroll and Sanbonmatsu 2013, 138) asked a number of questions related to party recruitment including, "Did leaders from your party actively seek you out and encourage you to run for the first office you ran for?"

at city councilors who are interested in pursuing a higher-level office. For the purposes of our interests, their work has the more serious flaw in that they also ignore race. Fox and Lawless (2011, 433) point to other, more personal, considerations: "Anyone who contemplates running for office ... must answer a series of questions. Is the time right to inject my family into the political arena? Where am I in terms of my professional goals? Do I know enough about the issues and the political system to run for office? ... Do I really want to take part in a political process that is so often associated with self-interest, corruption, and cynicism?" Lawless (2012) titles her first chapter, "Mudslinging, Money-Grubbing, and Mayhem: Who Would Ever Run for Office? These scholars do not, however, examine why women run from their own perspectives, and, again, while they include a small sample of Blacks and Latinos/as, their focus is on gender with considerably less attention to the intersection of race and gender.

For those who go on to run, influences within the political opportunity structure include, for example, open seats, term limits, legislative professionalization, and partisan composition of constituency, and, like Hedge, Button, and Spear (1996), we would argue, the racial makeup of the district. Paying one's dues helps as well: US Representative Barbara Lee's career (D-CA) illustrates this point; she "began her political career as an intern in the office of her predecessor, former Congressman and former Oakland Mayor Ron Dellums, where she eventually became his Chief of Staff."[8] Quoting Prinz (1993, 27), Fox and Lawless (2005, 644) indicate that "seats available and the hierarchy of positions for advancement give shape and definition to the political career." We discuss the impact of the opportunity structure on the political trajectories of elected officials of color in Chapter 5; at this point, we open the discussion of gender, race, and the decision to run for office using the words of the women and men of color who responded to the GMCL National Survey.

GENDER, RACE, AND THE DECISION TO RUN

We asked the GMCL Survey respondents: *"What was the most important reason influencing your decision to run for public office the very first time?"* After recording their verbatim responses, we then asked (twice), *"What was the next most important reason?"* – thus offering several opportunities

---

[8] Source: "U.S. Congresswoman Barbara Lee: Biography," http://lee.house.gov/about/biography (Accessed July 27, 2016). We should point out that before being elected to Congress, Lee also served in the California State Assembly and in the California State Senate.

for them to share their thoughts. Given that these questions invited open-ended responses, we analyzed them both qualitatively and quantitatively.[9]

The central themes that emerged are grouped into those that may be considered "Public Interest Focused" (such as a stemming from a sense of or relationship to community; issue passion; representation; and desire to make a change or difference) or stemming from a source that is more personal, or "Self Focused," such as being encouraged/recruited; strategic considerations (e.g., qualifications and likelihood of winning); political interest; and other personal reasons (including ambition). These categories are not mutually exclusive, and respondents typically cited more than one reason behind their decision to run for office. (See note in Figure 4.1 for coding decisions.)

The strongest motivations for running for office among elected officials of color clearly fall into the category of "issue passion" and "community." Half of the responses among all officials were coded as *Issue*, and half gave responses coded as those related to a sense of or relationship to *Community*. Another third expressed a need for greater *Representation* (especially for underrepresented groups), and one in five ran to *Make a Change* or *Make a Difference*. Over the three opportunities to respond, the minimum number of reasons given was 1 and the maximum out of 8 was 5, with a mean of 2.2.

Of course, a typology that clusters reasons into a "Public Interest Focus" and "Self Focus" may not reflect the reality for some race*gender groups. This rests on and is related to the way in which the person, especially a woman of color, focuses within and relates to a community, including the issues of concern, gaining greater political representation, and/or wanting to "make a change" or "make a difference." For many women, the ability to define the community, as distinct from one's personal experiences and/or interests, is hardly probable or even possible. Why? Because Black people, Black women in particular, and perhaps American Indians as well, are more likely to see some collective character to their environment. To survive, they have to protect themselves within the context of a community. It's true that the community may not be able to protect them, but their very survival is more dependent on a Black network or American Indian collectivity. Individuality or self-focused motivations in this world has a very different meaning than it would for White

---

[9] For a discussion of the coding system and protocol for the quantitative analysis used here, see Hardy-Fanta et al. (2007, esp. 32–36); a modified version of this section on motivations to run appeared in that paper as well.

Public Interest Focus	Community	50%		
	Issue Passion	50%		
	Representation	29%		
	Make a Change/Difference	21%	Personal Reasons (incl. Ambition)	21%
			Strategic Considerations	15%
			Encouraged/Recruited	16%
			Political Interest	11%

FIGURE 4.1 Typology of motivations to run.

Note: Verbatim responses, which are not mutually exclusive, were coded as follows. *Issue*: Have a passion or interest regarding a particular issue and/or problem, concern. *Community*: Focus is on the official's community, not on an issue; comments on what they can to improve, help, serve, or give back to the community, and so on; also included are mentions of community ties, prior or current connection to community, neighborhood, racial/ethnic "community"; and references to "my/the community." *Make a Change/Difference*: References to wanting to influence change or to make a difference externally, as in the community, in government, or in the city. *Representation*: Expression of being dissatisfied with current representation; wanting to increase the number of minorities and/or women in the political office; or believing there is a need for more/better representation for a particular group of people. *Strategic Considerations:* Focus on prospect being favorable to winning (e.g., "qualified," "could win," "no one else was running"); includes expression of political efficacy, meaning that they believe that they are competent or qualified to be in office. *Personal*: References to self and/or family/friends; includes mentions of emotion or personality trait as driving force; expression of a quest for power, to "get ahead, which were also coded into a subcategory of *Ambition*. Anyone who said she or he was encouraged or recruited or were picked for (or appointed to) a position was coded *Encouraged*. Political *Interest* was assigned to those who said they ran because of a general interest in politics, "being a part of politics," or wanting to be part of the decision-making process.

Source: GMCL National Survey, 2006–2007; N = 1,347.

women. The idea of a community-self dyad would work in quite different ways across racial group boundaries.

The evidence for this may be mostly historical: in an NPR broadcast commenting on the controversy over the portrayal in the film *Selma* of President Lyndon Johnson as lukewarm on civil rights, Joseph (2015), for example, notes,

Selma reminds us to honor not just the heroic figure making speeches, but the collective will of so many who made progress possible. Ultimately, the beating heart of this film rests not with its portrait of LBJ, or even King, not with what group has been left out or ignored, but with the larger truth that the civil rights movement's heroic period reflected our collective strengths and weaknesses as a nation, something Americans are loathe to recognize let alone acknowledge.

Motivations Focused on Public Interest, Public Service

Elected officials often speak broadly of being motivated by "public service." A study by Fox and Schuhmann (1999) finds that a commitment to public service is one of the key motivations for local officials (in their case, city managers). Svara (2003), one of the few scholars who has surveyed municipal elected officials in a way that includes attention to gender and race, for example, finds that 81 percent of municipal officials surveyed in 2001 cited a desire to "serve the city as a whole" as the motivation. Unfortunately, for the purposes of this book, his findings on motivations for running were not analyzed by race or gender. Within the broad category of public service, Fox and Schuhmann (1999, 235) include not only those who explicitly stated their goal of "public service," but also those who sought to "help the community," "make a difference," and "work with/serve citizens."

About one in five of the elected officials of color in the GMCL Survey responded in ways that spoke to a general desire or commitment to *serving* or helping the public, with men (at 24.0 percent) more likely than women (at 18.4 percent) giving responses such as "*It was just the right time to get involved. Time to devote to public service*"; "*I have a great passion for public service*"; and "*To improve the services of the city to the general public.*" Looking beyond this somewhat broad or even generic phrase, it is, rather, issue passion, concern about or relationship with community, increased representation, and making a change/difference that stand out for officials of color.

ISSUE PASSION AND COMMUNITY CONNECTION: EQUALLY IMPORTANT REASONS

As the Typology (Figure 4.1) and Table 4.1 show, half of all elected officials of color gave a reason to run that focused on an *Issue* that concerned them and/or the people they represented. Equally important was a reason related to *Community* (e.g., wanting to serve or help one's community, having been part of the community, and more; we discuss the complexity of meanings of "community" in the text that follows), with half again giving a reason reflecting that theme. A third said they were motivated by

TABLE 4.1. *"Public Interest–Focused" Motivations for Running for Office the First Time, by Race and Gender*

	Issue	Community	Representation	Make a Change/ Difference
All	50	50	29	21
Gender				
Female (N = 501)	52.0	47.3	29.0	22.2
Male (N = 846)	49.4	51.9	29.3	21.0
Race				
Black (N = 718)	46.2	48.7	28.4	21.5
Latino/a (N = 508)	58.1	51.4	28.5	22.4
Asian American (N = 94)	41.5	57.4	37.2	14.9
American Indian (N = 24)	45.8	41.7	33.3	25.0
Race*Gender				
Black women (N = 304)	50.2	46.1	27.1	22.4
Black men (N = 418)	43.4	50.6	29.4	20.8
Latina women (N = 157)	58.0	49.0	29.9	23.6
Latino men (N = 351)	58.1	52.4	27.9	21.9
Asian American women (N =30)	40.0	53.3	36.7	13.3
Asian American men (N = 64)	42.2	59.4	37.5	15.6
Amer. Ind. women (N = 10)	50.0	40.0	50.0	20.0
Amer. Ind. men (N = 14)	42.9	42.9	21.4	28.6

Note: Entries are percent of elected officials surveyed. Motivation categories are not mutually exclusive, and American Indians are mostly state legislators.
Source: GMCL National Survey, 2006–2007.

the lack of or need for better *Representation*; and one in five ran to *Make a Change* or *Make a Difference*.

Table 4.1 clearly shows that, for elected officials of color, there is remarkable consensus across race and gender for three of the four types of public-focused motivations to run for office for the very first time. Even for the one exception, *Issue*, where there are significant differences by race ($p < .0001$);

and race and gender in interaction ($p < .001$), a closer intersectional analysis shows that it is only Black women who are different from their Black male counterparts and the difference is only modestly significant (at $p < .1$).[10] Let us stay with "issues" for the moment and explore what elected officials of color said about them when asked why they ran for office the very first time.

Issue Passion

"Issue Passion," according to Fox and Lawless (2005, 2010, 2011), is a prime motivator for running for office. Issues raised by the elected officials in our survey range from the more general to the very concrete. An Asian American male state senator from Hawaii said, for example, that he ran "*to help small businesses*," and a Latino male county commissioner in Colorado responded, "*I felt I could give back and contribute to the surroundings with the health of the community. Lots of crime, not a lot for kids to do. Crime was out of line for the size of the town. I thought if I could help with that area of the community, it would be a plus.*"

At the most concrete level were reasons such as, "*There was no toilet in the park*," from a Latino male mayor in California. An alderman in Mississippi responded, "*My main reason to run was street improvement*," and a Latina school board member from California said, "*Getting more AP classes so that students could go further.*" A Black county commissioner in Georgia responded, "*A group of us was trying to get a city gym open[ed] back up so the kids would have somewhere to go play. That's why I ran the first time. And the City Council didn't want to open the gym back up.*" A Latino male city councilmember in Wyoming replied, "*I wanted to build a viaduct.*" Other responses were, for example, from an Asian female state legislator from Iowa: "*Education. Economic growth. Taking care of women and children.*" And a Latino county official in Texas said, "*I was trying to get a pothole filled in front of my house and I couldn't get it done. That's what got me interested.*"

Table 4.1 shows that Latinos were significantly more likely than Black, American Indian, and Asian American elected officials to point to a specific issue or issues as the reason they ran for office the first time. The gender difference alone on *Issue* was not significant, but the percentage of Black women who were motivated by an issue was significantly larger than that of Black men. The race*gender ranking on *Issue* suggests that

---

[10] The overall difference for race*gender (i.e., between each of the eight race*gender groups) is statistically significant, but it may be an artifact of race alone and gender alone.

it is for Latino men and Latinas that concrete issues are most salient, whereas they are least important for Asian American men and women.

Why would Asian Americans holding political office be less likely than all other groups to voice a concrete issue as a reason to run? One explanation is that their constituencies are relatively more affluent, compared to those represented by other elected officials of color. As we saw in Chapter 3, for example, not only do Asian American elected officials have considerably more personal and family resources, they also represent jurisdictions with more financial resources (see Table 3.4). And, as we discuss in Chapter 7, only 15 percent of Asian American officials considered their constituents as mostly of the working class; this compares to 41 percent among Latinos, 36 percent among Blacks, and 20 percent among American Indians. More than other groups, American Indian officials reported having half of their constituents living in poverty, compared to none of Asian officials. Greater affluence within a jurisdiction, in other words, is not just a resource for a candidate running for office, but also reflects a constituency with resources that may be directed at solving concrete problems, allowing their representatives to be motivated by other forces.

Community Connectedness

One of the contributions in the field of gender and politics has been the idea that women may approach politics from a perspective of "connectedness" (see, e.g., Flammang 1984, 1997; Hardy-Fanta 1993, 2002; García and Márquez 2001; Haywoode 1991) – and that relationships between people are an essential component of political participation. Scholars more recently have been exploring a related theme: whether women's paths to political office reflect a deeper connection to and rootedness in their communities. Fox and Schuhmann (1999, 235), for example, support the hypothesized relationship between gender and community among city managers: Female and male city managers mentioned public service by name equally often, but women and men defined public service in different ways. Specifically, women in their study identified helping the community, making a difference, and working with/serving citizens as their primary motivation significantly more frequently than did men.

A number of scholars have suggested that Black and Latina women, in particular, come to their candidacies and elected office with extensive ties to their communities and having honed their political skills in community organizations. Jennings (1991), for example, suggests that Black women mayors hone their skills in the church, civil rights movement, and as classroom teachers or community volunteers. Philpot and Walton (2007, 58–59) argue that "black women experience a political reality separate from that of white women and black men." Research by Hardy-Fanta (1993, 1997, 2002) and Montoya, Hardy-Fanta, and Garcia (2000) indicate that the politics of Latina women – including those in elected office – stem from concerns about specific issues affecting their communities. Takash's (1993) research on Latina elected officials in California finds that 61 percent claimed community activism as contributing to their election and 70 percent had served as board members of a local organization. Both Takash and Hardy-Fanta (1993) make an additional point: Latina political activism does not preclude conventional, electoral activity, including running for and holding elected office.

Because the literature suggests that women (including women of color) come to politics from a more relational or community focus, we were initially surprised to find no significant differences by gender in the percentages who said they ran for office for a reason connected to *Community*: 47.3 percent of women and 51.9 percent of men.

Complex Meanings of "Community"

Of course, the concepts embedded in a reason coded as *Community* – and the term itself – has many meanings: for instance, the "Black community," the "Latino community," or the "LGBT community." Like "public service," one may use the term as a general or abstract concept of solidarity and altruism, "*I wanted to help my community*," for example. With this in mind, we find that, when GMCL Survey respondents spoke of "community," the term may have been used to refer to a geographic area, a group of people, or as an appealing way of explaining the pursuit of office: "*I was asked by my community*." With such broad meanings, gender or racial differences may be obscured. And, of course, it is possible that, prior research to the contrary, *everyone* seeks a sense of connection. Frost and Meyer (2012, 36), for example, in their work on whether connectedness to the LGBT community fosters greater health and well-being among gay, lesbian, bisexual women and men, and racial/ethnic minorities, write, "Feeling connected to one's community represents an extension of the fundamental human need to belong, is associated with positive individual and social outcomes, ... and is central to establishing collective identity..."[11] All in

---

[11] They draw on and cite work by Ashmore, Deaux, and McLaughlin-Volpe (2004); Baumeister and Leary (1995); and Gamson (1997).

all, a careful examination of how the GMCL respondents used the term "community" sheds light on a dynamic that may be quite complex.[12]

In other words, just using the *word* "community," does not, in and of itself, reveal a deep-rooted connectedness to or focus on a group of people or those living within a set of geographical boundaries who share similar ethnic/racial or political beliefs or aspirations. For example, when a Black male mayor from Alabama says he ran for office because "*I am a firm believer in local government, and we established a government in my community, and I ran for a position in the government,*" he uses the word community, but the main emphasis of the statement seems to be on himself rather than his roots in – or what he can contribute to – a group of people he has ties to or a geographical location. He continued by saying, "*Government was an avocation when I was in school.*" In the following statement by another Black male municipal official, "*Due to the fact of the way I was raised, the chance I had to get where I am to develop me into a better person in the community where I live,*" the term "community" conveys a location, but not necessarily a focus on benefiting his community as a reason to run. And, as a corollary, a response that does *not* include the word "community" may, nevertheless, communicate a deep-seated rootedness to a particular group by race/ethnicity or within a set of geographical boundaries – even when these boundaries are social rather than drawn on a map.[13]

The elected officials gave many other responses that also indicated strong ties to or prior involvement in their respective community and/or serving groups of people. All of the following, for example, suggest some kind of community connection even when the word "community" is not mentioned: "*Opportunity to serve people in my neighborhood*"; "*I had been involved with the parent teacher group and decided it was time to*

---

[12] We would like to acknowledge the contributions of Rebecca Loya, PhD, who served as a graduate research associate at the University of Massachusetts Boston's Center for Women in Politics and Public Policy in 2010, for her contributions to this section on the complex meanings of "community." See also, Wong (2010).

[13] A simple counting of how often respondents used the words "community" and/or "communities" revealed 947 such responses by about half (642) individuals across all three invitations to respond, with a number of officials repeating the word(s) in more than one of the prompts. Although the differences by gender within each racial group were not significant, there were significant differences when comparing the various race*gender groups, with the mean number of mentions of the word "community" or "communities" the highest for Asian American men, followed by Asian American women (1.79 and 1.71, respectively). Black men and Latina women are next at 1.52 and 1.51, respectively; to our surprise, Latino men and Black women used the word "community" or "communities" least often, with means of 1.41 and 1.38, respectively.

go *the next level of involvement as an elected official instead of a volunteer"*; and "*It began in the Civil Rights Movement, and we were all asked to run for political office to promote economic development, education, and also to promote equal employment.*"

There are also mixed motivations: in the last example, race is implied, even if not explicitly stated, because of the reference to the civil rights movement and, in this context, "*We were all asked to run.*" In fact, a number of respondents specifically pointed to the civil rights movement as the source of their decision to run; witness the Black male municipal official from Louisiana who said, "*The civil rights movement and the people involved. We took on the system.*" In contrast, an Asian American male state legislator from Maryland, when asked why he ran for office the first time, demonstrated a perhaps weaker community-based reason when he responded first with, "*There were open seats,*" followed by, "*I wanted to serve my community.*" Service, including with a community focus, clearly motivated this Latino male state legislator from a large city in New Mexico, who said, "*To serve my state, my community, and my people.*"

What our analysis suggests is that a large number of elected officials color see serving, giving back to, and helping their own (racial/ethnic) community of people as a primary motivation for seeking office. Several used the phrases "community service" or "civic duty" to describe their commitment. On the other hand, it was also clear that simply using the word "community" does not necessarily indicate that deep ties within one's community are a major source of motivation for seeking office, and gender as well as racial differences may be obscured by the complexities of categorizing people's motivations to run.

GENDER, RACE, AND COMMUNITY AS MOTIVATION TO RUN: TESTING THE HYPOTHESIS

Because of the centrality in past research of community connection and concerns as motivators for women, especially women of color, to run, it is important to test it as a hypothesis and explore the relative weight of various contributing factors, rather than operate under the assumption that, based on prior scholarship, it is simply true. A multivariate analysis of *Community* as a reason to run for office the very first time (Table 4.2) provides strong evidence to the contrary. Controlling for other factors, Latino, Asian, and American Indian *men* are significantly *more likely* than other race*gender groups to give a *Community* response to why they ran for office.

TABLE 4.2. *Predictors of "Community" as the Most Important Reason for Running*

Contributing Factors	*b*	s.e.	Sig.
Race*Gender (*Ref. Black female*)			
Black man	.307	.241	.203
Latina woman	.441	.320	.168
Latino man	.585*	.259	.024
Asian woman	.820	.546	.133
Asian man	.791*	.396	.046
American Indian woman	.206	1.001	.837
American Indian man	1.967*	.884	.026
Level of Office (*Ref. municipal*)			
State legislator	−1.093***	.293	.000
School board	−.909***	.194	.000
County supervisor/commissioner	−.438†	.228	.055
Other			
Years of residence	−.003	.005	.592
Age	−.010	.007	.201
Foreign born	−.708*	.309	.022
College degree	.225	.175	.198
Married	−.062	.183	.733
Delegate view of representation (*Ref. trustee*)	.402*	.171	.019
Linked fate	−.233*	.094	.013
Constant	.894	.515	.083
Log likelihood: 933.886[a]; Nagelkerke R^2 = .063			

Note: The final two factors listed in "Other" (Delegate view of representation and Linked fate) are discussed in Chapters 7 and 8.
† $p < .1$; * $p < .05$; *** $p < .0001$.
Source: GMCL National Survey; N = 1,335.

    The lack of gender and race differences in the bivariate analysis and the puzzling findings in the multivariate analysis on a community-based reason to run requires some explanation. Why is there, overall, no gender difference between men and women of color elected officials on motivations reflecting solidarity with or connection to one's geographical location and/or identification with a racial/ethnic identity group? Why would we further see that, controlling for other factors, Latino, Asian, and American Indian men – but not Black men – would be significantly more likely to give a *Community* reason than Black women? One explanation may simply be that the women in politics literature is wrong – perhaps because a good deal of it reflects an essentialist perspective of women as more relational, connected, and community-focused and is supported by only a few studies of a scientifically rigorous nature. Qualitative research such as case studies, interviews with limited numbers of women (without or with men for comparisons), and studies based on a few geographical locations may simply be inadequate. At the same time, one might argue that, as we do above, the meaning of "community" is complex and difficult to tease out.[14] Another explanation is, of course, that women and men of color elected officials may be different from their White counterparts. In other words, when facing challenges within a contested political terrain, the trajectories of men of color may be as grounded in and rise from collective experiences and ties to their respective communities as are those of their female counterparts, especially given the relative disadvantages facing men of color as described in Chapter 3.

Although intriguing in their conclusions about the community ties of women of color, studies such as those by Hardy-Fanta (1993) and others (e.g., Flammang 1984; Jennings 1991; Montoya, Hardy-Fanta, and Garcia 2000; Takash 1993) may in fact not hold up when tested empirically. Even Hardy-Fanta (1997, 45–46), who conducted in-depth case studies of female and male Latino candidates who were successful in their election bids, finds that "...differences in the discourse of politics may hide commonalities across gender lines. For example, the men, thinking they should stay focused on election campaigns, may be suppressing a richer experience in community activities. They may simply be less verbally expansive about those aspects of politics." She concludes:

[R]eaching out seems more consciously constructed for Latino men – a way of staying in touch with constituents, as a candidate or officeholder – and less embedded, as it seems to be for Latinas, in their pre-electoral lives. It does, in many ways, represent an extension of themselves into the fabric of the community, an interpersonal skill, and a quality that reduces the apparent differences between the politics of women and men. They are building on a gendered style of interpersonal politics, but it is based on connecting to people in the community, nevertheless, and parallels the Latina style quite closely.

Level of office also contributes to a *Community* reason to run for office among elected officials of color. Table 4.2 shows that those serving at

---

[14] And, when coding verbatim responses for the purposes of quantitative analysis, there is certainly a potential for coding errors.

the municipal level more likely than all other levels to convey a sense of community as a primary motivation. In Chapter 7, we consider another factor that contributes to the model: those with a "delegate" role view of their representational role are more likely to give a *Community* response; paradoxically, those who have a greater sense of "linked fate" with others of their racial/ethnic group, which we explore in Chapter 8, are less likely. For now, we conclude that, despite prior research, the impact of community connectedness in the trajectories of male and female elected officials of color is not yet clear. The field of political science requires considerably more research into the meanings of community for the political trajectories of elected officials in a more diverse country.

REPRESENTATION AS A MOTIVATION TO RUN

Besides "issue passion" and "serving the community," there are a number of other motivations that we consider to be public rather than self-focused. Reasons related to *Representation* were given most often after those reflecting an *Issue* or *Community* (Table 4.1). Three in ten officials of color gave responses expressing dissatisfaction with current representation, a desire to increase the number of minorities (or women) in the political office, or a need for more or better representation for a particular group of people.

Variation by Level of Office and Race

There were significant differences by level of office, with larger percentages of those at higher offices giving responses reflecting a drive for a change in representation or an increase in (minority) representation. Examples of responses range from the general, where a Black male city councilor from South Carolina said, simply, *"Lack of representation within the community,"* to the more specific, in the case of a Black female member of the Board of Aldermen in a city in Florida who responded, *"The need for women, especially African American women."* An Asian American male school board member from California gave a response filled with multiple reasons, including minority representation: *"I knew the superintendent as well, and I felt I could work with her. I had a lot of encouragement from people in town interested in getting a minority on the school board."*

In contrast, for a Latino male school board member, also from California, representation was *the* reason: *"I'm an Hispanic, there never has been an Hispanic involved in the school board, so I wanted to get myself involved.*" And, when asked what his next most important reason was, he continued to focus on the need for a presence of underrepresented groups: "*To insure that there was diversity on the school board, both politically and ethnically and gender-wise also.*" A number of respondents focused on the inadequacy of the incumbents as a reason to run: "*The idiots who were in the office,*" said a Black male city councilor from a relatively small city in California.

American Indians: Representation as a Reason to Run

The number of American Indian elected officials in our survey was too small to include them in much of the analysis, and their sampling frame was based on state legislators only, limiting meaningful quantitative comparisons. They do, nevertheless, contribute to our understanding of why they run for office, and we find that representation is important to them as American Indians/Native Americans. An American Indian state legislator from Arkansas responded, "*I wanted more effective representation,*" and added, "*Disenchantment with the incumbent.*" A male state legislator from South Dakota replied: "*No tribal members [were] running for this office from the reservation. No tribal member living on this reservation was ever elected to the state offices, and they were open. Often, there was no challenger.*" An American Indian female state legislator from Montana said, "*Basically, they needed an Indian candidate to run for that position.*" This might seem like a call for merely descriptive representation, and she implies having been recruited (*Encouraged*), but she then added a more substantive – *Issue* – basis for her decision, "*I think it was because the representative who was in the position did not represent the Indian population or the constituents who I wanted to represent, like the poor, children, and education. I think also to try to impact economic development on the reservation.*"

PROMOTING CHANGE – MAKING A DIFFERENCE

Hardy-Fanta (1993, 30) studies Latinos/as in Boston and asserts that Latina women define politics as "promoting change...That's political, that's what I mean by politics, that's what politics means to me." Their male counterparts focused more on gaining positions in government, what Fox and Lawless (2005) refer to as "competitive traits" and that we include in the category of "self-focused" motivations. García and Márquez's (2001, 118) study of participants at a Latina Candidate

Development Conference as well as national delegates to the 1992 Democratic National Convention states:

> Most revealing about these findings is the combination of traditionally relevant political motivations with specific community-oriented motivations. That is, participants exhibited a commitment to getting particular candidates elected and certain policies addressed, as well as a commitment to both their own communities and the Chicano/Latino community at large. Participants *bridged* both traditional and community-oriented motivations for their political involvement. In effect, Latinas are entering traditional mainstream politics and bringing with them their experiences from grassroots politics and from their cultural networks and resources (emphasis in original).

The open-ended responses also lend support for the premise that Latinas bring with them a unique vision of politics – a *bridging* of both traditional and community-oriented motivations. This bridging suggests that Latinas bring their community with them, rather than "leave it behind" or "forget where they come from." One theme that emerged in our survey was "the need for change."

The literature on minority politics also suggests that Blacks and Latinos generally are open about their desire to gain political representation for their respective group, launch their candidacies based on perceived closeness to community, and campaign on what are the most important needs/issues facing geographic and ethnic communities. Pinderhughes (1993) argues that Black women are more likely to focus on horizontal, community-wide political mobilization, while Black men, based in the hierarchical institution of the African American church, narrow their goals toward achievement for a smaller sector of the population.

DISENTANGLING PUBLIC INTEREST REASONS TO RUN FOR OFFICE: INTERCONNECTED MOTIVATIONS

Despite the prevalence of issue- and community-based reasons to run, the preceding discussion and especially the quotes by the respondents make it clear that few elected officials of color are motivated by a single purpose. In one response, an individual may embed multiple reasons.[15] Based on our data, we find that 21 percent of all participants in the GMCL National Survey gave responses that were coded both as *Issue* and

---

[15] Carroll and Sanbonmatsu (2013, 61) suggest "an alternative conceptualization of relationally embedded decision making about running for office that moves beyond the individual, rational calculation of the ambitious politician."

Community: "*To create jobs for the community*" and "*Planning and smart growth, I wanted my community to develop with a plan in mind, capital improvements planning*"; "*To try to make positive changes in the community*" and "*Need a change in the community*"; "*To change the racial disparity that exists in our community*" and "*Safety and health programs were not in existence in our community, particularly for children and the elderly*"; "*Economics and welfare of our community*" and "*I saw the need to help my district and community. I saw a lot of needs in the community that weren't being met and I wanted to work to help meet those needs.*"

Many respondents also link *Representation* to their commitment to their communities. There seem to be three types of links between representation and community reasons: (1) representation of a given community within a larger governing structure; (2) representation of a racial/ethnic (or gender) group not bound by a specific governing structure; and (3) representation within a given government/community. Type 1 mentions the need for representation by a community but does not specify a racial/ethnic group identity. These responses are relatively rare; an example is a Latino male city councilor from a medium size city in Utah who said, "*Lack of representation for the west side of the community.*"[16] Type 2 includes responses that note representation concerns stemming from one's racial/ethnic (or other ascriptive) identity; an example is "*To ensure the minority Black community in the city [where] I live was being represented and their issues were being addressed.*" Type 3 involves concerns about representing the people's needs in government; examples include: "*Enhance the representation of government with input from different people and perspectives*"; "*Representation of the people; they had been ignored here for the last ten years*"; and "*What I felt was a lack of representation by the individuals elected by citizens of this district.*"

Local-Level Officials Drive Differences on *Issue* and *Community* as Reasons to Run

While it is only on motivations based on *Issue* that we find any significant differences by race (which led to differences between Black women and men), we do find large and significant differences by level of office.

---

[16] Of course, the phrase "west side" may have racial meaning, *a la* "South Side of Chicago" or Albuquerque's South Valley, which is heavily (immigrant) Latino. Latinos, in particular, may be dispersed in other places, but a geographic location such as "west side" may still imply a specific ethnoracial population.

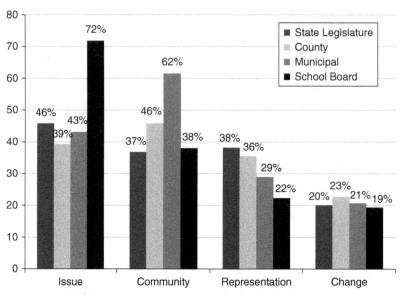

FIGURE 4.2 Public-interest reasons to run, by level of office.
Note: Entries are percents of respondents who gave each response; categories are not mutually exclusive. Differences for *Issue*, *Community*, and *Representation* are significant at $p < .0001$.
Source: GMCL National Survey, 2006–2007; $N = 1,344$.

As discussed earlier, half of all elected officials of color gave responses that focused on an issue and/or community, but, as Figure 4.2 shows, the strong showing for *Issue* as a reason to run for the first time lies with school board members: three-quarters at this level named an issue or problem as a primary reason to run the first time.

The explanation may be seen in a quote from an Asian male school board member in California: "*I care about what my children are learning in the school. I see this as education; it is not really a political position.*" Running for school board seats, in this example and others, appears to reflect a progression more from caring about what's happening in schools (beginning, often, with one's own children), and less from desiring to hold elected office per se.

And, in the case of *Community* as a reason, it is those serving on the governing boards of their cities or towns behind the relative weight of this motivation: six in ten of these municipal officials gave a response reflecting a concern about or ties to their community as their "most important reason for running the very first time" as compared to less than half of county supervisors/commissioners, and fewer than four in ten of either school board members or state legislators. Why might this be the case? Perhaps simply because representing a city, town, district, or neighborhood in essence means a geographical or "felt" community.

The percent who gave a reason reflecting dissatisfaction with those currently holding elective office or a desire for increased *Representation*, on the other hand, shows a smooth line by level with school board at the lowest percentage to state legislators at the high end (see Figure 4.2).

Variation by Race and Gender and Level of Office

The race*gender differences by level of office were modest among the four public interest–focused reasons given for why the officials ran for office in the first place. The only difference that was statistically significant by gender alone was among county officials who ran to *"Make a Change/Make a Difference"*: 36 percent of women of color at the county level compared to 18.3 percent of male county officials ($p < .01$). This was driven in large part by Black female county officials (34.2 percent) compared to their male counterparts (18.9 percent). Hispanic male county officials were twice as likely (at 56.4 percent) to give an *Issue* reason than their Hispanic women serving at that level (27.3 percent) ($p < .1$).

Although municipal officials overall are more likely than those at other levels to give a reason grounded in *Community* (see Figure 4.2), the only race*gender difference for municipal officials is on the reason linked to *Issue*: 54.9 percent of Hispanic men compared to 34.6 percent of Hispanic women holding municipal offices gave a response coded as *Issue*. Differences for school board members are as follows: 36.5 percent of Black men compared to 27.3 percent of Black women at this level gave a *Community* reason to run; 61.1 percent of Asian American male school board members were much more likely than their female counterparts (at 27.3 percent) to give a *Representation* reason; the differences were only modestly significant.

"SELF-FOCUSED" MOTIVATIONS

As shown in the Typology/Rankings of Motivations (see Figure 4.1), smaller percentages of elected officials of color offer "self-focused" reasons than those categorized as more publicly focused. Table 4.3 shows, for example, that just one in five officials surveyed gave a *Personal* reason

TABLE 4.3. *"Self-Focused" Motivations for Running for Office the First Time, by Race and Gender*

	Personal	Strategic	Political Interest	Encouraged
All (N = 1 ,348)	21.4	15.2	11.2	16.5
Race				
Black (N = 722)	20.8	18.0	12.3	20.2
Latina/o (N = 508)	21.1	10.4	10.7	12.6
Asian American (N = 94)	23.4	17.0	7.4	9.6
American Indian (N = 24)	37.5	25.0	4.2	12.5
Gender				
Female (N = 501)	24.4	14.2	11.4	18.8
Male (N = 847)	19.6	15.8	11.0	15.1
Race*Gender				
Black women (N = 304)	24.0	16.2	11.8	21.7
Black men (N = 418)	18.5	19.4	12.8	19.1
Latina women (N = 157)	24.2	10.2	12.7	13.4
Latino men (N = 351)	19.7	10.5	9.7	12.3
Asian American women (N = 30)	30.0	13.3	6.7	16.7
Asian American men (N = 4)	20.3	18.8	7.8	6.3
American Indian women (N = 10)	20.0	20.0	0.0	20.0
American Indian men (N = 14)	50.0	28.6	7.1	7.1

Note: Entries are percents of respondents. Motivation categories are not mutually exclusive. Differences by race are significant at $p < .001$ for Strategic and Encouraged; by gender for Personal ($p < .05$) and Encouraged ($p < .1$). All motivation categories are significant for race*gender: Personal at $p < .1$, Strategic and Political Interest at $p < .05$), and Encouraged at $p < .01$). The difference between Black women and men is also modestly significant ($p < .1$). *Source*: GMCL National Survey, 2006–2007.

(which includes, but is not limited to, personal ambition), compared to the half who gave a community- or issue-based response. *Strategic Considerations, Political Interest*, and *Encouraged/Recruited*, which we discussed earlier in this chapter, are all considerably lower than the others.

Again, these are not mutually exclusive. In other words, someone can be motivated by a public interest–focused reason such as an issue he or she cares about within a specific geographical or racial/ethnic community and, at the same time, run for office for a reason that refers to him/herself or family (*Personal*); she or he may also have been *Encouraged* to run, feel the time is right (i.e., a *Strategic* consideration), and have had a longstanding *Interest* in politics. In some cases, of course, one type of motivation stands out.

Personal Reasons: Occasionally Just Personal, More Likely in Combination with Others

While a great deal of the literature on gender and politics focuses on personal ambition as a reason to run for office – and we discuss ambition in depth in Chapter 5 – we find that elected officials of color convey many personal reasons other than ambition. An American Indian woman serving as a municipal official in an East Coast city,[17] for example, spoke of the pleasure she anticipated: "*I enjoy working with people*"; another reason she gave was "*Because I enjoy being involved with things that affect my life every day.*" An Asian American male school board member from California said, "*Personal fulfillment,*" followed by "*Development of attributes and character.*"

Others responded in ways that combined "the personal" with public interest–focused motivations. A Black female city councilor in North Carolina illustrates this multilayered set of reasons: When asked for the most important reason she initially ran for office, she first said, "*The need for representation*"; her second, equally succinct but different, answer reflected the theme of *Encouraged*: "*I was asked to.*" Her third was a personal reason: "*I just wanted to do it.*" Another Black female local official, also from the South, said, "*I like keeping busy*" and "*I had children growing up here.*" And, in the words of a Black male county official in North Carolina, "*I had recently retired, and I had some spare time on my hands. I didn't want to just sit around and let it go to waste.*" A response we found intriguing was "*Revenge,*" from a Latino male city councilor in California. Examples abound of personal reasons to run, alone or in combination with others; a quote from an Asian American woman in Alaska illustrates this point: her first reasons reflected both *Community* and *Representation*: "*I like to play a part of the judicial system and to do something for the community and be a representative for the Filipino community,*" but ended with something *Personal*: "*Also for my self-improvement.*"

Table 4.3 also shows that more women than men of color gave a *Personal* reason for running for office. There are no significant differences by race alone, and the differences by gender within each racial group, while occasionally large (e.g., in the case of Asian women and men) are significant only for Black women and men (and only at $p < .1$). Often, a public interest–focused rationale is grounded in a personal

[17] In cases where there are small number of individuals in a specific race*gender and level of office combination, we leave out names of cities and/or states to protect confidentiality.

experience: witness the Latina school board member in New Mexico who first offered "*To help children get educated*" as the most important reason she ran. When asked for her next most important reason, she responded, "*I raised seven children, and I raised another seven that weren't mine that my kids brought home because they couldn't live with their parents, so I just helped them out and raised them. I'm a Christian!*" Other personal reasons included "*It was spiritual,*" or "*My children,*" or "*I'm a people person.*"[18]

Again, most elected officials of color surveyed gave multiple reasons that mix self-focused motivations with those with a more public-interest focus. A Latina city councilor from Colorado provides a good illustration when she said, "*I actually was a victim of crime* [Personal], *and that led me to really become involved with neighborhood organizations* [Community], *and then when there was a vacancy* [Strategic], *the neighbors encouraged me to run*" [Encouraged].

Strategic Considerations

When a candidate decides to enter the electoral arena because the prospect is most favorable to winning (i.e., she or he feels qualified, believes she or he could win, and/or no one else was in the race), the decision to run demonstrates a sense of political efficacy tied to what Rudolph, Gangl, and Stevens (2000, 1,190) and others[19] refer to as "response outcome expectations" and reflects "strategic" considerations. Such considerations also reflect a sense of political efficacy, meaning that he or she believes that she or he is competent or qualified to participate. One of the Black women who gave a response we coded as *Strategic* was a female city councilor from South Carolina: "*I felt I was qualified. I felt I could bring a lot to the table if given that opportunity.*" And a Black female state legislator from Kansas illustrates this type of motivation when she says, "*I was interested and qualified.*" (Her motivations, in this case as in others, were not solely strategic, in that she added: "*People asked me to run.*")

Strategic considerations also include opportunities that emerge as a result of redistricting or lack of an opponent: "*It was a new district created by the legislature,*" responded an American Indian male state legislator from New Mexico. "*The filing deadline was approaching and no*

---

[18] Seven respondents specifically used the term "people person" to describe themselves.
[19] In note 2, Rudolph, Gangl, and Stevens (2000, 1190) write, "The external dimension of political efficacy, or perceived system responsiveness, is represented by Bandura's (1982) concept of "response outcome expectations."

Democrat had filed," was the answer given by an Asian female school board member from California. An Asian male state legislator from Maryland said, *"[It was an] open seat, and I always wanted to serve."* When asked for his most important reason to run, a Latino state legislator from Colorado, first said, *"To make a difference,"* but when asked for his next most important reason, gave one that was clearly strategic, *"One third of the House of Representatives was term limited. I would be more effective with a new freshmen group coming in."*

Other examples include: *"I felt like I had something to offer, I had been a resident of this town all my life, and being a minority I felt that I had something to offer that had not been brought to the table before"* (Black male vice mayor, Virginia); *"Because there was a vacancy here that they weren't interested in filling"* (Black male county commissioner, Tennessee); *"At the time, none of the candidates who were running I believed would do as good of a job as I would. I also thought I could win"* (Latina county board official from Oregon); *"Because there was a lack of direction in the township and I felt that I could make a contribution"* (Black male mayor from Michigan); and *"I could not find anyone else who was willing to do it, and I felt like my husband would have wanted me to finish his term and continue to serve"* (Black female municipal official from Texas, whose husband had died); she added, *"To fulfill my husband's legacy."*

While the differences by race and gender alone were not statistically significant nor were those by gender within race, an intersectional analysis reveals that, in general, men of color elected officials were more likely than women to report they ran for office for strategic reasons, with American Indian men the most likely and Latina women the least (see Table 4.3). We can conclude that, in most instances, a higher proportion of men than women run for *Strategic* reasons; one might suggest that this finding conforms to a "typical" – or perhaps "stereotypical" male model of rational behavior. Exceptions are American Indian women, the proportions of who ran for this reason were almost as high as that of their male counterparts[20] and Latino men, who were as low as their female peers.

"Political Interest" as a Reason to Run

Motivations to serve the "Public Interest/Service" are different from the more self-focused "interest in politics" at the heart of "political

---

[20] Because of small numbers, all findings related to American Indians should be viewed with caution.

interest" as a motivation to run, which we consider to be located in the "self." Examples of *Political Interest* include what a Latina city councilor from a very small New Mexico town said, "*I wanted to get/ be involved*"; for these officials, elected office is intrinsically a personal opportunity. They may run because, like the Black female state representative from Missouri, they "*just love politics*," or the Latina city councilor who says, "*I always wanted to be in politics.*" It is about the personal pleasure they get from the work, and from being engaged in decision making; the zest when dealing with challenges; in the words of a Black alderwoman from a small town in Louisiana, who wants "*to be a leader, a catalyst.*"

Political interest was not one of the motivations given very frequently – just over one in ten officials surveyed gave reasons suggesting a motivation tied to political interest, which in some cases is a thinly disguised desire for self-advancement. For example, responses from several male elected officials brought to mind a Latino male candidate in the study by Hardy-Fanta (1997, 31), when asked why he ran for office the first time, replied simply, "*Ego.*" One of the younger men in her study spoke in a similar vein, "*I always wanted to be somebody.*" An Asian city councilor from Virginia first responded to the GMCL Survey question about why he ran, "*Helping my community*, then said, "*The ability to make a difference.*" When asked, *Any other reason?* he replied, "*Pride – and ego.*"

As previously noted, most respondents offered multiple reasons, even within the same sentence. A Latina school board member's political interest was just one of a number of reasons she began with attesting to her qualifications: "*I was in education for a long time, and I felt that I was very qualified, and I understood the dynamics of the leadership,*" but then goes on to share an interest that was more personal: "*I wanted to see what it was like on the other side of the table.*" A Black city council member from a small town in Texas ended his list of reasons with "*To experience leadership.*"

Among those who replied with *Political Interest*, there is a wide spread at the intersection of race and gender, with Black men (at 12.8 percent) and Latina women (at 12.7 percent) leading the way in stating motivation driven by political interest, down to 6.7 percent for Asian American women. None of the American Indian women officials gave responses prioritizing political interest. There are few significant differences when the data are broken down by gender alone on these "Self-Focused" reasons to run for office. Women were more likely than men to give a personal reason – and to say they were encouraged or recruited, but this was only modestly significant.[21]

THE DECISION TO RUN: FIRST ELECTIVE OFFICE

We continue our examination of the paths to office for elected officials of color by looking at how they responded to the question: *Is this your first elective position?* Given the numbers who responded *"Yes"* to this question, the data initially suggested that about two-thirds could be considered "newcomers." Once we compared their answers to the office they said they currently held, we realized that almost eight in ten were elected to the office they currently hold (see "All" in Figure 4.3).

There is also considerable variation by level of office for elected officials of color: Nine in ten school board members and city/town councilors report being in their first elected office. This is higher than the seven in ten county officials and six in ten state representatives. State senators and those in mayoral positions are much less likely to report being in their first elective position, and members of color (in the 113th Congress) are the least likely of all.

One might say that it is not surprising that those in "higher-level" positions begin in a school board or city/county councilor position. The picture is more complicated, however, as we also find that, not only do the vast majority of elected officials of color report *not* having held prior office, but, on average, they also have been in their current office for more than ten years. This suggests that, especially in the case of local officials, they either seek or are fully committed to the positions they hold or ran unsuccessfully for a higher-level position. We explore these twists and turns of political trajectories by gender and race in the rest of this chapter.

First Elective Office, by Gender and Level of Office

We find that women of color elected officials, as suggested in the literature, do indeed report being in their first elective office more often than their male counterparts, but this difference is not statistically significant.

---

[21] Analysis by gender and race/ethnicity together shows significant differences on "encouraged" and "strategic." Asian men, for example, were more likely (19 percent) than their female counterparts (13.3 percent) to offer strategic reasons to run, but Asian women were more likely (16.7 percent) than Asian men to say they were encouraged or recruited to run. Latinas/os and Black women and men were not dissimilar.

TABLE 4.4. *In First Elective Position, by Gender and Level of Office*

Gender	Level of Office				
	All Levels	State Legislature	County	Municipal	School Board
All	78.7	55.9	73.3	78.5	91.6
Women	81.0	48.1	76.0	80.3	93.6
Men	77.4	60.4	72.5	77.6	89.8
N	1,359	145	217	638	359

Note: Entries are percents of elected officials; differences by level of office are significant at $p < .0001$; gender differences are not statistically significant. Note: "State Legislature" includes representative, senators, delegates, and members of the state assembly. County includes elected county supervisors or commissioners. Municipal includes elected city/town councilors, members of select boards or aldermen, and village board members, and those serving in mayoral positions.

Source: GMCL National Survey, 2006–2007.

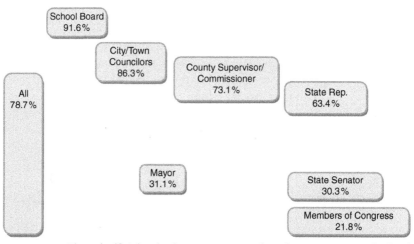

FIGURE 4.3 Elected officials of color reporting "in first elective position," by level of office.

Note: Entries are percents. The category "Mayor" includes those elected by popular ballot and city councilors who simultaneously serve in mayoral positions; it does not include Vice/Deputy Mayors or Mayors-Pro-Tempore, who are counted as "City/Town Councilors."

Sources: GMCL National Survey 2006–2007, N = 1,359, $p < .0001$; for members of the 113th Congress, GMCL Project, 2013; N = 96.

On the other hand, level of office does significantly affect the extent to which officials have held a local-level office (Table 4.4).

We see that, not surprisingly, more than nine in ten officials of color serving on elected school boards have held no prior office, as have close to eight in ten of those on municipal governing bodies. While the percentage decreases as one goes higher – to county supervisors/commissioners – the vast majority (73.3 percent) of those at that level are also in their first elective position.

At all three of these local levels of office, women are slightly more likely to be in their first elective position, but the gender differences for county, municipal, and school board officials are small and not statistically significant – especially in light of the much larger overall finding: that eight in ten of municipal, nine in ten of school board members, and three quarters of county officials did not hold a prior office. We also find no significant differences by race, and the only race*gender difference is among Latinos/as at all levels of office: 85.4 percent of Latinas reported first time in office versus 75.4 percent of Latino men ($p < .01$). However, as Table 4.4 shows, male state legislators of color are more likely than their female counterparts to report being in their first elective position.

But Are They Newcomers?

Simply looking at those who reported being in their first elective position obscures the fact that they are not newcomers to politics but rather were elected quite a number of years ago to the office they currently hold: on average 12.8 years. In other words, they are in their first elective position, in most cases, because they ran for and won election over and over again to the same seat. Those reporting being in their first elective position had been reelected and served, in most cases, quite a few terms; the mean years in office for this group is 11.1. Those who report having served in other offices prior to their current office have had an even longer tenure in politics, having served on average 18.7 years.

Women of color are significantly more likely to report being elected more recently, although the difference is not particularly large (Table 4.5). Racial differences are large and also highly significant: almost six in ten of Black officials compared to four in ten of Latinos and Asian Americans have been in office more than ten years.[22]

---

[22] This may be historically related since African American elected officials began to increase after the 1965 Voting Rights Act; minority language coverage began ten years later, therefore providing coverage to Latinos and eventually to Asian Americans.

TABLE 4.5. *Years in Office since First Election, for All and by Gender and Race*

Years in Office	All	Gender		Race		
		Women	Men	Black	Latino/a	Asian American
Mean years (s.e.)	12.8 (.24)	11.4 (.33)	13.6 (.32)	14.2 (.33)	11.3 (.37)	9.5 (.54)
		$p < .0001$		$p < .0001$		
N	1,338	493	845	711	507	96

Source: GMCL National Survey, 2006–2007.

Furthermore, when broken down by number of years and level of office (Table 4.6), we see that even if the vast majority reported being in their first elective office, very few of any level were newly elected (in the previous two years).

Perhaps somewhat surprising is the long tenures of those at the highest levels: eight in ten of all state senators (including not only those who are in their first elective position as state senator but also those who served in other offices prior to becoming senator) have served more than ten years, as have half of state representatives, and six in ten of country board members and mayors. It is only among municipal and school board members that we see the majority having been in office less than ten years. In sum, the elected officials in the GMCL survey have served a very long time – whether they are in their first elective office or in a different office. Hence, although most reported being in their first elective office, they are not newcomers to public office.

PRIOR OFFICE HOLDING: A "CAREER LADDER"
OR A HARD CEILING FOR WOMEN AND MEN
OF COLOR?

Political scientist Michael McDonald was recently quoted as capturing the conventionally understood, linear model of political trajectories: "Think of politics as a career ladder...You start out by running for school board or city council. From there you go to state representative or state senator, and that positions you to run for Congress" (Cobb 2014). To what extent does such a scenario apply to women and men of color? For women, especially, the trajectory of a career ladder has implied beginning their electoral ventures in lower-level offices, working themselves

TABLE 4.6. *Years in Office since First Election, by Level of Office*

Years in Office	State Senator	State Representative	County Board	Mayors	Municipal Board	School Board
0–2 years	0.0	0.9	2.3	0.0	2.0	4.0
	(0)	(1)	(5)	(0)	(10)	(14)
3–10 years	21.9	46.3	35.5	39.2	54.5	52.9
	(7)	(51)	(76)	(51)	(272)	(187)
More than 10 years	78.1	52.7	62.1	60.8	43.5	43.1
	(25)	(58)	(133)	(79)	(217)	(152)
N	32	110	214	130	499	353

Note: Entries are percents with N in parentheses; differences are significant at $p < .0001$. Year categories are from Svara (2003, 9). State Representative includes representatives, delegates, and members of state assemblies; County Board includes elected county supervisors or commissioners; Municipal Board includes elected city/town councilors, members of select boards or aldermen, and village board members but excludes mayors. The category "Mayors" includes those holding any mayoral position.

Source: GMCL National Survey, 2006–2007.

up to higher levels as they gain experience, support, and confidence. Prior office holding is also commonly linked to political ambition: "Those who ran for prior office are more likely to express ambition (compared to those without electoral experience) for other offices" (Williams 2008, 70).[23] Prior research has little if anything to offer on this subject at the intersection of race and gender.

In Chapter 3, we urged a shift from the traditional, individualistic view of demographic characteristics to one that is more dynamic – in other words, one that understands that, because of the barriers to educational and occupational opportunities as well as the sociopolitical and historical forces that shaped their political lives, there is likely no one path to increasingly higher-level offices for elected officials of color. These forces too often are personally devastating, as discussed in the Introduction to this book, which opens with the June 2015 shooting by a white supremacist that took the life of State Senator Clementa Pinckney, pastor of the Emanuel A.M.E. Church, and eight of his church members, in Charleston, South Carolina.

Similarly, we now challenge the ways the political science literature frames prior office holding in the context of a career ladder. Canon's (1990, 26) view, for example, that those who make the leap directly to the US Congress "are extremely ambitious and *do not want to waste time* in

---

[23] Williams draws on and cites Carroll (1994), Lawless and Fox (2005), and Schlesinger (1966).

lower office" (emphasis added) may do a disservice to the multitudes of individuals who intend to run for the same office but not for higher office. Moreover, describing those individuals of color who reach for and are elected to a relatively higher-level office (such as state senator or member of Congress) without beginning at a lower rung, such as school committee or city/town council, may miss a wealth of experiences and commitment to a larger cause that drive elected officials of color into office. We posit several additional reasons for caution.

First of all, some elected officials, especially those serving at the local level, may not run for higher-level office, but their public service – and what Schlesinger (1966) calls "static ambition" – may be far more intrinsic to the conduct of democratic politics than conventionally acknowledged. Second, the supposed lack of "progressive ambition" – that is, not running for higher-level office – may reflect not lack of ambition, but rather the hard ceiling they hit due to racism, sexism, or other constraints. Finally, we question the common assumptions that (1) women are more likely to need to "burnish their credentials" by holding lower-level office prior to either a state or federal legislative seat or statewide office; and (2) women's political progress is stymied by a lack of ambition. In fact, Maestas and Rugeley (2008, 530) conclude that, "The differences between serious amateurs, local officeholders,... or nonprofessional state legislative seat holders, and appointed officeholders are statistically indiscernible."

Women of Color: "Ambitious Amateurs," "Accidental Politicians," or Multiple Paths to Office?

One of the most important themes in the literature on women and politics is that women differ from men in their trajectories to public office. Rosenthal (1998a, 5) explains, "For many women, though not all, leadership style is shaped by the world of volunteerism, PTAs, community activism, family commitments, and church suppers." That women of color are more easily seen as informal leaders rather than positional ones is an extension of this argument, which has been suggested by a number of scholars. For women of color, their movement from one realm of politics into the other is largely unexpected or relatively rocky, in that they are not, as discussed earlier in this chapter, likely to be groomed by parties or elites to seek or win public office. Sharon Navarro (2008, 5) nicely sums up the argument: "All the existing research up to this point on Latina political behavior suggests that Latinas are *accidental leaders*; they are community activists or untraditional politicians who do not follow the typical paths or motivations that lead white males to politics" (emphasis in original).

Navarro's case study, however, shows Leticia Van de Putte, a public official in Texas, moving from an "accidental leader" to a "strategic politician." A pharmacist and mother of six, Van de Putte's political world was initially defined by her volunteer work with the Democratic Party and assisting in political campaigns of friends. Navarro traces her political career as she wins a seat in the Texas House of Representatives and subsequently moves up to the Texas Senate, exercising considerable leadership and proving herself a successful and influential politician. We will return to styles of leadership in Chapter 6; first we explore prior office holding to demonstrate further the nonlinear trajectories of elected officials of color.

Prior Office Holding: Members of Congress

Do members of the US Congress from communities of color achieve that level of office by climbing a "career ladder," that is, progress from lower-level to higher-level offices? And, given the emphasis in the women in politics literature on a "farm team" where women develop qualifications by starting at the local level and moving up, are women of color in Congress more likely than their male counterparts to start at the local level?

It is quite clear from Table 4.7 that the answer to these questions is a resounding *No*. For this group of elected officials, the vast majority have skipped the local-level-office route altogether; fewer than a third started as an elected city/town councilor, county official, or school board member. One in five (21.8 percent) held no prior office – moving directly into Congress – a percentage similar to that reported by Canon (1990, xi).

Like President Barack Obama, many (43.6 percent) skipped local-level elected office and served first as state legislators. And, even of those who did start in a local office, just one in ten of all members of Congress of color can be said to have climbed a "career ladder" – that is, started as a school board member, a city/town councilor or county commissioner/supervisor – and moved through a higher position as, for example, state legislator before winning a seat in the US House or Senate.

A gendered analysis of these women and men of color demonstrates quite clearly that, contrary to most of the literature on women in politics, women of color in Congress are *less likely* – not more – than their male counterparts

TABLE 4.7. *Career Ladder or Direct to Congress?*

Path to Office	All	Women	Men
No prior office	21.8	22.6	21.4
Started at local level	29.8	22.6	33.9
Direct to Congress	19.5	16.1	21.4
Career ladder	10.3	6.5	12.5
Started at state legislative level	43.6	54.9	37.5
Direct to Congress	27.5	35.5	23.2
Career ladder	16.1	19.4	14.3
N	87	31	56

Note: Entries are percents; total for all may not add up to 100 because of rounding. "Local level" in this table includes county-level positions. Because we are reporting on the universe of members of color in Congress, all findings are statistically significant. Members of the 113th Congress include US Delegate from the District of Columbia but not other nonvoting delegates.
Source: GMCL Project, 2013.

to start at the local level, by a difference of 10 percentage points. Slightly more than one-fifth of women and men of color were likely to hold no prior office before their congressional seats. Furthermore, more than half of women of color members of Congress start at the state legislative level rather than lower-level office compared to about a third of their male counterparts. Finally, those who did "climb a career ladder," starting in a position in a local office and moving up through a mid-level seat, are twice as likely to be men than women (12.5 percent men versus 6.5 percent women).

Nonlinear Paths for Black, Latino, and Asian American Members of Congress

Much of the literature on trajectories to the US Congress draws from candidate studies and is driven by notions of individualism and political ambition (see, Canon 1990; Jacobson and Kernell 1981; Maestas and Rugeley 2008). A central assumption of ambition theory is that politicians who form the bulk of those making "strategic candidate entry" are those who have carefully positioned themselves by moving from lower- to middle- to higher-level offices before making the move to the US Congress, statewide offices or the presidency. Canon (1990, xiii, note 7) also suggests that times of upheaval create conditions that foster "lateral entry" of amateurs, where " 'lateral entry' refers to election to a relatively high office in the career structure (such as the US House or Senate) without prior service in state and local office.

There are certainly many examples among elected officials of color that support the notion that conditions during "times of upheaval" lead some individuals to make the leap into higher-level offices without starting at a lower level and moving up, and the civil rights era certainly was such a time. For these officials, many of whom held office for a very long time, "career advancement" pales compared to other reasons.

Mervyn Dymally: Illustration of Complex, Nonlinear Trajectory

In the case of Mervyn Dymally (Figure 4.4), we see a Black man who, at the time of our survey in 2006–2007, held the position of California State Assemblyman (2003–2008) – for the second time. The office he held before that was, however, not a lower-level seat, but rather a higher one, in the US Congress (1981–1993). In fact, although there is a career ladder of sorts – state assembly, state senate, statewide office, and US Congress – Dymally's first office was *not* at the local level.

Over the course of his personal and political life, the demographics in his home town of Compton, California, had changed dramatically, from less than 5 percent Black in the 1950s to 90 percent in the 1970s. It was also a center of the school and housing desegregation battles in Los Angeles; these battles culminated in the "Watts Riots" of 1965 – certainly strong examples of "times of upheaval." From his work as a teacher and his 1962 election to the California State Assembly, one can certainly see a distinctive "career ladder" representing progressive ambition: Over the next thirty years Dymally was elected to the state senate in 1966, as lieutenant governor in 1974, and to the US Congress in 1980. He left that office in 1993 at the age of sixty-seven.

For elected officials of color – especially Blacks – who experienced and contributed to the civil rights era, activism for social justice and civil rights are the first step toward political office holding. Canon, Schousen, and Sellers (1996, 849), cite Dymally (1973) in writing,

These "traditional" black candidates often have backgrounds in the civil rights movement and black churches. They typically come from the liberal wing of the Democratic Party and embody the "politics of difference".... These candidates tend to think of themselves as political outsiders who must form political organizations separate from whites in order to battle for a greater share of the political pie. Many of the first blacks in Congress had little or no prior experience in party and elective politics, and more importantly, they valued their outsider status.[24]

---

[24] They also cite Holden (1973).

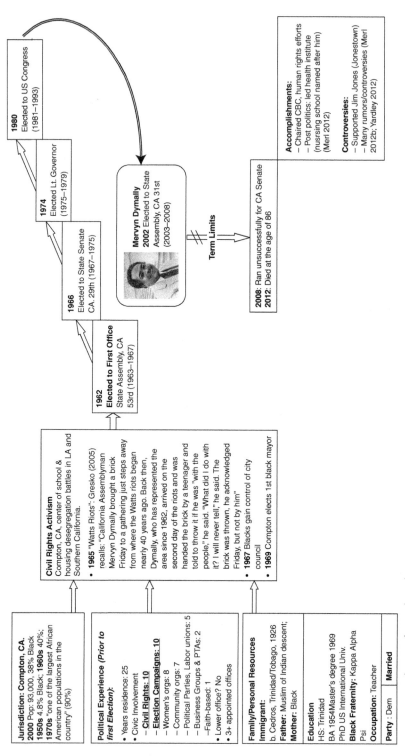

FIGURE 4.4 A complex political trajectory.

Sources: Canon et al. (1996); Dymally (1971); GMCL National Survey 2006–2007; GMCL Project 2013; Merl (2012); see also www.black-past.org/aaw/dymally-mervyn-1923. Photo courtesy of the Collection of the US House of Representatives.

Mervyn Dymally's later political life presents an equally complex picture: In 2002, "dissatisfied with the potential candidates for the Compton-area Assembly seat he first won in 1962 and dismayed at the dropping numbers of Blacks in the legislature, Dymally jumped into the race himself and won," coming full circle back to his original office (Merl 2012). With term limits in effect, he again sought a higher-level office – running unsuccessfully for the state senate in 2008. He died in 2012, at the age of eighty-six.[25]

Finally, while some might suggest sticking with one elected office reflects a lack of (progressive) ambition for higher office, Gerber (1996, 831), notes that the fact that "African American members of Congress are significantly less likely to exit from the House than other Democrats, ... will have important effects on the distribution of power among districts, and *will likely increase African American political influence and prominence*" (emphasis added).[26]

Prior Office Holding:
State Legislators of Color

Is there a "career ladder" at the state legislative level for elected officials of color? The findings are mixed. Notwithstanding the small number of state senators in our survey, we see that a third held no prior office and were elected directly to the state Senate. About a quarter went directly from a lower-level office to the state Senate; these include four city/town councilors, a school board member, a county treasurer, and two on other local boards. While we concede that the 27.3 percent who served first as state representative prior to becoming state senator is evidence of an upward path, only 18.2 percent climbed what would be considered a classic "career ladder," first holding a lower-level office, then moving up through an intermediate step before becoming state senator.

---

[25] Dymally is not the only one with a complex path, holding higher-level offices prior to the current position: Asian American Nestor Garcia served as city council member (Honolulu, HI, District 9) from 2003–2013. Prior to that, he was elected to the Hawaii State House (1995–2002). He also ran for the United States House of Representatives, Hawaii, District 2, 2006. His background includes press secretary for US Senator Daniel K. Inouye and Hawaii State Convention, Delegate, 1994. Nestor Garcia was not immune to scandals: He stepped down in 2011 and in 2012, "Former Council Chair Nestor Garcia Fined $6,500 – Largest Fine in City's History – for Failure to Disclose Conflicts of Interest on Rail Project." Source: www.hawaiireporter.com/former-council-chair-nestor-garcia-fined-6500-largest-fine-in-citys-history-for-failure-to-disclose-conflicts-of-interest-on-rail-project (Accessed November 20, 2014).

[26] Gerber does not mention gender in his article.

What about gender? As seen in Table 4.4, about half (55.9 percent) of state legislators of color were elected directly into a state legislative seat, without passing first through a lower-level office. Table 4.8 shows, however, that female state legislators we surveyed were more likely than their male counterparts to have held prior office. The 12.3 percentage points difference by gender among state legislators of color goes in the opposite direction from that reported by Carroll and Sanbonmatsu (2013, 48), who note that 61.3 percent of women compared to 55.6 percent of men did not hold a lower-level office prior to their election to the state legislature.

Because these differences, albeit large, are not statistically significant, we cannot say with any degree of certainty that there is a career ladder for state legislators; and any differences in degree of direction from that reported by Carroll and Sanbonmatsu – who do not report significance for their finding – may be illusory.

Prior Office Holding: Local-Level Officials

We find no significant differences either for municipal or county officials of color whose first position was one other than their current level of office. Overall, the overwhelming majority of city/town councilors (88 percent) held no prior office. School board officials present an interesting picture, however. Although, as shown in Table 4.4, the vast majority (91.6 percent) of school board officials held no office prior to their current position, there may be evidence of a "farm team" effect for women at this level: 75 percent of the women of color school board officials compared to 25 percent of men reported a prior office said it was on a board/commission or political/community position. In other words, women may have "prepared" themselves prior to their election to the school board.

Finally, given that traditional notions of a career ladder that one climbs, ever upward, we found that, at least among school board members of color, political life may be more fluid: 56.3 percent of male school board members reported that the office they held prior to their current position was as city/town councilor, and another 18.8 percent reported having come to the school board after holding a county position. In contrast, none of the women reported holding a municipal or county office prior to their current position on the school board.

CONCLUSION

The questions we addressed in this chapter include: Why do elected officials of color run for office in the first place? Is there a pipeline to elective

TABLE 4.8. *First Elective Position Held, State Legislators Who Ran for Prior Office, by Gender*

First Elective Position	Women	Men
In first elective position	48.1	60.4
	(26)	(55)
Held prior office	51.9	39.6
	(28)	(36)
First office held (as percent of those who held prior office):		
School board	29.6	19.4
Municipal	25.9	30.6
County	11.1	16.7
Lower-level state legislative	14.8	16.7
Other elective (including local, tribal offices)	7.4	5.6
Boards/commissions, political/community organizations	11.1	11.2

Note: Entries are percentages, with N in parentheses. "Lower-level state legislative": Virtually all of the state legislators who reported their first office was as a state representative held a current position of state senator; one was a legislator currently serving in that position but who, in between, served in a number of higher-level offices. Percentages may not add up to 100 because of rounding.
Source: GMCL National Survey 2006–2007.

office, as the literature suggests? How important are personal ambition and party recruitment as facilitating factors for someone to run for the first time? What is the role of "community" in the initial decision to run? Finally, is there a "career ladder" to higher office, or a "cement ceiling" for elected officials of color when it comes to running for higher office?

After analyzing a multitude of data from the GMCL National Survey, Database, and other new data, we find that for people of color holding political office, the initial decision to run is complex, and they are motivated to run for multiple reasons. By using a combination of qualitative and quantitative methods, we are able to hear – in their own words – why they ran.

We also hope we have put to rest the idea that the problem of how to increase women's descriptive representation can be "solved" by asking them to run as many times as possible; the evidence that "women need to be asked" before they consider running for office has been largely based on anecdotes, studies with limited generalizability, and embellished by activists' enthusiasm.

In fact, relatively few Black, Latino/a, Asian American, and American Indian respondents reported being asked to run. Women of color, especially state legislators, are somewhat more likely than their male counterparts to have received encouragement before they ran – but almost none of the elected officials of color surveyed by the GMCL Project reported having been specifically recruited by a political party. In fact, we wonder whether the literature might conflate two very different phenomena: being recruited by a party, for example, shows the value placed by an external agent on an individual to serve in office, but needing to be asked implies certain hesitancy or lack of confidence and leads to the conclusion that women are less likely to be "self-starters." More research clearly needs to be done to tease out whether the differences we found in party recruitment for elected officials of color compared to what has been reported in the literature (where upwards of 50 percent of female state legislators say they were asked to run by party leaders) mean that political parties refrain from recruiting people of color. Alternatively, is it because the respondents in our study are mostly local officials who run mostly in non-partisan races? Or is it simply that, by not asking directly, *"Did your run because you were asked to by a party leader?"*, we are left to infer a lack of party recruitment of people of color because they did not mention it among the many reasons they offered? In other words, they may have been asked but may simply not have regarded external encouragement as one of their most important reasons when responding to an open-ended question about why they ran. They are prioritizing their reasons, nevertheless, and, if we are to take them "at their words," our findings support the idea that people of color, men and women alike, are being ignored by political parties.

We must also conclude that, in contrast to previous research findings (including some of our own), men of color voiced reasons to run connected to *Community* at least as much as did women of color. And, few men and, for that matter, women of color were motivated to run for their first office by personal "ambition." Yet, are elected officials of color not "ambitious"? Nine in ten local-level officeholders we surveyed held no prior office – and, although they display discrete ambition by running for reelection, the vast majority do not seek higher office (i.e., display progressive ambition).

It turns out that elected officials of color – including women – are nevertheless, self-starters. Contrary to most of the literature on women in politics, women of color in Congress, for example, are *less likely* than their male counterparts to start at the local level. More than half of state legislators of color were elected directly into a state legislative seat, without first holding a lower-level office; we see that the state legislature also serves as an important entry point and stable location for office holding.

Finally, the evidence of a "career ladder" for elected officials of color is slim, with just two in ten having started at a lower-level – and complicated by the fact that the vast majority of officials of color report having held no prior office at all. From the survey alone, we were not able to determine whether staying in one position over many years is the result of high satisfaction with her or his current position or, perhaps, a "cement ceiling" with elected officials of color blocked from advancing to higher-level offices. We present new data on this topic in Chapter 5. Suffice it to say for now that what Black, Latino, Asian American, and American Indian elected officials have to say about their initial decision to run has much to contribute to the field and to perhaps a deeper understanding of why people in general run for office.

5

The Election Contest

Navigating the Campaign Trail

For elected officials from communities of color for whom the political landscape is often highly contested – the most important – and most concrete – contest is, no doubt, the election campaign. In Chapter 3, we described the personal and family backgrounds of the elected officials of color – and the contested nature of what often have been considered individual and static traits. In Chapter 4, we examined their motivations for running and trajectories to office, focusing on offices held prior to their current positions. Now we apply the intersectional perspective to examine the experiences within the election contests of elected officials of color.

We begin with an exploration of the extent to which elected officials of color report personal ambition as a motivation to run for office. We proceed to analyze evidence of "progressive ambition," that is, the desire to run for higher office. We then turn to explicate how, progressively ambitious or not, those who ran for office drew on a wide range of social and political experiences in their election contests, including the extent to which they are "embedded" in their local communities, a concept addressed in Chapter 4. We then examine the political experiences and extent of civic engagement elected officials of color drew on as they prepared to run for office the first time.

Focusing on the election contest, we review the opportunity structure that influences the election campaigns of Blacks, Latino, and Asian American women and men and analyze the possible impact it has on the experiences of the women and men of color in our survey. Turning next to the challenges and obstacles elected officials of color reported facing during their election campaigns, we examine the extent to which women and men of color see themselves as disadvantaged on the campaign trail.

What levels of support did they receive from political parties and other political organizations? Which race*gender groups felt they faced greater scrutiny over their personal qualifications and/or electability? And who reported that they had a harder time raising money? We conclude by comparing the perceived campaign disadvantage by level of office and between race and gender.

PREPARING TO RUN: POLITICAL AMBITION AND COMMUNITY CONNECTION

Prevailing political science research in the United States often points to an individual's personal ambition as the key factor behind the decision to run for elected office. The literature on women and politics has often bemoaned the fact that women do not run for elected office because they lack the same levels of political ambition as men, with ambition defined as wanting to "get ahead" or "move to the next level of office." For women, the apparent "lack of ambition" appears, in the end, to be largely regarded as a negative trait. Fowlkes (1984, 6) notes, however, that "[e]laborations of the ambition theory of political behavior have been developed from the utilitarian perspective of rational *men*" (emphasis in original). Burt-Way and May (1992, 23) make a similar point that "what constitutes political ambition has typically been defined by male political career patterns." Moore (2005) warns that existing studies of ambition tell men's and women's stories differently and that scholarly inattention to the ambitions of activists at the local level, particularly along racial lines, may lead to erroneous conclusions on peoples' motivations for engaging in politics. Having ambition in this sense appears to rule out any connection to community advancement – it applies only to individual advancement.

Personal Ambition as Motivation for First Election Contest

Personal ambition – or the supposed lack thereof for women – plays a central role in the political science literature on why women's representation lags behind that of men. We should first acknowledge that there are different types of political ambition. According to Schlesinger (1966), a politician's behavior is a response to his or her office goals. As an office-seeker, a person would evaluate the opportunities in the political structure and engage in political acts appropriate to gaining office. Schlesinger distinguishes among discrete, static, and progressive types of ambition. A politician is categorized as having *discrete* ambition when he or she expresses no intention to run for any office after the current term. If an official intends to run for the same office but not for higher office, then he or she is categorized as having *static* ambition. An official is labeled as having *progressive* ambition when he or she indicates a desire to run for higher office. In this typology, a public official who has low or no progressive ambition may have static or discrete ambition, which is different from being apathetic or having no interest in public service. Some elected officials, especially those serving at the local level, may be low in progressive ambition and, hence, regarded negatively by some political observers and scholars who regard self-advancement on a career ladder as a positive normative value. Yet, the public service of these officials may be far more essential to the conduct of democratic politics than conventionally acknowledged, as we explain in Chapter 2.

To what extent the elected officials of color in the Gender and Multicultural Leadership (GMCL) National Survey report a motivation reflecting personal ambition as a reason for running for office the very first time? From the survey results, the answer would seem to be: hardly ever. Virtually all of those surveyed gave reasons for running other than those associated with personal ambition, defined as a quest for power or personal/career advancement, or a desire to "get ahead" through or within an elective position. Just 3 percent included personal ambition among their reasons, but, even when the respondents did, it was embedded among other reasons.

A Black male city councilmember from upstate New York, for example, said, "*There are the issue[s] that are important to the community and those were the driving force, but I think I was interested before those issues, so a mixture of personal ambition and a desire to change the way things are. Desire to make a statement by running as a young student of color; I felt that by putting myself out there was something I wanted to do.*" Examples of personal ambition like this one were, for the most part, quite unambiguous – although, again, representing one among a variety of reasons. A Black male county official in Louisiana responded, "*Personal ambition.*" This was his second response, however, after, "*Concern for local improvement.*" His third was very general but on the altruistic side: "*Being serviceable. Service to mankind.*" A Latina city councilmember from Texas said, "*I wanted to be the first woman elected to the water board, and I was,*" followed by, "*I wanted to be a part of the community, and I thought that would be a good place to start.*" An Asian American female school board member first talked about her prior involvement with the PTA, then said, "*As an Asian American to be visible also as a model for young people,*" followed by "*Personal goals and an interest.*"

Racial differences were not significant and, although the gender differences were modestly significant ($p < .1$), the numbers and percentages are extremely small: just 3 percent of men compared to less than 2 percent of women gave such a reason. And, although Black men were statistically more likely than their female counterparts to give a response indicating personal ambition as the reason they ran for office, the percentages are so small that they should be taken with a great deal of caution.

There was some variation by level of office, with county supervisors/commissioners the highest at 3.7 percent; municipal board members next at 3 percent, and school board members at 2 percent. State legislators, at less than 1 percent, were the least likely to say that ambition was among the most important reasons to run for their first office. Of note is the finding that none of the state senators in our survey gave a reason reflecting personal ambition as a reason for running for office the very first time.

Progressive Ambition and Subsequent Runs for Higher-Level Offices

Besides examining the extent to which personal ambition plays a role in the initial decision to run, we also looked at elected officials' *progressive ambition* (i.e., whether they planned to run for a higher-level office in the future). When each respondent was asked how likely she or he would run for a higher level office in the future (using a scale of 0 to 10), the mean score for state senators (4.77) is found to be surprisingly lower than that of state representatives (5.17) and both are not much higher than that of city/town councilors (4.71).

From our discussion in Chapter 4 and the previous section, we suspect that the link for women between a statement/expression of progressive ambition (likelihood in 2006–2007 of running in the future) and subsequent actions (i.e., actually running for higher level office, as of 2014) may be weaker than heretofore understood. To explore the nature of ambition and paths to office, we supplemented data from the original survey with data collected in 2014 from public records to determine how many elected officials surveyed in 2006–2007 did later run for higher office.

The initial tally by gender shows that women state representatives were somewhat more likely than their male counterparts to have run for a higher-level office between the time of the survey and 2014 (regardless of whether they won or lost): 35 percent of the women compared to 27.8 percent of the men. This is despite the fact that, just seven years earlier, their mean scores of the likelihood of such a run in the future was lower than that of men: 4.76 to 5.39 on a scale of 0 to 10. For state senators of color, we see a reverse pattern: seven years earlier, women at this level, on average, were more likely than men to say they might run for higher office in the future (mean likelihood for women was 4.92 compared to 4.67 for men); but many more men than women at this level actually did run for higher office. Three men ran for lieutenant governor; one, David Ige, was elected in 2014 to serve as governor of the State of Hawaii; and another three men ran for the US Congress. In contrast, just one woman state senator ran for higher office in an unsuccessful bid for secretary of state.

When we analyze the data by race*gender, we see striking differences by race at both the state legislative and municipal levels of government. Six in ten Asian American state legislators – but just two in ten of Blacks at this level – ran for higher office in the eight years since they were first interviewed for the GMCL National Survey (Table 5.1). American Indians and Latinos/as are in the middle at three in ten. Although gender differences in the case of Latinas and Asian Americans seem relatively large, there are no statistically significant gender gaps within each race.

A similar pattern exists among municipal officeholders (see Table 5.2): Asian American municipal officials were more than twice as likely to have run for higher office between 2007 and 2014: 32.6 percent compared to Blacks (14.0 percent) and Latinos (13.7 percent). Our findings at the municipal level also suggest Latino and Black municipal officials who run for higher office might be equally likely to be women as men, whereas Asian American men are much more likely than their female counterparts to have run for higher level office.[1]

Beyond Political Ambition

However fascinating this exploration of political ambition among elected officials of color, ultimately we concur with Carroll and Sanbonmatsu (2013, 42) that "Ambition theory may not be an adequate framework for

---

[1] Because we gathered these data from public records, including Internet searches, the results may understate the frequency of an official running for office; we thank Julia Marin Hellwege for her assistance with these searches.

TABLE 5.1. *Progressive Ambition among State Legislators of Color, by Race and Gender*

	American Indian			Asian American			Black			Latino/a		
	All	Female	Male	All	Female	Male	All	Female	Male	All	Female	Male
Ran for higher office (%)	29.4	28.6	30.0	61.1	50.0	64.3	19.7	18.2	21.1	30.8	50.0	24.1
N	(17)	(7)	(10)	(18)	(4)	(14)	(71)	(33)	(38)	(39)	(10)	(29)

Note: Entries are percents, with N in parentheses, of state legislators who ran for higher office between the end of the survey in 2006–2007 and 2014. Differences by race are significant at $p < .0001$; gender differences within race are not significant.

Source: GMCL Project, 2014, using data gathered from public records, including news reports and officials' websites.

TABLE 5.2. *Progressive Ambition among Municipal Officials, by Gender and Race*

	Asian American			Black			Latino/a		
	Female	Male	All	Female	Male	All	Female	Male	All
Ran for higher office (%)	28.6	34.5	32.6	12.1	13.7	14.0	30.8	7.9	13.7
(N)	(4)	(10)	(14)	(4)	(8)	(12)	(4)	(3)	(7)
If Yes, ran for …									
Mayor	2	2	4	3	6	9	2	2	4
County supervisor/ commissioner	1	1	2	0	1	1	0	1	1
State representative	1	3	4	1	0	1	2	0	2
State senator	0	1	1	0	0	0	0	0	0
US Congress	0	3	3	0	1	1	0	0	0
N (sample)	14	29	43	36	50	86	13	13	38
N (total municipal)	14	29	43	158	214	372	53	164	217

Note: Entries are percents of municipal officials who ran for higher office between the end of the survey in 2006–2007 and 2014, and *N*'s, for those who did, show the offices they ran for. Differences by race are significant at $p < .0001$; "Yes" does not include mayors rotating in or chosen from within the city council, only those who were elected on a popular ballot in a mayoral election contest. *N* for Asians = All Asian municipal officials surveyed in 2006–2007; *N* for Blacks and Latinos = random sample at 23 percent of the total in the survey for each group.

Source: GMCL Project, 2014.

understanding how individuals decide to run for office...." They point to other factors such as candidate recruitment and note that "A community concern or issue may attract a citizen's attention, spur activism, and eventually lead to a bid for elective office" even for those who had not thought about, nor planned for, such a run. We discussed the motivations for running reported by elected officials of color in Chapter 4, and turn now to the fact that, politically ambitious or not, planned or not, those who run for office need to draw on a wide range of social and political experiences in their election campaigns.

For the discussion that follows, we propose that a number of indicators of civic and political engagement may be linked to the social and political capital an individual accumulates that can be useful in running for an elective office and merits empirical scrutiny. First is the level of community engagement, as measured by length of residence in their district as well as reported activism in community or neighborhood organizations. Second are the connections and experiences that come from working with election campaigns and political parties. Third is the role of civic organizations such as business groups, faith-based organizations, and PTAs/PTOs. Fourth are organizations most directly associated with political causes such as civil rights, labor unions, and women's rights.

COMMUNITY EMBEDDEDNESS

As can be seen in Table 5.3, Blacks, Latinos/as, and American Indians report living in their communities significantly longer, on average, than Asians American elected officials. That said, on this measure of community embeddedness, all four racial groups report having lived, on average, for decades in their communities. With a mean of thirty-one years, elected officials of color are similar, therefore, to officials in general. In his study of municipal officials, Svara (2003, 9) finds that the average number of years that council members have lived in the cities they represent is thirty-three years.

If, as we find, there are no significant differences by gender on how long they had lived in their communities before running for office, we did find some support that women of color are more active in community and/or neighborhood organizations than their male counterparts overall (see Table 5.4). Entries in this table also show that the greatest differences are by race, with Blacks significantly more likely than individuals of other groups to report a high degree of community activism. Whereas an intersectional analysis shows that differences by gender *within* race are

TABLE 5.3. *Ties to Community: Years of Residence, by Race*

Race	Mean Years
Black (N = 718)	32.9
Latino/a (N = 507)	32.0
American Indian (N = 24)	31.9
Asian American (N = 94)	22.7

Source: GMCL National Survey, 2006–2007; $p < .0001$.

neither large nor statistically significant, we find racial differences among women of color to be significant and large – with Black women having the highest level of community/neighborhood activism, followed by that of Asian American women, Latina women, and American Indian women.

Connections: Links between Political and Social Capital

Generally we think of political capital as the influence elected officials exert as politicians. Jacobs (2011, 1), for example, writes that "having political capital is having leverage to get things done." According to Flora and Flora (2008, 144), it consists of "organization, connections, voice, and power." In Chapter 3, we documented the impact of human capital resources, including those coming from being raised in a political family. Here, we examine the officials' own social and political backgrounds prior to running for office. Their experiences contribute to their social capital by building connections that may serve them well in running for office, not just for getting things done once elected. The questions we explore include: How active were they in election campaigns and/or with political parties? Did they work as a staffer for an elected official prior to running for the first time? Did they hold an appointed office? The role of these connections link this aspect of political capital to the resources embedded in one's social capital.

How much are political women and men of color engaged in political activities prior to running? Carroll and Sanbonmatsu (2013, 34), for example, state from their 1981 and 2008 surveys that women were significantly "more likely than their male counterparts to have worked both on the campaign of a candidate...and on the staff of an elected official" and to have "been active in their political parties." Respondents to the GMCL National Survey of 2006–2007 seem to be quite different (see Table 5.5): there is no significant difference, for example, between

TABLE 5.4. *Activism in Community/Neighborhood Organizations*

Identity Group	Mean
Gender	
Women (*N* = 503)	7.49
Men (*N* = 847)	7.16
Sig. by gender:	$p < .05$
Race	
Black (*N* = 721)	7.83
Asian American (*N* = 95)	7.07
American Indian (*N* = 23)	6.61
Latino/a (*N* = 511)	6.58
Sig. by race:	$p < .0001$
Race*Gender	
Black women (*N* = 304)	7.91
Black men (*N* = 417)	7.77
Latina women (*N* = 158)	6.86
Latino men (*N* = 353)	6.46
Asian American women (*N* = 31)	6.97
Asian American men (*N* = 64)	7.13
American Indian women (*N* = 10)	6.20
American Indian men (*N* = 13)	6.92
*Sig. by race*gender:*	$p < .001$
Sig. by gender within race:	n.s.

Note: Entries are mean levels of community activism on a scale of 0 to 10, where 0 is not at all active and 10 is extremely active.

Source: GMCL National Survey, 2006–2007; *N* = 1,359.

women and men of color on any of these measures. Because Carroll and Sanbonmatsu's study is on state legislators, we carried out additional analysis and discover that, even when controlling for level of office (not shown), there is no gender difference for state legislators or any office on prior activities such as having worked on election campaigns, served as staff of an elected official, or been active in the political parties.

Race, on the other hand, is significantly associated with the degree of political experience elected officials of color bring to their election contests. When asked how active they were before running for the first elective office, Blacks overall report the highest levels of working on election campaigns and being active in political parties of all the racial groups, and the mean level of their activism in election campaigns is significantly larger for Black men than it is for Black women (see Table 5.5). Gender gaps among elected officials in other minority groups are smaller and not statistically significant.

The same table also shows that having held a position as a staff member of an elected official prior to running for office did not turn out to play an important role in the trajectories of elected officials of color, with only about one in ten reporting this political experience. And, contrary to Carroll and Sanbonmatsu's (2013) findings, there was no difference by gender alone, nor by race*gender overall on this measure. Blacks were significantly more likely than Asians and Latinos/as to having served as staff, but American Indians, at 20.8 percent, were the most likely.

In contrast to serving as staff, about half of officials of color had held some appointed office prior to their first election contest. Table 5.5 shows that men of color were 4.5 percentage points more likely to have held appointed office prior to running than women of color. Larger gender differences were found between Asian American men and women and Black men and women (54.3 percent compared to 47.2 percent, respectively).

Party Involvement and Support: A Closer Look

In Chapter 4, we demonstrated that virtually none of the elected officials of color we surveyed ran for office the first time because they had been recruited by a major political party. When it comes to the degree of involvement in political parties – and party support – it is important to consider the fact that, like US officials in general (Svara 2003; Wright 2008),[2] the vast majority of elected officials of color (73.1 percent) in the GMCL National Survey ran in nonpartisan election contests.

In their study of state legislators, Carroll and Sanbonmatsu (2013, 57) acknowledge as well the nonpartisan nature of many races, especially at the local level, and note that "party sources were less influential for bids for local and county office than for state legislative bids." Our survey shows that, although there is no gender difference overall in the mean activity level in political parties, women of color who are running in partisan elections show a significantly higher level of engagement in political party activities than those in nonpartisan races: 6.07 to 5.33 out of a scale of 0 to 10 ($p < .05$).

Women in partisan elections also report receiving more party support: 8.11 (on a scale of 0 to 10) on average compared to 7.46 for those in nonpartisan races ($p < .05$). The difference for men of color in partisan versus nonpartisan elections is larger, but is significant for level of

[2] According to Wright (2008, 13), "More than three fourths of municipal elections and about half of all U.S. elections use the nonpartisan ballot."

TABLE 5.5. *Political Experience Prior to Running for Elected Office, by Gender, Race, and Race*Gender*

	Involved in Election Campaigns (Mean)	Involved in Political Parties (Mean)	Served as Staff (Percent)	Held Appointed Office (Percent)	# Appointed Offices Held (Mean)
Gender					
Women	5.58	5.65	13.1	49.0	1.06
Men	5.78	5.71	12.3	53.5	1.12
Sig. by gender:	n.s.	n.s.	n.s.	$p < .1$	n.s.
Race					
Black	6.21	6.33	14.8	51.4	1.14
Latino/a	5.17	5.08	9.4	51.2	1.02
Asian American	4.75	4.11	11.6	57.9	1.14
American Indian	5.67	5.54	20.8	54.2	1.33
Sig. by race:	$p < .0001$	$p < .0001$	$p < .05$	n.s.	n.s.
Race*Gender					
Black women	5.74	6.11	14.1	47.2	1.04
Black men	6.56**	6.48	15.2	54.3*	1.21[†]
Latina women	5.39	5.15	10.8	52.6	1.10
Latino men	5.07	5.06	8.8	50.6	0.99
Asian American women	4.84	3.94	12.9	46.7	1.00
Asian American men	4.70	4.19	10.9	63.1[†]	1.20
American Indian women	5.90	4.50	20.0	50.0	1.20
American Indian men	5.50	6.29	21.4	57.1	1.43

Significance by gender within race: [†]$p < .1$, *$p < .05$, **$p < .01$, ***$p < .0001$.

Note: Entries are means or percents for experiences of elected official prior to first bid for office; means for election campaigns and political parties are on a scale of 0 to 10, where 0 means not at all involved and 10 means extremely involved; percents of "served as staff" or "held appointed office" are those who responded yes.

Source: GMCL National Survey 2006–2007, $N = 1,359$.

activity only in political parties (6.22 to 5.25), not for party support. The only race*gender interaction that is significant is on the measure of support from own party for Latina women in partisan campaigns (8.39 to 7.18, $p < .1$). Asian American men also showed a significant difference, but it was based on just one man in a partisan and thirty-seven in nonpartisan races.

CIVIC ENGAGEMENT

Although some political theorists consider the term "civic engagement" too vague and difficult to operationalize, its key elements – political participation, social connectedness, associational membership, voluntarism – are deeply embedded in the cornerstone of American democracy (Berger 2009, 335). Nowhere is this more true than in the backgrounds of candidates for elected office. Engagement in civic organizations not only helps a prospective candidate build social networks, but it also provides a good training ground for honing political skills necessary for candidates to navigate the campaign trail. Furthermore, our prior research using multivariate regression shows that "being involved with civic organizations or groups may significantly facilitate one's likelihood for seeking a higher office," all else being equal (Lien et al. 2008, 16).

As previously noted in Table 5.4, activism in community/neighborhood organizations serves as an important dimension of involvement for these elected officials of color. When examining an expanded set of activities, as shown in Table 5.6, on average, Blacks report a greater degree of civic engagement than any other racial group, and these differences are highly significant. They are almost twice as likely to be involved in faith-based and civil rights organizations than Latinos and Asian Americans. Furthermore, other than labor unions, women of color overall report higher levels of engagement in all categories than men, although the sizes of the difference are neither large nor significant – with the noteworthy exceptions of PTA/PTO and women's organizations.

Women are also somewhat more likely to be engaged in faith-based organizations, but the difference is not as large, whereas for the other categories, the degree of gender significance is much higher. The findings by gender are not dissimilar to those reported by Carroll and Sanbonmatsu (2013, 55), who find: "Women were somewhat less likely than men to be involved in professional or business groups and labor organizations, and ...somewhat more likely than men to be active in children and youth organizations." They also anticipate our finding: "The most dramatic

TABLE 5.6. Civic Engagement, by Race, Gender, and Race*Gender

	Business Groups	Labor Unions	PTA/Os	Faith-based Organizations	Civil Rights Organizations	Women's Organizations
Race Sig. between groups:	$p < .0001$	$p < .001$	$p < .0001$	$p < .0001$	$p < .0001$	$p < .0001$
Black	5.35	3.28	6.68	6.24	6.94	4.22
Latino/a	4.47	2.66	5.36	3.92	3.26	2.57
Asian American	4.38	2.04	5.08	3.08	3.17	2.99
American Indian	4.22	2.13	6.46	4.29	5.25	2.74
Gender Sig. by gender alone and by gender within each racial group: $^{\dagger}p < .1$, $^{*}p < .05$, $^{**}p < .01$, $^{***}p < .0001$						
Women	3.4	2.7	6.9***	5.3†	5.4	5.6***
Men	3.2	3.1†	5.6	5.0	5.2	2.2
Race*Gender						
Black women	5.38	3.10	7.20**	6.42	6.71	6.31***
Black men	5.33	3.41	6.31	6.11	7.11	2.68
Latina women	4.18	2.04	6.46***	3.80	3.42	4.46***
Latino men	4.59	2.94**	4.87	3.97	3.19	1.72
Asian American women	4.07	2.03	6.29*	2.90	3.29	5.00***
Asian American men	4.53	2.05	4.50	3.17	3.11	2.02
American Indian women	4.00	2.90	7.20	4.40	5.20	4.44*
American Indian men	4.38	1.54	5.93	4.21	5.29	1.64

Note: Entries are means on a scale of 0 to 10, where 0 means not at all involved and 10 means extremely involved in activities, with each of the types of groups before the respondent first ran for elected office.
Source: GMCL National Survey 2006–2007; N = 1,359.

difference is that women ... were much more likely than their male counterparts to participate actively in women's organizations."

Although most researchers in the field of women in politics report gender differences in civic engagement and may point to the "women's movement" and the "year of the woman" as central contributing forces for the increase in women's political representation, missing from many of these narratives is the role of social movements in the socialization of women elected officials of color. Following our earlier exploration of the apparent contradiction between multiple forms of oppression and the degrees of political success for women of color – especially Black women (see Chapter 3) – it is wise to consider Darling's (1998, 153) perspective, that is, that the very struggle for freedom against sexism and racism "occupied much of black women's organizing work in the decades preceding the civil rights movement. Black women had to empower themselves to challenge many constructed forms of privilege and morality to create something emancipating and self-affirming." According to Darling (1998, 153), "Many African–American women have perceived their subordination and oppression as warranting a personal commitment to challenge and transform black institutions and American society." And, in words that may resolve the apparent contradiction, "Black women's sense that attainment of political office was possible for them came out of the activism and organizing that preceded it."[3] Similar observations and sentiments can also be found in Manuel (2006), Springer (1999), and Williams (2001).

The extent of this activism is borne out by data in Table 5.6 and in Figure 5.1. As shown, Black women lead the way among women of color on all these measures – and have higher mean scores than all the men in all categories (except Black men's activity levels in labor unions and civil rights organizations; even there, however, the within-race difference is not statistically significant).

Role of Black Sororities and Fraternities

Returning to Table 5.6, of particular note are the quite large and significant differences among women of color in their levels of activism in

---

[3] In this quote, Darling references Baxter and Lansing (1983) and Githens and Prestage (1977).

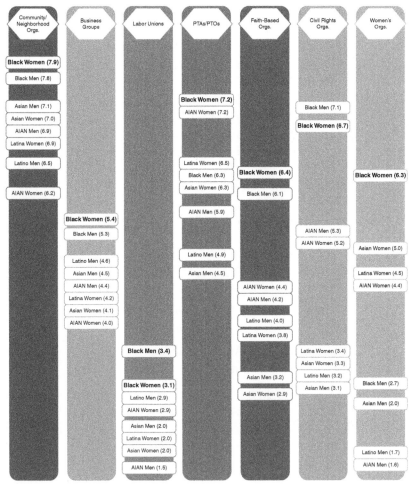

FIGURE 5.1 Civic activism of elected officials of color: Rankings by race*gender. *Note*: Entries are mean scores, which range from 0 ("not at all involved") to 10 ("extremely involved"); AIAN refers to American Indian/Alaska Native. Differences by race among women are significant at $p < .001$. *Source*: GMCL National Survey 2006–2007. $N = 1,359$.

women's organizations: the mean score can be as high as 6.3 for Black women and as low as 4.4 for American Indian women. Less surprising is how far down the chart are men of color. Among the many historical markers of civic engagement for Black women is the role of the women's club movement and Black sororities, which were as Darling (1998, 152) points out, the "work of the black women's club movement and ... the work of social action gospel women activists, especially in the Baptist denominations in the South, and activist sororities." Giddings (1988) earlier wrote that Black sororities were important leadership training grounds for Black women. What our analysis suggests is that Black Greek-letter Organizations (BGOs) have been as important, if not even more important, for Black male elected officials as their female counterparts – even in the South. These gender differences among Blacks are, however, neither large nor statistically significant. Furthermore, among all measures of activism, sororities and fraternities were reported by the respondents to be the least engaged civic organizations, next to that of labor unions (see Figure 5.1).

As Kimbrough (1995, 66) notes, "Celebrated women achievers such as Mary McLeod Bethune, Shirley Chisholm, Cardiss Collins, and Lena Horne can be counted among the members of Black sororities...."[4] At the same time, Kimbrough also states, "Distinguished civic, political, educational, and business leaders such as Martin Luther King, Jr., Thurgood Marshall, Jesse Jackson, Bill Cosby [*sic*], A. Phillip Randolph, and others fill the ranks of Black fraternities" (ibid.).

Social Movements and Adult Socialization: A Multicultural and Immigrant Perspective

Whereas Black women do take the lead in civic activism among elected officials of all other groups, we would be remiss in ignoring other contributing factors and other racial groups. The scores for activism in civil rights organizations, for example, should be viewed with some caution. First, a considerable literature exists attesting to the centrality of Black women as civil and voting rights workers (see, among others, Darling 1998, 153). Second, question wording may have suppressed reported activism by racial groups other than Blacks/African Americans: "*How active were you in the Civil Rights Movement?*" would not, for example, capture Latino/a activism in the Chicano Movement nor American Indians in the American Indian Movement (AIM) or sovereignty organizations. Finally, other forces, including other social movements such as those against the Vietnam War, point to the important role of adult socialization.

Mazie Hirono is the US senator representing the state of Hawaii (and the only woman of color serving in that body). In 2009, she participated

---

[4] Kimbrough ends his quote referencing Freeman and Witcher (1988) and Mills (1990).

in a panel at the National Archives in Washington, DC, that focused on women's diverse paths to political leadership. Her remarks clearly point to her mother as a source of strength, but in a way that suggests going against Asian cultural traditions: for her mother, the strength was in divorcing her husband and coming to the United States. In a 2009 interview she says, "I turned to politics when I was going to college, during the Vietnam War. I became politicized."[5] Adult resocialization – and engagement in social movements– may have as big an impact as pre-migration family socialization for immigrants.

ROLE OF THE ELECTORAL STRUCTURE

So far, we have focused on the political experiences of male and female elected officials of color drawing on their own perspectives of their first election campaigns. We consider now the *contours* of the opportunity structure or the contextual and structural conditions within which these officials ran for and were elected to office. In Chapter 4 we suggested that the opportunity structure may be a more flexible and effective concept than the pipeline notion to achieve our purpose of deconstructing a very complex phenomenon.

We have examined the importance of contextual factors such as the semiformal civic institutions linking government and the people as well as political parties, interest groups, community organizations, and professional associations. In the following sections, we explore the possible impacts of elements in the electoral structure such as the system of elections and legislative term limits. We subsequently discuss factors that shape the campaign environment such as candidate status, campaign competitiveness, and partisan elections from the perspectives of elected officials of color themselves. Candidates' perceptions of the political campaign environment due to their racial and gendered identities is the last topic for discussion in this chapter.

There is a long line of research looking into the possible impacts of electoral structure on electoral fates. Scola (2006, 2014), for example, studies the presence of women in state legislatures and points to the importance of various structural variables that explain the proportions for women legislators overall, for white women, and for women of color

---

[5] Hirono made these remarks at a panel discussion organized by the Center for Women in Politics and Public Policy and the National Archives: "Big Strides, Diverse Paths: Women's Journeys to Political Leadership." Washington, DC: National Archives, March 5, 2009. A video of the event is available on request.

legislators across the states. The variables she considers important include size of minority population, political ideology, political culture, and percent of professional women. In the end, none of these factors seems to be as important as state per capita income and accessiblity of single-member districts (Scola 2014). Nevertheless, much of the literature is segmented either by a singular focus on women (who are mostly White) or on Blacks and Latinos (who are mostly male). Largely missing from the literature is a systematic understanding of elected officials situated at the intersection of race and gender. Moreover, scholars seem to disagree on whether and how much political-institutional structure and social-political context matter for the election of political minorities to subnational offices such as state legislatures, city halls, county boards or commissions, and local school boards. In the text that follows, we begin with a review of literature on the impacts of single-member and majority-minority districts, followed by an analysis of the GMCL survey data. We hope to help settle some disputes in prior research with our multioffice, multistate, multiracial, and bigender data for elected officials of color nationwide.

Are Single-Member or Multimember Districts Better?

As discussed in Chapter 1, the rise of majority–minority districts following the enactment of the 1965 Voting Rights Act created opportunities for the election of people of color. Whereas past research tends to suggest that majority–minority, single-member districts (SMDs) help minority candidates, it is the Black male and Latino male candidates who seem to benefit most. Multimember districts (MMDs), on the other hand, tend to benefit women, mostly White women. Some other research, however, finds Black women to benefit from both the SMD and the MMD systems. In addition, although the *initial* creation of such districts may help Black women and men, the authors suspect that majority–minority districts with a Black male incumbent may have the more long-term effect of depressing the political representation of women of color.

Welch (2008) notes that one of the most consistent findings in this stream of research has been that women are more likely to experience electoral success in systems that facilitate proportional representation. Pritchard (1992) finds that when Florida changed its electoral rules for the state legislature in 1982 from MMD to SMD, the numbers of Black and Hispanic men in the state legislature increased considerably. Although Anglo, Black, and Latina women gained seats as well, Pritchard attributes this gain mostly to National Organization of Women (NOW) activities. Rule (1992) and Saint-Germain (1992) likewise provide evidence at the state level that MMD benefits the election of women. Darcy, Hadley, and Kirksey's (1993) study of the political representation of African Americans at the state and local levels concludes that the underrepresentation of Blacks is due almost exclusively to the underrepresentation of Black women and that women are more likely to run successful campaigns in MMD systems than SMD systems. Suspecting the potential interactive effects of demographic and electoral contexts, Darcy, Welch, and Clark (1994) argue that MMD systems may help improve the representation of Black women, without hurting the representation of Blacks in general, if they are in places where there is a significant African American population.

At local levels of elective office, SMD systems appear to work against women candidates as well. MacManus (1996, 67–68) observes that counties using the at-large election method have higher proportions of women board members than those electing board members from SMD systems; counties with mixed elections have the highest proportions of Black officials. Vengroff, Nyiri, and Fugiero's (2003) cross-national comparison of meso-level legislative bodies in 29 countries lends further support to the argument that as the proportionality of the electoral system increases, so too does the representation of women on those bodies. However, in a rare study on the election of Asian Americans to city councils, Alozie (1992) analyzes the 1986 International City/County Managers Association (ICMA) data and finds district and mixed election systems to not differ markedly from the at-large plan in the opportunities they grant for Asian Americans. Geron and Lai's (2002, 72) study may provide a possible explanation for this observation. Compared to the Latinos in their study who overwhelmingly run in districts where Latinos constitute a majority of the population, Asian American voters have limited electoral presence in most electoral districts. Unable to rely on population density, Asian American candidates must possess cross-racial appeals to win enough votes. Hence, the authors suggest that Asians and Latinos at all levels of government may need different pathways to political incorporation.

More recently, Trounstine and Valdini (2008) test the effects of electoral systems on representation by analyzing surveys conducted by the ICMA sent to city managers in 1986, 1992, 1996, and 2001. More than seven thousand cities are included in the sample and the dependent variable in the author's regression analysis is the proportion of Black, Latino, and female members on the city council. The authors find that the effects of electoral systems are not constant across all people of color, nor are they constant across gender. District elections facilitate the election of minorities and are a nominal detriment to women, but the key factor in getting African Americans elected is the proportion of their population. The same is true for Latinos, though the effect is weaker. This study also demonstrates that women do better in at-large elections at the municipal level (Trounstine and Valdini 2008, 561), though the authors argue that Black men and women were the only groups in their analysis substantively and significantly affected by electoral systems. Likewise, Smith, Reingold, and Owens (2012) find that at-large elections help women running for city council but the authors caution that the effect of electoral institutions may not be as pronounced as previously suggested.

At the school board level, Welch and Karnig (1978) find Blacks do better in at-large systems, but scholarship that is more recent suggests otherwise. Robinson and England (1981) argue that at-large systems hinder Black representation and Meier and England's (1984) study of America's eighty-two largest school districts revealed that Blacks did the most poorly in at-large elections but achieved near parity in mixed or ward systems. Stewart, England and Meier's (1989) survey of large urban schools supports Meier and England's (1984) findings but adds that at-large systems reduce Black representation more than appointment systems. Arrington and Watts (1991) find Black underrepresentation in North Carolina's largely rural school boards and note that Blacks appear to fare better in district-based systems. More recently, England, Hirlinger, and Kirksey (2002) and Hess (2002) demonstrate that at-large systems are a barrier to minority representation on local school boards and that Blacks do better in district-based systems. Similarly, in their study of nineteen jurisdictions in Indian Country, McCool, Olson, and Robinson (2007) find that American Indian candidates do better when at-large election schemes are changed to SMD systems at the school board level.

Findings of Latino representation on local school boards mirror those studies focusing on African American and American Indian representation. Fraga, Meier, and England (1986) examine the effect of electoral institutions on Hispanic representation on local school boards using data from urban school districts with at least 5 percent Hispanic enrollment. They find that at-large and appointment systems work to reduce Hispanic representation on local school boards, and this remains true even after controlling for population size. Polinard, Wrinkle, and Longoria (1990) compare school districts in Texas that recently switched to districted elections with those that maintained at-large systems and find that those districts using ward elections had greater numbers of Hispanics serving on the school board than those using at-large systems. Leal, Martinez-Ebers, and Meier (2004) also investigate the impact electoral institutions have on Latino representation on local school boards but, in contrast, argue that population proportion matters. Namely, when Latinos are a minority of the population, both ward and at-large systems systematically yield Latino underrepresentation, though at-large systems may do more harm than ward systems. The authors actually find appointment systems to be the best for Latinos. When Latinos are a majority of the population, they see no difference between ward and at-large elections in their impact on Latino representation.

There have been debates over the extent to which women, White women and women of color, in particular, benefit from district elections as opposed to running for at-large seats. Also, if in a district election, there are also questions concerning who benefits most from single-member or multimember districts. Thomas (2014, 10) provides a snapshot of the intriguing situation for incumbent women in the present day:

> The increase in majority minority districts has provided new opportunities for women of color. This is, in part, responsible for why African American women and Latinas are greater proportions of their representative groups in political office than [W]hite women. On the other hand, new district maps put in place for the 2012 elections resulted in districts being redrawn to pit female legislators against other legislators, including other women. The result was a reduction in the number of incumbent women who won reelection. In some cases, such as in North Carolina, Colorado, and Georgia, evidence suggests that women legislators and women legislative leaders were disproportionately targeted....

A typology by Scola (2014, 115–116) suggests that women in general and white women specifically benefit from MMDs, whereas legislators of color and specifically men of color benefit from SMDs. Her findings suggest that type of district does not seem to contribute to the expected level of representation of women of color state legislators. Prior research in the field (e.g., Darcy, Hadley, and Kirksey 1993) suggests Black women elected officials are more likely to come from MMDs.

According to the GMCL National Survey, virtually all (97.2 percent) state legislators are from SMDs due to the fact that only ten states have districts that send two or more members to its legislative chamber, and most of the states that do are among those with relatively low percentages of people of color.[6] As noted earlier, a limitation of most research on gender,

---

[6] The states with MMDs are Arizona, Maryland, New Jersey, Washington, New Hampshire, North Dakota, South Dakota, Vermont, West Virginia, and Idaho. A few Latino state legislators are from Arizona and American Indians from South Dakota.

race, and politics is the relatively exclusive focus on state legislators or members of Congress. If we are to understand the factors that lead to the increase in women of color in elected office – and given that the majority of all elected officials serve at the local level – it is essential to examine the data for a broader range of levels of office as well as by gender and race. One might suppose that Scola's (2006, 2014) findings, for example, may be due to the fact that she does not separate out Black, Hispanic, and Asian women and focuses exclusively on women state legislators.

We find that, once one includes those elected to county, municipal, and school board offices, we see that Black elected officials are significantly more likely than Asian Americans and Latinos/as to be elected in district than at-large systems. To wit, just three in ten Blacks (31.1 percent) are elected at-large compared to half of Latinos/as (52.2 percent) and more than six in ten of Asian Americans (63.9 percent).

Women of color are somewhat less likely than men of color to report being elected to at-large seats (39.5 percent to 42.4 percent) and more likely to be elected from MMDs (24.3 percent to 18.6 percent), but the differences are only modestly significant.

Table 5.7 shows that, when looking at all levels of office, within-group gender differences are small and, again, only modestly significant. It is the cross-race differences that are much larger and highly significant.

When we look just at those who are elected to a district seat, however, we do find the majority (64.5 percent) report being elected in an SMD rather than a MMD. Furthermore, there is a significant difference by gender – and by level of office. Six in ten (59.5 percent) of women of color are in single-member districts compared to almost seven in ten (67.5 percent) of men ($p < .05$) – seemingly providing some support for Scola's (2014) findings.

Level of office makes a difference, however. It is only at the municipal level of office (i.e., city/town councilors, mayors, aldermen, and members of selectboards) that we see a significant difference by gender within the ethnoracial groups – a difference that suggests a more complex picture. As can be seen in Table 5.8, for example, there is a twelve-point spread between Black female municipal officials and their male counterparts, with women more likely than men to be from MMDs and somewhat less likely to be from SMDs ($p < .1$); keep in mind that six in ten of Black municipal officials overall are from SMDs.[7]

---

[7] Asian American women at the municipal level are much more likely than their male counterparts to be from MMDs ($p < .01$), but their numbers are small and the findings should

TABLE 5.7. *Type of Seat, All Levels, by Race and Gender*

Type of Seat	Black		Latino/a		Asian American	
	Female	Male	Female	Male	Female	Male
Single-member	42.4	47.3	27.0	31.2	20.8	21.3
Multimember	25.9	22.1	22.6	15.8	20.8	10.6
At large	31.8	30.6	50.4	53.0	58.3	68.1
N	255	366	137	298	24	47

Note: Entries are percentages of elected officials of color in each type of seat; percentages may not add up to 100 because of rounding. We do not show American Indians in this table because their numbers were too small for meaningful analysis.

Significance by race: $p < .0001$; by race*gender: $p < 0.1$.

Source: GMCL National Survey, 2006–2007.

TABLE 5.8. *Type of Seat: Municipal Officials (Elected by District), by Race and Gender*

Race	Type of District	Female	Male	Total Municipal
Black[†]	SMD	55.1 (49)	67.5 (79)	62.1 (128)
	MMD	44.9 (40)	32.5 (38)	37.9 (78)
Latino/a	SMD	50.0 (11)	62.7 (37)	59.3 (48)
	MMD	50.0 (11)	37.3 (22)	40.7 (33)
Asian American**	SMD	25.0 (1)	100.0 (8)	75.0 (9)
	MMD	75.0 (3)	0.0 (0)	25.0 (3)

Note: Entries are percentages of municipal officials of color serving in district seats, with N in parentheses. SMD is single-member district and MMD is multimember district.

[†]$p < .1$; * $p < .05$; ** $p < .01$.

Source: GMCL National Survey, 2006–2007.

The majority (58.1 percent) of county officials of color are elected in SMDs – as are most officials at this level. This finding echoes what is reported by MacManus (1996, 56) in a 1993 survey of "large" counties – that 51.6 percent of county officials are elected from SMDs.

be taken with caution; the numbers are small because, in contrast to the other racial groups, the vast majority (65 percent) of Asian American officials are elected at large.

Impact of Term Limits

Difficulties in expanding the number of women in office (Thomas 2014) has been exacerbated by legislative term limits, which restrict the number of terms an elected official can stay in that office, so as to increase rotation. For proponents, it is considered a positive feature for minorities to gain more seats in legislative chambers dominated by non-Hispanic White males. However, despite some variation across the states, Carroll and Jenkins (2001a, 2001b) find the overall number of women serving in state house seats that were term limited actually decreased. They find that when term limits on seats held by women occur amidst a drop-off in the number of women running for office, the result is fewer women in the lower chambers of statehouses. However, their study on the impact of term limits on female African American state legislators is complex. In one of two years investigated, their numbers went down in the first year and increased by one in the second year (Carroll and Jenkins 2005).

Carroll and Jenkins (2001a, 197) conclude that unless efforts are made to recruit women to run for term-limited seats, the term limit itself may be insufficient as an electoral mechanism to increase the number of women state legislators. In another study, however, they end with a more positive, albeit puzzling, conclusion: "Thus far women have fared better in term-limited seats for state senates than for state houses because of a 'pipeline' effect whereby some women representatives who have been term-limited out or who face a term-limited future have successfully taken advantage of opportunities to seek senate seats that opened up because of term limits" (Carroll and Jenkins 2001b, 1).

Drawing from Carroll and Jenkins' research, Hawkesworth and Kleeman (2001, 8–9) focus some attention on the effects of term limits on women of color:

The number of women of color serving in term-limited house seats … declined, while the number of African American and Latino men in such seats increased. Of the seven African American women who were forced out of office by term limits in 1998, only one was replaced by another African American woman; one was replaced by a white woman, and the remaining five were replaced by African American men. Of the five Latinas forced out of office by term limits, only two were replaced by Latinas; the other three were replaced by Latino men.

According to the GMCL National Survey, a sizeable number of elected officials of color are in states favorable to term limits: four in ten are in states that, at the time they were surveyed, had term-limited state legislatures. A closer look at the impact of term limits for elected officials of color shows interesting patterns by level of office as well as gender: 42.9 percent of female state legislators served in states with term limits compared to 21.1 percent of the male legislators. However, one in ten of male state representatives in our survey were in states that previously had term limits.

More puzzling is that the strongest relationship by gender is for *county officials* – where women in these positions were significantly more likely than their male counterparts to serve in states with a term-limited *state legislature*. It is unclear how the political structure – in this case of a term-limited state legislature – would lead to a gender difference for county supervisors/commissioners. One might assume that county positions are more likely to be term-limited in states that have term-limited state houses; checking against data on county term limits (Bell 2011), however, we find that 52.1 percent of *all* elected officials of color serve in states with no term limits in either the state legislature or their county. Almost a third (29.3 percent) serve where there are limits for the state house terms, but not for county supervisors/commissioners. For about one in ten there are term limits for both, and another one in ten have term limits for their county positions, but none at the state level. A further exploration finds that just 12 percent of county commissioners/supervisors serve in term-limited seats – and that the percent of female and male was identical.

THE POLITICAL CAMPAIGN: DEGREE OF COMPETITION

Similar to the issue of term limit, a candidate's incumbency status and the possible effects it has on accessing elective office and political representation have been among the most important factors thought to influence the electoral fortunes of US women and minorities. In this section, we provide a review of literature on the topic, followed by empirical evidence from the GMCL National Survey. We also report findings from another measure of the perceived degree of competitiveness in our survey – the self-reported margin of victory in the most recent general election campaign.

Campaign Status: Incumbency versus Open Seats – Past Findings

Scholars generally agree that incumbency held by non-Hispanic White men reduces the proportion of women serving on elective bodies, while open seats may facilitate their representation. Just as the initial carving out of majority–minority districts created open seats in which women of color would not have to face a male challenger, Pritchard (1992) finds that women, primarily White but also Black and Latina, actually gained seats in the Florida state legislature in 1982 despite a change that year in the election system. The author concludes that the increase in open seats, in conjunction with NOW mobilization, was responsible for the increase. Conversely, Everson (1992) finds that the reduction of seats in the Illinois state legislature, a reduction that would presumably lower the amount of open seats, coupled with a change from cumulative voting (CV) to SMD, was tied to a reduction in the number of women serving in that elective body.

In Saint-Germain's (1992) study of Arizona state legislators, nearly twice as many male incumbents ran unopposed as did female incumbents, and even long-time incumbent women generally faced challengers. Darcy, Welch, and Clark (1994) compare state legislative candidates in six states and find that men and women generally run the same kinds of campaigns. They observe that although both generally are equally likely to face an incumbent or to run for an open seat, incumbency does have a drag effect, which slows down the replacement of the male legislature. This is true despite a growth in the pool of eligible female candidates. The authors note that the drag effect of incumbency might be higher in SMD systems because candidates have an easier time developing a personal reputation with their constituents than they would under a proportional representation system. Despite the different approaches of these two studies, the implications are the same: male incumbents faced few challengers in general.

In her review of the literature, Welch (2008) maintains that there is little evidence to suggest that voters' bias against women candidates put women at a disadvantage when compared to male candidates of similar incumbency and partisan status. Paxton, Painter, and Hughes (2009) test the effects of incumbency on women's political representation using reports from the Center for American Women and Politics (CAWP) at Rutgers University on the number of women in state houses from 1982–1996 and longitudinal latent growth models. They find little evidence that incumbency has a drag effect on women replacing men in legislatures. They argue, however, that a political climate focused more on "feminine" domestic issues would benefit women at the polls; a political climate focused heavily on "masculine" foreign policy issues hurts women electorally.

At the county level, MacManus (1996) notes that female representation is more extensive where there are term limits, suggesting an incumbency drag effect. However, she reports that whether a county had partisan or nonpartisan elections, campaign contribution limits, or staggered term limits do not have much effect on the representation of women, Blacks, or Hispanics (68–70). We know little about the effect of incumbency at the school-board level. However, Welch (2008) suggests that, since the publication of the Welch and Karnig article in 1978 on the election of Blacks to big city school boards, it has been established that incumbency is a major predictor of electoral success for both men and women. The fact that most incumbents are men, then, limits the rate at which women of color across all ethnoracial groups are entering legislative offices.

It is important to note that most of the work done on incumbency has focused on male incumbents with respect to female candidates rather than White incumbents with respect to candidates of color. It may be because there are few non-White challengers to begin with, especially those who can launch credible campaigns against White male incumbents. Nevertheless, the studies presented above clearly indicate that scholars have spent most of their time focusing on women as a whole rather than investigating the effect of incumbency on the various subsets of women. What we know about the effect of incumbency is largely specific to White women and not women of color or non-White men. What can we learn from the GMCL National Survey when the experiences of women of color are at the center of analysis?

Campaign Status: Incumbency versus Open Seats – GMCL Findings

Elected officials of color in the GMCL National Survey were asked to indicate whether they ran for their current office as an incumbent, a challenger, or for an open seat in their most recent election. Results in Table 5.9 show that the majority as a whole and in each racial group ran as incumbents, and the rate is highest among Asian males. Consistent with prior research findings, male elected officials of color are generally more likely to run as incumbents than female elected officials of color.

Among those who report having to run as a challenger, Asian women stand out as having a significantly higher percentage than Asian men. Gender differences in the rate of running as challenger are not significant among Blacks or Latinos. Among those who report running in an open seat election, the percentage is much higher for Latina females than Latino males, but the reverse is true among Asians. There is no gender effect among Blacks who won elections in open seat contests.

TABLE 5.9. *Campaign Status by Race and Gender, All Levels*

	All		Black		Latino/a		Asian American	
	Women	Men	Women	Men	Women	Men	Women	Men
Ran								
as Incumbent	59.4	66.8	61.1	65.5	55.1	66.5	67.9	73.4
as Challenger	15.9	14.4	15.5	14.5	14.7	16.5	21.4	4.7
for Open Seat	24.7	18.7	23.3	20.0	30.1	17.1	10.7	21.9
	$p < .05$		n.s.		$p < .005$		$p < .05$	
N	490	838	296	414	156	346	28	64

Note: Entries are percents of elected officials of color; American Indians are included in All, but breakdown by gender is not included because their numbers are small.

Source: GMCL National Survey, 2006–2007.

Similar gender patterns within each race exist when the analysis is run by each level of office. Studying the relationship between campaign status of our respondents and their residence in states with term limits in their state legislatures (38 percent do), we see that those who reside in states with no term limits are more likely to run as incumbents, while those who reside in states with term limits are more likely to run in open seats.

Perceived Margin of Victory

Another indicator of the degree of competitiveness in the campaign environment is the margin of victory, which we asked our survey respondents to help gauge retrospectively. As shown in Table 5.10, in their most recent general election campaigns, the majority of elected officials of color in the survey reported having a margin of victory over their closest opponent by a margin of 10 percent or higher. The proportion of elected officials having the 10 percent or greater margin of victory is highest among state legislators, followed in the order of those serving respectively at the county, municipal, and school board level. It is also higher among male than female officials, except at the school board level. Conversely, the proportion of elected officials of color running unopposed or in a very competitive race with a margin of victory of less than 5 percent is higher among women than men. The only exception is among male school board officials, 15 percent of whom report running in a tight race, compared to the 8 percent among female school board officials. At the municipal level, 16 percent of women compared to 10 percent of men report having run a competitive election campaign in the most recent general election. In each level of office and for either gender, the percentage of elected officials reporting having a margin of victory that was greater than 10 percent is much higher than those reporting having run an unopposed campaign which, in turn, is generally higher than those reporting having run a tight campaign.

Viewed from the intersection of race and gender, there is no racial difference among women of color in the reported margin of victory. However, among men of color, up to eight in ten among American Indians enjoy having a 10 percent or greater margin of victory than that for Black men (66 percent) or Latino men (62 percent) and Asian men (61 percent), while a higher percentage of Asian men (16 percent) than Latino men (13 percent), Black men (6 percent), or American Indian men report having run a tight election campaign. Studying the relationship between margin of victory of our respondents and whether they hold a partisan office (34 percent

TABLE 5.10. *Margin of Victory, by Gender and Level of Office*

	All		State Legislature		County		Municipal		School Board	
	Women	Men	Women	Men	Women	Men	Women	Men	Women	Men
Less than 5%	12.4	9.8	7.7	4.5	12.2	7.9	16.1	9.5	8.7	15.1
Greater than 10%	53.4	64.0	71.2	78.7	57.1	67.3	48.0	64.5	54.0	52.5
% Ran unopposed	20.2	12.2	15.4	10.1	26.5	10.3	19.3	12.5	21.1	14.5
	$p < .0001$		n.s.		$p < .01$		$p < .005$		n.s.	
N	485	833	52	89	49	163	224	402	160	179

Note: Entries are percents of elected officials of color who reported margin of victory in the most recent general election.

Source: GMCL National Survey, 2006–2007.

do), we note that up to seven in ten among elected officials who hold a partisan office report having a 10 percent or greater margin of victory, compared to the 56 percent among those who do not hold a partisan office.

PERCEIVED DISADVANTAGES IN THE ELECTION CAMPAIGN: FEWER OBSTACLES FOR WOMEN OF COLOR?

If findings from Chapter 3 suggest that experiences of successful political women of color as a whole in our study do not support the thesis of their being doubly disadvantaged politically by their dual identity at the intersection of race and gender, does each respondent see herself as facing fewer obstacles in the initial election contest for the current office compared to other candidates? What does each man of color elected official in our survey say about institutional and attitudinal obstacles? Before asking each elected official to indicate any obstacle faced during her or his first bid for the current office as compared to other candidates, we primed each respondent with this statement: "*Some people believe that minority candidates have to overcome special obstacles when they run for elected office.*" Each respondent was then asked to respond to a battery of seven scenarios listed in Table 5.11. Each question was followed immediately by a question asking the respondent to surmise the biggest factor – whether it be his or her race or ethnicity alone, or gender alone, or the combination of the two, or something else – to explain the given response.

When asked of the obstacles faced during their first bid for their current office, a large share of respondents in the GMCL Survey agreed or strongly agreed to the statements that, compared to other candidates, they received less support from political parties (39.6 percent) and other political organizations (35.8 percent); that they faced greater scrutiny over their personal qualifications and/or electability (37.0 percent), and that they had a harder time raising money (37.1 percent) than the reverse. That said, a majority of respondents did not report experiencing disadvantages.

Gender makes a difference in that about four in ten among men of color, but only three in ten among women of color, would indicate that they received less support from political organizations other than political parties and faced greater scrutiny over their personal qualifications than other candidates. About one in eight women of color would support the statements that they received greater scrutiny over their family's background and more comments on their personal appearances than their opponents. In comparison, about two in ten among men of color would

TABLE 5.11. *Perceived Disadvantages in Election Campaign, by Race and Gender*

Agreed/strongly agreed she or he received:	Black		Latino/a		Asian American		All	
	Women (N = 286)	Men (N = 396)	Women (N = 153)	Men (N = 341)	Women (N = 28)	Men (N = 64)	Women (N = 474)	Men (N = 817)
Less support from parties	37.0	45.9**	32.3	36.1	30.8	42.7*	34.6	41.9†
Less support from other political organizations	33.4	43.0**	25.4	32.9	8.3	42.0	29.8	39.2**
Greater scrutiny on qualifications	29.3	35.4	35.9	42.5	39.3	48.4	32.1	39.8*
Harder times raising money	38.8	45.9†	29.9	27.6	29.6	31.0	35.6	37.9
Less media attention	28.1	31.5	29.2	29.5†	14.3	19.7	27.2	30.4†
Greater scrutiny on personal appearance	11.8	20.4**	13.7	17.2	14.8	15.9	12.1	17.7†
Greater scrutiny on family background	12.8	20.4**	13.4	24.0*	18.5	17.7*	12.8	21.8***
Index of Perceived Campaign Disadvantage	2.18	2.34***	2.19	2.21	2.02	2.24†	2.17	2.28**

Note: Entries for perceived disadvantage are percents of those who agreed or strongly agreed with each of the seven statements; entries for Index of Perceived Campaign Disadvantage are means of the sum of scores in the seven variables listed in the table.

†$p < .1$ *$p < .05$; **$p < .01$; ***$p < .0001$.

Source: GMCL National Survey, 2006–2007.

indicate support for the last two statements. Also, higher percentages of men of color officials reported receiving less support from parties and other political organizations, less media attention, and greater scrutiny on qualifications and their family backgrounds. They were even more likely than their female counterparts to say they received more comments on their personal appearance than that of their opponents. These gender differences hold true for the officials as a whole and for all racial groups but with varying sizes and degrees of statistical significance.

This finding that, when there *are* gender differences, men of color would perceive more disadvantages on the campaign trail than women of color may be somewhat surprising given the attention in the literature to women's campaign disadvantages. It is consistent, however, with our findings in Chapter 3 that men of color are more disadvantaged in terms of their family backgrounds (see Table 3.6) (albeit not their current personal resources: see Table 3.4), and that they overwhelmingly disagreed that women have a harder time professionally or politically (see Table 3.9). We should, therefore, not be surprised that, as shown in Table 5.11, men of color might also perceive themselves as more disadvantaged in their *election campaigns* than their female counterparts.

To explore this dynamic further, we created a Perceived Campaign Disadvantage Index by taking the average of the summed scores from responses to the seven measures listed in Table 5.11. The mean of the Perceived Disadvantage Index scores in the final row substantiates the pattern shown for the individual measures: all of the men of color perceive a higher degree of disadvantage than their opponents during their first bid for elected office; the difference is not large (2.28 for men, 2.17 for women), but it is highly significant. The largest differences by race*gender are among Blacks and Asian Americans.

Perceived Campaign Disadvantages by Level of Office

Do minority candidates running for relatively higher levels of office perceive receiving higher levels of scrutiny over their personal attributes or lower levels of support from linkage institutions (i.e., mass media, parties, and organizations that link the mass with the governing elite) than their opponents? The answer is mixed. A higher percentage of candidates for state legislative (47 percent) and county offices (42 percent) than those for municipal offices (34 percent) and local school boards (30 percent) agreed or strongly agreed that they received less support from political organizations (other than parties). A similar order of responses by level of office is found in respondents' assessment of the amount of attention from the mainstream media.

The differences by level of office are greatest when involving the subject of raising money. As high as 56 percent of candidates for state legislatures and 47 percent of candidates for county offices, compared to the 34 percent among candidates for municipal offices and 28 percent among candidates for school board would indicate their having a harder time raising money than other candidates. However, when it comes to the level of scrutiny over one's personal appearances, those for the county and municipal positions report higher percentages of such than those for the state legislatures and local school boards. Finally, level of office does not make a significant difference to these minority candidates when it comes to their perception of levels of party support or scrutiny over one's qualifications for office and family background.

Explaining Perceived Campaign Disadvantages: Is It Race or Gender or Both?

When these candidates-turned-elected-officials were probed about the main reasons why they perceived relative campaign disadvantages during his or her first bid for the current office, a much higher percentage of men than women of color would nominate race, while a much higher percentage of women than men of color would nominate the intersection of race/ethnicity and gender, as the biggest factor behind their frustration over the perceived lack of support from political parties and organizations other than parties, having a harder time raising money, getting less mainstream media coverage, and facing greater scrutiny over their qualifications, personal appearances, and family background. However, a significantly higher percentage of men than women of color also identify factors other than race and gender as the biggest ones for their facing less party support and more scrutiny over personal qualifications and appearances. Given the weight of the issue, more research is apparently needed to explore the underpinning factors to explain the distinct response patterns given by the women and men of color elected officials in our survey.

CONCLUSION

This chapter continues our exploration into state and local minority elected officials' trajectories to office. Because of the prevailing literature's possessive investment in the concept of political ambition, we begin by checking if personal ambition was the primary motivation for the respondents in the GMCL Survey to launch their first campaign for a public office. We find that nearly none said so and that there are very few differences by race or gender or office level. The situation is different when we look at the responses to the question asking their likelihood of running for higher office. We find Asian men to exert the highest level of progressive ambition at both state legislative and municipal levels. Looking beyond the issue of political ambition, we find strong evidence of minority elected officials' leveraging community-based resources as social and political capital to help launch their political careers and women of color out-participated men of color as a whole in measures of community activism, but there are few gender differences in indicators of prior political engagement. Although hardly any elected official of color received any recruitment by political parties in their virgin campaign for office, we find women of color running in partisan elections to show a higher level of engagement (and report higher level of support from parties) than their male counterparts. Turning to civic engagement, we note the outstanding engagement of Blacks, especially Black women, and we attribute this high level of engagement to the Black community's legacy of involvement in spearheading social change and find that Black sororities play a constitutive role in the political socialization of Black women.

In our exploration of the role of the electoral structure, we find that, consistent with prior literature, minority elected officials in our survey were elected more from SMDs than at-large or MMDs. Black males lead this trend, followed by Black females. However, only among municipal elected officials do we see a significant gender advantage of Black and Asian males in accessing SMD seats than their female counterparts. We find some evidence of legislative term limits having a positive impact on cracking open the opportunity structure for minority women. However, the majority of elected officials of color did not reside in states with term limits at the time of the survey. On the issue of campaign status, we note that, consistent with the prevailing literature, the majority of our respondents ran as incumbents in their most recent general election campaign and the incumbency rate is higher among males than females and especially among Asians. The majority of them, especially males and state legislators, also report having a margin of victory that is greater than 10 percent, while there is no racial gap in these patterns. Thus, while political ambition carries different meanings for racial minorities than for Whites, several key elements in the electoral structure examined in our survey show consistency in their impacts on the electoral fates of both White women and women of color.

Checking against patterns of perceived campaign disadvantages reported by women and men of color officials in our survey, we find men of color and especially Black men report the highest incidence of feeling marginalized and discriminated against on the campaign trail because of their race. Interestingly and importantly, we find that women of color who perceived themselves as being disadvantaged in the campaign trail compared to other candidates tend to attribute the mistreatment to the intersectionality of their race and gender. This finding gives us hope that women of color's greater awareness of structural intersectionality may put them in a better position to support and champion political causes that require them to play a transformative role in bridging differences and building coalitions for social and/or political change.

PART III

LEADERSHIP, GOVERNANCE, AND REPRESENTATION

6

Leadership and Governance

In the book thus far we have demonstrated the impact race and gender have had on the growth in the numbers of elected officials of color; considered their personal, familial, and political backgrounds; explored why they ran for office; and described their paths to office within a contested political landscape. In Chapter 5, we also discussed at length the campaign experiences of women and men of color holding elected office today. At various junctures, we have reminded readers that our research is not on candidates but rather on the "winners" – those who gained a seat on the governing bodies at state, county, and local levels of office. We now examine important aspects of how these elected officials – the "winners" – govern. Our point of departure is how what we mean by the term "leadership" is both gendered and raced.

As we examine various definitions and meanings of leadership, we focus especially on debates informed by feminist, womanist, and other critiques of traditional theories within the field of political science. We recognize the potential influence of "gender power" on determining who comprises America's political leaders and how they exercise leadership in their representational and governing roles (see, e.g., Duerst-Lahti and Kelly 1995; Fletcher 2004). But we also extend the notion of gender power to race power, cognizant that elected officials of color exercise leadership in a political system dominated by both male-centeredness and "Whiteness" – that is, the predominance of White men among the nation's political and governing elite.

We begin the chapter with a theoretical discussion of "positional leadership," that is, that which is exercised by those serving in formal positions of authority and influence in our political institutions. We acknowledge the gender bias feminist research has unveiled in leadership studies as we point to scholarly neglect of elected officials of color, even as they have increasingly assumed the roles of positional leaders. We also interrogate essentialist and normative assumptions from the women in politics literature that have tended to overstate differences between female and male elected officials in their style of leadership and ways of governing. Accordingly, we question the extent to which women, as elected officials, constitute "transformational leaders" in American politics, a notion advanced in studies of women (mostly White) in terms of leadership style and governance.

In a more modest way, perhaps, we seek to question transformational possibilities in the exercise of leadership and governance by elected officials of color – women and men. This chapter begins to fill out answers by adding an intersectional analysis to existing research on perceptions of gendered leadership and governance. We examine evidence of political incorporation (or marginalization) of Black, Latino/a, Asian American, and American Indian elected officials with recent data on leadership positions they hold within their governing bodies. We conclude the chapter with findings on policy leadership, exploring whether women of color believe they can make a difference on policies benefitting marginalized groups in American politics.

CONTESTED NOTIONS OF LEADERSHIP IN AMERICAN POLITICAL SCIENCE

Scholarship on leadership in American politics is voluminous, diverse, and provocative. Yet, despite a substantial body of literature, leadership remains "an elusive concept" (Bennis 1999, 18); others point to its "amorphous" nature (Duerst-Lahti and Kelly 1995; Thomas 2003). And, according to Hardy-Fanta (2002, 193), "Most studies of political leadership reflect certain assumptions about how leadership is conceptualized, who is counted as a leader, and how leadership should be studied." Varied approaches to the study of leadership, emanating from political science and business as well as other disciplines, include analyses of "specific traits, skills, styles, or personality characteristics that leaders possess" (Han 2010, 6), as well as their socialization experiences, motivations, behavior, and impact (Duerst-Lahti and Kelly 1995, 13).

Even more salient within political science and popular culture, perhaps, is the focus on *positional leadership*, whereby the term "leader" generally brings to mind those in positions of power, influence, and authority. Individuals who serve in official positions in government are de facto leaders, given their influence and authority over policymaking and political institutions. Definitions of leadership as well as the criteria for identifying leaders are, nevertheless, subjects of debate and contention, and this is nowhere truer than when considering leadership bestowed on individuals because of their positions in government. Feminist scholars have long criticized the conflation of position and leadership, as well as its gender bias; they have been joined by women of color, who add a womanist critique.

Positional Leadership: Feminist Critiques

Contending that gendered meaning is embedded in the very definition of leadership, the feminist critique of existing theory is among the most provocative challenges to notions of leadership. Scholars such as Bligh (2010, 639) point to "the *great man theories*, which were based on the assumption that the capacity for leadership is inherent – that great leaders are born, not made or developed" (emphasis in original). Under this rubric, it is men who are most likely to be identified and studied as leaders (see, e.g., Hardy-Fanta 2002, 195–196); and traits and characteristics generally associated with men and male behavior are deemed to be qualities of leaders. Hence, feminist scholars Duerst-Lahti and Kelly (1995) identify "masculinism" as an "ideology" as well as a "way of being" that firmly places leadership and leaders within a framework of patriarchy and male-centeredness.

The masculinist bias identified by feminist scholars in leadership studies derives to a great extent from the preponderance of men who hold formal positions in government; similarly, the lack of women or their relatively smaller numbers as public office holders (regardless of the level of government) has produced widespread notions that men are leaders and women are not. Gendered assumptions on positional leadership may be based on logical fallacies. Every high school student is familiar with the concept of logical conclusion: if A = B and B = C, then A = C. When applied to positional leadership:

Premise 1: Most positions are held by men.
Premise 2: Those in positions of influence = Leaders.
Logical conclusion: Men = Leaders (and Leaders = Men).

The problem with logical conclusions that are fallacious such as these lies with the fact that, although Premise 1 may not be wrong, without acknowledging the gendered reasons most positions are held by men, it is incomplete and does not cover the relevant facts necessary to argue the conclusion.

The underrepresentation of women in positions of government has generated a large body of work on gender and politics that investigates electoral structures and processes, socioeconomic variables, and attitudinal factors (especially political ambition) to explain barriers to office holding and why more men than women seek elective office (Fulton, Maestas, Maisel, and Stone 2006; Lawless and Fox 2010). Offering a macro-level analysis, McDonagh (2009, 6) points to the nature of the state itself. She contends, "The state's public policies teach voters which traits are associated with political governance and, by extension, who are suitable as political leaders. The key to women's political leadership, therefore, is a political context generated by state policies that teach voters that the traits associated with men as well as with women signify inclusion in the public sphere of political governance."

Feminist scholarship also assails positional leadership as a narrow conceptualization of political leadership overall. (For a review of feminist scholarship on political leadership, see Carroll 1984; Sjoberg 2014; Zerilli 2008.) The focus on leaders in official government positions neglects other forms of leadership, such as those that emerge through informal networks and community-based endeavors, in which women – and especially women of color – participate. Thomas (2003, 89) states, "leadership can be exerted in a wide variety of ways, informally and formally …. One need not be an elective or appointive officeholder… to be a leader, and many authors point to instances in which informal community leaders play large public sphere and political roles." Emphases on the relational aspects of being a leader can more easily accommodate women's roles as community activists and organizers. Quoting a management expert, Rosenthal (1998a, 20) observes that "the only real requirement is that 'a *leader* is someone who has *followers*'" (emphasis in original). In like manner, Han (2010, 6) offers a more inclusive definition of a leader as one who has "the ability to encourage, influence, or inspire others to act in pursuit of a common goal or agenda."

A number of scholars have explored these connections between informal and formal expressions of political leadership for women of color. In one of the few (and early) studies to conduct a statewide survey of Latina elected officials, Takash (1993, 33) challenges a contention she finds prevalent in scholarship on Latina political participation: that a relatively wide gulf exists between nonelectoral and electoral activities for Latina women. She finds instead that both nonelectoral and electoral activities are present in these women's backgrounds. Majorities of the women surveyed had experience in both community activism (61 percent) and political campaign work (68 percent) prior to their first elected or appointed position. In her study of Latino politics in Boston, Hardy-Fanta (1993) likewise finds Latina women deeply involved in grass-roots endeavors, using their personal connections to informal networks to mobilize community members to solve social problems through collective action. Rather than preclude their involvement in more traditional politics, however, their activism leads to more engagement in electoral politics, including voting and running for public office. In a similar vein, García and Márquez 2001) conclude that both traditional and community-oriented motivations spurred Latina women to be active in party politics or as candidates for political office.

Positional Leadership: Womanist Critiques and Contributions

"Womanist is to feminist as purple to lavender."
   –Alice Walker, *In Search of Our Mothers' Gardens: Womanist Prose*

Walker (1983) was the first to offer the term "womanist" as an alternative to – and critique of – traditional (White) feminism.[1] It refers to Black feminists or feminists of color who are, in her words: "Responsible. In charge. *Serious.*" Womanists are women who appreciate women's culture and strengths; and are not separatists but are rather, "Committed to survival and wholeness of entire people, male *and* female" (Walker, 1983, xi–xii; emphasis in original).

The term "womanist" is, of course, not just a linguistic alternative to "feminist" but also the result and reflection of "an internal insurgency" by women of color who, during the 1970s–1980s, fought against the "sexual politics of the previous decade only to be confronted by

---

[1] According to Walker, the term "womanist" comes: "From womanish....A black feminist or feminist of color. From the black folk expression of mothers to female children, "You acting womanish," that is, like a woman. Usually referring to outrageous, audacious, courageous, or willful behavior. Wanting to know more and in greater depth than is considered "good" for one ... [A womanist is also a] woman who loves other women sexually and/or nonsexually. Appreciates and prefers women's culture, ... and women's strength. ...Committed to survival and wholeness of entire people, male and female. Not a separatist ... Womanist is to feminist as purple to lavender" (1983, xi–xii; emphasis in original).

the feminist politics of exclusion a decade later" (Nnamaeka 2015). Nnamaeka underscores the multiple intersectionalities for women of color: "Excluded from and alienated by feminist theorizing and thinking, women of color insisted that feminism must account for different subjectivities and locations in its analysis of women, thus bringing into focus the issue of difference, particularly with regard to race and class." She provides a sweeping endorsement of how, by "weaving the separatism and black moral superiority of the black nationalist philosophy, the pluralism of the black empowerment variant, and the interrogation of white feminism, womanism seeks to give a voice, a standpoint to black women" (Nnamaeka 2015).[2]

In light of the womanist challenge – issued more than thirty years ago – it is ironic that the very literatures that seek to broaden analyses of leadership beyond men and formal politics tend to neglect the role of women of color. Scholars who have centered their work on women of color in politics fault mass attitudes, the social movement literature, and feminist scholarship for rendering "invisible" women of color who have been leaders within their own racial/ethnic group's political movements as well as the women's movement in the United States. Barnett (1993, 162–164) points to flaws in social movement scholarship, with its almost exclusive focus on "great men and elites as movement leaders." She observes, "Most of the leadership recognition and pioneering research covering the civil rights movement of the 1950s and early 1960s, in particular, has concentrated on the leading roles and charisma of elite male professionals within the Black community, such as ministers or on the resource-providing role of elite supporters outside the Black community." She remedies holes in this literature by stipulating that "Black women were much more than *followers* in the modern civil rights movement; many were also *leaders* who performed a variety of roles comparable to those of Black male leaders" (emphasis in original).

Simien (2006, 22) argues that "[b]y ignoring the fact that black women experience racism in ways different from black men and that black women have different experiences with sexism from those of white women, the group consciousness literature fails to address the unique situation of black women." Smooth (2010, 183) argues that, ultimately, there must be more receptivity in the political system, among voters and

---

[2] For more on the concept of womanism, see, for example, Allan (1995); Cannon (1988); and Hill Collins (1996).

elites, especially political parties, to accept Black women as "viable, appropriate political leaders."

Hardy-Fanta (1993) challenged the invisibility of Latina women as political actors, a common misconception in mainstream political science literature, first by reviewing the numbers in traditional political roles and then by examining the ways Latina women's politics broaden the definition of the nature of politics. She observed that the leadership of Latina political women often remains invisible even when they hold elected positions. Fifteen years later, Navarro (2008, 11) noted how women of color are still overlooked as political elites; she identifies only a handful of published works on Latina elected officials and calls attention to the many dimensions of their lives and political careers that are in need of investigation. Then as now, the failure to recognize Latina women as leaders betrays "a particular mindset: leaders must be men" (Hardy-Fanta 2002, 198). Since that time, there have been a number of important additions, including, for example, works by Fraga et al. (2006, 2008); Fraga and Navarro (2007); García et al. (2008); and Sierra (2010).

Increasingly we see scholars of Asian American politics likewise decrying the lack of attention to Asian American women's political experiences, while simultaneously challenging gender stereotypes and recognizing their leadership roles. Kawahara (2007, 18) notes:

Little scholarship exists regarding the experiences of Asian American women compared to that of European American women.... What is available has focused on topics such as familial roles and relationships, cultural values, attitudes and beliefs. Unfortunately, some popular literature and media continue to perpetuate the stereotypes of Asian American women as passive, exotic, or victims of a patriarchal 'traditional' Asian culture.... Research on leadership among Asian American women is even more sparse....Despite the continued growth of the Asian American population and the increasing diversity within this group, the rising visibility of advocacy and activism among Asian American women leaders is seldom addressed.[3]

Although small in number and fragmented by differences in ethnic origin, religion, and immigration generation, Asian American women in elective offices have had their share of the political firsts and monumental accomplishments among political women in the United States. US Representative Patsy Mink (1927–2002), for example, was the first woman of color elected to the US Congress, who has been fondly

[3] See also Chu 1989; Kawahara, Esnil, and Hsu 2007; Lien and Swain 2013; Lim 2014; for a discussion of feminism and Asian American women, see Chow 1987.

remembered for her leadership role shepherding the passage of the Title IX Amendment of the Higher Education Act that aims to ensure equal rights for girls and women of all origins in educational opportunities. In honor of her lifelong campaign to advance women's rights, Title IX was renamed the Patsy Mink Act a few days before her funeral.

It has been more difficult to assess American Indian women's leadership roles as elected officials because research on their activism is closely connected to tribal politics, rather than non-tribal elected leadership. That said, a number of scholars point to the importance of American Indian women's activism historically (see, for example, Ford 1990; Jaimes 1992, 1997); on environmental issues (see, for example, Prindeville and Bretting 1998; Prindeville 2004a); and on issues of sovereignty (Prindeville 2004b). Diane-Michele Prindeville compares the demographic characteristics and "leadership trajectories" of American Indian and Hispanic grassroots activists and public officials[4] and reports that all of the American Indian women leaders she studied said they felt politically efficacious (Prindeville 2002, 2003). She also writes, "Tremendous variation exists in the politics and governance of the over 550 federally recognized American Indian tribes. For example, women are barred from participating in tribal politics in most Pueblo Nations, yet in other Southwestern tribes they are political leaders" (Prindeville 2004b, 101).

Positional Leadership Revisited

This book pursues positional leadership as a central research concern for a number of reasons, notwithstanding scholarly criticism of its masculinist features. First, there is a paucity of data or analysis on elected officials that includes women and men from multiple racial/ethnic groups; few studies that exist are national in scope; and few include multiple levels of office. Despite their increasing numbers and importance, leadership based on positions in government among people of color – women and men – remains understudied in political science. The neglect of women of color in the literature on political elites with this level of detail is especially glaring.

Second, the distinct nature and significance of positional leadership to the practice of democratic politics and, ultimately, to the quality of

---

[4] Twenty-six of the 60 participants in her study were indigenous women who belonged to 17 Indian nations; the public officials in her research include elected and appointed officials. Her research focuses exclusively on New Mexico and other areas in the Southwest.

life experienced by people of color, cannot be denied. Indeed, two of the leading feminist critics of masculinism in the study of politics acknowledge the influence of positional leadership. Duerst-Lahti and Kelly (1995, 13) state, "...merely holding a position of public authority places one in a leadership role in governance by virtue of positional power alone. Political leadership occurs through formal aspects of government and a multitude of ways surrounding formal governing."

Recognizing the potential power of positional leadership does not preclude understanding its limitations as well. There is, unfortunately, ample evidence of the limits of influence for elected officials who are not White men. Research by Hawkesworth (2003, 2006) for example, suggests that, even on reaching one of the highest levels of elected office, women of color in Congress often voice frustration over their sense of marginalization. She finds that "Congresswomen of color provided narratives that differed markedly from those of their white counterparts. African American Congresswomen, in particular, related tales of insult, humiliation, frustration, and anger that distinguished their responses from those of their white counterparts" (Hawkesworth 2003, 533). Further discussion of institutional constraints on the full incorporation of elected leaders of color, especially women, appears toward the end of this chapter.

Third, in seeking to fill the scholarly gap on elected officials of color, we are cognizant of the role of informal leadership among communities of color. Indeed, an important body of literature draws attention to the participation of women of color in nonelectoral politics, such as labor union organizing, community-based organizations, and protest activities (see, e.g., Bookman and Morgen 1987; Cohen, Jones, and Tronto 1997; Hardy-Fanta 1993, 2002; Mora and Del Castillo 1980; Pulido 2006; Sierra and Sosa-Riddell 1994; Wong 2006; Wong et al. 2011). Rather than overlook informal leadership, we seek to investigate more systematically its connections to women in formal office holding.

Fourth, in writing about Black politics and leadership, Davis (2007, 48) underscores the presence of elected officials, among others, as influential leaders. Though academics and theorists may argue over what defines leadership, "... the concept and the *praxis of leadership* endure. That is, some acts and patterns of behavior that are generally regarded as influential, if not determinative, continue to be carried out by individuals with an impact that may be consequential for the many. Elected officials ... are regularly engaged in decision making which directs and impacts large numbers of people" (emphasis in original).

Hancock (2004) draws attention to the power and influence of elected leaders in their ability to frame policy debates and shape public discourse that ultimately legitimizes or delegitimizes certain groups (e.g., welfare mothers) as they pursue their interests in American politics. She argues that policymakers, regardless of race, gender, class, and party, participate in the construction of public identities that may support or oppose the interests of those they seek to represent. Her book reveals the problematic role of Black members of Congress speaking about welfare mothers from the framework of a "politics of disgust." Jordan-Zachery (2009, 2), using similar conceptions, "evaluates the racing and gendering of policymaking in the United States…[and shows] how key decision makers use race and gender cultural images and symbols to frame policy… [and] how these frames and the resulting policies impact the lives of African American women and their quest for social justice."

For these reasons, examining the experiences of men and women of color in elected positions has the potential to expand our understanding of those holding positions that confer leadership. Although not all public officeholders are equal in influence, either as individual politicians at the state or local level or as actors in various institutional settings, we nevertheless submit that all officeholders in our study are important leaders as they engage in the workings of democracy. Commenting on variations in power and influence within legislative bodies, Duerst-Lahti and Kelly (1995, 30) state, "…although legislatures have institutional leadership structures and posts, almost any legislator can be seen as a leader by virtue of the capacity to respond or not, give direction to policy, or influence interests of a legislative district. So, doing the work of a public post can readily be understood as *doing leadership*" (emphasis added). Let us now turn to theoretical questions and arguments associated with "doing leadership."

"DOING LEADERSHIP": A TRANSFORMATIONAL VIEW OF WOMEN?

Intrinsically related to definitions of who is a leader is what a leader does, that is, how leadership is exercised. Feminist scholars argue that gender bias appears in definitions of "doing leadership" as it does in definitions of who is a leader. Contested notions of leadership such as action, activity, influence, and power emerge in theoretical debates (McDonagh 2009; Rosenthal 1998a). Numerous scholars have asked the question: Do women lead and/or govern differently than men? (See, e.g., Epstein,

Niemi, and Powell 2005; Rosenthal 1998a, 1998b; Thomas 1998, 13; Whicker and Jewell 1998.)

Lawless and Theriault (2006, 175) suggest that "female legislators are more likely than their male counterparts to conduct business in a manner that is egalitarian, cooperative, communicative, and contextual."[5] Rosenthal's study (1998a, 18–19) of state legislators provides an example of gendered differences in leadership styles, which she distinguishes as "aggregative" versus "integrative." Aggregative – also known as transactional – leadership means the exercise of "who gets what" and "at whose expense" through legislative decision making that involves competing "interests, power, and exchange." Rosenthal observes that such leadership is generally associated with a male way of doing things.

Drawing from Burns (1978), Rosenthal posits that the integrative style of women's leadership may be considered transformational. As Burns defines it, transformational leadership moves beyond "transactional" bargaining and compromise to implement day-to-day policy. It implies challenging the conventional ways of doing things, creating broader changes in the political system. For Rosenthal (1998a, 21–22),

...integrative leadership contradicts existing structures or norms of leadership. The orthodox view of leadership qualities depicts a man who leads from a position of authority and hierarchy, who has vision, who can take charge and move others forward, who is the source of motivation for followers, and who tells others the meaning of their work. The antithesis of these qualities is the integrative leader who leads through interpersonal networks, who focuses on the ordinary, who empowers others, who relies on community as a source of motivation, and who participates with others in the discovery of meaning.

Numerous studies have found evidence of a "politics of difference," suggesting the potential for "transformational" change as a result of women "doing leadership" differently from men. Flammang (1997, 198), for example, contrasts "male careerism versus female public service" and describes "transformational female-based typologies" based on a redefinition of power from "power over" to "power to." Studies of women of color have addressed the feminist critique of power and leadership as well. According to Hardy-Fanta (1993), women gravitate toward an integrative style that emphasizes mutuality, collaboration, collectivity, consensus, and the empowerment of others. Along a similar vein, García and Márquez (2001, 117) find that the Latina party activists and candidates in their study expressed a desire "to see others like themselves involved

---

[5] They refer to studies by Rosenthal (1998a) and Thomas (1994).

in politics." In short, integrative leaders seek to invite participation rather than impose dominance or make deals behind closed doors. According to this model, relationships tend to be nonhierarchical, involving power sharing rather than bald competition for power and working to get the job done more than being in the limelight.

Though the question of gendered difference among political elites would be subject to further scrutiny by researchers employing a variety of investigative methods, women activists appeared to seize on the central themes generated by this body of scholarship to promote what one group of researchers (Pittinsky et al. 2007) called, the "great woman theory of leadership." Books and other publications portrayed or assumed that women leaders are, in essence, "better than men." Influential activists such as Marie Wilson and Linda Tarr-Whelan have written volumes that have strongly normative and prescriptive messages: *Closing the Leadership Gap: Why Women Can and Must Help Run the World* (Wilson 2004), which was reissued with a new subtitle: *Add Women*, Change Everything (Wilson 2007; emphasis added); and *Women Lead the Way: Your Guide to Stepping Up to Leadership and* Changing the World (Tarr-Whelan 2009; emphasis added). Others in the same vein include: *Enlightened Power: How Women Are Transforming the Practice of Leadership* (Coughlin, Wingard, and Hollihan 2005). From this perspective, the ways women demonstrate leadership will transform politics – including governmental institutions – in significant and profound ways.

Such pronouncements carry deeply essentialist perspectives on women's leadership: women make better leaders and the world would be a better place if women were in power. Journalistic accounts, along with some academic studies, mostly anecdotal in nature, added to the "great woman" theory drumbeat.[6]

Researchers have pointed to the importance of scholarly inquiry not falling prey to simplistic and essentialist understandings of political behavior. Han (2010, 6) warns not to overgeneralize about gendered styles of leadership. The line between men and women is not crystal clear, and "[d]ifferences between male and female leadership styles are sometimes subtle and should not be overstated." For some groups, especially, men may also exhibit an inclusive and participatory approach to leadership. Reingold (1996, 2000) articulates a healthy skepticism in pursuing

---

[6] Weisman and Steinhauer (2013) provides an interesting journalistic account of women in the US Senate. Although not deeply essentialist, it is anecdotal in nature, based on selective interviews with women senators.

her own studies of gendered differences (assumed or to be tested) among female and male state legislators, insisting that elite politicians may have more similarities than differences in their legislative behaviors. After all, they are "strategic politicians" driven by institutional constraints and norms (party, district preferences, etc.) that may dictate behavior regardless of gender.

In her own review of the literature on women as political leaders, Rosenthal (1998a) critiqued empirical limitations of work largely biographical or "exploratory" in nature, based on small and/or nonrandom samples. She noted that as larger numbers of women occupied elected office and assumed important positions (e.g., committee chairs), researchers adopted improved and more empirical research methods to test gender differences in legislative behavior. Kathlene's (1994, 572) study of leadership style serves as a case in point. Not relying on self-reports among legislators of their own behavior, she codes by gender the content of what was said during committee hearing debates; she finds that, among male and female state legislative committee chairs, "women are more likely to act as facilitators of the hearing," whereas "men used their position of power to control [the] hearings."[7]

In *When Women Lead*, Rosenthal (1998a, 16–17) herself follows a "triangulated research strategy" that involves a survey of state legislators across fifty states, focus groups with committee chairs, fieldwork, and direct observation of committee chairs in three legislatures. She maintains that although she discovers gendered differences in leadership styles among women and men, she makes no normative claim that "one particular style is more effective, appropriate, or preferable than another." Rather, she notes that legislatures, as complex institutions, may require different sets of skills, styles, and behavior for members to be effective. A contrast, to be sure, from the normative and unequivocal pronouncements of essentialist (female) perspectives that women – by their nature – make better leaders than men.

We note that the literature represented and summarized here overwhelmingly studies White women and men. Broadening the scholarly focus to include women and men of color – and understanding a larger community context for their experiences and roles as elected officials – provides a counter-perspective to essentialist or overgeneralized studies that draw clear and elevated distinctions between (all) women

---

[7] Lawless and Theriault (2006, 175) refer to and quote from this work by Kathlene (1994). See also Kathlene (1995) for a discussion of gender and consensus building in leadership.

and (all) men in public office. We turn again to literature on women of color who call attention to a womanist framework of political analysis that casts electoral behavior and office holding in more historical and collective terms.

Rejecting Female Essentialism: "Necessity Was the Midwife of Our Politics"

According to Nepstad and Bob (2006), leadership is most definitely about more than the actions of an individual within an official position; it is as much about community connection, the awareness of repression and grievances, and the social movements generated and sustained by those who struggle for redress and change. Leadership in the face of – and as a response to – racial repression and community grievances is at the heart of the experiences of each of the groups being considered in this book (see, e.g., Manuel 2006).

As Rosser-Mims (2010, 3) notes, "Historically, Black women have been at the forefront of the struggle for human and civil rights pro-mulgating [*sic*] their blood, sweat, and tears with the goal of sustaining families, communities, and to building the very foundation upon which the United States is built." Black women scholars challenge not only tra-ditional views of leadership based on the White male experience, but also those of White women. Instead of admonitions, for example, to *Lean In*,[8] with the implication that women can get ahead in business and politics if they act more like men – Black women activists and scholars affirm a vision of "Lifting as we climb."[9] In fact, "the emergence of Black female leadership in the United States represents a history of their struggle for liberation from oppression to 'lift' the Black community out of racial, economic, and educational subjugation" (Rosser-Mims 2010, 4).

From her studies of Black women's political leadership develop-ment, Rosser-Mims (2005, 2010), concludes, first, that, "...they shared

---

[8] Not only is there the book, *Lean In: Women, Work and the Will to Lead* (Sandberg 2013), but there is also a movement of sorts: www.leanin.org, with thousands of "Lean In Circles" as well as 17 million (and counting) news stories generated since its publication.

[9] The motivational phrase "Lifting as We Climb" seems to have originated as a motto of the National Association of Colored Women's (NACW) Clubs, which was "founded in 1896 through a merger of the Colored Women's League, of Washington, DC, and the National Federation of Afro-American Women, of Boston, Massachusetts" (Myers 1997, 260). For a more current application, see Springer (1999), *Still Lifting, Still Climbing: African American Women's Contemporary Activism*; for a review of the role of Black women in the civil rights movement and in African American politics, see Pinderhughes (1993).

a philosophy of uplifting the Black community, collectiveness, and communality, in addition to the belief in a higher being, *which differs from traditional leadership models*. Second, the participants developed a political consciousness due to their experiences with resistance and oppression from birth to adulthood as Black females. This experience uniquely prepared them for applying a political analysis as the basis of their worldview" (2005, 2; emphasis added). Referencing Hill Collins (2000) and Allen (1997), she concludes that, Black women "developed a 'culture of political resistance' that required them to 'expand their roles as homemakers and laborers to incorporate that of caretakers of the race" (Rosser-Mims 2010, 7). Leadership for community betterment and change as compared to personal ambition and an abstract goal of "parity for women" extends to the policy arena: Grayson (1999, 131), in discussing Black women's activism in health policy during the 1980s–1990s, declares, for example, that, "Necessity was the midwife of our politics."

Abdullah and Freer (2008, 104) present the candidacies of two Black Panther Party members, Bobby Seale and Elaine Brown, as means to an end – community empowerment. Both ran for public office; neither won, but they drew a significant number of votes. Mobilization of the Black community was their objective. Through their candidacies, Black residents were "actively connected to the formal political system." Abdullah and Freer, working from within a womanist framework, suggest that a feminist definition of leadership – enhancing others' capacity to act – is not gender bound, as seen in the candidacies of this Black man and Black woman. Recall from Chapter 4 that almost a quarter of elected officials of color reported that they decided to run for office the very first time because they wanted to "make a change/make a difference" (see Chapter 4, esp. Figure 4.1), and that, although women of color in general and Black women and Latinas in particular, did give this type of reason more than their male counterparts, the differences were not statistically significant, thus affirming Abdullah and Freer.

Hardy-Fanta (1997, 45), in a study of all Latino/a candidates who ran for office in Massachusetts over a thirty-year period, concluded that "differences in the discourse of politics may hide commonalities across gender lines." Despite often being cited in studies of gender differences in leadership styles, Tolleson–Rinehart (2001, 164) concludes that "[g]endered *expectations* are more influential than any measurable gender *differences*" (emphasis in original).

In drawing attention here to commonalities across gender among people of color, it is imperative to note that we are not saying that gender differences are absent from their politics. Simien (2006, 12), for example, points out that in real life, political movements have treated race and gender identities as separate, in competition or opposition with one another. Invoking a different perspective from Abdullah and Freer, mentioned earlier, she critiques the Black Panther Party, which she contends equated the experience of African American men with the black political agenda," thereby treating "the struggle of black women against patriarchy as antithetical to the larger community narrative of racial discrimination." Social movements of other racial/ethnic groups similarly criticized and dismissed the concerns of women of color (or other subpopulations, such as gay minority men) as subordinate to those of (straight) men (Cohen 1999; Gay and Tate 1998; Pulido 2006).

Revisiting "Gendered Leadership Style"

Overall, scholarship investigating gendered differences in leadership have employed a variety of research methods, among them case studies (Flammang 1997); studies with small sample sizes (Rinehart 1991); self-reported descriptions of elected officials' legislative behavior (Thomas 1994, 1998); participant observation, that is, researchers' observations of legislative behavior (Brown 2014; Kathlene 1994); mixed methods (Rosenthal 1998a); and surveys of elected officials' perceptions of their own and others' style of decision making (CAWP [Center for American Women and Politics, 1991). We submit that the earlier, more qualitative research studies, while limited in generalizability, contributed to the development of "grounded theory," generating hypotheses for further – and more empirically rigorous – research.

Our study seeks to extend previous work by employing quantitative methods involved in administering and analyzing a national survey of elected officials of color. We note that, like research cited earlier, our explorations of leadership style rely on the perceptions that elected officials report of perceived gender differences. While our quantitative methodology provides for more generalizability, at the same time other issues may be present (e.g., social desirability in responses). Future scholarship will likely provide further empirical tests of gendered differences in leadership that move beyond survey research. We now draw on our national survey of elected officials of color to investigate their perceptions of how women and men "do leadership," exploring the gendered styles often presented in prior research.

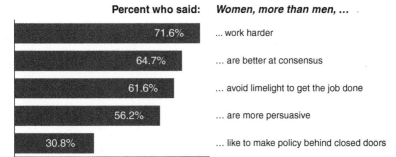

FIGURE 6.1 Style of leadership, by gender.
Source: GMCL National Survey, 2006–2007; N = 1,203–1,236.

GENDER AND LEADERSHIP STYLE: PERSPECTIVES
OF ELECTED OFFICIALS OF COLOR

We approach the question posed earlier about whether women in governing positions are "transformational" from an intersectional perspective: What are the differences – and commonalities – between women of color elected officials and their male counterparts in their opinions about leadership style? The majority of men and women surveyed by the Gender and Multicultural Leadership (GMCL) Project –across all racial groups and on all measures – view women as working harder, being better at achieving consensus, avoiding the limelight to "get the job done," and being more persuasive than men (see Figure 6.1). Seven in ten elected officials of color say women work harder than men; over six in ten judge they are better for achieving consensus, not caring about being in the limelight, and well over half on women being more persuasive than men.

Furthermore, there is strong agreement on women's openness in policymaking: fewer than a third agrees with the statement: *"Female elected officials are more likely to conduct policymaking behind closed doors compared to their male counterparts."* One can make the case, then, that seven in ten believe that women (and by implication, women of color) are *not* more likely than men to be secretive in the policymaking process.

That said, there are also differences by gender and at the intersection of race and gender – differences that are highly significant for most groups. For example, women of color are significantly *more* likely than their male counterparts to see women as working harder, being better at achieving consensus, avoiding the limelight to get the job done, and not preferring to make policy behind closed doors – by about 20 percentage points (Table 6.1). This is driven almost entirely by Black and Latina women.

TABLE 6.1. *Perspectives on Style of Governance: Elected Officials of Color, by Gender and Race*

Perspective	All		Black		Latino/a		Asian American	
	Female	Male	Female	Male	Female	Male	Female	Male
Agree/Strongly Agree that Women:								
Work harder than men	82.3***	65.1	84.7***	62.7	78.0***	67.7	82.1*	67.9
	(458)	(765)	(281)	(378)	(150)	(319)	(28)	(56)
Are better at achieving consensus than men	78.6***	56.4	78.0***	53.6	81.1***	59.5	78.6†	55.2
	(458)	(768)	(273)	(377)	(148)	(321)	(28)	(58)
Avoid limelight to get job done	73.6***	54.4	73.7***	55.6	70.7***	50.2	81.5	66.7
	(462)	(758)	(278)	(374)	(147)	(315)	(27)	(57)
Are more persuasive than men	61.0†	53.4	63.5*	50.8	55.1	54.0	71.4	62.1
	(462)	(774)	(277)	(380)	(147)	(324)	(28)	(58)
Disagree/Strongly Disagree that Women:								
Like to make policy behind closed doors	74.9***	65.9	77.5*	72.2	69.7*	60.1	68.0	55.4
	(447)	(756)	(271)	(370)	(142)	(318)	(25)	(56)

Note: Entries are percents of elected officials in survey, with *N* in parentheses.

†$p < .1$; *$p < .05$; ***$p < .001$.

Source: GMCL National Survey, 2006–2007.

For Asian Americans, other than for those who believe that women work harder than men, the gender differences are less significant.

It is only on the effectiveness (i.e., persuasiveness) measure that variations across race*gender groups appear, but not all carry statistical significance: Black women (at 63.5 percent) are significantly more likely than Black men (at 50.8 percent) to report women are more persuasive than men ($p < .05$). Latina women and men are comparable in slight majorities responding that women are more persuasive than men; a larger majority of Asian women than men agree with this statement, but none of these differences are statistically significant.

The findings on leadership style appear to provide considerable support for the idea that women do bring a different style to the exercise of leadership. Although it is valuable to add the perspectives of women (and men) of color to these debates, subjective opinions on gender and style of leadership have their own limitations. In the end, much more research is needed. First, more (and more rigorous) studies with an intersectional lens are critical, given how rare they are. Second, from a methodological perspective, how we measure leadership style needs to move beyond the subjective evaluations of elected officials themselves.

CONGRESSIONAL LEADERSHIP POSITIONS

From subjective perceptions of leadership *style*, we turn now to another dimension of positional leadership: What evidence is there of the political incorporation of elected officials of color, as measured by their shares of leadership positions in their governing bodies? To what extent do these differ by race and gender? To gauge the extent of political incorporation of women (and men) elected officials of color, we gathered data on and calculated their shares of leadership positions in Congress and state legislatures, as well as the prestige and distribution of their committee assignments. In many ways, how power is distributed through both formal leadership positions (e.g., speaker of the house, majority/minority leader, whip, and committee chairs) or through "informal leadership teams" determines to a great extent the influence positional leaders wield (Smooth 2008, 182–188). Although the GMCL Survey focuses on elected officials in state legislatures and local government, we have been able to update the GMCL National Database with information on the leadership positions of members of the 113th and 114th Congresses.

Race*Gender and Congressional Leadership

As reiterated by Lawless and Theriault (2006, 173), "...the push to increase women's numeric representation in the House and Senate is predicated on the notion that women will bring a 'different voice' to the legislature. Perhaps no 'voices' are as important as those of the congressional leadership." But as Dolan, Deckman, and Swers (2007, 256–257) note: "Seats and leadership positions on prestigious committees such as Appropriations, the committee that determines how to allocate government funds across various programs, and Ways and Means, the tax-writing committee, are generally awarded to more senior members." Furthermore, "majority party members have more influence on the direction of policy than do minority party members." Since "women make up a larger proportion of the Democratic caucus than the Republican caucus [and] Republicans have held the majority in Congress and thus controlled the policy agenda" for more than a decade, the lack of women in top committee positions is not surprising.

According to Manning and Brudnick (2014, Summary), between 1917 and 2014, "Nineteen women in the House, and 10 women in the Senate, have chaired committees."[10] Moreover, other than Speaker of the House Nancy Pelosi, "no woman has ever approached the top of the parties' leadership pyramids, either in the House or the Senate..." and, for many years, the record was, "perhaps, even more dismal when we move from party leadership to committee leadership" (Lawless and Theriault 2006, 173). Until very recently, no women chaired any of the most exclusive committees: Appropriations, Rules, and Ways and Means in the House; and Appropriations, Armed Services, Finance, and Foreign Relations in the Senate (Dolan, Deckman, and Swers 2007, 256; Lawless and Theriault, 2006).

How have women in general fared in the roughly ten years since these studies were published? At least incremental progress seems apparent. In the 108th Congress (elected in 2002, serving from 2003 to 2004), women chaired just two committees out of the forty-one available in the House and Senate. By the 113th Congress (elected in 2012, serving from 2013 to

---

[10] Though these numbers may be true, a perusal of the historical record suggests that women in Congress have been offered gendered and "fluff" committee leadership posts: Corinne C. (Lindy) Boggs (D-LA) was chair of a committee in the 99th–100th Congresses, but it was the Commission of the Bicentenary of the US House. Even more ludicrous was the assignment of Yvonne Burke (D-CA) as chair of the Select Committee on the House Beauty Shop in the 94th–95th Congresses; a post held earlier by Martha Wright Griffiths (D-MI) (Manning and Brudnick 2014, 10–11, 30).

2014), women served as chair on nine Senate committees and one House committee (CAWP 2014, 2–3; Manning and Brudnick 2014). There has even been some progress for women on the most prestigious congressional committees in recent years.

In the 113th Congress, Barbara Mikulski (D-MD) presided over the Senate Appropriations Committee; Barbara Boxer (D-CA) chaired both the Senate Environment and Ethics committees; Patty Murray (D-WA) chaired the Senate Budget Committee; Senator Debbie Stabenow (D-MI) chaired Agriculture, Nutrition, and Forestry; and Senator Dianne Feinstein (D-CA) chaired the Select Intelligence Committee, a position she held in previous Congresses. Though not as prestigious as the Senate committee chair positions, Candice Miller (R-MI) chaired the House Administration Committee (CAWP 2014, 2–3).

Party Control of Congressional Leadership: Chair and Committee Assignments

Chairmanships and committee assignments in the US House and Senate are made by party leaders. Gitelson, Dudley, and Dubnick (2016, 372) point out that chairs of committees and subcommittees are "always members of the majority party in the body." Further, a seniority system guides – if not determines – committee leadership positions. Generally, the senior member of the majority party with the longest continuous service on a committee becomes its chair. The most senior member of the minority party on a committee generally becomes its "ranking member." Party leaders also make committee assignments, with the respective chambers simply ratifying their choices. Membership on committees entails competition among members, as they seek assignments on the committees they prefer. They may seek placement on "prestigious" committees considered of major importance within the chamber and in specific policymaking areas, or on committees whose jurisdiction oversees policymaking in areas of special interest to members' constituents. Research notes consideration of both types of committees in the preferences of members of color in Congress (discussed further later).

Given that, as we mentioned in the Introduction, and discuss at more length in Chapter 7, the vast majority of elected officials of color – including most women and people of color in the US Congress – affiliate with the Democratic Party, party control of the legislative chambers greatly impacts their potential rise in the leadership ranks of the institution. For example, in the 114th Congress (as of December 31, 2014), which was in

Republican control, only two out of a total of forty-three Black members in the House were members of the majority party; among Hispanics, only six out of twenty-nine were Republicans; and the sole Asian American (Mazie Hirono) in the Senate and all nine members in the House were Democrats. Similarly, majorities of women in the Senate (fourteen out of twenty) and House (sixty-two out of eighty-four) were Democrats (see Hellwege and Sierra 2014). Hence, the party in control of the chambers of Congress – in this case the Republican Party– carries major implications for institutional leadership among elected officials of color. Given that most members of color and women are in the minority party in the 114th Congress, the availability of institutional leadership positions for them is reduced. Further, very small numbers of people of color, regardless of party affiliation, hold positions in the US Senate, lessening even further their potential to wield influence as leaders within the Senate.

As suggested earlier, the rise in the number of women as committee chairs is related, in part, to party control of each chamber. Republicans controlled both chambers of the 108th and the House in the 113th Congress. Democrats were in control of the Senate as the women cited previously assumed their chairmanships in the 113th Congress. Adding the component of race to this gender profile reveals that all the women who assumed committee chairmanships in the 108th and 113th were White women. Hence, White women increased their numbers as committee chairs (from a total of two to a total of ten), but women of color did not enjoy even those incremental advances.

Few women of color have broken through to congressional committee leadership: none served as committee chairs in either the House or Senate of the 113th Congress; and just one chaired a subcommittee in the House (Table 6.2).[11] Men of color do not seem to fare much better: In the Senate, Robert Menéndez (D-NJ) rose to chair the prestigious Senate Foreign Relations Committee when John Kerry became secretary of state; with the change to Republican control in 2015, he now serves as ranking member. No men of color served as chair of any committee in the House (a total of only nine Republican men of color –seven Hispanics and two American Indians – served in the 113th Congress). Given their party's minority status in the House, four elected officials of color – two men and two women – served as ranking members: Bennie Thompson (Black, D-MS), Homeland Security; John Conyers (Black,

---

[11] We would like to thank Marla Aufseeser (MPA, MA) for her research assistance in gathering these data.

TABLE 6.2. *Committee Leadership, by Gender, Race and Party Control, in the 108th and 113th Congresses*

	Committee Leadership				Subcommittee Leadership			
	White Women Chairs		Women of Color Chairs (Ranking Members)	Men of Color Chairs (Ranking Members)	Subcommittee Chairs Held by Women (Ranking Members)		Chairs Held by Women of Color (Ranking Members)	Chairs Held by Men of Color (Ranking Members)
	(108th)	(113th)	(113th)	(113th)	(108th)	(113th)	(113th)	(113th)
US Senate	2-Rep.	9-Dem.	0 (0)	1-Dem. (0)	5-Rep. (n.a.)	11-Dem. (4-Rep.)	0 (0)	1-Dem. (5-Rep.)
US House	0	1	0 (2-Dem.)	0 (2-Dem.)	7-Rep. (n.a.)	7-Rep. (16-Dem.)	1-Rep. (5-Dem.)	1-Rep. (11-Dem.)

Note: Because the analysis is based on the universe of members of Congress – that is, not a sample – all differences are statistically significant. Committees include sixteen standing committees, plus four select committees; the latter include Select Committees on Ethics, Intelligence, Indian Affairs, and Aging but not special committees, such as Benghazi.

Source: GMCL Project, 2015. Data from the 108th Congress were calculated from Table 2 in Lawless and Theriault (2006, 174); data for women committee chairs in the 113th Congress are from Manning and Brudnick (2014) and the *Fact Sheet: Women in Congress: Leadership Roles and Committee Chairs, Previous Congresses; 113th Congress 2013–2015* (CAWP 2014 [February]); data on subcommittees in the 113th Congress are from CQ Roll Call; for the House: http://media.cq.com/pub/committees/index.php; for the Senate: http://media.cq.com/pub/committees/index.php?chamber=senate (Accessed May 20, 2015); n.a. = not available.

D-MI), Judiciary; Linda Sanchez (Latina, D-CA), Ethics; and Maxine Waters (Black, D-CA), Financial Services.

What is the picture for leadership at the next tier – chairs of congressional *subcommittees*? Research conducted at the end of the twentieth and beginning of the twenty-first centuries finds few women serving as subcommittee chairs (Lawless and Theriault 2006). Our analysis of data for the 113th Congress shows that women and men of color held very, very few such positions. Subcommittee chairs in the 113th included: Ileana Ros-Lehtinen (Latina, R-FL), chair of the House Foreign Relations Subcommittee on the Middle East and North Africa (the other five women in leadership positions at this level, as Democrats, are ranking members); Bill Flores (Latino, R-TX), House Veterans Affairs Subcommittee on Economic Opportunity; and Robert Menéndez (Latino, D-NJ), Senate Banking Subcommittee on Housing, Transportation, and Community Development (at the same time as chairing the Senate Foreign Relations Committee).

As with chairmanships of full committees, White women Democrats in the Senate increased their numbers as subcommittee chairs, numbering eleven in the 113th Congress. With just one woman of color in the Senate (Mazie Hirono, D-HI), it is not surprising that there was no presence for women of color in that chamber. Five Senate subcommittees had Republican men of color as their ranking members.[12] Sixteen subcommittees had female (Democratic) ranking members, of which five (31.3 percent) were women of color (four Black and one Latina). None of the ten Asian Americans or two American Indians in Congress at that time held leadership positions as chairs or ranking members of congressional committees or subcommittees.

In summary, our intersectional approach to the study of congressional leadership reinforces how party control has a major effect on the numbers of elected officials of color – women and men – holding committee chair positions. Elected officials of color are quite limited in the number of leadership positions they hold in either chamber, and the interaction of party with race seems to be determinative: Blacks make up half of all elected officials of color in the 113th Congress, with three-quarters

---

[12] A person may hold more than one leadership position on subcommittees, so that, although five subcommittees in the US Senate have ranking members who are men of color, in fact there are only three men in those positions: Ted Cruz (2); Marco Rubio (2), and Tim Scott (1). House ranking members of color hold just one each. Cory Booker, the sole Black senator, did not arrive in the US Senate until late in 2013; he held no leadership position until the 114th Congress.

of those serving as ranking members. While ranking members exert a presence on legislative committees, they have less power and influence in the chamber and over public policies of concern to their communities. Overall, men of color, aside from one Hispanic Republican from Texas, held no positions in the House as chairs of either committees or subcommittees; just one Republican woman of color (Latina) served as chair of a House subcommittee. Women, overall, fare not much better when Congress is in Republican hands – at least to date. When Republicans retook the Senate in 2014, women not only lost any gains, but also were reduced to pre-108th levels: in the 114th Congress they currently hold just two of the twenty Senate chair positions.[13]

Additional research addressing institutional leadership among members of color provides some evidence of career advancement over years past with implications for further possibilities in the future. Gerber (1996, 832–833) examines congressional career patterns for African American members in the House from 1974 to 1992. Comparing them to all other Democrats in the House, he finds that they "are significantly less likely to exit" the lower chamber than their non-African American colleagues. Their longer tenures as members of Congress are associated with their high reelection rates in heavily Democratic (safe) districts. Moreover, he finds that they "rarely" seek higher office; noting that winning statewide elections (e.g., senator, governor) would be difficult for many, if not most, of them. Hence, as they rise in seniority within the House and their party, Gerber predicts that when Democrats control the House, African American representatives are likely to claim "a sizable number of … chairs of important committees and subcommittees." Brief analysis of the 103rd Congress (1993–1994) showed they held twelve of ninety-seven Democratic seats on prestige committees and, otherwise, enjoyed a seat on every committee (Gerber, 1996, 841). Gerber concludes with a rather sobering prediction, perhaps reflecting our own analysis of the continuing effects of party: when Democrats are in the minority, "African American Democrats will likely labor in obscurity" (Gerber, 1996, 840).

In an additional effort to gauge the effects of race and ethnicity on the institutional mobility of members of Congress, Rocca et al. (2011) examine the rate by which members attain committee leadership positions. Their research focuses on the attainment of members' first leadership

---

[13] Source: "Special Report: Committee Guide: Complete House and Senate Rosters, 114th Congress, First Session," *CQ Weekly*, March 2, 2015; we would like to thank Alex Gangitano of CQ Roll Call, for providing data and assistance.

positions on subcommittees in the House, as either chairs or ranking minority members. Their study spans from the 101st through the 108th Congresses (1989–2004). They focus their analysis on Black and Latino representatives in comparison to White and non-Latino members. They examine gender (sex as a variable) but do not look at women of color, specifically.

Rocca et al. (2011) provide interesting and rather unexpected results. They find that Black legislators attain leadership positions faster than White legislators: this may be because of the tendency for Black members of Congress to sit on less prestigious committees than White members, allowing for greater opportunity for institutional advancement. As they say, "There is typically greater opportunity for upward mobility on these committees because of the relatively high rates of transfer out of such committees" (Rocca et al. 2011, 905). Their finding for Blacks does not hold for Latinos, who acquire leadership positions at the same rate as non-Latino legislators.

These studies, alongside our own descriptive analysis, present perhaps a glass-half-full/ half-empty scenario for the further incorporation of people of color within Congress. They are making progress as their seniority increases and they become chairs of committees and subcommittees. But their ability to wield influence as policymakers will remain constrained by which party controls Congress. Longitudinal and quantitative studies of more recent Congresses incorporating intersectional analysis that includes specific attention to women of color may produce yet more and perhaps unexpected results.

We add a footnote here of research that addresses committee leadership at the state legislative level. Orey, Loverby, and Larimer (2007) conducted a study of all state legislative chambers at two time periods, 1989 and 1999, and found that overall, Blacks remained underrepresented as committee chairs. However, disparate results applied to committees of high importance (not significantly underrepresented) vis-à-vis those with jurisdiction over "social services" (overrepresented). The authors concluded that advances for African American state legislators "have been limited almost entirely to chambers where the black caucus is a critical element of a Democratic majority" (Orey et al. 2007, 619). Reingold and Smith (2014) adopt an intersectional approach to assess the institutional mobility of women of color, men of color, and White women across twenty-five state legislatures. Preliminary findings reveal a "complex" portrait of interacting factors affecting each group.

Congressional Committee Assignments

Before we turn to the governing aspect of leadership for elected officials of color, it is worthwhile to describe briefly the distribution on the most prestigious and influential committees for women and men of color in Congress. Among the members of color on the most powerful House committees in the 113th Congress, women's proportions ranged from a high of 44.4 percent on Foreign Affairs to 37.5 percent on Armed Services and one-third on Ways and Means. They constituted about one-quarter on three others: Appropriations, Judiciary, and Rules. Remarkable is the fact that, of the five women on the Foreign Affairs committee, four were women of color; they gained even more ground in the 114th Congress, where five of the six are women of color. In comparison, White women made up just 2.8 percent of White members on this committee in the 113th House.

A similar pattern is evident for all of the most exclusive committees (see Table 6.3), including Appropriations, where women of color made up 27.3 percent of committee assignments held by members of color, in contrast to the 18.4 percent White women held as a share of Whites on this committee.

Although these percentages are intriguing and should encourage further research by gender*race, there are a few caveats: First, the numbers on some committees are quite small (which is why we did not include analysis for the Senate). Second, owing to limitations of space and as this is not the central focus of the chapter, we have not included a fully intersectional analysis, that is, the percentages for Black, Latina/o, and Asian women and men. Third, without holding a position of leadership, Lawless and Theriault's (2006, 175) words for women in general ring true as well for women of color: "The lack of women's voices emanating from committees and party leadership roles would be somewhat less disconcerting if the words coming from members' mouths did not appreciably differ across gender lines." And we would add "across party lines."

Recent work by Michael Minta (2011) explores committee oversight by Black and Latino/a members of Congress, finding that they pay careful attention to their constituencies' interests inside and outside of their specific legislative districts. Minta (2011, 17) argues that "strategic group uplift" distinguishes minority and white legislators' policy focus. Let us now look at how women and men of color do in congressional party leadership.

TABLE 6.3. *"Exclusive Committee" Assignments for Women of Color and White Women, 113th House of Representatives*

Committee	Women of Color (N/All Committee Members of Color)	White Women (N/All White Committee Members)	Women of Color (N/All Women Committee Members)
Appropriations	27.3 (3/11)	18.4 (7/38)	30.0 (3/10)
Armed Services	37.5 (3/8)	15.1 (8/ 61)	27.3 (3/11)
Foreign Affairs	44.4 (4/9)	2.8 (1/36)	80.0 (4/5)
Judiciary	25.0 (3/12)	7.4 (2/27)	60.0 (3/5)
Rules	25.0 (3/12)	11.1 (3/27)	50.0 (3/6)
Ways and Means	33.3 (1/3)	20.0 (2/10)	33.3 (1/3)

Note: Entries are percents of members of House of Representatives; in parentheses is the number on the committee over the total of each group. "White" refers to those whose race is non-Hispanic White. Because the analysis is based on the universe of members of Congress – that is, not a sample – all differences are statistically significant.

Source: GMCL Project, 2015, based on data from CQ Roll Call, http://media.cq.com/pub/committees/index.php (Accessed May 20, 2015), and from http://ballotpedia.org/United_States_Congress# Congressional_committees; membership on the House Select Committee on Intelligence was gathered from the "Annual Report on the Activity of the House Permanent Select Committee on Intelligence for the One Hundred and Thirteenth Congress," www.congress.gov/congressional-report/113th-congress/house-report/717/1 (Accessed May 23, 2015).

Congressional Party Leadership

We extend our discussion of positional leadership to the political parties in Congress. At the beginning of the 114th Congress, Black party leadership in the House is mostly male: James E. Clyburn (D-SC) serves as Assistant Democratic Leader (the third highest position in the chamber after minority leader and minority whip); John Lewis (D-GA), as Senior Chief Deputy Minority Whip; G. K. Butterfield (D-NC) and Keith Ellison (D-MN) are Chief Deputy Minority Whips. Donna Edwards (D-MD) is Policy Committee Co-Chair and the only woman in party leadership. (There are no members of color holding party leadership in the US Senate.) On the Latino side in the 114th Congress, we have Xavier Becerra (D-CA) as Democratic Caucus Chairman, Ben Ray Luján (D-NM) as Chair of the Democratic Congressional Campaign Committee, and Joaquin Castro (D-TX) as Chief Deputy Minority Whip. No Asians serve in party leadership positions. The leadership of the Republican Party is entirely White, with White women holding three out of nine positions.[14]

It is important to document the ascension to party leadership by congresspersons of color, even though their ascension to the most powerful positions (speaker of the house, majority/minority leaders, and majority/minority whips) has not yet been achieved. As their numbers increase and Black, Latino/a, and Asian American members of Congress gain seniority, will we see significant change in the institution's power structure, that is, real power at the top for both men and women of color? Can this happen when the vast majority of elected officials of color are Democrats serving in a Congress controlled by Republicans? The experiences of White women would suggest not.

Leadership within Congressional Caucuses

Leadership opportunities also exist within congressional caucuses organized to promote the interests of ethnoracial groups and women. Founded in 1977 – in part, under the leadership of Patsy Mink, the first woman of color elected to Congress – the Congressional Caucus on Women's Issues has a relatively long tenure, but the role and impact of women of color in that institution has received relatively little attention. Gertzog (2004, 36), following a chapter titled "Transformation and Growth: 1982–1992," affirms that, in the early 1990s, newly elected African American women "brought a new dimension to the largely white, male House. All were seasoned politicians, and they readily affiliated with the Women's Caucus. One remarked, 'Women's issues are almost like African American issues'." (He also notes new Latina Democrats joining the Caucus, but has little else to add on the ways these women changed the Caucus.) Times may

---

[14] Source: Schneider (2015); unless otherwise noted, the individuals holding the following positions are White men. Republican Party leadership includes Speaker, Majority Leader, Minority Whip, Chief Deputy whip, Republican Conference chair (W-F), Republican Conference vice-chair (W-F), Republican Conference secretary (W-F), Republican Policy chair, and NRCC chair. Democratic Party leadership includes: Minority Leader (W-F), Steering Committee Co-Chair (W-F), Democratic Whip, Assistant Democratic Leader (B-M), Chair, Policy Communications (W-M), Democratic Caucus Chair (H-M), Democratic Caucus Co-Chair, Policy Committee Co-Chair (B-F), Senior Chief Deputy Whip (B-M), DCCC chair (H-M), and eight Chief Deputy Whips (including two Black men and one Latino man).

have changed since then: During the 113th Congress, three of the four leaders of the Congressional Caucus for Women's Issues were women of color.[15] For the 114th Congress, Doris Matsui (D-CA) rose to co-chair, but the other leadership posts were filled by White women. As the Spotlight on the Congressional Black Caucus (see Box 6.1) shows, two of its five leadership positions for the 114th Congress are women (although not the chair).[16]

Box 6.1. Leadership of the Congressional Black Caucus (114th)

 CHAIR:
Rep. G. K. Butterfield

 FIRST VICE CHAIR:
Rep. Yvette Clarke

 SECRETARY:
Rep. Karen Bass

 WHIP:
Rep. Hakeem Jeffries

 SECOND VICE CHAIR:
Rep. André Carson

Note: Reproduced from CBC website; images are official photographs, used with permission of members, courtesy of Government Printing Office.
Source: CBC website. http://cbc-butterfield.house.gov/cbc-leadership/ (Accessed February 5, 2015).

---

[15] Reps. Jaime Herrera Beutler (R-WA) and Donna F. Edwards (D-MD), and Doris Matsui (D-CA) served as vice chair; www.womenspolicy.org/source/women-elected-caucus-leadership-114th-congress/ (Accessed May 20, 2015).

[16] Cardiss Collins (D-IL) was the first female chair of the CBC in the 96th Congress; Maxine Waters (D-CA) in the 105th; Eddie Bernice Johnson (D-TX) in the 107th; Barbara Lee (D-CA) in the 111th; and Marcia Fudge served as chair during the 113th Congress.

The leadership of the 114th Congressional Hispanic Caucus (CHC), comprising only Hispanic Democrats, is evenly split between Latinos and Latinas. The CHC made national news (Gamboa 2015) by selecting women to hold the two top positions: Linda Sánchez (D-CA) ascended to chair, and Michelle Lujan Grisham (D-NM) moved from whip to first vice chair (see Box 6.2).

Box 6.2. Leadership of the Congressional Hispanic Caucus (114th)

 CHAIR:
Rep. Linda T. Sánchez

 1ST VICE CHAIR:
Rep. Michelle Lujan Grisham

 2ND VICE CHAIR:
Rep. Joaquin Castro

 WHIP:
Rep. Ruben Gallego

Note: Images are official portraits used with permission of members.
Source: Congressional Hispanic Caucus. http://congressional hispaniccaucus-sanchez.house.gov/ (Accessed May 21, 2015).

On the other side of the partisan divide, six Hispanic Republicans form the Congressional Hispanic Conference. Mario Diaz-Balart (R-FL) serves as its chair. No other leadership positions for the Conference are identified.

Asian Americans also present a new face of caucus leadership (Box 6.3): Judy Chu (D-CA) has served as chair of the Congressional Asian Pacific American Caucus since the 112th Congress. And a woman delegate, Madeleine Bordallo (D-Guam), serves as first vice chair.

Box 6.3. Leadership of the Asian Pacific American Congressional Caucus (114th)

CHAIR:

Rep. Judy Chu

1ST VICE CHAIR:

Rep. Madeleine Bordallo

CHAIR EMERITUS:
Rep. Mike Honda

WHIP:
Rep. Mark Takano

Note: Images are official portraits used with permission of members. *Source*: Congressional Asian Pacific American Caucus. http://capac-chu.house.gov/ (Accessed February 12, 2015).

POSITIONAL LEADERSHIP AT THE STATE-LEGISLATIVE LEVEL

Scholars have tracked gender and leadership in state legislatures for quite some time, focusing on the same eight positions as discussed earlier (senate president, speaker of the house, senate president pro tempore, speaker pro tempore, senate/house majority leader, senate/house minority leader).[17] According to the Center for American Women and Politics (CAWP 2013b [April]), women hold 17.5 percent of all leadership positions at the state legislative level. This is a substantial increase from the 7.2 percent in 1980, but less than the 19.2 percent in 1996 reported by Whicker and Jewell (1998, 164).[18] CAWP also reports that women made up 19.0 percent of state legislators chairing standing committees (CAWP 2013b). At the same time, as Reingold and Smith (2014, 1) note, "Despite a growing body of research on the causes and consequences of women and racial/ethnic minorities' numerical representation, little attention has been paid to their institutional incorporation and power." They go on to say, "the political incorporation of women of color, men of color, and

---

[17] The precise titles for these positions differ by state: the title in New York, for example, is Speaker of the State Assembly.
[18] The higher percentage in 1996 reported by Whicker and Jewell (1998, 165) may be due to variation in the positions counted as "leadership"; see, for example, their comment about variation by states.

white women depends, to varying degrees, on the interacting effects of gender, race/ethnicity, partisanship, and seniority – as well as the leadership position in question" (35). Little, Dunn, and Deen (2001, 32) also report that the number of women state legislators in leadership positions rose from nine in 1983 to 36 in 2000; they also confirm the effects of party rule we noted in the earlier discussion on Congress: "Interestingly, women comprised a larger proportion of the Republican leadership (13.7%) than Democratic (10.3%)."

Haynie (2001, 47) helps frame the factors that have shaped African American state legislators' participation and advancement: "Efforts to advance [African American state representatives'] legislative careers and efforts to become more incorporated into the 'mainstream' of the legislative institution [may be] "potential explanations for the apparent decline in the saliency of black interest committee assignments to African American legislators. Obtaining seats on those committees deemed to be the most prestigious in the legislature is an important vehicle for accomplishing both of these outcomes."

As we saw in Chapters 1 and 2, the presence of African American women in state legislative office (now for more than forty years) is on the rise and noteworthy. Smooth (2008, 185), however, finds that African American women were largely absent from power positions within their respective legislatures. Using data from state legislatures in Maryland, Georgia, and Mississippi during the 2000 session, she concludes, "As is the case with party leadership positions, white men held the majority of committee leadership positions while few, if any, African American women did."

Little if anything has been documented previously about the leadership positions of Latinos/as or Asian Americans at this level. Fraga et al. (2008, 167) briefly discuss gender differences in committee assignments of a sample of Latino/a state legislators serving in 2004–2005, but they do not include analysis of leadership positions. In a note, they write that they "found no major differences in the propensities of Latinas and Latinos to serve as committee chairs...[and] no significant differences in the types of committees on which they served as chairs" (174, n. 3).

What can we ascertain about women of color in these types of positions at this level of office? Perhaps the best to say would be: "Bad news, good news." There are a number of ways to show the extent to which women of color, White women, and women in general have achieved a measure of leadership parity in state legislatures (Table 6.4) such as by number of leaders, share within racial group, share of all leadership

TABLE 6.4. *State Legislators in Leadership Positions, by Gender and Race, 2013*

Group	A	B	C	D	E	F
	Number Leaders	Members in Legislature	Leaders as Percent of (Group) Members	Leaders as Percent of All Leaders	Percent in Legislature	Parity Ratio
Women of color	11	364	3.0	3.3	4.9	.673
White women	47	1,417	3.3	14.2	19.2	.739
All women	58	1,781	3.3	17.5	24.1	.726
All men	274	5,602	4.9	82.5	75.9	1.09
All	332	7,383	4.5			

Note: "Parity Ratio" is calculated as "Leaders as Percent of All Leaders" divided by "Percent in Legislature." Note, also, that because this table reports on all elected officials at this level – in other words, it is not a sample – all differences are statistically significant; "White" refers to those whose race is non-Hispanic White. Percentages may not add up to 100 because of rounding.

Source: GMCL Project, 2013, for number of and leadership data on women of color state legislators. Numbers for "All Women" are from the Center for American Women and Politics (CAWP 2013a); "White Women" and "White Men" were computed from CAWP (2013b). The model for the table comes from Whicker and Jewell (1998, 164).

positions, and parity ratio. Our analysis shows that women of color hold a paltry number of leadership positions in state legislatures (column A). When viewed as a share of their group (i.e., women of color, White women, all women, all men), women of color state legislators make up 3.0 percent of their membership (column C), which might be seen as comparing favorably to that of White women (3.3 percent), especially in light of the fact that, with just 332 total leadership positions, leadership positions only make up 4.5 percent of the total. Yet their share of all leaders is only 3.3 percent, compared to 14.2 percent for White women (column D).

It is clear that women of color do still lag by this measure, and again when we use the parity ratio as an index of proportional representation: women of color make up 4.9 percent of the members of the legislature (column E) and, therefore, parity would be achieved if their share of the leadership positions were also 4.9. With their share of all leadership positions at 3.3 percent (column D), their parity ratio (calculated as D/E) shows that they are only about two-thirds of the way to parity (column F) in state legislative leadership positions.

TABLE 6.5. *Women of Color State Legislative Leadership Positions, 2013*

Names and Race	State	Position
Asian American		
Donna Mercado Kim	HI	Senate President
Black		
Adrienne A. Jones	MD	Speaker Pro Tempore
Sharon Weston Broome	LA	Senate President Pro Tempore
Nia H. Gill	NJ	Senate President Pro Tempore
Andrea Stewart-Cousins	NY	Senate Minority Leader
Leah Landrum Taylor	AZ	Senate Minority Leader
Sheila Y. Oliver	NJ	House Speaker
Stacey Abrams	GA	House Minority Leader
Latina		
Lucia Guzman	CO	Senate President Pro Tempore
Leticia Van de Putte	TX	Senate President Pro Tempore
Nora Campos	CA	Speaker Pro Tempore

Source: GMCL Project, 2013, for women of color; Center for American Women and Politics for data on leadership positions.

White women – with a parity ratio of .739 – are closer to three-quarters there. And, of course and not surprisingly, both are much smaller than the percentage held by men (82.5 percent), whose parity ratio is 1.09, indicating that they are overrepresented in the leadership. The parity ratio for the "All Men" category is misleading, however, as it includes male state legislators of color, who, like their female counterparts, occupy fewer leadership positions; the actual parity of White men is likely to be significantly higher.

Who are the women of color who hold these positions? Of note in Table 6.5 is that in 2013 an Asian American woman, Donna Mercado Kim, served as Senate President in the state of Hawaii; Black women are well represented, and, while smaller in number, Latinas have a presence as well.

There are, of course, a number of limitations to these data. Striving as we do to fully interrogate the data intersectionally, it is troubling to use the broader "women of color" category; it is necessary, however, because of the small numbers. And, further research is needed to document the leadership of male legislators of color, as well as leadership at other levels of office besides Congress and our state Houses. Leaving this research for others to pursue, we now turn to leadership in governing as another aspect of political incorporation.

POLICY LEADERSHIP:
DO WOMEN OF COLOR LEADERS
(BELIEVE THEY CAN) MAKE A DIFFERENCE?

As discussed in the introduction to the chapter, the women in politics literature, based primarily on research on White women, promulgates the
idea that women have a different leadership style than men. Numerous
scholars have, over the years, also asked whether women holding leadership positions as elected officials have an impact on public policy.
O'Connor (2003) responded to the question: *"Do Women in Local,
State, and National Legislative Bodies Matter?"* with *"A Definitive Yes
Proves Three Decades of Research by Political Scientists,"* and cites numerous studies as evidence. Thomas (1998, 10) points to women as the
direct beneficiaries of more women in office: "[w]omen officeholders are
more likely than men to consider representing the interests of women to
be very important.... Women politicians of both parties also tend, more
often than their male peers, to be supportive of issues relevant to women,
including funding for domestic violence shelters, funding for medical research on women's health issues, and child support enforcement."

According to Thomas and Welch (2001, 168), "Most tellingly, attitudes translate into direct legislative support. Women legislators tend,
more often than men, to make priorities of issues of women and to introduce and successfully usher those priorities through the legislative process." Given general patterns of Democratic Party affiliation and liberal
policy positions among women officeholders (Carroll and Sanbonmatsu
2013; Reingold and Smith 2012), further explorations have investigated
whether women policymakers would also support substantive interests
of ethnoracial minorities.

We performed a simple test of the hypothesis that women are more
likely than men to support policy positions to benefit not just women and
families, but also minorities. To answer this question, we analyzed data
from the National Hispanic Leadership Agenda's (NHLA) Congressional
Scorecard for the 113th Congress, which tallied the "number of times
that U.S. Senators and U.S. Representatives voted in line with NHLA
positions" (NHLA 2014, 3). Table 6.6 shows that women senators, on
average, voted with NHLA's position 86.9 percent of the time compared
to 56.8 percent of the men; in the House it is 76.3 percent for women and
just 38.9 percent for the men.

And, when we look at differences between minority and White members of Congress by gender (Table 6.7), we see that the small gender

TABLE 6.6. *NHLA Score, Members of 113th Congress, by Gender and Chamber*

Voted in Line with NHLA Position	House		Senate	
	Men	Women	Male	Female
Mean percent	38.9	76.3	56.8	86.9
(s.e.)	(2.44)	(4.69)	(4.96)	(5.93)
N	361	77	83	20
	$p < .0001$		$p < .0005$	

Note: Entries are mean percent who voted in line with the National Hispanic Leadership Agenda (NHLA) position, followed by standard error (s.e.) and N.
Source: GMCL Project, 2015, analysis of data from the National Hispanic Leadership Agenda's 113th Congressional Scorecard (NHLA 2014).

TABLE 6.7. *NHLA Score, Members of Congress, by White/Minority*

Voted in Line with NHLA Position	Non-Hispanic White		Minority	
	Male	Female	Male	Female
Mean percent	36.1	72.0	83.8	94.4
(s.e.)	(2.29)	(5.09)	(4.46)	(4.05)
N	387	69	57	28
	($p < .0001$)		(n.s.)	

Note and *Source*: See note in Table 6.7.

difference on their NHLA scores between women and men of color serving in the US Congress is not statistically significant – as opposed to the almost 40-point gap among Whites, which is highly significant.

A survey by the Center for American Women and Politics (CAWP 2001, 11) asked a sample of state legislators whether they thought that having more women in office would "make a difference in terms of helping pass policy initiatives to benefit women *and minorities*" (emphasis added) and reported that women state legislators were more likely to agree.[19] To explore this more deeply, we decided to replicate the CAWP survey question so as to offer an intersectional perspective and serve as

[19] The executive summary to the CAWP (2001, n.p.) report, *Women State Legislators: Past, Present and Future*, states that "the increased presence of women in the legislature has made a difference in the extent to which the economically disadvantaged have access to legislatures and the extent to which legislatures are sympathetic to the concerns of racial and ethnic minority groups."

TABLE 6.8. *Women's Impact on Helping Pass Policies to Benefit Racial Minorities: Perception of Elected Officials of Color, by Gender and Race*

Percent Reporting Women Make....	A Lot of Difference	Some Difference	Little or No Difference
All (N = 1,247)	43.5	44.7	11.8
By Gender***			
Female (N = 469)	53.7	38.8	7.5
Male (N = 778)	37.4	48.2	14.4
By Race*Gender***			
Black women*** (N = 282)	57.4	35.8	6.7
Black men (N = 381)	40.7	47.2	12.1
Latinas** (N = 149)	47.7	46.3	6.0
Latino men (N = 326)	34.4	49.1	16.6
Asian American women (N = 28)	50.0	35.7	14.3
Asian American men (N = 59)	33.9	45.8	20.3
American Indian women† (N = 10)	50.0	20.0	30.0
American Indian men (N = 12)	33.3	66.7	0
By Race*			
Black (N = 663)	47.8	42.4	9.8
Latino/a (N = 475)	38.5	48.2	13.3
Asian American (N = 87)	39.1	42.5	18.4
American Indian (N = 22)	40.9	45.5	13.6

Note: Entries are percents of responses to the question: *Would you say that women have made a lot of difference, some difference, very little difference, or no difference at all in terms of helping pass policy initiatives to benefit racial or ethnic minorities?*
†$p < .1$; *$p < .05$; **$p < .005$; ***$p < .0001$.
Source: GMCL National Survey, 2006–2007.

a corrective for studies with exclusively or predominately White respondents. We introduced the topic by saying, "*In recent years, the number of women serving in public office has increased across the country. We are interested in whether you think the presence of **women** has affected the way your particular governing body works*"; then we asked "*Would you say that women have made a lot of difference, some difference, very little difference, or no difference at all in terms of helping pass policy initiatives to **benefit racial or ethnic minorities?**"* We revisit this question using multivariate analysis in Chapter 7 (see Table 7.7), but, for now, as shown in Table 6.8, it is clear that about nine in ten of all elected officials of color concur, saying that it either makes a lot of difference or at least some difference. Furthermore, women are driving this result: 53.7 percent of women compared to 37.4 percent of men say women make a lot of difference.

Recent research provides additional evidence – beyond the subjective responses of legislators – of the particularly significant role women of color play in advocating and legislating for the interests of women and minority communities. Reingold and Smith (2012) study welfare policymaking at the state legislative level and conclude that it is women of color – more so than men of color or White women – who were the strongest defenders of the interests of poor and minority women in need of government assistance. And, despite evidence of marginalization within their respective chambers, they still "managed to make a difference" in policy outcomes (143). Similarly, Brown (2014) provides insights on how Black women in the Maryland state legislature adopt both individual and group strategies to provide substantive representation for marginalized populations.

EVIDENCE OF POLITICAL INCORPORATION FOR ELECTED OFFICIALS OF COLOR: DO THEY VOTE WITH THE MAJORITY?

Years ago, Browning et al. (1984) identified another dimension of political incorporation for minority public officials – whether they were members of a dominant coalition (voting majority) on their governing bodies. As such, they were likely to achieve success in seeing their policy positions prevail. Officials on the losing side of votes overall risked marginalization, achieving only "token" influence in local government. We adapted this measure of political incorporation by asking GMCL Survey respondents about their voting records in the governing body within which they serve: *"Are you part of a voting majority on important public policy issues, part of a voting minority, or do you vote with the majority and the minority equally?"*

As seen in Table 6.9, there is strong evidence of political incorporation when it comes to self-reported voting records: four in ten said they vote with the majority; another half split evenly between the majority and minority; and only a small percentage see themselves as consistently in the minority on their governing bodies. Asian Americans serving in elected office are the most likely (55.1 percent) to report voting with the majority. Reflecting the legacy of Black racial segregation and the prolonged and lingering resistance to the incorporation of Blacks into the political system, it may not be surprising that the percent of Black officials who vote with the majority is the smallest of all four racial groups; that said, half responded that they vote equally with both.

At the same time, American Indians also indicate a voting pattern distinct from those of the other ethnoracial groups. American Indian state

TABLE 6.9. *Self-Reported Voting Records, by Race*

Reported Votes....	All	Black	Latino	Asian American	American Indian
...with voting majority	39.5	35.4	41.9	55.1	42.1
...equally with both	49.1	51.1	48.4	40.4	36.8
...with voting minority	11.5	13.5	9.7	4.5	21.1
N	1,221	638	475	89	19

Note: Cell entries are percents of elected officials of color reporting votes. American Indians are mostly state legislators, and their findings should be viewed with caution for this reason and due to their small numbers.
Source: GMCL National Survey, 2006–2007; $p < .01$.

legislators report a relatively high rate of voting with the majority *and* the highest rate of voting with the minority. Perhaps their unique status as public officials at once immersed in American governmental processes as well as their identity and ties to (semi) sovereign peoples (and governments) underlie these differences.[20] To determine whether the difference for American Indians was due to the fact that most of them in the GMCL Survey are state legislators whereas the majority in other groups are local officials, we compared the voting records by race of state legislators alone.

Although their numbers are small, we find that the difference may be real: 30.8 percent of American Indian state legislators reported voting in the minority, compared to 35.5 percent of Black and 19.4 percent of Latino/a legislators. Remarkably, and possibly reflecting their concentration in two very multicultural states, almost all (94.4 percent) of Asian American legislators said they vote with the majority – and none with the minority. In Hawaii, both legislative chambers have been dominated by Democrats since the early 1950s. Other groups serve in legislatures where partisanship is more contested.

There were few significant gender differences. Among state legislators, men were more likely than their female peers to report voting with the

[20] At the time this manuscript was being written, news broke that "The Penobscot and Passamaquoddy tribes withdrew their representatives to the Maine Legislature on Tuesday in the latest sign of a growing rift in the historically troubled relationship between the sovereign tribes and the state." Maine is the only state where tribes send representatives. "The tribal representatives' role in and recognition by state government have been tempestuous, however. An effort in 1939 to give Indian representatives full speaking and voting rights failed and, two years later, lawmakers ousted the tribal representatives altogether. Their status was gradually restored, and in 1975, tribal representatives were once again given seats and the ability to speak during floor debates" (Miller 2015).

majority (56.8 percent compared to 45.8 percent, respectively), but this difference was not statistically significant. Among elected officials as a whole, the only difference by gender is for Latinas, who are significantly more likely than their male peers to vote with the majority (47 percent to 39.6 percent; $p < .05$).

CONCLUSION

We began this chapter by interrogating the meanings of leadership, which, in our analysis, are based on questionable assumptions, built primarily on experiences of White men, and more recently, White women. A robust body of literature now disrupts and expands old and traditional definitions of leadership and its praxis toward more inclusionary visions that count people of color – women and men – among the nation's governing elites. In that vein, our study seeks to contribute to empirical understandings of people of color as they increase their numbers as positional leaders and seek to exercise influence in the political system. To what extent does – or will – their presence in government lead to a "politics of difference" – significant change, even transformational change – in how government operates?

Recognizing the difficulties involved in providing definitive answers to this question, we turned our attention to more modest examinations of important aspects of leadership and governance.

In the case of leadership style, largely drawn from subjective perspectives of elected officials themselves, we add our own survey data. Women and men of color elected officials think women – like the literature on White women suggests – work harder, are better at building consensus, avoid the limelight to get the job done, are more persuasive, and more transparent when developing public policy. Hence, our study supports the notion that gender does matter in how elected officials engage in the policymaking process within their governing bodies. To be sure, we have no additional, rigorously objective measures of leadership style; like other scholars, we rely on self-reports of elected officials. But our study is unprecedented in its generalizability and focus on elected officials of color nationally, so that our findings of gendered difference carry the debate further.

We add an important assessment of political incorporation by examining a wide array of leadership positions – on committees in Congress and state legislatures, and in the political parties – which demonstrates some progress but also continuing underrepresentation for women and men of color. Institutional constraints and characteristics weigh substantially on the prospects of continued advancement for these officials in their quest to wield power in their respective governing bodies. And, yet, the elected officials of color in our study – overwhelmingly local office-holders – report they belong to voting majorities for the most part, suggesting a level of effectiveness as substantive representatives for various constituencies.

More expansive research agendas on the links between descriptive and substantive representation for elected officials of color continue to emerge. They include, for example, studies of bill sponsorship and passage among elected officials of color (see, e.g., Bratton, et al. 2006 and Reingold and Haynie 2014). Perhaps by putting elected officials of color – especially women – at the center of ongoing research, a deeper understanding – more complex and more accurate depictions of how government works for all – may be attained.

In Chapter 7, we continue to challenge existing tenets of political science by delving into the relationships between elected leaders and their constituents and incorporating a gender*race analysis as we tackle the equally complex meaning and nature of representation from the perspectives of Black, Latino/a, Asian American, and American Indian elected officials.

7

Perspectives on Representation

A common theme in popular media and the academic literature is that by the time an elected official of color gets into office she or he is either so changed by the process, or was different to start with, that she or he is no longer *representative* of the people she or he serves (see, e.g., Reed 2000; Tate 2003). Pundits and scholars portray Black and Latino (and perhaps Asian) elected officials as so different from their constituents in terms of class, ideology, and/or partisanship, that a gulf exists between them and their constituents, and they no longer act in sync with the preferences and desires of their communities.

King, Shaw, and Spence (2010, 109) summarizes research of Adolph Reed (2000) and other scholars who argue that the liberal and "'upper-class bias' of Black elected officials often confounds their ability to be accountable to impoverished Black constituents." Specifically, Reed comments that the apparent unity in Black electoral leadership really reflects the domination of middle- and upper-class Blacks, who often neglect the interests of lower and working class Blacks in their legislative agenda setting process. According to Bowler and Segura (2012, 174), scholars such as Tate (2003) have "raised the possibility that African American representation has strayed from black voter preferences by being more liberal than the constituencies they represent." Bowler and Segura also note that there is less research on this topic vis à vis Latinos, and that "[f]or Asian Americans, there is an almost total absence of information by which to evaluate co-ethnic representation. As such, it is far harder to assess the responsiveness of Asian American legislators at any level of government" (174).

Embedded within this narrative is of course the question of whether a representative who is of a "minority" racial group – whether he or she be the president, member of Congress, or local official – can represent nonminority constituents at all. The number of permutations, although not infinite, are several: Can White elected officials represent minority groups? Can the wealthy represent the poor and working class? And can men represent women? Separate from questions about the foundation of this narrative is the fact that, heretofore, research has focused almost exclusively on those holding office at the national or state level; virtually nothing is known about the extent to which municipal, county, and school board officials – who make up the vast majority of all elected officials – can represent the interests and preferences of their jurisdictions.

Furthermore, to what extent do similarities between the representatives and the people in their jurisdictions (by race or other social attribute) influence the elected officials' views about what they should do as representatives or what they perceive as the adequate or preferred representational role for their constituents? Addressing the vision of John Adams (1776) for the representative assembly that it "should think, feel, reason, and act like them," we ask how closely elected officials of color should "think alike" or "stand for" the majority political values of their constituents. We also wonder if there are substantive impacts from being congruent in personal, social, or political characteristics with the majority of constituents on taking policy positions to advance social justice for disadvantaged racial minorities and women.

This chapter proceeds with a theoretical exploration of the concept and dimensions of political representation, followed by a discussion of how elected officials of color might perceive their representational role.[1] Anchoring on the concept of congruence between views and experiences of the representatives and the represented, we then conduct empirical scrutiny of the various dimensions of representation and explore their interrelationships to each other among elected officials of color situated at the intersection of race and gender serving in state and local offices in the Gender and Multicultural Leadership (GMCL) National Survey. This is followed by an exploration of the possible implications or impact of descriptive/symbolic representation on the substantive dimension of representation. Several guiding questions to wrap up the chapter are: Does congruence on race, class, ideology, and partisanship contribute to the representatives' views on their representational roles? Are those who

---

[1] Sections of this chapter appeared in a modified way in a paper presented at the 2011 Annual Meeting of the American Political Science Association, Seattle, Washington, September 1–4; see Lien, Pinderhughes, Sierra, and Hardy-Fanta (2011).

"match" their constituents in these ways more likely to support legislation that protects minority rights?

THEORETICAL CONSIDERATIONS: DIMENSIONS OF POLITICAL REPRESENTATION

How representative elected officials of color are of the constituents hinges, first and foremost, on the various meanings of the concept of representation. In her seminal work *The Concept of Representation*, Hanna Pitkin (1967, 209) identifies several dimensions of political representation. The descriptive dimension refers to the extent to which the social characteristics of the representatives "look alike" or resemble in important ways the characteristics of the represented. The symbolic dimension refers to the extent that representatives "think alike" or "stand for" the values of the represented through the taking of a certain stance or making a certain speech that may earn the constituents' trust and confidence. In the substantive dimension, the representatives are expected to be "acting in the interests of the represented, in a manner responsive to them" (209). The formalistic dimension refers to the institutional arrangements that regulate the selection and removal of representatives such as through the electoral mechanism.

Pitkin (1967) herself did not recommend studying the four dimensions in isolation or paying attention only to the substantive dimension. Rather, her idea of representation is a multifaceted and interconnected one. To be truly representative, a legislative body must achieve some minimum quality on *all* dimensions of representation. Schwindt-Bayer and Mishler (2005) believe that Pitkin sees strong intercorrelations among the dimensions. For instance, in their study of women in thirty-one democracies, when representatives are elected through systems with free, fair, and open elections, they are more likely to reflect the social diversity of the represented, encourage policy responsiveness, and enhance public support for democratic institutions. They find that the structure of electoral systems exerts powerful influences on women's descriptive and symbolic representation. Their unit of analysis is the national political system and their focus is solely on women's interests, however.

Groups that historically have been marginalized based on their racial, ethnic, gender, and other social attributes may create a special problem for Pitkin and other theorists who treat representatives as an undifferentiated body of decision makers presumed to be male in gender, White in race, and who experience no systemic disadvantages in the seeking and exercising of power in the electoral process. Many recent scholars on political inequality have contended that the prolonged political exclusion of women and men of certain racial and ethnic groups is more than unjust: the failure to recognize their indispensable and constitutive roles (in the building of their own local and the national communities) and their bridging roles (linking underprivileged sectors of the society) is also undemocratic (Hill Collins 1990; Guinier and Torres 2002; Philips 1995, 1998, 1999; Young 1990, 2000). Within the women in politics literature, most scholars focus on descriptive representation, especially on increasing the numbers of women in office, comparing women's personal backgrounds and political characteristics to those of men, and, as we saw in the last chapter, promoting the idea that women have a transformative (substantive) impact on leadership style and public policies.

Envisioning the representative assembly to be a miniature portrait of the people, John Adams (1776) argues that achieving descriptive representation is essential for a democratic system of government. However debated the value of descriptive representation for people of color and women, we believe it is one of the most important ways in this democracy to measure progress in civil rights, racial justice, and equality. Given the varied types of representation described previously, it is of considerable interest to find out the extent to which our elected officials of color meet the "look alike" criteria Adams urges.

When former New York City mayor Rudy Giuliani said, "I do not believe ... that the president loves America....He doesn't love you. And he doesn't love me. He wasn't brought up the way you were brought up and I was brought up..."(Samuelsohn 2015), he was communicating to his White male (and wealthy) audience that President Obama is not "like you and me" (Cillizza 2015), and he was speaking directly to the "look alike" dimension of descriptive representation: "It's not just the questioning of Obama's patriotism but also the suggested 'otherness' of Obama that is at work here." Obama's symbolic, descriptive – and, as Blow (2015) among others assert, substantive – impact as the Black chief executive of this country, conveys to those like Giuliani and his audience that he does not represent *them* – that is, White upper-class men. During his first run for the White House, because of his biracial background and upbringing in Hawaii and Indonesia, innumerable politicians and media questioned, *Is he Black enough?* Context and perceptions matter, of course, and when it came time to decide whom to support – a White women or a biracial man – in the 2008 presidential nomination process, most pundits, scholars, as well as the vast majority of Black voters, responded with, *He's Black enough for me.*[2]

Numerous scholars have revisited Pitkin's (1967) construct as they have tackled "[t]he crucial issues of responsiveness, quality of democracy, and inclusiveness" – especially in light of the underrepresentation of women and certain racial/ethnic groups (Celis and Mazur 2012, 509; see also Celis 2012; Minta 2012). Williams (1998), for instance, insists that, to ensure fair representation, politically marginalized groups must be able to elect their representatives to help articulate and defend minority interests. Mansbridge (1999) sees the improvement in the quality of deliberation as a benefit of having minority representatives. In her theory of the politics of presence, Philips (1995) argues that achieving levels of representation by women and minorities that more closely match their shares in the population may enhance perceptions of legitimacy and increase legislatures' responsiveness to policy concerns affecting these groups. These ideas point to the importance of exploring empirically the interrelationships between descriptive, symbolic, and substantive representation for communities of color. Before that, in the next section we would like to address the issue of perceived representational role or how the representatives see their proper role as representing the constituents.

REPRESENTATIONAL ROLES: DO ELECTED OFFICIALS OF COLOR SEE THEMSELVES AS TRUSTEES OR DELEGATES?

How do elected officials of color think of their representational role? In theory, those representatives who subscribe to the *delegate* view of representation see themselves as acting on instructions from their constituency via the latter's expressed preferences. James Madison is the best-known advocate for the delegate view of representation. Those representatives who follow the *trustee* view see themselves as free agents acting on their own understanding of the best interests of the constituency and the principled directives of their own conscience. The trustee view of representation is best articulated by Edmund Burke. Representatives who do not subscribe strictly to either the delegate or the trustee view

---

[2] See discussion on National Public Radio between Juan Williams, David Bositis, and Carol Swain, "Black Voters Aren't Fully Sold on Obama." Radio broadcast, www.npr.org/templates/story/story.php?storyId=7299432 (Accessed June 29, 2016); see also Samuelson (2009).

of representation are considered *politicos*, whose representational acts depend on the particular circumstances of the decision-making process.

In Pitkin's (1967, 209) vision, "[t]he representative must act independently; his action must involve discretion and judgment; he must be the one who acts.... The representative must act in such a way that there is no conflict, or if it occurs an explanation is called for." Here, a representative's ability to know or assess accurately the interests of his or her constituents is not questioned but assumed. Her notion of substantive representation is also both idealistic and paradoxical in that a representative is expected to strike a balance between a desire to reflect the perceived preferences of the represented (as delegates) and a wish to use his or her judgment to decide how to advocate for the best interest of the constituency (as trustees).

Not surprisingly, the trustee–delegate distinction has been challenged. Rehfeld (2009), for example, argues that, if the three key aspects of their lawmaking process – aims, sources of judgment, and degree of responsiveness (to electoral sanctions) – are simultaneously considered, there should be eight, rather than only two, ideal types of representatives. With this rethinking, Rehfeld lays out the possibility of having seemingly paradoxical types of representatives who may be trustees but who also depend on the judgment of others and are responsive to electoral sanctions, or delegates but who may exert independence from constituency influence and the threats of electoral sanction. He does not specifically address the representation of minorities and he seems to assume minority group interests to be no different from other pluralistic interests. Yet, his theory opens up the possibility that the empirical evidence of the conventional trustee–delegate distinction may not be as clear cut and drawn by the same fault line as previously thought.

Nonetheless, in our survey we followed the convention of treating representational role orientation as a dichotomous measure, that is, as a choice of being either a delegate or a trustee type of representative. We gauge minority elected officials' view of their representational role in acting for constituents by a question asking respondents to choose from a pair of statements on the representational role that came closest to their view: "A. *In a situation when the views of my constituents conflict with my own, it is more important that my vote reflects the views of my constituents.* or B. *In a situation when the views of my constituents conflict with my own, it is more important that my vote reflects my informed judgment and trust that my constituents will support me.*" We treat respondents who chose statement A as "delegates," and those who chose statement B as "trustees."

Three in five (63 percent) of our respondents consider themselves subscribing to the trustee concept of substantive representation; only one in three (34 percent) consider themselves as delegates of their constituents. This finding on the popularity of the trustee view of representation among non-White elected officials differs significantly from early studies on White women serving in local offices where delegate is the more popular role (Antolini 1984; Bers 1978; Flammang 1985, 1997; Mezey 1980). It is consistent, however, with the pattern identified in a recent review of legislative women in state and congressional offices (Reingold 2008b) as well as studies of state legislators (e.g., Cooper and Richardson 2006; Wahlke, Eulau, Buchanan, and Ferguson 1962). Reingold (2008b, 134) explains that few women or men would identify with the delegate role, "perhaps because it could easily be associated with passiveness, subservience, weak leadership, and indecisiveness – all gender stereotypes that haunt female politicians in particular."

For officials of color, we might speculate that they also do not wish to be associated with the negative connotations of being preferential to the minority community. However, in the analysis that follows, we show that officials who view their legislative role as closer to the delegate form/model are more likely to perceive a correspondence between their own respective racial, partisan, and ideological identities as well as what they perceive as the most important issue stance and that of their constituents.

We also find that respondents' race and level of office appear to matter more than gender in their view on representational role. Although respondents in each race all identify more with the trustee role, Asians register a particularly high percentage (72 percent), while others all hover around 58 percent. In terms of the level of office, local school board members report a significantly higher frequency of identification with the trustee role (70 percent) than officials in other offices. Those serving at the municipal level report a somewhat higher identification with the delegate role (38 percent) than state legislators or school board members. Women and men of color do not differ in their representational role orientation.

GAUGING CONGRUENCE IN POLITICAL REPRESENTATION FOR COMMUNITIES OF COLOR

Scholars such as Dovi (2002) voice doubts as to whether Blacks and other minority groups need representatives who descriptively "look like" them to represent adequately the interests of the respective racial group. She argues that not all descriptive representatives are preferable – only those who have strong mutual relationships with dispossessed subgroups of historically disadvantaged groups. In response, Minta (2012) investigates *how* descriptive representation leads to substantive representation of Black and Latino interests in the US Congress and points to the significant role of racial group consciousness, identification, and minority community organizations in the process. Burden (2007) also provides empirical evidence that descriptive representation may often result in substantive representation. His thesis is that personal traits of legislators – not just race or gender but also values, interests, and expertise – shape legislative decisions in important ways. Because voters often do not have sufficient information to judge the (prospective) performance of political candidates, they are better off electing someone who is like them than hoping to change a representative who is not. His research bolsters the value and importance of electing representatives with like-minded background and provides another justification why minorities should be elected to represent minority communities.

We provided a baseline portrait of elected officials in previous chapters that examined aspects of descriptive, symbolic, and substantive representation. By looking at the election contests of Black, Latino/a, Asian American, and American Indian elected officials, we examined, to some extent, formalistic representation in Chapter 5. We turn now to describing how well elected officials of color "match" their constituents on key measures of representation: race, ideology, partisanship, and class.

DESCRIPTIVE REPRESENTATION: HOW REPRESENTATIVE ARE ELECTED OFFICIALS?

Studying political representation has often meant developing methods to measure actions (e.g., legislation proposed) or outcomes (e.g., policies implemented). Nowhere is this more true than in seeking links between descriptive or symbolic and substantive representation. We argue that one way that representation can be understood is to gauge the extent of *congruence* between elected officials and their constituents. In this meaning, we believe how similar the democratically elected officials are to their constituents by race, class, ideology, among other factors, is, despite protests from others, an equally important question.

In Chapter 6, we explored the relationship between elected officials and their constituents from the perspective of leadership: How often and with what goal in mind do their constituents – as "followers," voters, potential voters – contact their elected leaders? We now expand our understanding of this relationship by determining the degree of congruence between constituents and their Black, Latina/o, Asian American, and American Indian representatives on some of Pitkin's dimensions. We first measure descriptive representation by the degree of congruence between the racial identity of the elected officials and their perceptions of the dominant race among their respective constituencies. Second, we gauge how well the representatives' own political partisanship and ideology matches the partisan-ideological makeup of their constituents. For an indication of issue responsiveness, which is tied to the substantive dimension, we measure the extent to which men and women of color who represent constituencies disadvantaged by class also view class as the most important issue facing minority communities.

We then return to whether congruence between the representatives and their constituents might affect their views about representational roles (i.e., do they see themselves as "delegates" or "trustees"?) and explore the possible impact of the increased presence of women and minorities in governing positions on passing policy initiatives to benefit women and/or minorities. Lastly, we explore the feedback link to representation through a variety of constituent relationship and gauge the extent to which indicators of these constituent linkages may be associated with minority elected officials' attitudes toward protecting the interests of minority communities – in this case, perceived importance of affirmative action for women or racial minorities and expressed support for renewing minority voting rights).

One might well ask, why examine the officials' *perceptions* of their constituents? One reason is that, as Fenno (2007, 11) writes, "In the study of representation...perception matters a lot.... A constituency is, to an important degree, what the elected representative thinks it is." We must acknowledge, nevertheless, that with a few exceptions (e.g., Fenno 1978, 2007; Miler 2007, 2010), our emphasis on representatives' perceptions of constituencies is a departure from most prior research that strives to establish a linkage between the descriptive and the substantive form of representation for those members of Congress or state legislatures who are either women (who are mostly White) or racial minorities (who are mostly Black men). The preponderance of the evidence in this growing line of research points to a positive relationship between increased presence of elected officials who are women and/or minorities and improved likelihood that the interests of women, Blacks, and Latinos/as will be represented in the legislative process. Furthermore, there is value in focusing on the attitudes and opinions of the representatives themselves. Their perceptions of constituencies may be influenced by personal background and values, which, in turn, may influence their concepts of representational role, evaluations of the meanings of descriptive representation, and policy opinions on protecting minority interests. Finally, although we do not question the knowledge and judgment of our elected officials and their estimations of the constituencies, we use, when possible, other data sources such as jurisdiction-level data from the US Census to assess the extent perceptions match actual numbers "on the ground."

Do Elected Officials of Color Think They "Look Like" Their Constituents?

Do Black, Latino, Asian American, and American Indian elected officials represent jurisdictions where the majority of constituents are coethnics, that is, share their racial identity? Because of the history and legacy of racial discrimination against these minorities (see "Narratives of Exclusion," Chapter 1), proponents of minority voting rights have argued for the creation of majority–minority districts to help bridge the substantial gaps in descriptive political representation between non-Hispanic Whites and those of other ethnoracial groups (discussed in Chapter 1; see also Davidson and Grofman 1994). In an earlier publication, we demonstrated that, as the result of the 1965 Voting Rights Act and subsequent amendments, the racial makeup of a district correlates highly with the election of people of color to offices at the national, state, and local levels (Lien, Pinderhughes, Hardy-Fanta, and Sierra 2007). To gauge the congruence by race for respondents in the GMCL Survey, each elected official is asked to indicate whether his or her jurisdiction is made up mostly of (non-Hispanic) Whites, Blacks, Latinos, Asian Americans, American Indians, other, or mixed with no dominant race. For the racial "look alike" dimension (descriptive representation), respondents who are of a certain racial identity and perceive their constituency as made up mostly of coethnics are assigned a code of 1 and 0 otherwise.

Perceived Congruence on Race

About six in ten Blacks and Latinos/as, and close to half of American Indians believe their jurisdictions are made mostly of their coethnics (Table 7.1). Asian American elected officials show a distinctive pattern of

TABLE 7.1. *Perceived Racial Makeup of Jurisdictions, by Race of Elected Officials*

Said Race of Majority of Constituents Is...	Race of Elected Official				
	All	Asian American	Black	Latino/a	American Indian
Mixed	21.7	29.8	21.3	21.1	13.6
Non-Hispanic White	19.5	44.7	17.7	17.0	27.3
Black	32.2	0	59.5	0.6	13.6
Latino	24.4	10.6	1.6	60.4	0
Asian American	1.2	13.8	0	0.6	0
American Indian	0.8	1.1	0	0	45.5
N	1,305	94	696	493	22

Note: Entries are percent of elected officials of color; differences are significant at $p < .0001$.
Source: GMCL National Survey, 2006–2007; $N = 1,359$.

representation: only a small portion (13.8 percent) of them believe that they represent predominantly Asian districts, while close to half think they represent mostly White districts. Thus, with the exception of Asian Americans, the majority of elected officials of color in our survey report that they do descriptively represent constituents who resemble their racial characteristics.

Perceptions Vary by Race*Gender and Level of Office

When gender is added to the analysis by race, a slightly higher percentage of male than female officials (62 percent vs. 57 percent) of Blacks, Latinos, or American Indians report their jurisdictions as made up mostly of their coethnics. Conversely, a higher percentage of female than male officials of Asian American, Black, and Latino descent report their jurisdictions as made up mostly of mixed-raced people. For Asian Americans, a higher percentage of male than female officials (16 percent vs. 10 percent) report having a mostly Asian constituency. In comparison, a much higher percentage of both Asian American women and men (47 percent and 44 percent respectively) report having a constituency that is mostly made up of Whites than persons of other ethnoracial backgrounds. As the following discussion shows, level of office held by elected officials also makes a difference in their perceptions of racial congruence.

State Legislators

We find that almost two-thirds of Black state legislators represent districts that are "majority Black" and about half of Latino state legislators thought their constituents are majority Latino, while fewer than a quarter of Asian American state legislators thought they represent "majority Asian" districts. In contrast, half of Asian American and four in ten Latino/a legislators thought they represent "majority non-Hispanic White" jurisdictions. Asian Americans are also more likely than other groups to report their jurisdictions being "mixed" in racial makeup – and this percentage (26.8) is larger than the share of those who report being elected from "majority Asian" jurisdictions. Black, Latino/a, and Asian American state legislators are also unlikely to be elected from jurisdictions that have majorities of other groups of color that do not match their own. It is clear from these findings, which are highly significant (Figure 7.1), that the role of perceived racial composition within jurisdictions as a factor in the growth of elected officials of color is not as simple as might be construed from previous studies and that it varies considerably by racial group.

The only significant gender difference for state legislators is among Blacks, with Black women being much more likely than their male counterparts to report being elected in jurisdictions that are "mixed, with no dominant race" (34.8 percent women vs. 8.8 percent men) and much less likely to be elected from "majority Black" jurisdictions (73.5 percent men vs. 50.0 percent women).

Local-Level Officials

When it comes to local-level officials, Latinos/as are more like Blacks, with six in ten of both groups being elected from jurisdictions that match their respective ethnoracial identities (Figure 7.2). Asian American local officials again are more likely to represent jurisdictions that are majority White (43.4 percent), mixed (30.3 percent), and even more Latino (13.2 percent) than Asian (11.8 percent).

And the role of gender among Latina/o local officials is different from that among Black state legislators. Although a majority of all Latinos are elected in majority-Latino jurisdictions, Latinas are somewhat more likely to represent jurisdictions that are more mixed, and somewhat less like likely (at 58 percent) to report representing "majority-Latino" jurisdictions, than their male counterparts (at 63 percent). Why would the constituent-elected official racial match be so much closer for Blacks, Latinos, and American Indians compared to Asian Americans? First, of course, is simply the fact that,

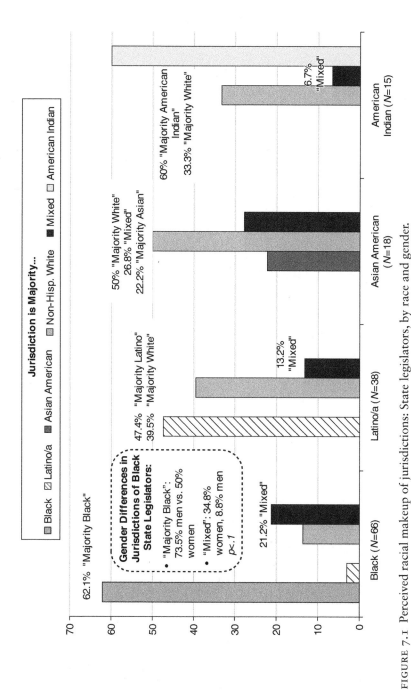

FIGURE 7.1 Perceived racial makeup of jurisdictions: State legislators, by race and gender.

Note: In this analysis, the racial makeup of the jurisdiction is based on the response to the following survey question: "*Would you say that the racial or ethnic makeup of your jurisdiction is mostly: non-Hispanic White, Black, Hispanic or Latino, Asian, American Indian or mixed with no dominant race?*" Entries are percents of state legislators of color by race.

Source: GMCL National Survey and Database, 2006–2007; *N* = 137; *p* < .0001.

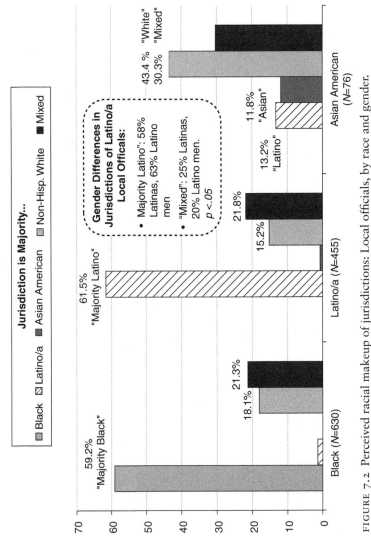

FIGURE 7.2 Perceived racial makeup of jurisdictions: Local officials, by race and gender.
Note: In this analysis, the racial makeup of the jurisdiction is based on the response to the following survey question: *"Would you say that the racial or ethnic makeup of your jurisdiction is mostly: non-Hispanic White, Black, Hispanic or Latino, Asian, American Indian, or mixed with no dominant race?"*
Source: GMCL National Survey, 2006–2007. N = 1,168; p < .01.

outside of Hawaii and, to a lesser extent, California, Asian Americans make up a smaller share of the population overall and in localities as well. Second, it is also possible that Asian American candidates are more "acceptable" to non-Hispanic Whites given their overall socioeconomic status and racial image. One must also ask whether they have either benefited less from majority–minority districting decisions than Latinos/as and Blacks – or, perhaps, even when they have the numbers in the population, been hurt by them (Saito 2009). These are important issues for future explorations.

Congress

Considerable amount of ink has been used to report the racial makeup of the districts represented by members of Congress. Few provide, however, multi-racial portraits; an exception is our earlier finding that "Neither Asian nor American Indian House members were elected from districts in which the majority of the population is of their own race" (Lien et al. 2007, 491). In fact, in our research the percent in non-Hispanic White districts was, on average, 62.8 percent for Asians and 77.6 percent for American Indians, compared to 32.9 percent for Blacks and 26.2 percent for Latinos. In contrast, Black and Latino districts were made up of a majority Black or Latino population, respectively (490). These numbers provide stronger evidence of descriptive racial representation among Blacks than found in an earlier study by Button and Hedge (1996, 203), who report that "districts represented by black law-makers contain, on average, 60% blacks, compared to just 13% for their white counterparts. Indeed, only 5% of the white lawmakers in our sample represent black majority districts (versus 75% for our black legislators)."

How Well Do the Elected Officials Know Their Constituents?

Since legislators' perceptions of their constituents are important for the quality of representation and governance (Fenno 2007), we are cu-rious: *How well do minority elected officials know their constituents?* We gained insights into this by checking whether the survey respondents' perceptions of the majority racial group in each of their jurisdictions (i.e., state legislative districts and municipal places) match the comparable fig-ures in the US Census.[3] We find that, remarkably, the vast majority of state

---

[3] Please see Appendix A for details on how we matched each elected official in the GMCL Database with the racial makeup of district or jurisdiction; since the survey data are from 2006–2007, we used jurisdictional data from the 2000 US Census.

TABLE 7.2. *Congruence between Officials' Perception of Racial Makeup in Jurisdiction and Race of Elected Officials, by Level of Office*

Level of Office	Race of Elected Official			
	American Indian	Asian American	Black	Latino/a
State legislators	93.3	100.0	78.8	92.1
	(15)	(18)	(66)	(38)
Municipal officials	n/a	93.0	71.6	84.5
		(43)	(352)	(206)

Note: Entries are percent, with N in parentheses, matched for each cell, according to US Census, by race of elected official and (selected) levels of office; differences are significant at $p < .05$ for state legislators and at $p < .0001$ for municipal officials.
Source: GMCL National Survey and National Database, 2006–2007.

legislators – almost nine in ten – correctly estimated that their districts were made up of coethnics; the same is true for three-quarters of municipal officials. Furthermore, Asian American elected officials at both state and municipal levels turn out to be the *most* accurate judges of racial makeup in their jurisdictions (Table 7.2). The small size of the population of Asian elected officials might also help reduce the error margins, as Black elected officials who are the most numerous in size are accorded with the lowest, despite still respectable, congruency rates.

Among Blacks, whose perceptions are relatively less likely to match the population in their districts according to the US Census than the other groups, their estimates are still quite accurate, with about three-quarters yielding a "match." We note the "errors" tend to be in some of them seeing their districts as not being "majority Black." Curiously, three-quarters of the Black state legislators whose reported perception that their jurisdictions were *not* majority Black do in fact represent districts that are majority Black, in some cases by a substantial margin – with Blacks making up 60 to 70-plus percent of the population in those jurisdictions. For municipal officials, we find that a quarter of those whose perceptions did not match also underestimated the percentage of the jurisdiction that was Black. Exactly why a greater portion of the Black officials underestimate the size of their Black coethnics in their jurisdictions than other minority officials is a subject for future exploration. Nevertheless, the "takeaway" from this exercise is that these elected officials are clearly in tune with the racial composition their districts – and we can have confidence in using their perceptions in the analysis that follows.

SYMBOLIC REPRESENTATION: AN UNTAPPED
RESOURCE FOR CONSTITUENTS?

Although policy responsiveness has been considered a most important and commonly used gauge of quality representation, Eulau and Karps (1977) have maintained that it is only one of the ways representatives may respond to constituents' interests. They complain that the values of policy responsiveness have been overemphasized while the psychological impacts of symbolic speech or gestures on the opinions of the represented have been underappreciated. For them, legislators may respond to constituency needs by bringing in nontangible benefits in a manner that builds constituency trust and confidence in their leadership. In fact, according to Wahlke (1971), symbolic representation might be the most realistic standard for quality representation. Certainly, students of US Congress and state legislators have found the institutions loaded with acts of symbolic representation such as through position taking, credit claiming, and advertising for the particularistic activities affecting their constituents (Fenno 1978, 2003; Hall 1996; Mayhew 1974; Smith 2003).

In his study of the Congressional Black Caucus, Whitby (2007) makes the observation that virtually all incumbents engage in symbolic acts to enhance their electoral fortunes. In his earlier work, he notes that the presence of Blacks in Congress symbolizes the group's inclusion in polity, progress achieved in US race relations, and their political empowerment in the US system (Whitby 1997). Thus, "the symbolic value of descriptive representation may be especially important for racial minority groups as they continue to struggle for full inclusion in mainstream American society" (Whitby 2007, 207). Mansbridge (1999) makes a similar point that, through symbolic actions taken on behalf of their minority constituents, legislators of racial and gender minorities may be better able to enhance the perceived legitimacy of governmental authority and increase the levels of political efficacy and political trust among disadvantaged social groups than their nonminority colleagues.

Nevertheless, Whitby (2007, 206) notes when the focus is on African American congresspersons' symbolic representation, the majority of the literature has been "generally focused on CBC [Congressional Black Caucus] protest activities..." Those who view these activities with a critical tone cite the reliance on symbolic rhetoric and even dramaturgical politics to placate their constituents. This attitude may partially account for the paucity of empirical research on symbolic representation. Unlike the studying of other dimensions of representation, symbolic representation is said to be concerned not so much with who the representatives are or what they do, but how they are perceived and evaluated by those they represent, that is, the "stands for" and "thinks alike" dimension of representation.

Past research on the attitudinal components of symbolic representation, with its efforts to assess its value from the perspectives of the represented, is limited and produces mixed results. Whereas studies on Blacks generally find positive effects on constituents' evaluations of their representatives, levels of political efficacy and trust in government, and propensity to participate politically (Banducci, Donavan, and Karp 2004; Gay 2002; Tate 2003; Tate and Harsh 2005), some have found that presence of women officeholders does not produce the anticipated benefits (see, e.g., Lawless 2004). Despite the somewhat celebratory tone of many scholars and activists about the "transformational" effect of women's leadership discussed in Chapter 6, Minta (2012) critically observes that the literature presents conflicting findings on whether female legislators provide better representation of women's interests than male legislators. In another study, Huddy, Cassese, and Lizotte (2008) suggest that political differences among women based on race, religion, and economic status may be much larger than the gender gaps between men and women.

Do Elected Officials of Color "Think Like" Their Constituents?

If the majority of elected officials of both sexes do believe that they represent constituents who racially "look like" them, we ask now whether congruence on this measure of descriptive representation might extend to the "think alike" dimension of representation such as shared political partisanship and ideology? To proceed, we first compare the degree of similarity between elected officials' own political party affiliation and the political party with which they believe the majority of their constituents would identify. We do the same for correspondence on political ideology. Then, we explore the linkages among measures of representation by race, party, and ideology.

Outlook on Partisanship: Just How "Democratic" Are Elected Officials of Color?

Before we examine the congruence on partisanship, we note that, not unexpectedly, the vast majority of elected officials of color (81.4 percent) report a Democratic Party affiliation with the balance evenly split between

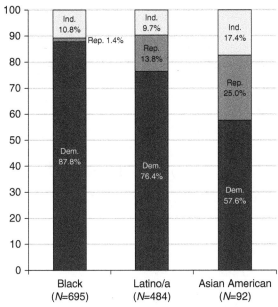

FIGURE 7.3 Party by race, all levels.
Note: Entries are percents of officials who reported party affiliation.
Source: GMCL National Survey, 2006–2007; N = 1,271; *p* < .0001.

Republicans (8.0 percent) and Independents (10.7 percent). There is variation by race (Figure 7.3), with Blacks and Latinos (at 87.8 percent and 79.4 percent, respectively, significantly more likely to be Democrats compared to 57.6 percent among Asian Americans. Women of color are more likely than men of color to report a Democratic Party affiliation (84.3 percent compared to 79.6 percent), but these differences are statistically significant only at *p* < .1.

Level of office makes a difference, with Democratic Party being able to count nine in ten state legislators and county officials in their column; the figure is eight in ten for municipal and school board officials (*p* < .0001). And, among state legislators of color, a higher percentage of women than men identified more strongly with the Democratic Party.

Congruence on Partisanship
Among the respondents who identify with being Democrat, three out of four perceive the majority of their constituents to be Democratic in partisanship as well (see Table 7.3). Six in ten of the self-identified Independents

TABLE 7.3. *Congruence on Political Partisanship*

Constituent Partisanship	Partisanship of Elected Officials				
	Democrat	Republican	Independent	None	All
Democrat	74.6	35.0	59.7	34.6	69.1
Republican	8.5	31.1	17.9	11.5	11.3
Evenly divided	16.8	34.0	21.6	53.9	19.3
Mostly Independent	.1	0	.7	0.0	.2
None/Don't Know	0	0	0	0	.1
N	996	103	134	26	1,259

Note: Entries are percent of elected officials who share partisan identification with their constituents; differences are significant at $p < .0001$.
Source: GMCL National Survey, 2006–2007.

also perceive voters in their jurisdictions to be more Democratic in partisanship. Among the 103 Republicans, only 31.1 percent perceive their constituents to be Republicans, while about one-third each perceive their constituents to be Democrats or evenly split between the two parties. Of those who are not sure of or mum on their partisan affiliation, just over half perceive their constituents as being evenly split between the two parties, while a third perceive their constituents to be more Democratic.

This exercise shows that the degree of correspondence in partisanship depends on the party in question. Elected officials of color who are Democratic in partisanship have the highest degree of correspondence with the perceived partisanship of the majority of their constituents. Those who are Independent also tend to perceive having a more Democratic constituency. However, those who identify with the Republican Party may be cross-pressured by being in the partisan minority among communities of color. Their ability to perform symbolic representation for minority groups may be limited by this fact, a finding that is also reported by Reingold and Harrell (2010). For these officials, not only is the degree of correspondence between personal and constituent partisanship lower, but also a higher share of these elected officials believe they represent a constituency that is either sympathetic with the opposite party or mixed in partisan identity. Nevertheless, the observed relationships can vary by level of office, racial, and gender identity.

In terms of level of office, those Democrats serving as state legislators and county officials report a higher degree of correspondence between their own and the perceived partisanship of their constituents than those serving as municipal officials and school board members (82 percent vs.

72 percent). A similar but weaker pattern is found among Republicans where six in ten state legislators perceive their constituency to be more Republican in partisan orientation than not. However, no more than one-third of Republicans in county and local offices would report their constituency as more Republican. Instead, 49 percent of school board members and 44 percent of county officials who are Republican perceive their constituency to be more Democratic in orientation, while close to half of Republican municipal officials think of their constituents as evenly divided between the two parties. Among respondents who are partisan Independent, at least seven in ten of state legislators and county officials report a Democratic-leaning constituency, compared to the 64 percent among municipal officials and 49 percent among school board members.

Looking from the angle of gender and racial identity, about three in four Black and Latino and two in three Asian Democrats perceive having constituencies that share in large part their partisan affiliation. Among Republican officials, those who are Black report a higher level of Democratic constituency than other groups, while Asian Republicans report a higher Republican constituency than other non-White officials. In terms of gender, although female Democrats are about as likely to report a Democratic-leaning constituency as male Democrats, female Republicans are more likely to report a Democratic-leaning constituency (41 percent) than male Republicans (32 percent).[4]

Outlook on Ideology: Just How "Liberal" Are Elected Officials of Color?

Despite a highly Democratic skew in political partisanship among elected officials of color, Table 7.4 shows a much more balanced personal ideological outlook across the board. Roughly equal shares of the respondents indicate that their views on most matters having to do with politics would fall under the liberal, conservative, and middle-of-the-road banners. Asians report the highest level of being middle-of-the-road (44 percent); Blacks report the highest level of liberalism

---

[4] Among Independents, a significantly higher share of Black (70 percent) and Asian (60 percent) than Latino (46 percent) officials perceive their constituencies to be more Democratic in orientation, while a higher share of Latinos than Blacks or Asians perceive their constituencies to be evenly divided. For male Republicans, they are more likely to perceive a constituency that is evenly divided (36 percent) than female Republicans (28 percent). Male Independents are also more likely to report a Democratic-leaning constituency (63 percent) than their female counterparts (54 percent), while a higher percentage of female Independents report an evenly divided constituency than male (30 percent vs. 17 percent).

TABLE 7.4. *Personal Political Ideology of Elected Officials of Color,*
by Race

	Asian	Black	Latino/a	All
Very liberal	7	11	9	10
Somewhat liberal	21	27	18	23
Middle of the road	44	36	34	36
Somewhat conservative	25	21	29	24
Very conservative	3	5	9	6

Note: Entries are percent of self-reported political ideology of elected officials.
Source: GMCL National Survey, 2006–2007; $N = 1,258$.

at 38 percent, while Latinos report the highest level of conservatism (37 percent). Not surprisingly, women in each group are significantly more likely than their male counterparts to self-identify as being very or somewhat liberal. Specifically, 43 percent of Asian female versus 21 percent of Asian male elected officials place themselves on the liberal camp. The similar figures for Blacks are 46 percent among women and 32 percent among men. Among Latinos, 39 percent among Latina and 24 percent among Latino elected officials identified themselves as liberals.

Congruence on Political Ideology

Next, we gauge the degree of "think-alike" between representatives and the represented by estimating the correspondence between an official's own political ideology and the perceived ideological stance of the majority of his or her constituency. Table 7.5 show that, among the respondents who are very liberal, only one in five perceive the majority of their constituents as very liberal, while more think of their constituents as somewhat liberal (39 percent) or moderate (24 percent).

Among the respondents who are somewhat liberal, two in five view their constituents as somewhat liberal, while one in three view them as middle-of-the-road. Among those who think of their political ideology as middle-of-the-road, close to half think of their constituents as sharing their moderate stance (46 percent), while a higher proportion view their constituents as somewhat conservative (26 percent) than somewhat liberal (17 percent).

Among the 305 respondents who self-identify as somewhat conservative, two in five view most of their constituents as sharing their ideological stance, but 36 percent view most of their constituents as being more

TABLE 7.5. *Congruence between Officials' Perception of Constituent Ideology and Their Own Ideology*

Ideology of Constituents	Ideology of Elected Officials					
	Very Liberal	Liberal	Middle of the Road	Conservative	Very Conservative	All
Very liberal	19	4	5	3	2	6
Somewhat liberal	39	40	17	12	4	23
Middle of the road	24	34	46	36	28	38
Somewhat conservative	13	18	26	40	39	27
Very conservative	5	3	6	10	27	7
N	127	297	450	305	79	1,258

Note: Entries are percent of elected officials whose perceived ideology of their constituents matched their own; differences are significant at $p < .0001$.
Source: GMCL National Survey, 2006–2007.

moderate than themselves. Finally, among the 79 respondents who self-identify as very conservative, 27 percent think their constituents share the same view on politics, while 39 percent think their constituents are somewhat conservative and 28 percent believe them to be moderate in view.

Are Black and Latino/a Officials More Liberal than their Constituents?

Considerable criticism has been levied against officials of color – Blacks in particular – for "incorrectly representing" their constituencies on ideology. Some argue that Black elected officials are far to the left of the ideological position of their constituents. We find, however, that while some of these officials consider their constituents to be more moderate in political views than they themselves, more than half of Black officials and four in ten of Latinos/as and Asians who consider themselves personally being liberal or very liberal represent constituents who share their ideology. Relatively few liberal/very liberal Black (at 15.7 percent) and Latino/a (at 11.7 percent) elected officials report constituencies made up primarily of those with conservative or very conservative ideologies.[5] We also do not believe this discrepancy to be an issue, as the majority of our elected officials prefer to think of themselves as trustees than delegates.

[5] Variation within racial groups was significant for Latinos and Blacks at $p < .0001$.

Congruence in Political Representation:
A Brief Summary

In sum, the majority of respondents report sharing the predominant racial identity with their constituents. The extent of descriptive racial representation varies significantly by race, with Latinos and Blacks reporting
higher rates of correspondence than American Indians and Asian
Americans. Close to three in five respondents on average report sharing a predominant party identity with their constituents, with Blacks the
highest and Asians the lowest. Political ideology is a different case where
only a minority of respondents report sharing the predominant political
ideology with their constituents,[6] with the highest degree of perceived
ideological correspondence being found among those who are moderate
in view.[7] These numbers do not vary much across racial groups. However,
gender matters in that a significantly higher percentage of Asian women
(50.0 percent) than Asian men (26.6 percent) report sharing the predominant political ideology with their constituents. The reverse is true among
Blacks, where 43.0 percent of Black men while 33.9 percent of Black
women show evidence of ideological correspondence with the majority
of their constituents; these gender differences are significant at $p < .05$.

LINKAGES BETWEEN RACE, PARTY, AND IDEOLOGY

A visual presentation of linkages between race, party, and ideology may
be found in Figure 7.4. Viewed as a group, the vast majority (71 percent)
of officials of color who perceive their constituents to be made up mostly
of persons who share their racial identity *also* believe their constituents
share their partisanship. Not unexpectedly, two-thirds (67 percent) share

---

[6] This figure is higher for Blacks (61 percent) and American Indians (59 percent) and
Latinos (57 percent) than for Asians (44 percent). Neither measure varies much between
the men and women of each racial group.

[7] Race still matters in that a higher percentage of very liberal Blacks than Latinos (25 percent vs. 11 percent), but a smaller percentage of very conservative Blacks than Latinos
(18 percent vs. 34 percent) perceive their constituents to share their political views.
Analyzing the relationships by level of office, we note that moderate state legislators
report the highest level of correspondence with their constituents' political views (66 percent) than moderates in other offices. State legislators who are very liberal or very conservative are also more likely than other office holders in the survey to perceive a constituency that is more moderate in political views than their own. In contrast, up to two in
five county officials who are very conservative, which is the highest percentage of extreme
conservatism among all levels of office holders, perceive their constituents to share their
brand of politics.

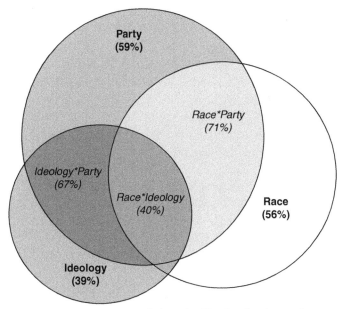

FIGURE 7.4 Congruence of elected officials of color and constituents on race, party, and ideology, alone and in interaction.
Note: Percentages in bold are for Race, Party, and Ideology alone; those in italics are for the interactions, with size of circles and segments proportionate.
Source: GMCL National Survey, 2006–2007; N = 1,276 for (Race*Party) and (Race*Ideology); N = 1,253 for (Party*Ideology).

not only party identification but also ideology. In contrast, just 40 percent of those who perceive their constituents are their coethnics believe their constituents share their political ideological stance.

Among those who believe their constituents to be mostly coethnics and also perceive the majority of them to share their ideological stance, with Asians having the highest rate of 46 percent and Latinos having the lowest rate of 37 percent. Furthermore, between 40 percent and 50 percent of officials of color who perceive their constituents to be mostly copartisan also believe them to be mostly ideological pals. This rate is highest among American Indians (50 percent) and lowest among Latinos (40 percent). There is no significant gender-based difference in any of the racial groups.

FACTORING CLASS INTO THE DEBATE

During the 2016 presidential primary season, we have seen a simultaneous focus on income inequality and disparities in educational access and outcomes by race as well as an increasingly anti-immigrant sentiment on the conservative side. Our interest in the congruence on race, class, education, and immigrant status between elected officials' perceptions of the communities they represent thus reflects more than an academic or methodological question. If one aims to delve into the linkages between descriptive and substantive representation, we believe it is worth looking at the match between the represented and the representative and not only the latter's perceptions but also the actual characteristics of his or her constituents that drive minority policies, that is, the "demand side" of politics. For example, if, as political elite, the elected official is of a higher socioeconomic class than that of the constituency or jurisdiction, does that make her or him more likely to be view her or his representational role as a delegate rather than a trustee? And can she or he be expected to support policy initiatives that benefit the disadvantaged minorities in her or his jurisdiction?

Congruence on Class

In Chapter 3, we demonstrated that elected officials of color have attained (or entered politics with), on average, higher socioeconomic status than that of the general population. To assess whether they, as socioeconomic elites, may be "out of touch" with their disadvantaged constituents we quantified the level of class-based congruence between them (the elected representatives) and their constituents (the represented).

Each elected officials of color was asked to estimate the class makeup of his/her constituency with following question: *"Would you say that your constituency is mostly poor, working class, middle class, upper class or mixed w no dominant class?"* Nearly half of those surveyed responded that their constituents are mostly poor or working class people (14 percent and 34 percent, respectively), with significant variation by race. Whereas only 15 percent of Asians considered their constituents as mostly of the working class, this percentage is 41 percent among Latinos, 36 percent among Blacks, and 20 percent among American Indians. More than other groups, American Indian officials reported having half of their constituents living in poverty, while more than a quarter (28 percent) of Asian officials reported having upper-middle class constituents.

We determined congruence between the elected officials and the people in their districts by matching his or her class category[8] with that of their

---

[8] To determine the class category of the elected officials, we coded their responses on their own household income during the previous year (reported in $10K increments) into a

TABLE 7.6. *Congruence between Elected Official's Class and Perceived Class of Constituents*

Race	Match, by Race	Match, by Race*Gender	
		Female	Male
Asian American	66.3	66.7	66.1
	(55)	(18)	(37)
Black	52.0	56.7	48.6
	(314)	(144)	(170)
Latino/a	49.5	50.4	49.2
	(219)	(68)	(151)
Match (All)	52.5	55.9	50.5
	(603)	(237)	(366)
Total N	1,149	424	725

Note: Entries are percent matched for each paired cell; *N* is in parentheses; differences on match by race overall are significant at $p < .01$ and by race and gender overall at $p < .1$; the gender differences within race are only significant for Blacks (at $p < .05$). Income of elected officials: "*Was the estimated annual income for your household in 2005; Less than $50,000; At least $50,000 but less than $100,000; At least $100,000 but less than $150,000; or $150,000 or more?* "Class of constituents: "*Would you say that your constituency is mostly: Poor, Working Class, middle class, upper class or mixed with no dominant class?*" We do not report American Indians because their numbers are small and they serve primarily as state legislators.

Source: GMCL National Survey, 2006–2007.

estimates of their constituents; if they matched, they were coded 1, all else, 0.[9] We call this the "Elected Official-Constituent Perceived Class Match" (Table 7.6). Comparing reported class of each official with his/her perception of the class of his or her constituents, we find that, for at least half of elected officials of color, their class "matches" their perceptions of constituent class, but with significant differences by race. Two-thirds of Asian Americans, followed by half of Blacks and Latinos, share the same economic class as their constituents. Women – and Black women,

class that corresponded to those of their constituents: Poor/Working Class (less than $50,000); Middle Class ($50,000 to less than $100,000); Upper Middle Class ($100,000 to less than $150,000), and Upper Class ($150,000 or more).

[9] To determine the elected officials' perceptions of their constituents' class, we asked, "*Would you say that your constituency is mostly: Poor, Working Class, Middle Class, Upper Class, or mixed, with no dominant class?*" To determine the class category of the elected officials and to reduce classification errors we coded survey respondents as 1 if they were in the Upper Middle Class category and their constituents were either in Upper, Middle, or Upper Middle; and to avoid eliminating or misclassifying those who said their jurisdictions were "mixed, with no dominant class," we coded them as 1.

especially – were also significantly more likely than their male counter-parts to report income that matched the class of their constituents.

As we discussed in earlier chapters, achieving a certain socioeconomic status is the result of considerable collective and individual effort for US women and men of color and, as we say elsewhere, is a continuing story of struggle, not only for the elected officials but also for the communities they represent. For this reason – that what may matter more than a precise match on income is "standing for" and representing their interests – we turn now to the question of class congruence and issue responsiveness.

Class-Based Issue Responsiveness

Our interest in class status, of course, goes beyond a mere "academic exercise"; our goal is rather to explore linkages between the representa-tive and the represented to see if the class-advantaged representatives may feel responsible to "act in the interests of" of their class-disadvantaged constituents and perform substantive representation to help advance interests of those in the disadvantaged class. We go beyond gauging the extent to which the representatives and their constituents are of the same class to hypothesize that elected officials of color whose constituencies are mostly poor or working class people[10] *and* who select class as "the most important problem" facing minorities in their jurisdictions are more likely to be responsive to the policy needs of their impoverished constitu-encies, thereby exercising a nascent version of substantive representation.

When asked whether race, class, or gender were the most important issue facing minorities in their communities, eight in ten said class, either alone or in combination. In fact, a third said class alone, while 17.8 per-cent of respondents named all three issues, including class, as the most important problem. On the measure of how many not only consider themselves representatives of the poor or working class, but also name class as the most important problem facing minorities in their communi-ties, we find four in ten (41.4 percent) of respondents to be in the cate-gory of greatest potential for possessing class-based issue responsiveness. Among them, Latinos (46.5 percent), American Indians (42.9) and Blacks (41.3 percent) stood out from and Asian Americans (15.7 percent) on this measure ($p < .0001$). Only among Blacks is gender difference signifi-cant. Importantly, a higher share of Black men (44.9 percent) than Black

---

[10] As measured by the survey question about whether their constituents were mostly poor or working class.

women (35.3 percent) not only perceive their constituencies as made up mostly of the poor and working class but also show concern over the class challenges facing these disadvantaged groups ($p < .05$).

Our hypothesis is that congruence (a "match") between elected officials and their constituents on descriptive dimensions of representation (such as race) as well as on symbolic dimensions of representation (such as partisanship, and ideology) may lead to greater class-based issue responsiveness. Bivariate analysis shows that the vast majority of respondents who reported class to be the most important problem for minority communities are from communities made up mostly of persons who share the same racial identity with them. Based on the long history of racial oppression against ethnoracial minority groups in the United States, we further believe that there may be a close relationship between the perceived constituency linkages by race and partisanship and class-based issue responsiveness among representatives of color, and indeed we find that two-thirds of elected officials who demonstrate class-based issue responsiveness come from jurisdictions dominated by copartisans. We therefore anticipate that congruence by race and by partisanship will contribute significantly to a class-based issue responsiveness. As there is not a significant relationship between ideology and issue responsiveness in the bivariate analysis, we do not predict a significant contribution in the multivariate analysis.

The logistic regression results are reported in Table 7.7.[11] As predicted, when the race, gender, and level of office differences across GMCL Survey respondents are controlled, we find the likelihood of non-White elected officials' issue responsiveness to the disadvantaged classes among their constituents be strongly and significantly increased by one's having a constituency that is mostly made up of coethnics or copartisans. We also find those who hold an office at the school board level to be more likely to show responsiveness to class-based issues than their colleagues in other levels office. We find the intersection of race and gender matter in that, when compared to being Black and male, being an Asian male

---

[11] In the multivariate analysis reported here and later in the chapter, to control for the intersecting effects of race and gender for the four groups of women and men of color officials in the survey, we create interactive terms of race and gender groupings for the multivariate analysis. Other control variables are office level, personal partisanship, and personal ideology. For the "think-alike" dimension of symbolic representation by shared partisanship, respondents who are of a certain party and perceive their constituency to be made up mostly by copartisans are assigned a code of 1 and 0 otherwise; for symbolic representation by shared ideology, respondents who are of a certain ideological orientation and perceive their constituency as made up mostly by people who share the same orientation are assigned a code of 1 and 0 otherwise.

TABLE 7.7. *Logistic Regression Predictors of Class-Based Issue Responsiveness*

Contributing Factors	b	s.e.
Constituent/Elected Official Congruence		
By race	.881**	.126
By partisanship	.323*	.130
By ideology	.017	.123
Race*Gender (*ref = Black men*)		
Latino men	−.008	.156
Asian men	−1.113**	.389
American Indian men	.565	.694
Black women	−.448*	.166
Latina women	.432†	.259
Asian women	.329	.674
American Indian women	.069	1.048
Office Level (*ref = Municipal*)		
State Legislative	−.083	.218
County	−.113	.173
School board	.281*	.146
Ideology (Liberal)	.202	.130
Partisanship (Republican)	.278	.219
Constant	−1.218	.163
Percent predicted correct	66.0	
−2 log likelihood	1673.495	
Nagelkerke R^2	.114	

Note: b = unstandardized logistic regression coefficients, s.e.= standard errors.
†$p \leq .1$, *$p \leq .05$ **$p \leq .005$.
Source: GMCL Survey 2006–2007; N = 1,359.

or Black female is associated with being less likely to hold issue responsiveness when other conditions are equal. This finding of Black males being significantly more likely to be responsive to their constituents on class-based issues may be linked to our earlier findings of the least disadvantaged class status of Black men as a whole. The relationship is not affected by the personal political ideology or partisanship of the officials or by the perception having a constituency that shares one's ideology.

IMPLICATIONS FOR SUBSTANTIVE REPRESENTATION

Thus far, we have described the extent of representational congruence between the elected officials and their constituents. The preceding section also demonstrates the possibility to link up dimensions of representation from the perspective of class-based issue responsiveness. It is now time to address the question: So what? What are other possible linkages between these various dimensions of representation? And, even more important, what impact do they have on substantive issues of concern to communities of color and their elected representatives?

Are officials' views on representation influenced by the nature and extent of congruence between them and their constituents – that is, a sense that they are "like" the people they represent? In the text that follows, we consider the scenario when representational congruence or the lack thereof may influence an elected official's view of his or her representational roles as a delegate or trustee as well as on the prospects for substantive policy impact when we control for the possible confounding factors of group attributes by race and gender, office level, political ideology, and political partisanship.

Cross-tabulation results (not shown) suggest that those officials who believe the majority of their constituents share their race or partisanship or ideology all show a significantly higher tendency to hold a delegate view of representation. Around four in ten respondents who perceive their constituents as mostly coethnics or copartisans or ideological pals, also hold the delegate view, compared to three in ten of those who do not hold such a view. The relationship between representational role and class-based issue responsiveness is slightly weaker: 35 percent of respondents who express class-based concerns for their poor or working class communities subscribe to the delegate view of representation, compared to 30 percent of respondents who do not demonstrate congruence by class with their constituents. We do not see the same pattern for respondents who hold trustee view of representation. We conclude, then, that perceptions of constituencies may be associated with officials' representational role orientation, but *only for those* who hold the delegate role. Further, among the types of constituent linkages, perceived ideological correspondence appears to be more useful in predicting delegate role orientation than perceived racial correspondence, even if both are significant predictors.

CONSTITUENT RELATIONSHIPS: THE FEEDBACK LINK TO REPRESENTATION

In many ways, constituents are an integral part of the representational equation for elected officials: as current, potential, and future voters, citizens, and taxpayers, they make up the feedback link for the elected.

Hearing from constituents may help an elected official become more responsive to community concerns, more effective and, all other things being equal, more likely to be reelected. In her research, Maestas (2000, 665–667) suggests that keeping tabs on constituent concerns helps legislators "become better informed about the interests of current constituents, and presumably, future 'potential' constituents" (667) and may also help them "build a base of support to run for higher office" (665). Even constituents who cannot or do not vote may have considerable influence and, like voters, need to believe that their representatives are responsive to them.

Nowhere is this more true than in communities of color, with a historically (and, in many cases, currently) greater share of grievances. Although it is true that, "...leaders cannot know everything about a particular community's grievances," it is equally true that communication from community members to their elected officials is an important measure of the "doing" of leadership. In other words, "to galvanize aggrieved populations, leaders need deep understanding of their community's circumstances and experiences, a factor which we call 'localized cultural capital' " (Nepstad and Bob 2006, 4).

In this section of the chapter, we explore the gender and racial dimensions of the amount and types of constituent contact with their elected officials. The following are of particular interest: How many constituents are reported by their elected officials to have reached out to voice a community concern? Are there differences by racial group? By gender? On this latter question, we are continuing to examine the notion of women's "transformational" leadership style discussed in the previous chapter, as women in politics scholars have reported views that "women were better at constituency service, more honest, more sensitive, more idealistic, more courteous, better listeners, and more understanding" (Flammang 1997, 248). We conclude the chapter with policy representation and impact: What are the issues the constituents in their communities care most deeply about? And, finally, to what extent do elected officials of color believe having women in elected office helps women and minorities?

Gender, Race, and Amount of Self-Reported Constituent Contacts

Past investigation by Thomas (1992) of city councilmembers finds Blacks and women in general to spend more time on constituency service than average Whites or men. Speaking of state legislators, Donovan, Mooney, and Smith (2011, 261–262) write, "...women may also engage in *more*

TABLE 7.8. *Self-Reported Amount of Constituent Contacts, by Gender of Elected Officials*

Number per Week	Female	Male	All
0	8.3	2.7	4.7
1–4	25.0	26.1	25.7
5–19	36.0	39.4	38.2
20+	30.7	31.8	31.4
Total percent	100	100	100
N	436	767	1,203

Note: Entries are percent of elected officials who reported the number of contacts; differences are significant at $p < .001$.
Source: GMCL National Survey, 2006–2007.

constituent service and be more cooperative, consensus-building, and egalitarian in the legislative process" (emphasis added).

Looking at elected official of color in the GMCL National Survey, it is very clear that overall they are very connected to their constituents, reporting high levels of contact: seven in ten report at least five constituent contacts per week; and three in ten say twenty or more. There were, nevertheless, some surprises. At first it seemed women on average had more contacts: a mean of 33.0 for women compared to 26.8 for men; on closer examination of the data, however, this is likely to be an artifact of more women than men reporting what we might consider "outlier" numbers, which make means not the best measure.[12] Using categories rather than means, we see that, in fact, more women than men of color officials reported zero contacts, and, in general, men reported more contacts than women (Table 7.8).

There were relatively large differences by race (Table 7.9), with Blacks and American Indians reporting the highest numbers of constituent contacts, followed by Asian Americans and Latinos/as. There were no gender differences by race, except for Latinos/as. Latinas (at 12.3 percent) were significantly more likely than their male counterparts (at 2.8 percent) to report none.

Latino men were also more likely to report higher numbers, with three in ten Latino men at 20+ contacts and four in ten at five to nineteen

---

[12] These were in the range of 1,000 or more per week: one man is recorded as 1,100, and six men with 500 or more; there were two females coded as 1,000+ and another 6 at 500; it is unclear whether these were input errors or valid responses. In subsequent analyses, we removed these outliers.

TABLE 7.9. *Self-Reported Amount of Constituent Contacts, by Race of Elected Officials*

Number per Week	Black	Latino/a	Asian American	American Indian
0	3.9	5.7	6.7	0
1–4	21.2	32.2	25.6	20.0
5–19	41.2	35.2	30.0	45.0
20+	33.6	27.0	37.8	35.0
Total percent	100	100	100	100
N	633	460	90	20

Note: Entries are percent of elected officials who reported the number of contacts; differences are significant at $p < .005$.
Source: GMCL National Survey, 2006–2007.

contacts per week, compared to two in ten for Latinas at the highest category, and three in ten at five to nineteen ($p < .0001$).

Why Constituents Make Contacts

Six in ten officials of color reported that their constituents contacted them to "voice a community concern," and women are more likely than their male counterparts to receive this type of contact (63.1 percent to 58.1 percent). This is true for all gender*race groups, except Latinos, with the biggest differences for Blacks (64 percent for women and 53.9 percent for men) and Asian Americans (70 percent for women; 60.3 percent for men). Of course, based on these data, we cannot determine why women would report more contacts to voice a community concern than men: Is it that they are viewed as more responsive? That they are more attuned to community concerns? Or, as Hardy-Fanta (1997, 46) suspected, men "may simply be less verbally expansive about those aspects of politics."

If large percentages of elected officials of color report that their constituents contact them to voice community concerns – and that there are gender differences in some groups – we must ask: What are the other reasons for constituent contacts? The second most common reason that constituents contact their representative is to get help with a family or personal problem. What stands out in Table 7.10 is that the vast majority (63.6 percent) of American Indian officials gave this as the reason they heard from their constituents – not "to voice a community concern." This might reflect the uniquely intimate nature of the relationships American Indians maintain with their elected leaders as well as the overwhelming poverty, drug and alcohol abuse, and other mounting challenges facing

TABLE 7.10. *Reported Reasons for Constituent Contact, by Race of Elected Officials*

Reason Given	Black	Latino/a	Asian American	American Indian
Voice community concern	51.3	59.2	58.1	18.2
Help solve family or personal problem	25.1	24.2	19.4	63.6
Influence government policy	7.3	5.9	15.1	4.5
Help find a job	6.7	3.3	0	0
Multiple reasons	7.3	4.1	5.4	13.6
Other	2.3	3.3	2.2	0
Total percent	100	100	100	100
N	686	488	93	22

Note: The percentages for "voice community concern" do not match those in Table 7.10 because in this table, the categories are mutually exclusive and include a "multiple reasons" and "other category," whereas, in Table 7.10, the percentages reflect those who gave this response as well as others.
Source: GMCL National Survey, 2006–2007, N = 1,359; $p < .0001$.

the indigenous population in the present day.[13] For the other groups, it is one-quarter or less. Asian American officials are also more likely than those of other groups to report their constituents having reached out to them to influence public policies.

CONSTITUENT RELATIONSHIPS: POLICY REPRESENTATION

Much of the literature on women in politics, based as it is on the views and experiences of White women, brings with it a normative, essentialist perspective, as we discussed earlier. Scholars often describe gender differences on the issue priorities of women and men in office (Dodson 2006; Dodson and Carroll 1991; Saint-Germain 1992; Thomas 1991, 1994, 2005; Welch and Sigelman 1982). Boles and Scheurer (2007, 39–40) reiterate long-held views that "women in elective office tend to be more liberal and more supportive of issues of concern to women, children, and families than are men, differences that conform to gender stereotypes held by voters" but that

---

[13] For a glimpse into the unique scope and depth of challenges facing American Indians on a daily basis, see the 2014 Native Youth Report released by the White House in June 2014, www.whitehouse.gov/sites/default/files/docs/20141129nativeyouthreport_final.pdf (Accessed June 29, 2016).

their public policy positions are also shaped by "broader constituency concerns [as well as] partisan loyalty." The link between women's supposed personal and legislative interests are tempered, therefore, by communication from their constituents about their concerns and those of their communities. Furthermore, as Dodson (2006, 21) remarks, "operationalizing gender in ways that capture its diversity, embedding our analysis of gender and gendered behavior within the institutional and cultural contexts, and rethinking the model that describes the way gendered behavior does (and does not) occur should free us to devote more attention to ...matters that strike at the conceptual heart of any analysis of women's [leadership, including] the contested meaning of gender difference."

Perceptions of the Top Policy Issues for Constituents

Given that leadership for elected officials of color takes place within these institutional contexts of governing, and that effective governing must include being responsive to the issues of greatest concern to one's constituents, we turn now to how those surveyed by the GMCL Project responded to the questions: "*What do you think is the most important policy issue facing your constituents? What is the next most important issue? The next?*" After coding their verbatim responses,[14] what we find is remarkable unanimity that carries across gender and racial lines. Almost half (46.2 percent) of all officials of color gave a response indicating that Education is the top policy concern of their constituents (see Figure 7.5) – and, although women of color were significantly more likely to mention education as one of their top issues, the difference was relatively small. Employment and Wages ranks second at 32.1 percent, and again there is no gender difference. The next five top issues were cited by about one in five of all officials: Development, Healthcare, Public Safety, Infrastructure, and Housing, with the next cluster Budget/Funding and the Economy) not far behind. Twelve percent gave responses that reflected social justice issues (i.e., the desire to see people treated fairly/equally).

---

[14] Coding their verbatim responses, we arrived at twenty-eight categories, which are not mutually exclusive, as a response could and typically did include more than one issue. Categories (in alphabetical order): Budget, Community Appearance, Development, Economy, Education, Employment and Wages, Environment, Ethics, Gasoline, Government, Healthcare, Housing, Immigration, Infrastructure, Language, Minority Issues, Municipal and Social Services, No Child Left Behind (which was a subcategory of Education), Participation, Public Safety, Quality of Life, Representation, Taxes, Treating All Equally/Fairly, Utility Costs, War, Zoning, plus Other.

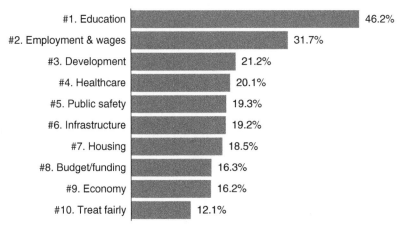

FIGURE 7.5 Top ten policy Issues, all elected officials of color.
Note: Entries are percent of officials who mentioned an issue that was coded into one of these (nonmutually exclusive) categories.
Source: GMCL National Survey, 2006–2007; N = 1,180.

Any gender differences pale in the face of agreement overall about issues of concern to their constituents: The top two most important issues receive the same rank for women as for men: Education is no. 1 and Employment and Wages no. 2; Development ranks no. 4 for both, and the Economy no. 8. The largest variation in terms of rank (and significant difference) is Infrastructure, no. 3 for men but no. 9 for women (*p* < .001). Somewhat in keeping with traditional views of women's concerns, women of color's responses lead to Healthcare to be ranked no. 3 for them.

With virtually all studies of this type having ignored the intersection of race and gender in politics, it is not surprising to find that our findings for elected officials of color do not square with findings based solely on White men and women. The remarkable convergence in perspectives among elected officials of color regardless of gender challenges the numerous other studies suggesting that women elected officials are more likely to be concerned about "issues relevant to women" (Thomas 1998, 10). What are these issues? Clark (1998, 119), in a chapter on women at the national level, begins by declaring, "Women and men do have different attitudes on many political issues" ... and points to "a divergence of attitudes among the two sexes on ... social issues, including the role of women, minority rights, social welfare, and protection of the environment." Kahn (1993, 489), for example, states that "men are more likely to discuss economic issues such as taxes and the ...budget"... while women focus on "social issues and social policy, such as education and health policy. We find, instead, that "Taxes" (mentioned by 9.3 percent of the respondents) did not make it into the Top Ten issues of concern to their constituents, and there is no significant difference by gender. And taxes were no more likely to be mentioned than issues related to "Community" (also mentioned by 9.3 percent), such as community improvement, appearance, and so forth. Men gave responses reflecting concerns about the "Environment" slightly more (5.5 percent) than women (3.9 percent), but the overall concern was low and not significant, especially in comparison to the degree male and female elected officials of color reported constituent concern with Education.

Few Gender Differences, What about Race?

In looking at percentages by race (Table 7.11), we again see remarkable similarities, with most of the same ten issues mentioned by all three racial groups – and Education the no. 1 issue facing the constituents of all three groups. Issues related to jobs and wages rank no. 2 for Blacks and Latinos. The "concrete needs" discussed as a motivation to run in Chapter 5, show up as issues related to "Infrastructure," which ranks no. 2 for Asian American elected officials and no. 3 for Latinos; for Blacks, these issues drop to no. 9, with Development, Healthcare, Housing, and the Economy well ahead. Public Safety issues, which include law enforcement and criminal justice system issues, are no. 5 for Latinos and no. 3 for Asian Americans. Black elected officials are the only group for whom issues of equal/fair treatment were of such importance that it made it into the Top Ten (no. 8).

Despite the overall similarities in what are considered to be the issues of greatest concern to their constituents, the percentages of mentions by each group are significantly different (at $p < .0001$) for Education, Employment and Wages, and Healthcare; and at $p < .005$ for Housing, the Economy, Infrastructure, and Budget/Funding issues.

Given how rare data are for American Indians, it is worth pointing out that, like the other groups, Education ranks no. 1 for American Indian state legislators; Healthcare is no. 2, followed by Employment and Wages, Development and Infrastructure. Public Safety issues, which are no. 3 for Asian American officials, drop to no. 6 for this group, followed by Budget, Taxes, and the Economy. In contrast to Blacks and Latinos/as, who did not mention issues related to the Environment, for

TABLE 7.11. *Top Ten Issues for Constituents, by Race (Ranked by Percent)*

	Black		Latino/a		Asian American	
No. 1	Education***	42.1	Education	48.3	Education	56.3
No. 2	Employment and Wages***	38.9	Employment and Wages	23.8	Infrastructure	31.0
No. 3	Development†	23.4	Infrastructure	21.6	Public Safety	27.6
No. 4	Healthcare***	21.6	Budget/Funding	19.4	Budget/Funding	25.3
No. 5	Housing**	21.5	Public Safety	19.0	Housing	25.3
No. 6	Economy**	18.7	Development	18.3	Employment and Wages	18.4
No. 7	Public Safety	18.5	Healthcare	17.7	Development	17.2
No. 8	Treat Fairly/ Equally**	15.5	Housing	13.9	Economy	17.2
No. 9	Infrastructure**	15.3	Economy	13.0	Environment	16.1
No. 10	Budget/Funding**	12.7	Immigration	11.9	Healthcare	13.8
	N	626	N	447	N	82

Note: Entries are percent of each racial group ranked by categories for "most important policy issue facing your constituents"; percentages sum to more than 100 because respondents were probed twice for "the next most important issues." Significance (at $^{†}p < .1$; $^{*}p < .05$; $^{**}p < .005$; $^{***}p < .0001$) between racial groups is shown next to each ranked category only in the first column.

Source: GMCL National Survey, 2006–2007.

Asian American elected officials and American Indian State Legislators, this issue is no. 9 for the former and no. 10 for the latter.

Gender differences within race are small and rarely rise to a level of statistical significance. Education is clearly the top issue for all races and both genders. Black elected officials – men and women alike –are consistently on the same page for every issue. There are few other gender differences: Latinas, mentioned education issues significantly more than their male counterparts: (60.9 percent and 42.9 percent, respectively; $p < .0001$); the salience of education for Latinas and Latinos alike, nevertheless, confirms findings by Fraga et al. (2008, 165–167). In the study of Fraga et al. of Latino state legislators, Latinas were *more* likely than their male peers to mention issues related to Budget ($p < .05$); they also found a large and significant difference among Latino/a state legislators on Economic Development and Jobs, with 16.7 percent of Latino men compared to just 2.9 percent of Latina reporting that as a top policy issue. In contrast, Latinas/os in our study saw this as an issue of concern to their constituents at percentages that were identical (24 percent). In addition, we find Asian and Latino men (at 37.3 percent and 24.8 percent, respectively) to be significantly more likely than their female counterparts (at 17.9 percent for Asian women and 14.5 percent for Latinas) to mention issues related to Infrastructure (significance was $p < .1$ for Asians, and $p < .05$ for Latinos).

The relative lack of variation by gender for issues such as the environment, taxes, and healthcare is revealing since a number of these are supposedly gendered for elected officials. For example, mainstream scholars often cite the environment as an area of particular concerns to women in governing positions, but less than 5 percent of elected officials in our sample mentioned environmental issues – with women slightly *less* like than men to give mention it as an issue of concern.[15] And, given prevailing views about war being a policy issue of greater concern to men, it is of note that there are no gender differences for any of the racial groups on issues related to war. This is noteworthy because debates about the Iraq War were raging during the period when the GMCL Survey was in the field and despite the fact that male elected officials of color are substantially more likely than elected officials in general to be veterans: 31 percent of males in our survey reported having served in the military.[16] This is substantially higher than the 22 percent of all officials who are veterans

---

[15] And this small difference (3.9 percent for women to 5.5 percent for men) was not statistically significant.

[16] Two percent of women in our survey also reported that they had served in the military.

(Seth Lynn, Veterans Campaign, quoted in Zhang 2009).[17] Although Asian men were about half as likely (17 percent) compared to Black and Latino (about 31 percent each) to be veterans, these differences are not statistically significant. American Indian male state legislators were the most likely (42 percent) to report having served.[18] Furthermore, the Army reports that, as during the Vietnam War when White men were able to avoid the draft to an extent not possible for young men of color, during the wars following the attacks of September 11, Blacks made up a greater share of enlisted men than their share of the population (Brook 2014). And yet, we saw no gender difference for this group either.

SUBSTANTIVE IMPACT ON POLICY: CAN ELECTED
OFFICIALS OF COLOR ADVANCE RIGHTS THAT
BENEFIT WOMEN AND MINORITIES?

In Chapter 6, we showed that elected officials of color overwhelmingly believe that women and/or minority elected officials make a difference in helping pass policy initiatives that benefit women, racial minorities, and the economically disadvantaged, but that there are some distinctive variations by gender and race. (We also confirmed this finding with other evidence – i.e., voting patterns of Black, White, Latino/a, and Asian women and men in Congress). It would seem logical to hypothesize that elected officials who believe there is such a policy impact would be more likely to advance minority rights, defined here as perceived importance of affirmative action for women or racial minorities and expressed support for renewing minority voting rights, while controlling for influence from the type and degree of congruence by race, partisanship, ideology and class, discussed earlier in this chapter.

As Table 7.12 shows, having a constituency made up mostly of copartisans may increase the chance of the elected officials' expressed support for legislation to protect minority rights such as affirmative action and voting rights. However, we do not see the same effect when the constituency is made up of people who share their race or ideology with the elected officials. Neither do we see a significant relationship between

---

[17] Lynn's research revealed that the 22 percent of current elected officials who are veterans is far short of the 75 percent of politicians in 1969 who were former military personnel.

[18] The American Indian numbers are small and should be viewed with caution; that said, a recent report from the US Department of Veterans Affairs suggests that American Indians do serve at a higher rate than other groups, www.va.gov/TRIBALGOVERNMENT/docs/AIAN_Report_FINAL_v2_7.pdf (Accessed June 29, 2016).

TABLE 7.12. *Predictors of Support for Proposed Legislation to Protect Minority Rights*

Contributing Factors	OLS Regression Predicting Support for Minority Rights	
	b	s.e.
Congruence		
By race	−.007	.087
By partisanship	.293**	.088
By ideology	.052	.083
By class	−.074	.084
Delegate view	.134	.085
Perceived impact	.601**	.072
Race*Gender (*ref = Black men*)		
Latino men	−.777**	.110
Asian men	−1.716**	.207
American Indian men	−.363	.532
Black women	.062	.112
Latina women	.136	.179
Asian women	.612†	.355
American Indian women	.662	.799
Office Level (*ref = Municipal*)		
State legislative	.132	.145
County	.113	.119
School board	−.185†	.100
Ideology (Liberal)	.251**	.088
Partisanship (Republican)	−1.155**	.149
Constant	7.639	.208
Adj. R^2	.30	
F-score	28.14	
N	1,141	

Notes: b = unstandardized slope coefficient; s.e. = standard errors. The dependent variable is a three-item summed index of questions asking respondents to indicate the degree of importance for them to support affirmative action for women, and affirmative action and voting rights for persons from one's own racial and ethnic background (adjusted alpha = .81).
†$p \leq .1$; * $p \leq .05$; ** $p \leq .005$.
Source: GMCL National Survey, 2006–2007.

perceived benefits of descriptive representation and the incidence of issue responsiveness among respondents representing the poor or working class or the representational role orientation.

However, when differences in group attributes, office level, and political ideology and partisanship are controlled, we find a strong and positive influence of having perceived policy impact as minority repre- sentatives on taking legislative action to help protect minority rights. Moreover, everything else being equal, we note that respondents who are Latino or Asian American men, liberal, and Republicans are significantly less likely than other individuals to exercise substantive representation by supporting legislative proposals to protect and advance the interests of racial and gender minorities.

CONCLUSION

In this chapter we have explored the meanings, contours, and possible substantive impacts of descriptive representation for elected officials of color. At the end of the long journey, we find that, with important excep- tions, the majority of the minority elected officials in our study perceived their jurisdictions as made up largely of constituents who shared their racial and partisan, but not necessarily ideological, outlook. And our elected officials are amazingly accurate in their estimation of the con- stituent makeup by immigration generation. However, the degrees of "look alike" and "think alike" differ across race and gender groups and by level of office. Also, the directions of partisanship and political ide- ology are found to matter in gauging the extent of perceived partisan and ideological congruence between minority officials and their constituents. In terms of representation by class interest, we find that at least half of elected officials of color correctly identified the majority class status (by household income) of their constituents. We also find that their reported degrees of responsiveness to issues related to disadvantaged constituents can be predicted by the degrees of congruence in race and partisanship.

In terms of their views on the representational role, most of our elected officials believe they are expected to serve the trustee function of electoral leadership and this view is better predicted by the degree of congruence in ideological outlook than in racial or partisan outlook. However, every- thing else being equal, it is the degree of partisan congruence that seems to matter more in predicting support for minority-targeted legislation. These patterns are illustrative of the complicated relationships between dimensions of representation among minority elected officials.

Finally, gauging the extent and content of reported contacts between elected officials of color and their constituents, we find the vast majority of our elected officials to report a great deal of contacts with their con- stituents, especially those holding higher levels of office. However, con- trary to the literature on women and politics, minority women are not necessarily having more contacts with constituents than their male counterparts. Although women of color elected officials do report more contacts by constituents to voice a community concern, there are few racial or gender differences among minority elected officials in their perceptions regarding topic policy issues for their constituents. This remarkable convergence in perceived policy concerns between men and women of color elected officials is also different than the prevailing literature in women and politics and suggests a good foundation for solidarity and coalition building on representing common issue concerns and policy needs.

PART IV

ADVANCING DEMOCRACY IN THE UNITED STATES

8

Prospects for Building Coalitions across Race and Gender

An important question in political science is whether, as the United States moves toward a "majority–minority" nation, the various ethnoracial groups will work together on issues of concern, or whether the differences between these groups will lead to a contested set of "identity politics." This chapter revisits the observation made in the Introduction that elected officials of color have the capacity – or at minimum the potential – to impact public policies. In other words, it is elected officials at various levels of office who propose and vote on policy proposals that affect their constituents. As minorities in a majoritarian democracy, if they do not or cannot find common ground and fail to build coalitions across race, the growth in population and descriptive representation described in earlier chapters may limit their capacity to lead and exercise substantive representation. In a worst case scenario, the opportunity for transforming conditions on the ground for their respective communities will be lost, and prospects for advancing democracy in the United States will diminish.

In Chapter 7, we discussed how elected officials of color ranked the issues of greatest concern to their constituents. In this chapter, we address their policy positions on issues being debated at the time of the survey – such as voting rights, immigration, women's rights, and education inequality – issues that remain core concerns in contemporary American politics. Many of these policies are interpreted as race-based and affect the groups in different ways, which explains why coalition building across racial groups might be important but complicated.

Furthermore, we ask if Black, Latina, and Asian American women have political experiences and hold policy positions that are shared by their male counterparts, or do they share more in common with women from other racial/ethnic backgrounds? The answers to this question may help shed light on how likely women of color are to support building coalitions across various identity groups. Some scholars have proposed that women of color may offer a bridging function to political endeavors. Fraga et al. (2008), for example, introduce the concept of "strategic intersectionality" in their analysis of the legislative behavior of Latina elected officials. They find that Latina state legislators are able to draw on their multiple identities to enter more effectively into coalitions with other race*gender groups than their Latino male counterparts. Moreover, Latinas exercised more fluidity in whose legislative agenda they supported, choosing at times a women's caucus position when in conflict with that of a Latino caucus. According to a number of theoretical and empirical studies (Dawson 2001; Fraga and Navarro 2007; García et al. 2008; Simien 2006), the shared experiences of intersectionality for women of color may lead to the development of a bridging function, which can create opportunities for coalitions across race and gender.

On issues of concern to women, another question is to what extent do Black, Latina, and Asian American women elected officials hold more similar policy positions with each other because of their racialized gender than they do with men of their own groups – and, perhaps, with non-Hispanic White women? So-called "women's issues" tend to focus on reproductive rights, health, affirmative action in higher education, and the quality of K–12 education. For Black and Latina women, who, on average, have poverty rates much higher than White women, other issues surface as well: child care subsidized by or provided by the government, for example, and college education counted as part of the "work requirement" for women receiving welfare. The potential for building coalitions within and between the various race*gender groups is the core focus of this chapter.

We begin this chapter with a brief discussion of the theoretical considerations underlying interracial coalition building, followed by what we know about the efforts of women elected officials from diverse backgrounds to work together across gender and race. We then present analysis of the positions held by respondents from the Gender and Multicultural Leadership (GMCL) National Survey on a range of policy issues.[1] The chapter concludes with a discussion of the factors that support the prospects for coalition building across race/ethnicity and gender

---

[1] Portions of this chapter appeared in modified form in a paper prepared for presentation at the 2009 American Political Science Association Annual Meeting (Pinderhughes et al. 2009).

within our multicultural leaders, and the significance of our findings for answering the question: *How* **do** *we get along* in an increasingly diverse and complex political world in the United States?[2]

CONSTRAINTS OF COMPLEX COALITION BUILDING

In analyzing the possibilities and constraints of building interracial coalitions, Lien (2001, 126–127) argues that intergroup coalitions across racial groups "may be assessed at three separate but interconnected levels … [First] is the between-group level, or factors related to racial interactions." Second is the "within-group level, or factors dealing with the formation and maintenance of a multiethnic community…" and third, "the beyond-group level, or factors related not to group characteristics but to the very nature of the U.S. racial system."

Given the varied and diverse histories and experiences of the ethnoracial populations in the GMCL Project, it does not seem wise to assume that the empirical conditions for forging common policy interests may exist. In fact, it may be difficult to anticipate the natural formation of long-lasting, harmonious interracial relationships across communities of color, given the highly unstable politics of race in US history and society.[3]

Opportunity for "Friendly Contacts" That Facilitate Interracial Coalition Building

Based on Blalock's theory of interminority coalition building, Lien (2001, 126) hypothesizes that "[c]ross-racial coalition is more likely to occur between groups that have high levels of friendly contacts and low incidence or sense of intense economic competition, that are similar in language, religion, beliefs, and values, and are not too far apart in social and political rankings." Analysis of the distribution by county of the more

---

[2] Rodney King, the subject of police beatings in Los Angeles in the early 1990s, commented, "*Can we all just get along?*" (For an analysis of this phrase for cross-racial coalitions, see McClain and Stewart 2014).

[3] As we complete this manuscript, we wonder whether moves made by the Republican Party may have already pushed Asians much further to the left as evidenced by their vote in 2012 than we could have predicted in 2006–2007. And, of course, the 2016 Republican field is encouraging even further movement by Asians and Latinos based on their continuing hostility based on immigration, race, and so on. We cannot state that this will be stable, but we can take note that the continuing rightward move by the Republican Party would seem to enhance other non-Black racial/ethnic groups in directions that would make collaboration with African Americans more possible.

than 11,000 elected officials of color in the GMCL National Database suggests that, when top counties are ranked by the numbers of elected officials in the various counties for each group, the elected officials appear to have little potential for interaction.

"Top Counties" for Black, Latino, and Asian American Elected Officials: Limited Opportunities?

Table 8.1 shows that, at the turn of the new millennium, there were only two counties (Los Angeles and Fresno) in which relatively large shares of Asian American and Latino officials overlapped.[4] And Cook County (home of Chicago) was the only county in which both Blacks and Latinos shared a high number of representatives. Los Angeles was the single county in which each of the three non-White groups can claim to have a relatively good share of representation – and to be able to show that we had to go beyond a "Top Ten" list of counties – for Blacks, the City of Angels reaches a rank of only 13.[5]

As we go beyond the Top Rank counties, however, the opportunity for cross-racial coalition building appears to increase: First, of the 81 counties with Asian representation, 56 (69 percent) have Latino elected officials and 57 or 70 percent have Black elected officials; second, of the 326 counties with Latino representation, 154 (47 percent) have Black elected officials and 56 (17 percent) have Asian elected officials; and finally, of the 790 counties with Black representation, 154 (19 percent) have Latino elected officials and 57 or (7 percent) have Asian elected officials. It remains to be seen whether, in recent years and into the future, the Black, Latino, and Asian American elected officials are more – or less – likely to share geographical space.

Gender, Race, and the Potential for Coalitions within a Contested Political Framework

Gender brings another dimension to the already complex political framework for interracial coalitions. How the various permutations of race

---

[4] We acknowledge that these data may be somewhat dated, as they are based on an early iteration of our database (with elected officials who were in office in 2004–2005). Ten years later, with immigration and mobility, conditions on the ground may have changed.

[5] We should point that, since Kings County, NY, encompasses Brooklyn, which is contiguous to Queens County, there may be possibilities of coalition between Blacks and Asians in these two boroughs of New York City (ranked no. 9 and 8, respectively, in Table 8.1).

TABLE 8.1. *Top Counties Ranked by Number of Elected Officials for Each Racial Group*

County Rank	Black (N = 7,557)	N	Latino (N = 3,929)	N	Asian (N = 308)	N
1	Cook, IL	248	Los Angeles, CA	263	Los Angeles, CA	49
2	St. Louis, MO	108	Hidalgo, TX	222	Honolulu, HI	45
3	Bolivar, MS	77	Cameron, TX	113	Santa Clara, CA	27
4	St. Clair, IL	71	El Paso, TX	95	Alameda, CA	17
5	Prince George, MD	70	Maricopa, AZ	93	Maui, HI	14
6	Wayne, MI	67	Fresno, CA	90	Hawaii, HI; Kauai, HI	12
7	Crittenden, AR; Cuyahoga, OH	58	Bexar, TX	71	King, WA	10
8	Jefferson, AL	54	Nueces, TX	61	Queens, NY; San Mateo, CA	9
9	Kings, NY	52	Tulare, CA	54	Orange, CA	8
10	Philips, AR	49	Webb, TX	50	Sacramento, CA; San Francisco, CA	7
11	Essex, NJ	42	Cook, IL	49	Fresno, CA	6
12	Camden, NJ; Kankakee, IL; Sumter, AL; Washington, MS	39	Kern, CA	47	San Joaquin, CA; Thurston, WA	5
13	Anne Arundel, MD; Charleston, SC; Los Angeles, CA	38	Duval, TX; Imperial, CA	46	Merced, CA; Solano, CA; Humboldt, CA	4

Note: Entries are the number of elected officials (of any level) found in each of the counties; the county rank in the left column applies to each group.
Source: GMCL National Database, 2004–2005; N = 11,794.

and gender among multicultural political leaders – that is, Black women and men, Latinas and Latinos, and female and male Asian Americans office holders – will come together or not on issues related to race, gender, and class to have some impact on their respective community's or groups' status, has been a primary question in US political inquiries for quite some time.

Each race*gender group in the GMCL study brings perspectives based on their different social and economic standings and histories to its public policy decision making. For those of immigrant backgrounds, patterns of gendered relationships vary across the groups due to cultural variations and practices in their home countries as well as those developed after immigration. In the post-1965 era, the differential growth rates between the foreign- and the native-born population as well as the relative socioeconomic mobility of the foreign-born and the relative immobility of the native-born population have been the sources of increasing social and political tensions. In light of this increasingly contentious political arena, are interracial conflicts inevitable and could interracial coalitions be impossible?

EVIDENCE OF COOPERATION – AND CONFLICT

To be sure, under certain conditions, racial minorities historically have been able to form cooperative relationships among and across their various populations as well as with White liberals at the individual and group level. Cooperative relationships have emerged out of common interests and needs as well as shared concerns over racial grievances and aspirations for liberty and equality (Lien 2001). At the same time, in specific historical and contemporary contexts, racial conflicts and competition have also been observed for these groups. For example, in some analytical frameworks (e.g., Saito 1998), the issues and interests of Latinos and Asians are different from those of Blacks. There are significant internal divisions within each race, and each group is being affected differently by global economic forces. In others, Blacks and Latinos align more closely with each other than they do with Asians (see, e.g., Muñoz and Henry 1990). Scholars have observed competition and conflicts in governance in multiracial cities such as Los Angeles and other major US cities (Jones-Correa 2011; Telles, Sawyer, and Rivera-Salgado 2011).

On top of the continuing racial segregation and discrimination in housing and public education, Blacks, Latinos, and to an increasing extent Asian Americans, have been in direct competition with each other for housing, jobs, access to educational and health institutions, and political office holding (Chang and Diaz-Veizades 1999). Black–Korean conflicts have been the subject of several studies (Abelman and Lie 1995; Kim 2000, 2001; Park and Park 2001) in which economic and political competition are heightened by differences in cultural orientations and practices. Latino-Korean relations are observed to be equally multidimensional (Chang and Diaz-Veizades 1999, 7). On the other hand, accounts of multiracial coalitions have also been observed, especially among the radical left (Pulido 2006) and feminists in the 1970s (Gilmore 2008).

Besides socioeconomic issues, a basic source of tension is the different concept of race and racial positions across the three ethnoracial groups (Robinson and Robinson 2006). And gender, that is, the positions and roles of women within specific groups, as a way of understanding how the groups differ or cohere, can also be seen as another strategy for exploring group political development and dynamics (Carroll 2008; Pulido 2006).

Political Incorporation and Interracial Coalitions

Reviewing the political incorporation of people of color in American cities – defined as the extent of their role in dominant coalitions that control city government – Browning, Marshall, and Tabb (2003, 366–373) maintain that, because of the significant entry of Latinos and Asians into local politics, the ground for political coalitions has been transformed by immigration. In many cities the future of political incorporation will be very different from the coalitions they observed between Blacks and Whites that advanced the incorporation of Blacks in some American cities at the end of the twentieth century. Instead, they note that "[r]acial politics will be increasingly multiracial, multiethnic politics in many cities" (366) and characterized by concrete and fluid formations of crosscutting and shifting, issue-oriented coalitions.

On an optimistic note, Lien (2001) maintains that monumental changes in the social, economic, and political orders on both the domestic and international fronts in the post-1965 era may have improved the opportunity structure for racial minorities to construct interracial connections under certain circumstances. She observes that new grounds for interracial coalition building between people of color at the *mass level* have emerged because of increased opportunities and means for personal and organizational contacts and improved economic and political status for the disadvantaged compared to the pre-1965 era.

At the beginning of the new millennium, there seemed to be greater tolerance of and appreciation for cultural diversity in US society and politics. With its continuing commitment to the founding principles of liberty and equality, the nation seemed poised to address issues of social justice and empowerment for all. Lien's analysis of public opinion data from that period suggested that "[c]oalitions between Asians and Latinos and Blacks can be established based on their shared concerns over race-related social redistributive issues at the local level, even though Latinos and Blacks have distinct issue concerns and different social distance to Asians" (Lien 2001, 168). She also finds that racial bridges are easier to build between Asians and Whites based on interpersonal relationships and shared ideology. Moreover, participation in group- or organization-based activities may reduce racial tensions between Asians and others by increasing the opportunity to forge a sense of common identity or linked fate with each other.

Of course, Lien's (2001) previous analysis is based on analyzing mass data, while this chapter rests on studying political elites. And, within a few short years, the socioeconomic and political situation changed dramatically. First came the 9/11 attacks in 2001, the seemingly never-ending "War on Terror," and the economic crash of 2008 following the bust of the housing bubble.

Then we saw the election of Barack Obama in 2008 and his reelection in 2012. On the one hand, his success was the result of a coalition among Blacks, Latinos, Asians, and select groups of Whites (especially women and those with higher levels of education and wealth) (Teixeira and Halpern 2012).[6] Some point to the fact Obama's election has brought about an *increase* in racial tensions, especially between (lower-class) Whites[7] and communities of color. The divide between lower-class Whites (especially in the Republican Party) and minorities and women, who are more likely to be Democrats, although not new, may be increasing. Whether that coalition of minority voters will be sustained and extended to the political leadership of color remains to be seen.

---

[6] They write, "According to the national exit poll, President Obama achieved victory by carrying 93 percent of African American voters, 71 percent of Latino voters, 73 percent of Asian American voters, ..." (Teixeira and Halpin 2012, 1).

[7] Teixeira and Halpin (2012, 1) conclude the earlier quote by noting that Obama won with "only 39 percent of white voters."

Historical Struggles of Women in the United States: Parallels and Potential Partners

The history of American women demonstrates some parallels, especially when examining the diversity of experiences in the struggle for basic civil rights. While for centuries middle- and upper-class White women enjoyed certain privileges, especially in comparison to Black and American Indian women, their legal status as women was a hotly contested arena for centuries. Women, regardless of race, were not allowed to vote until 1920.

Rights we take for granted today are the result of legal battles: the right to execute contracts; practice certain professions, including the law; own property; retain custody of children after a divorce, to name just a few. "It was not until 1978 … that marital rape was outlawed anywhere in the United States" (Ford 2011, 16). The prospect for coalitions among women across race is even more fraught with obstacles. Although there are certainly bright spots – including the strong links between those working in the suffrage and abolition movements – there are even more examples of tensions and racism between white women and women of color. Locke (1997) also points out that passage of the Fifteenth Amendment, which granted the right to vote to former slaves, reduced African American *women's* status "from three-fifths to zero." Ford (2011, 42) reminds us that "The suffrage movement was filled with "ugly nativist and racist rhetoric and action."

Later, within the modern Black Civil Rights, Chicana/o, Yellow Power, and Red Power Movements, each group of non-White women, respectively, was marginalized by its male counterparts. (White women's) feminism's current focus on reproductive rights, to the relative exclusion of concerns of greater importance to women of color/poor women (e.g., economic rights, the incarceration of minority men), has continued to create strains between women from different racial/ethnic groups. The rifts between Black women and White women, in particular, have generated mistrust; the literature on this topic is large (see, e.g., Cohen, Jones, and Tronto 1997; Hull, Scott, and Smith 1982; Moraga and Anzaldúa 2015). Thus, as in the question of whether elected officials of color can form coalitions across the divides of race/ethnicity, one must ask as well whether non-Hispanic White women can join women of color in building bridges across gender and race/ethnicity.

When looking at the full range of diversity by race/ethnicity, gender, and other dimensions, we examine the extent to which women and men of color elected officials' political interests converge and offer promise of potential coalitions to tackle social justice issues that affect communities of color, and how divergent they are from each other. To explore the degree of convergence and divergence between the various groups by race and gender alone, and in interaction, we examine their respective positions on key policy issues using data from the GMCL National Survey.

POSITIONS ON POLICY ISSUES UNDER
DEBATE – THEN AND NOW, AGAIN

It seemed, in the years immediately following the completion of the survey in 2006–2007, that many of the issues discussed in this chapter had faded from view. The protections of voting rights seemed settled when the Voting Rights Act Reauthorization and Amendments Act of 2006 received almost unanimous bipartisan support in the US House and Senate and was signed into law, with considerable fanfare, by Republican President George W. Bush.[8] President Bush also stated that "immigration reform [was] a top priority of his second term" (Shrestha 2006, 25; Wasem 2012, 28) – reform, we should point out, that included a path to citizenship.

Both of these issues have resurfaced, however, as hotly contested fights. For many people, the Supreme Court ruling of *Shelby County v. Holder* in 2013, which "put a dagger in the heart of the VRA" (Vagins and McDonald 2013), and the new impasse on immigration reform, represent steps backward in the ongoing struggle for civil rights in this country. Nativist rhetoric during the summer leading up to the 2016 presidential Republican primaries has advanced policy proposals that include, not only rejecting any semblance of a path to legal status for the more than 11 million people in this country without documents, but has also touched upon the repeal of birthright citizenship, enshrined in the Fourteenth Amendment of the US Constitution.

As we close this writing in early 2016, with a still-fragile economic recovery after the recession that began in 2007, chances of advancing policies that benefit poor women also seem remote – and the conservative position on abortion rights appears to have hardened in the political realm, with continued efforts to limit access to health clinics

---

[8] Its official name – the *Fannie Lou Hamer, Rosa Parks, and Coretta Scott King Voting Rights Act Reauthorization and Amendments Act of 2006* – paid tribute to Black women civil rights activists.

that provide this service, even as half of the country favors keeping *Roe v. Wade* intact and protecting a woman's right to an abortion, at least in some cases, if not all. Education represents another area of policy debate with the fights continuing over the renewal of "No Child Left Behind"[9]; whether states will adopt the "Common Core" curriculum and testing standards[10]; school vouchers; and other school practices, such as permitting prayer and the teaching of creationism instead of evolution in public schools.

At a time when tensions around race appear to be on the rise, and women's rights (including birth control and abortion) are under renewed assault, there seems to be one area where rights have been extended, rather than curtailed: same-sex marriage. After decades of struggle, the Supreme Court ruling in *Obergefell et al. v. Hodges* in 2015 made same-sex marriage legal across the entire country.

In this section of the chapter, we explore variation by gender and race on policy positions such as these among our nation's state and local minority female and male elected officials. We also develop an analytical scheme that tests the elected officials' perspectives on their sense of linked fate and support for these positions to explore if and how much they can be considered as a politically cohesive community.

The following series of tables show how elected officials in the GMCL National Survey responded to a wide variety of issue propositions, which are grouped into the following categories: Minority Civil Rights, Women's Rights, Immigration, Rights for Same-Sex Couples, and Changing Education Policies, with results analyzed by gender, by race, and by race*gender.[11]

---

[9] For information about the original legislation, signed into law by President George W. Bush in 2002, and its reauthorization in 2015, see www.ed.gov/esea (Accessed June 30, 2016).

[10] The "Common Core" is an initiative of the Obama administration; according to its website, "State education chiefs and governors in 48 states came together to develop the Common Core, a set of clear college- and career-ready standards for kindergarten through 12th grade in English language arts/literacy and mathematics. Today, 43 states have voluntarily adopted and are working to implement the standards, which are designed to ensure that students graduating from high school are prepared to take credit bearing introductory courses in two- or four-year college programs or enter the workforce" (Source: www.corestandards.org/wp-content/uploads/FAQs.pdf; accessed June 30, 2016); it has been a controversial program debated during the lead up to the 2016 presidential primaries.

[11] The decision to report means rather than percentages is based on our desire to present findings in the simplest and clearest manner for the sake of the reader; we also followed a model used in prior studies (see, e.g., Carroll and Sanbonmatsu 2013, 81).

Minority Civil Rights

In Table 8.2 we see clearly that elected officials of color are, as a whole, extremely supportive of minority civil rights, saying that the Voting Rights Act was extremely important ($\bar{x}$ = 9.17 out of 10), as is affirmative action for achieving both equity for their own racial group as well as for women ($\bar{x}$ = 8.58, for both). "Opposition to the death penalty" is also strong ($\bar{x}$ = 2.51 out of 4); the smaller mean is, to some extent, an artifact of the different response option. Table 8.2 also shows significant differences by gender and race, with women of color as a group reporting positions that are more pro-minority civil rights than their male counterparts on every measure. (Question wording and response options may be found in the notes to each table.)

The racial differences are also highly significant, with the means for questions on voting rights and affirmative action for Blacks higher than for Latinos, and much higher than for Asian Americans. We see the same pattern on support for affirmative action to achieve equity for one's own racial group. The differences by race are smaller but still substantial on whether it is important to achieve equity for women.

Some readers may be surprised that the death penalty is included in a category focused on minority civil rights. We include it here because numerous activists, legal experts, and scholars point to the racial disparities in its application (see, e.g., "The Color of Death: Race and the Death Penalty," in Walker, Spohn, and DeLone 2012, 345–402). According to a fact sheet on *Innocence and the Death Penalty* (DPIC 2015), more than 150 individuals have been exonerated and had their convictions overturned; of these, 52.3 percent were Black. Further, some prisoners are being freed from death row through the efforts of groups such as the Innocence Project, which have called into question the validity of the evidence in death penalty cases. For these reasons, it is worth seeing the positions elected officials of color hold on this policy. Our survey findings suggest a shared opposition to the death penalty (see Table 8.2), with Black respondents most opposed; Asian American officials, even more than their Latino counterparts, may be more likely coalition partners on this issue (p < .0001). The strongest opposition, however, comes from Black women; and the only significant difference by gender within race (not shown) is between Black women ($\bar{x}$ = 2.75) and Black men ($\bar{x}$ = 2.51) on opposition to the death penalty (p < .001).

TABLE 8.2. *Issue Positions on Minority Civil Rights: Elected Officials of Color by Gender and Race*

Issue Position	All	Gender		Race			Race*Gender					
							Women			Men		
		Women	Men	Black	Latino	Asian American	Black	Latina	Asian American	Black	Latino	Asian American
Importance of Voting Rights Act	9.17	9.32	9.08	9.69	8.63	8.05	9.72	8.68	8.64	9.68	8.61	7.79
(Scale: 0–10; N = 1,162)		*p < .05*		*p < .0001*			*p < .0001*			*p < .0001*		
Importance of affirmative action programs for racial equity	8.58	8.78	8.51	9.32	8.01	6.51	9.19	8.17	6.89	9.33	7.94	6.33
(Scale: 0–10; N = 1,197)		*p < .05*		*p < .0001*			*p < .0001*			*p < .0001*		
Importance of affirmative action to help women achieve equity.	8.58	8.77	8.47	9.14	8.00	7.53	9.19	8.13	8.14	9.11	7.94	7.25
(Scale: 0–10; N = 1,197)		*p < .05*		*p < .0001*			*p < .0001*			*p < .0001*		
Opposition to the death penalty	2.51	2.63	2.44	2.61	2.38	2.50	2.75	2.42	2.48	2.51	2.36	2.51
(Scale: 1–4; N = 1,149)		*p < .001*		*p < .0001*			*p < .005*			n.s.		

Note: Entries are mean values with higher values representing more pro-minority/civil rights responses. Question wording on Voting Rights Act: "*Using a scale from zero to ten, where zero is not at all important and ten is extremely important, in your opinion, how important are the protections of equal political access in the current voting rights act for persons of your racial or ethnic background?*" Question wording on the Death Penalty: "*Please tell me whether you strongly disagree, disagree, agree, or strongly agree with each of the following policy proposals: "The death penalty should be an option as punishment for those who commit murder."* For affirmative action: "*Using a scale from zero to ten, where zero is not at all important and ten is extremely important, in your opinion, how important are affirmative action programs in terms of helping persons women/of your racial or ethnic background achieve equity?*" Responses for the Death Penalty were reverse coded: 1 – Strongly Agree; 2 – Agree; 3 – Disagree; 4 – Strongly disagree. Means for All and Gender do not include positions of American Indians. The differences by gender within each racial group were significant between Black women and men on the death penalty (*p < .001*), and between Latinas and Latino men on same-sex marriage (*p < .05*).
Source: GMCL National Survey, 2006–2007.

Women's Welfare and Reproductive Rights

Table 8.3 shows that elected officials of color are remarkably supportive of women's issues, including support for abortion rights ($\bar{x} = 1.52$ on a scale of 0–2, where 2 is the most progressive/feminist response: "*By law, a woman should always be able to obtain an abortion as a private decision to be made with her physician*") and on opposition to repealing *Roe v. Wade* ($\bar{x} = 3.03$ scale of 1–4, where 4 is strongly opposed). The strength of support on these two issues would seem to be driven by Asian American respondents – and by Asian American women in particular.

In a similar vein, elected officials of color are strong supporters of policies designed to help poor women, with all respondents, on average, agreeing that women receiving government assistance should be able to count college attendance toward the "work requirement"; and the government should provide and subsidize child care. Although women are more likely than their male counterparts to agree, and the differences are highly significant, they are not very large.

With these findings, we can say with some confidence that elected officials of color – male and female alike – clearly support women's rights and are potentially strong allies with women who, in general, are pro-choice and progressive on such issues. But coalitions on these issues may fail when elected officials and voters in general are more divided on government initiatives to benefit women who are poor. The Center for American Progress offers a measure of hope: "More than two-thirds of Americans agree that the government or businesses should be doing more to help fund child care for working parents" (Glynn 2012, 3; see also Boushey and O'Leary 2010). They also note, "Our nation's lawmakers, however, have yet to take a serious look at this issue." And, of course, factors besides gender and race such as party affiliation and socioeconomic status, may contribute. We test these factors in a multivariate analysis to help answer the question of whether elected officials of color will join forces with progressive White women and men on these issues.

Immigrant Incorporation

On immigration issues (Table 8.4,) we see a potential for allies among Latino and Asian American elected officials to provide driver's licenses for undocumented immigrants, with these groups showing significantly more support than Blacks. This is not surprising in light of the fact that, as discussed earlier (see esp. Table 3.6), Asians and Latinos are significantly

TABLE 8.3. *Issue Positions on Women's Welfare and Reproductive Rights: Elected Officials of Color, by Gender and Race*

Issue Position	All	Gender		Race			Women			Men		
		Women	Men	Black	Latino	Asian American	Black	Latina	Asian American	Black	Latino	Asian American
Support for abortion rights (Scale: 0–2; N = 1,146)	1.52	1.59	1.47	1.55	1.43	1.71	1.59	1.53	1.89	1.52	1.39	1.62
		$p < .005$		$p < .0001$			$p < .05$			$p < .005$		
Opposition to repeal of *Roe v. Wade* (Scale: 1–4; N = 1,139)	3.03	3.12	2.97	3.07	2.92	3.21	3.15	3.01	3.43	3.02	2.89	3.10
		$p < .005$		$p < .01$			$p < .05$			$p < .1$		
College education should count toward the "work requirement" for women receiving welfare. (Scale: 1–4; N = 1,140)	2.99	3.01	2.97	3.00	2.97	3.00	2.99	2.95	3.02	2.99	2.95	3.02
		n.s.		n.s.			n.s.			n.s.		
Government should provide childcare services with fees according to ability to pay. (Scale: 1–4; N = 1,195)	3.00	3.10	2.94	3.05	2.95	2.93	3.14	3.04	3.04	2.98	2.91	2.88
		$p < .0001$		$p < .1$			n.s.			n.s.		
Subsidized childcare should be increased for poor working mothers in welfare-to-work programs. (Scale: 1–4; N = 1,193)	3.07	3.14	3.03	3.13	3.00	3.06	2.98	2.91	2.88	3.01	2.97	3.03
		$p < .005$		$p < .001$			n.s.			n.s.		

Note: Entries are mean values with higher values representing more progressive/feminist responses. Question wording: *"Which of the following statements best agrees with your view on abortion? (A) By law, abortion should never be permitted; (B) The law should permit abortion only in cases of rape, incest, or when the life of the woman is in danger; or (C) By law, a woman should always be able to obtain an abortion as a private decision to be made with her physician."* This was coded as 0, 1, 2, with a maximum mean of 2. *Roe v. Wade:* "Please tell me whether you strongly disagree, disagree, agree, or strongly agree with each of the following policy proposals: *The United States Supreme Court should overturn the Roe v. Wade decision, which made abortion legal during the first three months of pregnancy."* This was reverse coded to match direction, with 4 – Strongly Disagree; 3 – Disagree; 2 – Agree; 1 – Strongly Agree. For others, questions are as stated, response options: 1 – Strongly Disagree; 2 – Disagree; 3 – Agree; 4 –Strongly Agree.
Source: GMCL National Survey, 2006–2007.

TABLE 8.4. *Issue Positions on Immigrant Incorporation: Elected Officials of Color by Gender and Race*

Issue Position	All	Gender		Race			Women			Men		
		Women	Men	Black	Latino	Asian American	Black	Latina	Asian American	Black	Latino	Asian American
As a matter of public safety, driver's licenses should be made available to immigrants, regardless of their legal status in the United States.	2.35	2.34	2.35	2.12	2.63	2.54	2.14	2.66	2.65	2.10	2.62	2.49
(Scale: 1–4; N = 1,166)		n.s.		p < .0001			p < .0001			p < .0001		
Noncitizen legal immigrants should be allowed to vote in school board elections if they have children in the public schools.	2.43	2.54	2.34	2.41	2.43	2.48	2.53	2.52	2.75	2.33	2.39	2.35
(Scale: 1–4; N = 1,186)		p < .0001		n.s.			n.s.			n.s.		
Government agencies should provide services in a variety of languages to help non-English-speaking clients	2.90	2.93	2.89	2.86	2.95	2.96	2.91	2.99	2.86	2.83	2.93	3.00
(Scale: 1–4; N = 1,189)		n.s.		p < .1			n.s.			p < .05		
Favors mandating bilingual education	2.82	2.81	2.83	2.83	2.88	2.51	2.84	2.85	2.33	2.82	2.89	2.56
(Scale: 1–4; N = 1,173)		n.s.		p < .001			p < .01			p < .05		

Note: Entries are mean values with higher values representing more pro-immigrant responses. Question wording for the first three: *"Please tell me whether you strongly disagree, disagree, agree, or strongly agree with each of the following policy proposals:* [policies as shown]." Response options: 1 – Strongly Disagree; 2 – Disagree; 3 – Agree; 4 – Strongly Agree. Response options for "A law banning preferential school admission on the basis of race or ethnicity": 1 – Strongly Favor; 2 – Favor; 3 – Oppose; 4 – Strongly Oppose. For "A law mandating public schools to provide instruction in other languages for students not proficient in English," responses were reverse coded: 1 – Strongly Oppose; 2 – Oppose; 3 – Favor; 4 – Strongly Favor. Means for All and Gender do not include positions of American Indians. The differences by gender within each racial group were significant only on noncitizen voting: Blacks (p < .001), Asians (p < .05), and Latinos/as (p < .1).

Source: GMCL National Survey, 2006–2007.

more likely to have an immigrant background, with more than half of Asian American and a third of Latino officials reporting that one or more parents were foreign-born.

Results are more mixed on the other measures of support for pro-immigrant policies. Women of color reported stronger support than men for noncitizen voting in certain elections. Asian American and Latino men were also the most supportive of having government agencies provide services in languages other than English. However, Blacks and Latinos were significantly more likely to agree with a policy mandating bilingual education than Asian Americans surveyed – with this pattern holding up between both Black and Latina women and men. To try to account for these somewhat puzzling differences is the reason we test a set of factors in addition to gender and race – including political and sociodemographic variables – in a multivariate regression later in this chapter.

Rights of Same-Sex Couples

Some of the most heated political fights in recent years have been around rights of same-sex couples, including the right to marry. At times, as Robert Siegel of National Public Radio said (Bates 2015), "The campaign for same-sex marriage has often been compared to the [B]lack civil rights movement of the 1960s" – a characterization that "has irritated many African Americans" because, as Bates (2015) counters, Blacks believe "[W]hite LGBT folks have always had the option, no matter how painful, to keep their orientation private and escape discrimination."

Nevertheless, in a short period of time, advocates pursued court cases as well as other political strategies to achieve what was almost unthinkable just a few years ago: In June 2015, the Supreme Court handed down a decision (*Obergefell et al. v. Hodges*) that recognized the rights of gays and lesbians to marry anywhere in the nation. Shocking to many on the Right, who have continued to resist implementation of the law, and shocking to many Blacks, who may resent how seemingly quickly and painlessly the change came to be compared to the centuries of struggle from slavery to the Civil Rights Act of 1964.

Although we have no evidence that the elected officials in our survey had any impact (by voting on local or state legislation, we do know the extent to which, in 2006–2007, they affirmed the possibility that *"Gay and lesbian couples should be allowed to legally form civil unions, giving them some of the legal rights of married couples."* Table 8.5 shows that Black elected officials are significantly less likely by race to report that

TABLE 8.5. *Issue Positions on Rights of Same-Sex Couples: Elected Officials of Color by Gender and Race*

Issue Positions	All	Gender		Race			Race*Gender					
							Women			Men		
		Women	Men	Black	Latino	Asian American	Black	Latina	Asian American	Black	Latino	Asian American
Support for same-sex marriage rights (Scale: 1–4; N = 1,104)	2.37	2.43	2.31	2.22	2.45	2.89	2.28	2.60	3.08	2.18	2.38	2.80
		$p < .05$		$p < .0001$			$p < .0001$			$p < .0001$		

Note: Entries are mean values with higher values representing a position that is more pro-gay rights. Question wording on Same-Sex Marriage: "*Please tell me whether you strongly disagree, disagree, agree, or strongly agree with each of the following policy proposals: Gay and lesbian couples should be allowed to legally form civil unions, giving them some of the legal rights of married couples.*" Response options for Gay marriage: 1 – Strongly Disagree; 2 – Disagree; 3 – Agree; 4 – Strongly Agree. Means for All and Gender do not include positions of American Indians.
Source: GMCL National Survey, 2006–2007.

they favor civil unions, with Black men (mean 2.18 out of 4) the least of all. This matches findings from public opinion polls: According to the Pew Research Center (2015a, 2), for example, "51% of blacks oppose gays and lesbians marrying legally, while 41% are in favor. Majorities of whites (59%) and Hispanics (56%) now favor same-sex marriage."

Women of color elected officials, in general, are more supportive of extending marriage rights to gays and lesbians than their male peers. This expands on previous research by Carroll (2003, 138)[12] and Herrick (2010, 937), who find women officials to be more supportive of civil unions or gays and lesbians than their male counterparts, but whose research only looks at state legislators and does not provide an intersectional analysis. Furthermore, according to the same report by the Pew Research Center, the gender gap on this issue has shrunk, with majorities of both women (58 percent) and men (53 percent) in favor of gay marriage (Pew Research Center 2015b).

Looking at the opinions of Asian American officials, initially we were somewhat surprised that they reported the most support among all racial groups, with Asian women ($\bar{x} = 3.08$) showing the strongest support of all.[13] With this group somewhat more likely to claim a Republican Party affiliation(see Figure 7.3) than the other groups, they are actually less likely (at 28.7 percent) than Latinos at (37.4 percent) to voice a conservative or very conservative ideology nor hold much more conservative views than Blacks (at 25.3 percent). And, whereas four in ten Blacks report being liberal or very liberal, three in ten of Asians and Latinos are in that ideological camp (see Table 7.4). Where we find most Asians is in the "middle of the road" ideologically speaking (with more than four in ten reporting as such). Lewis and Gossett (2008, 5) support this, at least among the general population in California, where

… opinions on homosexuality and gay rights issues today are much more strongly split along ideological, partisan, and religious lines. Liberals, Democrats, and the less religious have become more supportive of same-sex marriage, but conservatives, Republicans, and Protestants have not. Similarly, African-Americans' support for same-sex marriage has not risen, while that of non-Hispanic whites, Latinos, and Asian-Americans has.

---

[12] Carroll's measure, like ours, was testing support for civil unions; interestingly, when the data were collected in 2001, the only group for which the difference was not significant was between Republican female and male state representatives.

[13] The differences between Latinas and Latino men shown in the table were significant ($p <$ .05, not shown).

Research on the views of same-sex marriage for elected officials of color is very sparse and limited to state legislators and members of Congress. Herrick (2010) finds that Black legislators were also more likely – and Latinos less likely – to support civil unions than other races, but she does not report the positions of Asian legislators.[14] Studies of public opinion data suggest that "the issue of same-sex marriage varies by generation, ideology, and region of the country" (Ford 2011, 366), factors that we will explore in the multivariate analysis in the text that follows.

Changing Education Policies

Among racial and gender groups, we see strong opposition to school vouchers, with Blacks and women in the forefront (Table 8.6). With no significant difference by gender within race, women of color seem to be in agreement, whereas Black men are stronger in their opposition than other men to this issue. At the intersection between religion and public school education, that is, the teaching of creationism and permitting prayer in public schools, we see strong variation by race but not by gender alone.

Asian American women and men in political office are much more likely to oppose the teaching of creationism, with means ranging from a high of 3.31 for Asian American women to a low of 2.78 for Black men. A similar pattern exists for permitting prayer in public schools with, on average, Asian American women significantly more opposed ($\bar{x} = 3.11$) than Black men ($\bar{x} = 1.86$). On the question of support for the No Child Left Behind policy, which mandated "high-stakes" testing at various stages of elementary, middle and high school, the only significant difference is between male and female elected officials, with opposition of women stronger than that of men.

Making Sense of the Findings: A Brief Summary

What stands out? First, elected officials of color show strong support for policy positions that promote civil rights and women's rights, affirming the importance of the Voting Rights Act; affirmative action programs; and two measures of reproductive rights – policies that seemed settled but which are

---

[14] Herrick (2010, 937) reports that "The probability for the average black legislator was .49 compared to .38 for others" and this is significant at $p < .05$, but her finding that Latinos were less likely to offer support (probability of .15) was not significant. She also notes that the "other races" category in her study includes "mostly White legislators, but also a handful of Asian Americans and Native Americans" (934).

TABLE 8.6. *Issue Positions on Changing Education Policies: Elected Officials of Color by Gender and Race*

Issue Positions	All	Gender		Race			Women			Men		
		Women	Men	Black	Latino	Asian American	Black	Latina	Asian American	Black	Latino	Asian American
Opposes school vouchers for public, private, religious schools	3.00	3.07	2.96	3.08	2.90	2.98	3.06	3.05	3.22	3.09	2.83	2.86
		$p < .1$		$p < .01$			n.s.			$p < .001$		
(Scale: 1–4; N = 1,176)												
Opposes No Child Left Behind	2.57	2.69	2.50	2.53	2.60	2.74	2.64	2.74	2.93	2.45	2.53	2.64
		$p < .001$		n.s.			n.s.			n.s.		
(Scale: 1–4; N = 1,169)												
Opposes teaching creationism instead of evolution	2.83	2.83	2.84	2.79	2.82	3.18	2.80	2.78	3.31	2.78	2.84	3.11
		n.s.		$p < .005$			$p < .05$			$p < .05$		
(Scale: 1–4; N = 1,060)												
Opposes permitting prayer in public schools	2.11	2.08	2.13	1.98	2.18	2.82	1.86	2.34	2.96	2.06	2.10	2.76
		n.s.		$p < .0001$			$p < .0001$			$p < .0001$		
(Scale: 1–4; N = 1,175)												

Note: Entries are mean values with higher values representing more progressive responses. Question wording: "The following questions are specifically about policies concerning education. For each one, please tell me whether you would strongly favor, favor, oppose, or strongly oppose each policy: The No Child Left Behind Act mandating public schools to meet certain testing standards for federal funding; A law giving parents government-funded school vouchers to pay for tuition at the public, private, or religious school of their choice; A constitutional amendment to permit prayer in public schools; A law mandating the teaching of creationism instead of evolution in public schools. Response options for each: 1 – Strongly Favor; 2 – Favor; 3 – Oppose; 4 – Strongly Oppose. Means for All and Gender do not include positions of American Indians.

Source: GMCL National Survey, 2006–2007.

contested once again. They also are in favor of policies to support women economically including college counted toward the work requirement for women on welfare and childcare subsidized by the government. On education policies, they firmly oppose school vouchers, the teaching of creationism instead of evolution, and any ban on race-based school admission.

On policies promoting immigrant incorporation they favor mandating bilingual education, and, in essence, reject the notion of "English only" in government services. On some issues, such as gay unions/marriage, No Child Left Behind, opposition to prayer in public schools, and the death penalty, their positions were somewhat less supportive. Others with support that is more obvious are in the area of expanding some rights and privileges (e.g., driver's licenses and noncitizen voting in certain elections) for undocumented immigrants.

In addition to substantial differences across racial groups, where Black elected officials are generally more supportive of traditional minority civil rights, while Asian American office holders seem more supportive of extending "new" rights, we find significant differences by gender for thirteen of the nineteen questions shown in these table measures. And, in every case, women hold more liberal, progressive positions than those of their male counterparts. The more liberal positions women of color public officials revealed in our survey are consistent with findings on women in general, as reported in the literature. Carroll, Dodson, and Mandel (1991), for example, show a large gender gap between state legislators, with women substantially more likely than men to oppose prohibiting abortion and the death penalty.

Partisanship may help explain the differences in issue positions. Carroll and Sanbonmatsu (2013, 81) find that differences between Republican women and men state legislators' positions on the death penalty, *Roe v. Wade*, affirmative action programs for women and minorities, and school vouchers were large and significant, and "represented more liberal and/or feminist responses" than men holding the same positions. Their argument for specifically studying Republican women is pertinent in that these women are supposedly more likely to represent the moderate wing of the Republican Party. Other research challenges the one-to-one link between party, gender, and more liberal views on contested rights, including, for example, gay marriage (Casey, O'Mahen, and Puccio 2011).

As noted earlier in this volume, eight in ten elected officials of color report a Democratic Party affiliation, with one in ten being Republican or Independent. Party affiliation varies significantly by race, with nine in ten Blacks and eight in ten Latinos/as being Democrats compared to fewer than six in ten Asians. On the policy positions discussed previously, for elected officials of color in our survey, there are fewer gender differences when comparing Republican and Democratic women and men than the literature might predict. In contrast to previous studies, we find that Republican women of color were more likely to support school vouchers than Republican men but only at $p < .1$; no other differences were significant by gender with this party. Among those who identified as Democrats, women were significantly more likely than men to oppose the death penalty and school vouchers ($p < .05$).

Let us move now to exploring some of the factors besides gender and race that may contribute to the potential for building coalitions between and among these groups.

PROSPECTIVE ALLIES: KEY TO COALITIONS

Political influence may be elusive for elected officials unless they form part of a broader voting majority and have political allies who support them in their respective governing bodies. As we saw in Chapter 6, there is strong evidence of political incorporation and the potential for coalitions when it comes to self-reported voting records: four in ten said they vote with the majority; another half split evenly between the majority and minority; and only a small percentage see themselves as consistently in the minority on their governing bodies. In this section, we examine survey respondents' potential to form political alliances among themselves and build coalitions with other groups.

In addition to how they vote, a measure of political incorporation is the extent to which a legislator – whether at the state or local level – has political allies. Fraga et al. (2005, 12) points to the importance of such allies in helping – in their case – Latino/a state legislators to position themselves to influence public policy making and to form coalitions with a variety of groups. We agree that "[b]onds of solidarity based on ethnicity and gender seem plausible given the raced and gendered hierarchies that predominate in state legislatures."

We find that elected officials of color are most likely to draw their allies from those who share their ideology, race/ethnicity, and party affiliation. Women of color are significantly more likely than their male peers to find prospective allies with elected officials who share their ideology and are fellow minority women (Figure 8.1). They report equal likelihood of getting support from other elected officials of their own race/ethnicity and/or own party. Women of color are also slightly more likely

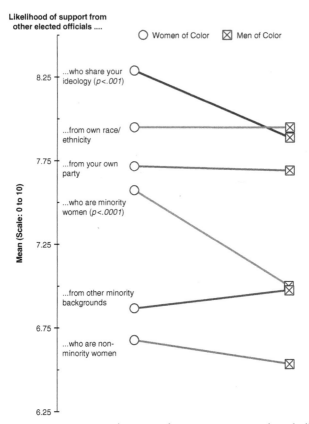

FIGURE 8.1 Perceived support from prospective political allies.
Note: Entries are means of female and male elected officials, on a scale of 0–10;
N for ideology = 1,245; own race/ethnicity = 1,197; party = 1,194; minority
women = 1,162; other minorities = 1,140; nonminority women = 1,170. A line
that declines sharply indicates a significant difference between women and men.
Source: GMCL National Survey, 2006–2007.

to see allies in White women, whereas men are more likely to find allies
in other minority elected officials. These latter differences are, however,
neither large nor significant.

LINKED FATE: EVIDENCE OF POTENTIAL FOR COALITIONS?

We asked the GMCL National Survey respondents three questions to
gauge if they feel a sense of linked fate with other minority groups: "*Do
you think what happens generally to other minority groups in this country affects what happens in your life and how you view politics? Do you*

think what happens to people of your own racial or ethnic background in this country affects what happens in your life and how you view politics? Do you think what happens to women in this country affects what happens in your life and how you view politics?" To assess the strength of their bonds for those who responded in the affirmative, we then asked, *"Is it a lot, some, or not very much?"*

On average, there is a relatively strong sense of linked fate elected officials of color, scoring close to 2 on a four-point scale from 0 to 3, where a 0 indicates a response of *"No"* to the questions, and a 3 indicates *"Yes, a lot."* (See Table 8.7.) Blacks clearly have the strongest sense of linked fate on all three measures, with Black men driving the difference on linked fate, not only with one's own racial group, but also with other minority groups.

Dawson (1994), Gay (2004), Gurin, Hatchett, and Jackson (1989), Philpot and Walton (2007), and Tate (1993), and others have consistently found evidence on the importance of linked fate among Blacks. Importantly, Jones-Correa (2011, 84) finds a majority of Latinos report having linked fate with Blacks, between 60 and 70 percent for those surveyed in seven states, some traditional receiving and others new immigrant destination states. Latino/as having commonalities with Blacks, that is those with closer contact with African Americans by living in neighborhoods with Blacks or having children in the same schools and other associations were also more likely to perceive linked fate with Blacks.

Research on Black linked fate has found it confirmed over time, when controlled for sociodemographic status, that is both by class and economic location. Gay (2004, 559–560), for example, discusses the "central paradox in black public opinion, the well-documented tendency of middle-class blacks to be more racially oriented than lower-class blacks." She notes that it may be that Blacks, especially those in the middle and upper class, have been frustrated by their inability to obtain economic well-being in housing that reflects progress in employment. She quotes Landry (1987, 111) that "it may be the tarnished success of life in the middle" generating these beliefs. Yet, she argues that reinforcement of race consciousness, linked fate may fade "[i]f the residential returns to middle-class status improve …" (Gay 2004, 560). Unlike our research, most of the linked fate analysis is centered on mass rather than elite opinion. The routine activities of elected officials representing their constituents, which typically include significant proportions of Blacks, may also reinforce or even strengthen their linked fate.

On the question of whether *"what happens to* women *in this country affects what happens in your life and how you view politics,"* we find

TABLE 8.7. *Sense of Linked Fate: Elected Officials of Color, by Gender and Race*

Linked fate (i.e., own life and view of politics are affected by what happens to others in this county) with…	All	Gender		Race			Women			Men		
		Women	Men	Black	Latino	Asian American	Black	Latina	Asian American	Black	Latino	Asian American
…other minority groups	1.82	1.77	1.85	1.93	1.72	1.53	1.79	1.77	1.45	2.03	1.70	1.67
(Scale: 0–3; N = 1,281)		n.s.		p < .0001			n.s.			p < .0001		
…people of own racial or ethnic background	1.94	1.90	1.97	2.09	1.77	1.73	2.00	1.73	1.86	2.16	1.79	1.67
(Scale: 0–3; N = 1,286)		p < .0001		p < .01			p < .1			n.s.		
…with women	1.87	2.03	1.77	1.97	1.78	1.66	2.12	1.89	1.87	1.84	1.74	1.56
(Scale: 0–3; N = 1,283)		p < .0001		p < .0001			p < .1			n.s.		

Note: Entries are mean values with higher values representing a greater sense of linked fate, ranging from 0 to 3. Question wording: "*Do you think what happens generally to other minority groups in this country affects what happens in your life and how you view politics? Do you think what happens to people of your own racial or ethnic background in this country affects what happens in your life and how you view politics? Do you think what happens to women in this country affects what happens in your life and how you view politics?*" For those who responded yes, we asked, *Is it a lot, some, or not very much?* Responses options: 0 – No; 1 – Yes, not very much; 2 – Yes, some; 3 – Yes, a lot.

Source: GMCL National Survey, 2006–2007.

significant gender differences among elected officials of color that can be attributed to the larger gaps among Blacks, with a mean of 2.12 for Black women.[15] Philpot and Walton (2007, 59) conducted experimental research on the support that Black women voters might offer Black women candidates for elective office. They conclude that "[B]lack women have created an identity that is greater than the sum of its parts ..." and that, in this case Black women voters maximize "the utility for those standing at the intersection of the competing identities." They explicitly discuss Black women, but they recommend their findings should apply to "individuals who simultaneously possess overlapping and competing interests, especially where these interests are both inescapable and subordinate." The GMCL analysis is of course based on the views of women of color who are already in elective office, but there is no reason to assume they would differ significantly from ordinary individuals, and the data at least offers some support for this position.

A MULTICULTURAL AND GENDERED CONTEXT FOR COALITION BUILDING

It is important to describe the positions elected officials of color hold on these contested policies, and to explore differences by race and gender separately and in interaction. A more robust analysis is needed, however, to explain the variation – an analysis that includes other factors besides gender and race. We first proceed to use ordinary least squares (OLS) regression on a broad measure of the potential for coalitions: the extent to which they have a sense of "linked fate" with other minority groups. We then test the independent effects of various factors indicating greater support for key public policies related to minority civil rights, immigrant incorporation, rights of same-sex couples, and women's welfare and reproductive rights potential coalitions around on.[16] In this way, we may be able to understand the relative contributions to the likelihood of inter- and intragroup coalitions among Black, Latino, and Asian American female and male elected officials in the United States at the start of the twenty-first century.

Each of the multiple regression models is based on the idea that minority elected officials' policy attitudes and political networks may be a

---

[15] The gender differences within race evident for Blacks are also significant at $p < .01$ for linked fate with women and other minorities, and at $p < .05$ with those of coethnics.

[16] While we included a bivariate analysis of positions on education (Table 8.5), we did not include a multivariate analysis here.

function of a variety of factors, which we covered in the previous chapters: *group-based identities* at the intersection of race and gender; the respondents' *personal and family backgrounds and resources*; the various *political factors*, such as political orientations, social ties, views on minority rights; and, finally, those related to the opportunity structure, in this case, *level of office*.

Prior research has used these models to explain a number of dimensions of political participation and influence by elected officials of color. In the previous chapters, bivariate data on the various factors we propose as independent variables have been presented in earlier chapters. Among group identity factors, we hypothesize that elected officials with strong racial and gender identities, either individually or in combination, might also have high levels of linked fate.

Explaining Variation on a Shared Sense of Linked Fate and on Policy Positions

Because of the long and shared history of slavery and subsequent de jure segregation and de facto discrimination among Blacks, we predict that, all other things being equal, Blacks would have the strongest sense of linked fate. With political histories of Latino and Asians in this country that are much shorter and complicated by considerable diversity by nationality, their sense of linked fate is likely to be less than that of Blacks. American Indians, having originated in North America, could also have strong group identity, and hence high levels of linked fate, but it is also possible that as a result of the genocide, discussed in Chapter 1 (see Narratives of Exclusion), and the federal government's attempts to wipe out a sense of "Indianness," discussed in Chapter 3 (esp. "Educational Access and Attainment: The Historical Context").

The various waves of the women's movement have documented that, while some women live privileged lives, others – especially women of color – have had to fight to secure equal rights under the law. Our model tests whether there are common bonds by gender among these women of color elected officials. We hypothesize that sociodemographic factors also play a significant role in predicting political perspectives and policy positions, independently of race/ethnicity and gender.

Higher levels of attainment on sociodemographic factors such as education and income typically are associated, whether at the mass or elite levels, with higher levels of political participation and political influence.

Given the life experiences and backgrounds of people of color, including elected officials these reflect personal and family *resources* rather than simple demographic measures of individual choices (see discussion in Chapter 3 of this volume). We also go beyond traditional socioeconomic status models (Hardy-Fanta et al. 2007) and include additional variables: marital status, age, and immigration generation. Finally, where elected officials hold similar views ideologically, are associated with the same political party, and have been involved in civic organizations – all discussed in earlier chapters – we hypothesize they would also hold similar views on the policy positions in question.[17]

The results of our analysis are reported in three tables: Table 8.8, which reports on the sense of Linked Fate, which has potential as a foundation for coalition building. Table 8.9 follows, with OLS-regression models to gauge the independent effects on "Traditional" Minority Civil Rights, Immigration Rights, and Rights of Same-Sex Couples of respondents' backgrounds and resources, political experiences, and level of office. In Table 8.10, we conclude the series with Women's Welfare and Reproductive Rights. The dependent variables are index measures constructed from the items reported in the related bivariate tables; see note to tables for an explanation of the how we constructed each of the measures and table notes for question wording.

To gauge the respondents' sense of linked fate, we constructed a three-item summed index measure of responses to survey questions asking whether what happens generally to other minority groups, people of their own racial and ethnic background (coethnics), or of women, in the United States would affect what happens in their life and how they view politics. We report the findings in Table 8.8. When only group identities

---

[17] Michael Minta (2011, 1) notes that the US Congress's Congressional Black Caucus, the Congressional Asian Pacific American Caucus, and the Congressional Hispanic Caucus, formed the Congressional Tri-Caucus in the wake of Hurricane Katrina. A 2015 review of state legislative minority and women's caucuses in 2015 found a variety of types of single-group caucuses and combinations, as follows: Five with women's caucuses; eighteen with Black caucuses; five with both Latino and Black caucuses; one has an Asian caucus; two have American Indian/Native American; and three states with combined minority caucuses. These are the states – especially the eight with large multiracial populations – that form the ground on which the potential for coalitions (or for a variety of types of interactions between or among these groups) rests. Continued observation will be required.

TABLE 8.8. *OLS Estimations of Sense of Linked Fate with Own and Other Minority Group(s) and Women in the United States*

Predictors	Model I		Model II		Model III	
	b	s.e.	B	s.e.	b	s.e.
Race*Gender (*Ref. = Black men*)						
Latino men	−.089**	.028	−.118***	.033	−.027	.034
Asian men	−.105*	.052	−.174**	.060	−.022	.061
AIAN men	.113	.121	.107	.121	.177	.119
Black women	−.032	.030	−.036	.031	−.042	.030
Latina women	−.004	.048	.002	.048	−.009	.046
Asian women	.025	.095	.034	.094	−.022	.091
AIAN women	.073	.195	.093	.195	.052	.187
Personal and Family Resources						
Income			.000	.003	−.000	.003
Education			.031*	.016	.028†	.015
Married			−.008	.025	.004	.025
Age			−.003*	.001	−.004***	.001
Immigration generation			−.020	.015	−.019	.014
Political Orientations, Ties, and Concerns over Minority Impact and Rights						
Ideology (5 = very liberal)					.033***	.010
Partisanship (Republican)					−.137***	.039
Prior involvement in civic organization					.012*	.005
Perceive minority impact on governing					.028	.020
Support minority rights					.033***	.008
Level/Type of office (*Ref. = Municipal*)						
State legislature					−.015	.038
County					.024	.030
Local school board					−.020	.025
Constant	.845***	.019	1.007***	.096	.520***	.118
Adj. R^2	.015		.025		.107	
F-score	3.195		3.121		7.015	
N = 1,002						

Notes: b = unstandarized slope coefficient, s.e. = standard errors. For question wording, see note in Table 8.7; dependent variable is a three-item summed index of responses to survey questions asking whether what happens generally to other minority groups, people of their own racial and ethnic background (coethnics), or of women, in the United States would affect what happens in their lives and how they view politics (adjusted alpha = .81).

†$p < .10$, *$p \le .05$ **$p \le .005$ ***$p \le .001$.

Source: GMCL National Survey, 2006–2007.

are considered (Model I), we see that Latino and Asian men register significantly lower degrees of linked fate than Black men, but there are no significant differences from Black men for any of the different groups of women of color (or AIAN men).[18]

What do we learn from this analysis? First, we should not be surprised that, among elected officials of color, the groups with the strongest sense of linked fate would be Black men as well as all women of color. Blacks – women and men alike – in this country have a long tradition of "we rise and fall together,"[19] so it is not surprising that the same pattern would hold among their elected officials. Second, we posit that the "dual oppression" of women of color by race/ethnicity and gender might lead them to a similar sense that their fates are linked. This holds true even when sociodemographic factors (personal and family resource) variables are added to the model, with women of color not dissimilar from Black men in their sense of linked fate. Additional education may be the result of its leading to greater understanding of the structural sources of discrimination; the negative direction of age may be because younger elected officials may have had less exposure to legislative experience and they may also have come to age in a time when rampant discrimination is no longer legal and acceptable.

Third, what is striking about these three models is that, in looking at Model III, race and gender are not significant when compared with the extent to which the elected officials share a political and civic perspective (i.e., the added political variables). And, other than age, the sociodemographic variables are also not significant (the respondent's level of education is significant, but only at the $p < .1$ level). Thus, a respondent's political ideology, partisanship, social ties, and support for minority rights may facilitate the forging of a sense of common identity as minorities in US society and politics, even more than their race/ethnicity and gender. We should also note that the adjusted R^2 is also more robust than when simply considering race/ethnicity in combination with gender. These findings suggest that our hypothesis that sociodemographic

[18] When constructing the database of all elected officials of color that formed the sampling frame for the GMCL Survey, we included American Indian/Native American mostly from the level of state legislator. The N for the AIAN group is therefore small (24) and findings for this group should be approached with caution.

[19] In a chapter titled, "Becoming a Collective Representation," Alexander (2010, 27) writes that as he accepted the Democratic Party nomination on August 28, 2008, Barack Obama said, "That's the idea of America, the promise that we rise and fall together, that I am my brother's keeper, my sister's keeper."

factors would be as influential as race/ethnicity and gender is clearly not supported. Finally, the findings are not unidimensional, but are complex. Some of the findings are based on what we already understand, involving stronger findings of linked fate, and for minority issues among Blacks – male and female – but they also seem to move in the same direction with relatively strong support for linked fate among women of color elected officials.

POLICY POSITIONS OF ELECTED OFFICIALS OF COLOR: POTENTIAL FOR COALITION BUILDING

Table 8.9 examines factors associated with respondents' level of support for a set of civil rights that include "traditional" minority rights (i.e., support for voting rights and affirmative action for minorities and women), immigrant incorporation, and contested "new rights" (i.e., same-sex marriage). Note that, in this table and the next, we show only the final models.

"Traditional" Minority Civil Rights

The first set of results in this table shows that, compared to Black men, Latino and Asian men are significantly *less* likely to support traditional minority rights, as measured by their responses to questions on support for the Voting Rights Act and affirmative action. Women of color are much more cohesive on this measure, with no significant differences between them. It also shows that variations among them in personal and family backgrounds and resources have little effect. In fact, the only sociodemographic variable that has a significant contribution to the model is age: The older the respondents are, the greater the support they evidence for traditionally defined minority rights. We suggest that older elected officials of color in our survey (of whom half are Black), may have strong ties to the Civil Rights Movement, resulting in stronger support for minority rights than their younger counterparts.

We also note that one's political ideology and political partisanship are strong predictors of support for these policies. In addition, the degree of prior engagement in civic organizations, and perception of the impact of the increased presence of women and minorities in public office in facilitating the making of policies beneficial to both non-White and White women, racial minorities, and the economically disadvantaged, also have

TABLE 8.9. *OLS Estimations of Support for Minority Rights*

Contributing Factors	"Traditional" Minority Rights		Immigrant Incorporation		Rights of Same-Sex Couples	
	B	s.e.	B	s.e.	b	SE
Race*gender (ref. = Black men)						
Latino men	−.682***	0.14	.356***	0.05	.455***	.086
Asian American men	−1.716***	0.25	.263**	0.10	.880***	.159
American Indian men	−0.553	0.47	−0.057	0.18	.075	.284
Black women	0.018	0.12	0.074	0.05	.054	.077
Latina women	0.086	0.19	−0.056	0.07	.608***	.104
Asian American women	0.517	0.38	−0.095	0.15	.979***	.217
American Indian women	1.134	0.72	0.334	0.27	.956*	.375
Personal and Family Resources						
Income	−0.011	0.01	0.001	0.00	.037***	.007
Education	−0.014	0.06	0.033	0.03	.068†	.039
Married	−0.028	0.10	0.043	0.04	−.229***	.063
Age	.010*	0.00	0.000	0.00	−.001	.003
Immigration generation	−0.081	0.06	−0.021	0.02	.078*	.037
Political Orientations, Resources, and Concerns over Minority Impact and Rights						
Ideology (5 = very liberal)	.178***	0.04	.080***	0.02	.127***	.027
Partisanship (Republican)	−1.135***	0.16	−.280***	0.06	−.282**	.101
Prior involvement in civic organizations	.078***	0.02	.017*	0.01	−.003	.014
Perceive minority impact on governing	.552***	0.08	.065*	0.03	−.082	.050
Support for Minority Rights			.060***	0.01	.084***	.020
Level/Type of office (ref. = Municipal)						
State legislature	0.183	0.16	.197**	0.06	.200*	.098
County	0.15	0.13	0.004	0.05	−.248**	.079
Local school board	−.178†	0.11	0.036	0.04	−.103	.065
Constant	6.889***	0.44	1.374***	0.19	.739*	
Adj. R^2	.318		.167		.197	
F-score	26.043		10.517		11.810	
	N = 951		N = 951		N = 950	

Notes: b = unstandarized slope coefficient, s.e. = standard errors. For question wording, see note in Tables 8.2, 8.4, and 8.5; for dependent variables, Minority Rights is a three-item summed index of questions asking respondents to indicate the degree of importance for them to support affirmative action for women, and affirmative action and voting rights for persons from one's own racial and ethnic background (adjusted alpha = .81); for Immigrant Incorporation it is a four-item index of survey items asking respondents their attitude toward policy proposals that would have government agencies provide bilingual services; permit driver's licenses regardless of one's legal status; allow parents who are not citizens to vote in school board elections; and mandate bilingual education in public schools (adjusted alpha = .67); and for Rights for Same Sex Couples it is a single item asking the extent respondents support civil unions for gays and lesbians giving them some marriage rights.

†$p < .10$, *$p \leq .05$ **$p \leq .005$ ***$p \leq .001$.

Source: GMCL National Survey, 2006–2007.

statistically significant impacts on the degree of support for minority rights among minority elected officials in the survey.

Immigrant Incorporation

The second set of findings in Table 8.9 reports factors associated with respondents' support for immigrant incorporation, which is an index based on respondents' positions on policies that would permit driver's licenses regardless of one's legal status; allow parents who are not citizens to vote in school board elections; and ensure that government agencies would provide services in a variety of languages to help non-English-speaking clients and mandate bilingual education.

While there are no gender differences between Black men and women, a racial gap exists between Asian men and Black men. Thus, all else being equal, both Latino and Asian men are more supportive of policy proposals favoring immigrant incorporation.

Here again, we observe that one's political ideology, political partisanship, the degree of prior civic ties, and perception of the minority impact on passing policies to benefit minorities by race, gender, and class, all have statistically significant impacts on the degree of support for immigrant incorporation. In addition, other conditions being equal, being more supportive of traditional minority rights may significantly increase the degree of support for immigrants' rights as well.

Rights of Same-Sex Couples

At the time we developed the GMCL National Survey, a national right to same-sex marriage was a distant and unlikely prospect. At the beginning of 2004, for example, there were no states where same-sex marriages were performed; just two states and the District of Columbia permitted civil unions or domestic partnerships. Massachusetts became the first to allow gay marriage on May 17, 2004, but, by the time our survey data collection was complete (February 2007), it still stood alone – and twenty-six states had passed *constitutional bans against same-sex marriage.*[20]

The final model in Table 8.9 shows that, all else being equal, Black women holding public office are more like Black men in support for gay rights, with no significant difference between them. As in the bivariate results (Table 8.5), Latinos and Asian Americans of both genders

---

[20] For the interactive timeline (and source for these numbers), see *Boston Globe* (2016).

continue to show greater support than the other groups. Higher family income adds to the model substantially, but those who are married offer less support. Consistent with findings in the previous regression models, we find political ideology, partisanship, and attitudes toward minority rights to matter significantly in predicting support for this contested new right. However, unlike previous findings, prior engagement with civic organizations does not matter and, curiously, respondents who perceive fewer benefits from having more women and minorities in office in passing policies to benefit the socially and economically disadvantaged may be the ones who are likely to lend support for these new rights.

We should note that we included level of office as a control variable, and find that, compared to elected officials in other offices, state legislators are significantly more likely to promote "contested new rights," including policies favoring immigrant incorporation, and permitting civil union rights for gays and lesbians. County elected officials seem to be most concerned about the implications of providing childcare and other welfare services to needy women and parents. They are joined by locally elected school board members in expressing reservation regarding contested new rights. We find also that school board members may show less support for traditional minority rights and report a higher likelihood of receiving support from potential policy allies on their respective school boards.

Women's Welfare and Reproductive Rights

Recall that, in Table 8.3, we saw elected officials of color were very supportive of women's welfare and reproductive rights – and that the strength of the support seemed driven by Asian Americans, especially Asian American women. To determine how that support holds up after controlling for other factors, we constructed an index on Support for Women's Welfare that consists of respondents' attitudes toward proposals for the government to subsidize or provide childcare for poor working women and whether college education should count toward any work requirements for women receiving welfare. Women's Reproductive Rights uses a two-item summed index of respondents' views on abortion (never, in cases of rape or incest, or always; see question wording in Table 8.3) and opposition to repealing *Roe v. Wade*.

Table 8.10 shows that, controlling for other factors, there is a significant contribution to the model for Women's Welfare by elected officials

TABLE 8.10. *OLS Estimations of Women's Welfare and Reproductive Rights*

Contributing Factors	Women's Welfare		Reproductive Rights	
	b	SE	b	SE
Race*Gender (Ref. = Black men)				
Latino men	0.07	0.05	−0.09	0.12
Asian American men	.172*	0.08	0.31	0.22
American Indian men	0.18	0.15	0.03	0.42
Black women	.065†	0.04	0.09	0.11
Latina women	−0.02	0.06	0.08	0.14
Asian American women	−0.10	0.13	0.497†	0.29
American Indian women	0.08	0.23	−0.06	0.48
Personal and Family Resources				
Income	.006†	0.00	0.043***	0.01
Education	0.00	0.02	0.11	0.05
Married	−0.02	0.03	−0.337***	0.09
Age	−.003*	0.00	0.00	0.00
Immigration generation	0.02	0.02	−0.090†	0.05
Political Orientations, Ties, and Concerns over Minority Impact and Rights				
Ideology (5 = very liberal)	.087***	0.01	0.239***	0.04
Partisanship (Republican)	−.113*	0.05	−0.733***	0.14
Prior involvement in civic organizations	.019**	0.01	−0.02	0.02
Perceive minority impact on governing	0.00	0.03	−0.09	0.07
Support for Minority Rights	.067***	0.01	0.093***	0.03
Level/Type of office (Ref. = Municipal)				
State legislature	0.06	0.05	0.239†	0.14
County	−.090*	0.04	−0.06	0.11
Local school board	2.09	0.16	−0.240*	0.09
Constant	2.09***	0.16	3.42***	0.42
Adj. R^2	0.16		0.19	
F-score	9.99		11.96	
	N = 958		N = 944	

Notes: b = unstandarized slope coefficient, s.e. = standard errors. For question wording, see note in Table 8.3; for dependent variables, Women's Welfare is a three-item summed index that consists of items from the survey asking respondents their attitudes toward proposals for the government to subsidize or provide childcare for poor working women and whether college education should count toward any work requirements for women receiving welfare (adjusted alpha = .62); for Women's Reproductive Rights it is a two-item summed index of questions asking respondents to indicate their views on abortion (never, in cases of rape or incest, always- it's a woman's decision) and opposition to repealing *Roe v. Wade* (adjusted alpha = .57).
†$p < .10$, *$p \le .05$ **$p \le .005$ ***$p \le .001$.
Source: GMCL National Survey, 2006–2007.

who are Asian American men and Black women, those with more income, and those who are younger.

The race*gender effect also exists for Women's Reproductive Rights, with Asian American women the most supportive, as expected from Table 8.2, but only modestly, suggesting that, controlling for other factors, there are similar levels of support among all groups. In fact, as we saw in the other multivariate analyses, sociodemographic characteristics (i.e., personal and family resources), income, marital status have a much bigger effect than race and gender – matched only by, again, a liberal ideology, a Democrat party affiliation, and an overall support for minority rights.

IMPACT OF SHARED POLICY POSITIONS ON
POTENTIAL FOR COALITIONS

Analysis of data from the GMCL National Survey offers a unique opportunity to examine the potential for political coalitions among elected officials of color with full attention to the diverse and complex nature of the groups. Multivariate analysis including the intersection of race/ethnicity and gender together with class and other sociodemographic factors reflecting personal and family resources, plus political dimensions demonstrate the parameters (and policy positions) within which coalitions are possible. From these findings, we stress the importance of political factors such as partisanship and ideology in building governing coalitions.

For the most part, the analysis shows that women of color and Black men tended to be more similar, with Latino and/or Asian men less likely than the other race*gender groups to support most of the measures. In two models, Women's Welfare and Rights of Same-Sex Couples, Black women elected officials stood out as showing greatest support, which is not unexpected given the socioeconomic status of Black women and the relatively high educational levels the Black female elected office holders have achieved.

In the instance where the dependent variable was whether the elected officials shared a sense of "linked fate" – surely a key element in coalition building across race and gender – the political factors reduced the race*gender variables to insignificance. The only significant sociodemographic variable was age, but four out of the five political variables were significant. Black men and women of color share similar supportive stances in support of Minority Civil Rights and Immigrant Incorporation (Table 8.9), even while political factors were strongly significant. In these two cases, however, again we saw a weak showing for the predictive impact of sociodemographic factors. With the exception of Asian male elected officials, a similar pattern held for the support of expanded welfare and work policies for women (Table 8.10) and support from political allies (Figure 8.1). Race/ethnicity and gender variables maintained significance (with Black men and women of color sharing similar supportive stances) in support of Minority Civil Rights and Immigrant Incorporation even while political factors were strongly significant. In these two cases, however, again we saw a weak showing for the predictive impact of factors reflecting personal and family resources.

What can we conclude, therefore, about the intersection of race/ethnicity, gender, class (and other sociodemographic factors), when seeking to explain shared political perspectives and policy positions among elected officials of color? First, that Latino and Asian men are, generally, less supportive of many of the perspectives and positions examined here than women of color and Black men (and, for the most part American Indian men). While Black men and women of color are generally more supportive, the striking pattern shown here is the lack of cohesion among the men of color, especially when compared with the cohesion among women of color. Thus, we can assert that, across the different measures, women of color do present a relatively consistent opportunity for political coalitions among elected officials of color. Second, that, for the most part, sociodemographic variables (even income and education) did not add as much to the explanatory value of the model as we hypothesized.

Third, shared political ideology, partisanship, and other political factors seemed to contribute the most to the models, all else being equal. Clearly, shared partisanship (being Democrats) and ideology (being more liberal) matter most in building coalitions across race and gender. Finally, and most provocatively for the larger field of intersectionality research and the prospects for coalitions across race/ethnicity and gender, women of color of any race/ethnicity and Black male elected officials share perspectives and positions that may offer the best hope for multiracial coalitions among the political elite.

Having reached these conclusions about intersectional prospects, it's also important to acknowledge that the patterns that shaped this first significant generation of African American elected officials are likely to change in the coming years. Ironically, the very existence of access to the American polity may lead to different patterns of participation, socialization, and complexity within the Black population. President Barack Obama claims all dimensions of his identity while successfully mobilizing beyond the Black American population. Increased immigration from Africa, South America, and the Caribbean may also lead to a more heterogeneous Black population than was present before the end of de jure and de facto discrimination. For the moment, however the composition of elected officials by race and ethnicity may only change marginally, while the gender profile seems to be changing more rapidly (Bratton, Haynie, and Reingold 2006).

CONCLUSION: PROSPECTS FOR ADVANCING AMERICAN DEMOCRACY

The title of this book, *Contested Transformation*, reflects the contingent and contentious nature of politics at the heart of race and gender in the United States of America today: whatever progress has been achieved has taken place within the context of a contested political terrain. Any transformation that has occurred has come with a fight, is vulnerable to setbacks, and has been resisted at every point in time and in numerous ways. In Part I of this book, we tackled the question: Given the dramatic growth in minority populations and elected officials in the post-1965 era, has there been change in the American political landscape? At the most basic level the answer is, "*Yes*," owing to the growth in numbers of elected officials of color from the very highest levels of office (the presidency and the US Congress) to those serving in state legislatures and in local-level offices. As we describe in detail in Chapter 1, the recent growth in descriptive representation has been impressive, and that growth has been driven by women of color.

The answer is also "*Yes*," when we consider the demographic changes in Latino, Asian American, and Black women and men in electoral politics, including in presidential elections, as well as in public policy. In answering the question of when and why minority legislators (to the US Congress and state legislatures) matter, Griffin (2014) finds that minority elected officials, especially African Americans and Latinos, are much more likely to support and initiate policies favored by minorities in their jurisdictions. He also finds their elections stimulate the participation of minority constituents; the presence of minorities in legislative bodies has also altered the major party coalitions and encouraged the adoption of minority-friendly policies. Our book does not assess constituents' opinions, only those perceived by their representatives. We also do not study their voting patterns. However, our elected officials are quite adamant about their positive impacts on advancing minority rights and addressing their issue concerns.

The answer is, at the same time, a resounding, "*No*." Even with the growth in descriptive representation among elected officials of color, their levels of representation continue to lag behind their shares in the population. Why after fifty years of considerably reformed immigration and civil rights policies do we find this paradox of growth accompanied by continuing underrepresentation? We contend that it is due to the fact that despite the important moves toward political equality, efforts to make gains have been contested every step of the way. As we have demonstrated in this volume, the answers are complex, multifaceted, and challenging.

One of the "takeaways" of this chapter and book must be that, despite the many differences between Black, Latino/a, Asian American, and American Indian elected women and men office holders in their backgrounds, reasons for running, political experiences, and in this chapter their policy positions, their *commonalities outweigh their differences.* Furthermore, given how much in common they have, we see the prospects for coalitions across race and gender – at least on voting rights, immigrant incorporation, and women's welfare and reproductive rights, as well as on same-sex marriage.[21] (See Figure 8.2.)

Let us return to some of the images from the Introduction: the horrors of the murder of churchgoers in South Carolina; police violence against young minority men and women; anti-immigrant rhetoric and policies; continued race-based inequities in income and access to quality education; and the chipping away of women's reproductive rights by emphasizing the protection of religious freedom. And yet, we saw elected officials of color, most remarkably Republican South Asian Governor Nikki Haley, at the forefront of successful efforts to remove symbols of the Confederacy. Protests – including rallies by the Ku Klux Klan (Borden 2015) – did continue in the weeks following the removal of the Confederate flag in South Carolina. Even after the Supreme Court ruling giving same-sex couples the right to marry, Kentucky county clerk Kim Davis, for example, went to jail rather than allow marriage licenses to be issued to same-sex couples. Protests may likely continue on these issues – along with the violence against minorities that we discussed in the opening to this book.

---

[21] And, we might add that support for these positions – and the potential, therefore, for coalitions – may be greatest among those who are young, unmarried, liberal Democrats.

FIGURE 8.2 Cartoon by Andy Marlette. (From *This Week in American Flags*, June 26, 2015; used with permission.)

The competing narratives we described in Chapter 1 – the growth in population and descriptive representation of people of color existing simultaneously with continued underrepresentation within a contested political landscape – means that positive change is often followed by retrenchment, for their communities and elected representatives. An important recent example is the Supreme Court's 2013 *Shelby County, Alabama v. Holder* decision, which struck down Section 4 of the 1965 Voting Rights Act. In most of the chapters in this volume, we have provided a detailed and intersectional analysis focusing on who the elected officials of color are; where they serve; the differences and similarities in their backgrounds; their complex political trajectories; the multiplicity of their motivations to hold office; and their perceptions of leadership and representation. The struggles of the communities they represent will continue – as will successes and setbacks for their elected officials and the interests they are trying to advance. But through the messiness of government and politics, the presence and contributions of women and men of color will, however slowly, make their mark, ultimately leading to the strengthening of American democratic processes and institutions.

Appendix A

Data and Methodology

The research for this book draws heavily from two primary sources constructed for the Gender and Multicultural Leadership (GMCL) Project: the GMCL National Database of minority elected officials and the GMCL National (Telephone) Survey of a national sample of those elected officials serving in state legislative or local office during 2006–2007. Certain data were added and/or updated in 2012–2014. In this appendix, we provide a detailed description of the GMCL National Database and the National Survey as well as the added/updated data. Following that, we include a note on our decisions regarding race/ethnicity and a discussion of data limitations.

GMCL NATIONAL DATABASE

The GMCL National Database includes the universe of Black, Latino, and Asian American elected officials serving in federal, state, and local offices who were in office in 2006–2007. The 10,160 individuals in the Database consist of elected officials in congressional, statewide, state legislative, county, municipal, and school board offices. Congressional elected officials include only voting members (except for the delegate for the District of Columbia). Statewide elected officials are limited to governors and lieutenant governors, state treasurers, secretaries of state, attorneys general, auditors, and controllers. County office refers to members of county legislative bodies, such as county councilors, commissioners, and supervisors. Municipal officials include mayors and members of city/town/village governing bodies, such as city/town councils and boards of aldermen/selectmen. Our database does not include judicial or law enforcement positions, party officials, or miscellaneous officials elected to boards and commissions such as water, utility, railroad, and so on. Neither does it include those elected from Puerto Rico or territories such as Guam or American Samoa. The database also includes American Indians, but, for reasons discussed later, only those serving in state legislators and Congress.

Construction of the Initial Database

The first step was to consult the most current directories provided by the Joint Center for Political and Economic Studies, National Association of Latino Elected and Appointed Officials (NALEO), and the UCLA Asian American Studies Center. We used data from the National Conference of State Legislatures and other sources to identify American Indian state legislators and one congressperson.[1]

Verification of Data Accuracy and Consistency

The second step was to verify the directory information for accuracy and recode the information to make it consistent across groups. The verification process determined that the extent to which the database captures the officials in office at that time was more accurate for different racial groups than others and for different levels of office.[2]

Updating and Adding New Data

To address concerns that some data may be out of date, we updated aspects of the database in 2012–2014. We updated the National Database to include members of the 113th Congress and gathered data on their occupations, prior offices held, religion, marital status, and so forth. We also updated the database for the state legislators of color in 2012–2013 and gathered data on whether the state legislators who were surveyed in 2006–2007 had subsequently run for higher offices. We gathered comparable information on a sample of local officials in 2014. And, finally, we gathered information on leadership positions and committee assignments for members of color in the 113th Congress. Analyses that draw on these updated data are clearly

---

[1] To build the initial database, we referred to McClain and Stewart (2002); their total of forty-three at that time included forty-two state legislative officeholders and one member of the US Congress who were American Indian.
[2] We determined that the accuracy rate was higher for Latino and Asian Americans than for African Americans.

labeled in the tables using the convention GMCL Project [YEAR], which distinguishes them from data derived from the GMCL National Survey, 2006–2007, or the GMCL National Database, 2006–2007.

A Note on the Enumeration of Elected Officials Studied

The total number of elected officials of color in the United States is greater than the approximately 10,160 elected officials in our database. For example, at the time the database was constructed, there were more than 9,000 Black and 5,000 Hispanic/Latino elected officials, according to the most rosters of the Joint Center for Political and Economic Studies (JCPES) and NALEO. The difference is due to the fact that the GMCL database does not include judicial or law enforcement positions; party officials; county and municipal officials who serve on a variety of boards and commissions such as water, utility, and so on; nonvoting members of Congress; and, finally, elected officials from Puerto Rico or territories such as Guam and American Samoa.[3]

Expanding the Database: Linking Contextual Jurisdictional Data

Once the database of elected officials was constructed, we expanded the data by linking contextual data from the US Census by district, county, or Census place to each elected official. Congressional district information on the racial makeup of each district comes from the Census 2000 "Profiles of General Demographic Characteristics: U.S., Regions, Divisions, Metropolitan Areas, American Indian Areas/ Alaska Native Areas/ Hawaiian Home Lands, States, Congressional Districts."[4]

We included the racial breakdown for each state legislative district using demographic information for all ages (not just voting age and older) from the Census 2000 Redistricting Dataset.[5] As Lien et al. (2007)

---

[3] Including the nonvoting member from the District of Columbia, but not other nonvoting delegates.

[4] We use the "race alone and in combination" and "Hispanic or Latinos and Race" categories to compile the racial makeup of each district from the Census 2000 Profiles of General Demographic Characteristics. (For more details on these data, see "2000 Census of Population and Housing. Technical Documentation. Issued May 2001," https://www.census.gov/prod/cen2000/doc/ProfilesTD.pdf, accessed July 7, 2006)..

[5] Source: U.S. Census 2000 Redistricting Data (P.L. 94–171) Summary File, PL1 and PL2. American Fact Finder.

note, it is the total population, not just the voting age population, that determines reapportionment.

To link county-level demographic data to each official, we first determined the county in which his/her primary address was located (generally his or her office). From 2000 Census population data we were able to construct the percent African American, Latino/Hispanic, Asian/Pacific Islander, and American Indian/Native Alaskan, as well as percent non-Hispanic White. We also included the median household and per capita income; and percent of the population below the poverty level, foreign born, and those speaking a language other than English.[6]

We were also interested in gathering contextual information at the municipal level to determine who lives in the places these elected officials represent, that is, their constituents. Gathering and analyzing jurisdictional data at the municipal level represented a challenge because it was not possible to determine with reliable consistency whether the municipal officials were elected at-large or by district, and, even when known, district-level demographic data are not routinely available for those elected at the district level. Therefore, we used the demographic data by "Census Place"[7] as a proxy for municipal jurisdictions for census places with populations of 5,000 or more. The data gathered included percent Hispanic/Latino; percent Non-Hispanic White, Black, Asian/Pacific Islander, and American Indian/Alaskan Native; percent non-White; median household income; and percent of the population below the poverty level, speaking a language other than English, foreign born, high school graduates, and college graduates.

The primary data source for the jurisdictions of school board members was the US Department of Education's National Center for Education Statistics (NCES); we downloaded school district data for all fifty states from the State Education Data Profiles.[8] These data include racial makeup

---

[6] County data are from US Census Bureau: Profile of General Demographic Characteristics: 2000 Census Summary File 1 (SF 1) 100-Percent Data, available by state and county from American FactFinder.

[7] In this article a "place" is "a concentration of population either legally bounded as an incorporated place, or identified as a Census Designated Place (CDP)... Incorporated places have legal descriptions of borough (except in Alaska and New York), city, town (except in New England, New York, and Wisconsin), or village" (Source: "Glossary," US Census Bureau, p. 294). www.census.gov/population/www/cen2000/censusatlas/pdf/16_Backmatter-Glossary.pdf [Accessed July 7, 2016]) Data are from US Census 2000, Summary File 1 (SF1) and Summary File 3 (SF3); we would like to thank Anthony Roman of the Center for Survey Research at the University of Massachusetts Boston for his assistance.

[8] Source: Census 2000 School District Tabulation (STP2) prepared by the US Census Bureau's Population Division and sponsored by the National Center for Education

of the school district; percent of students receiving high school diplomas; dropout rates by race and gender; per capita income; total population below the poverty level; and, in a smaller number of cases, the per student expenditure.

GMCL NATIONAL SURVEY

Besides being a valuable source of data for analysis, the GMCL National Database also served as the sampling frame for the GMCL National (Telephone) Survey, which was conducted with a nationwide sample of African American, Latino/a, and Asian American elected officials, women and men, at the state and local levels. American Indian and Alaska Native state legislators are also included in the survey. The GMCL National Survey is a systematic telephone survey of the nation's nonwhite elected officials holding state and local offices across the fifty states of America. The complete survey instrument, with response options, skip patterns, and so forth, is available for download from on the GMCL Project website (www.gmcl.org/pdf/GMCL_SurveyInstrument.pdf). A version modified for ease of reading is available in Appendix B of this volume.

The survey was conducted between June 2006 and March 2007 mostly by the Institute for Public Policy (IPP) at the University of New Mexico, whose interviewers telephoned a sample of randomly selected individuals from a population of non-White elected officials grouped by race, gender, and level of office. They interviewed officeholders across the United States to gather information on their experiences in seeking and gaining elected office, their policy positions on a number of policy issues, efforts to work together with the constituents they represent and their colleagues in office, and other topics reported in this volume.

The IPP interviewers, equipped with a computer-assisted telephone interviewing system and a nineteen-station survey laboratory, trained interviewers to conduct the survey under full-time supervision, using a protocol that included at least ten attempts per number, respondent appointment tracking and follow-up, and reluctant respondent persuasion where necessary. In the event the eligible respondent from the list-based component was not at a particular number, interviewers tried to acquire a valid number for the designated point of contact. The protocol utilized to track calls and respondents was designed to maximize both

Statistics, http://nces.ed.gov/programs/stateprofiles (Accessed first July 20, 2006; last accessed July 6, 2016).

the survey response rate and the consistency with which the survey was applied to ensure maximum data validity and reliability. On request, the IPP survey research staff faxed and/or emailed a general study description to potential participants in an attempt to validate the study and the IPP as the survey implementers for this project.

Multiple lists of elected officials in the population grouped by their office levels and complete with their first and last names, official titles, phone numbers, and their reported race and gender identification were prepared by the GMCL project team and handed to IPP for field work, which lasted from June 5 to November 9, 2006. A follow-up phase aiming to enhance the participation of American Indian and Asian American elected officials was conducted by the Center for Women in Politics and Public Policy (CWPPP) at the University of Massachusetts Boston and took place between December 15, 2006 and January 31, 2007. Overall, 1,378 interviews were completed between June 5, 2006 and March 21, 2007, with 1,359 valid. These included 727 Black/African American, 512 Latino/a, 96 Asian American, and 24 American Indian elected officials who were state legislators, county officials (at the level of county commissioner), municipal officials (city/town councilors, members of select boards/boards of aldermen, mayors), and school board members. The survey response rate as a percentage of the total successful contacts was 72 percent, the cooperation rate was 77 percent, and the refusal rate was 22 percent.

It is worth noting that, overall, the refusal rates for this study were quite low for most groups and the completion rates are very respectable considering the difficulty of identifying valid telephone numbers where elected officials in state, municipal, and county offices, as well as serving on school boards can be easily contacted. Also affecting the ability to complete interviews was the degree to which elected officials – or staff members – were willing to comply with requests via cold-call from an unknown entity to participate in research, especially during an active campaign season such as was true during the implementation phase of this endeavor. The average length of interviews is forty-four minutes. There are no statistically significant differences in the interview length by race, gender, level of office, or implementation stage.

Differential quota or unequal selection probability rates are assigned for each of the population groups to permit gathering enough cases for analysis by race, gender, and office. For example, the quota rate for Asian male municipal officials is .5, but that for their female counterparts it is

1.0; the quota rate for Black female state legislators is .5, but that for their male counterparts is .33; and the quota rate for Latino male county officials is .33, but that for their female counterparts is 1.0. The overall quota rate is .24.

A Note on Terminology of Race and Ethnicity

As discussed in the Introduction, African American is used interchangeably with Black, and Hispanic is used interchangeably with Latino. The Asian category includes native Hawaiians and other Pacific Islanders. We use the term American Indian rather than Native American. The American Indian category also includes Alaskan natives. For reference to all non-White groups in our study, we sometimes use the term "elected officials of color." We are aware of the scholarly argument that "White" is itself a "color" in a social and political sense. We respect the differences in scholarly opinion on this issue. For our purposes, references to people of color do not include non-Hispanic Whites.

Data Limitations

Although the survey is designed to be a probability study of the population, our ability to generalize the findings is limited by the scarcity of the population in some offices and for some racial and gender groups as well as the idiosyncratic nature of the elite population that facilitates the participation of those who have more time in hand (fewer responsibilities, less campaign need) and are more accessible for the survey interviewers (have valid contact information on record, have no or friendly gatekeepers). To the extent that the survey approximates a probability sample of the nation's nonwhite elected officials at subnational levels of office, we estimate the margin of error or the measure of the variation one would see in reported percentages if the same survey were taken multiple times for the total N at the 95% level of confidence to be ±3%. That is, the "true" percentage for the entire population would be within the margin of error around the survey's reported percentage 95% of the time. Note that the margin of error only takes into account random sampling error. It does not take into account other potential sources of error such as bias in the questions, bias due to excluding groups who could not be contacted, people refusing to respond or lying, or miscounts and miscalculations, as well as other limitations mentioned above.

Appendix B

GMCL National Telephone Survey Questionnaire

The following is a copy of the questionnaire used during telephone interviews with the sample of Black, Latino/a, Asian American, and American Indian elected officials who participated in the survey. For the sake of readability and length, it has been modified from the version designed for computer-assisted interviewing and coding. Many of the questions were closed-ended; for these we provide the choices offered to the respondent. Responses to open-ended questions were typed verbatim and coded later by our research team. For other questions that may appear open-ended, the interviewers coded according to a drop-down box of possible responses. Items in brackets were not read to the interviewee. Codes for non-responses included −99 DK/NA, −98 Refused, −97 Drop Out; for the sake of simplicity, these are not shown below. The full survey instrument, with all introductory text, response options, skip patterns, and so forth, may be found at www.gmcl.org/pdf/GMCL_SurveyInstrument.pdf.

* *

1. [Introduction] Are you ready to begin?
   1 Continue
2. As a part of the survey, I am required to ask: are you male or female?
   1 Male
   0 Female
3. Now I would like to ask you a few general questions about your elective office. Our records indicate you are a <<Title in Database>>. Is this correct?
   1 Yes
   0 No

[Asked if answered No] What level of elective office do you currently hold?
1 State Legislator
2 Municipal Official
3 County Official
4 School Board Member
0 Not in elected position
5 Other <<Verbatim>>[1]

4. What is the official title of your elective office? [Check List Open[2]:]
  1 Alderman/Alderwoman
  2 Assembly Member
  3 Board of Supervisors
  4 Board of Aldermen
  5 Board of Selectmen
  6 City Commissioner
  7 City Councilor
  8 County Board of Supervisors
  9 County Commission
  10 County Council
  11 County Freeholder
  12 County Judge
  13 County Legislator
  14 County Supervisor
  15 Delegate
  16 Deputy/Vice Mayor
  17 Freeholder
  18 Judge
  19 Mayor
  20 Mayor Pro-tem
  21 Representative
  22 School Board Member/Trustee
  23 School Committee Member
  24 Selectman/woman
  25 Speaker of the Assembly 26 Speaker, House of Representatives
  27 State Assembly Member 28 State Representative

[1] In cases such as "Other," interviewees were offered the opportunity to explain in their own words; their responses were typed verbatim and coded later by the GMCL Research Team.
[2] This indicates the items in the list were not read to the interviewee, but rather used by interviewer to check off frequently used responses.

29 State Senator
30 Town Councilor
31 Township Committeeman
32 Township Supervisor
33 Village Trustee
36 Other <<Verbatim>>

5. Is this your first elective position?
   1 Yes
   0 No

6. What year were you first elected to public office?
   <<Year: Integer>>

7. [Asked of those who answered "No" to question 5] What was your first elective office?
   [Check List Open: See Q4]

8. [Asked of those who answered "No" to question 5] What year were you first elected to your current office?
   <<Year: Integer>>

9. [Asked of those who answered "No" to question 5] How many elected offices did you hold prior to your current position?
   <<# Offices: Integer>>

10. [Asked of those who answered "No" to question 5] What was the most recent elective office prior to your current position?
    [Check List Open: See Q4]

11. [Asked of those who answered "No" to question 5 and said they held two or more elected offices in question 9] What was your most recent elective office before you were a [response given in Q10]?
    [Check List Open: See Q4]

12. [Asked of those who answered "No" to question 5 and said they held more than two elected offices in question 9] What was the most recent elective office before you were [response given in Q11]?
    [Check List Open: See Q4]

13. How many appointed positions did you hold prior to your current elected position?

o None
1 One
2 Two
3 Three or more

14. [Asked of those who answered "School Board Member" to question 3] We know there are many kinds of school systems; could you tell me which of the following best reflects your school board or committee system? Is it:
    1 City- or Town-wide
    2 County School District
    3 Independent School District
    4 Unified School District
    5 Consolidated School District
    6 Local School-based Board
    7 [Other:] <<Verbatim>>

15. [Asked of those who answered "Mayoral Position" to question 4] Which of the following best describes your election as mayor? Were you:
    1 Listed on the ballot as a candidate for mayor and popularly elected
    2 Popularly elected to the municipal governing body and selected by your colleagues to serve as mayor
    3 Popularly elected to the municipal governing body and, as the top vote getter, serve as mayor
    o None of the above

16. How did you become mayor?
    <<Verbatim>>

17. Is your current position full or part-time?
    2 Full-time
    1 Part-time

18. How long had you lived in the district or area you represent before you were elected to your present office?
    <<Year in district: Integer>>

19. Next we would like to ask you a few questions about your experiences before you were elected to your current office. On a scale from zero to ten, where zero means not at all involved and ten means extremely involved, how involved were you in activities

with each of the following groups before you first ran for elected office?

20. Political parties   <<0...10>>
21. Labor unions   <<0...10>>
22. Business groups   <<0...10>>
23. Parent teacher's organizations or associations   <<0...10>>
24. Election campaigns   <<0...10>>
25. Civil rights organizations   <<0...10>>
26. Faith-based organizations   <<0...10>>
27. Community or neighborhood organizations   <<0...10>>
28. Women's organizations   <<0...10>>

29. Did you ever serve on the staff of an elected public official prior to your first bid for office?
    1 Yes
    0 No

30. [Asked of those who answered "Yes" to question 29] Was this person a male or female? [If served more than once] We are interested in the time last time you served on the staff of an elected public official prior to your first bid for office.
    1 Male
    0 Female?

31. [Asked of those who answered "yes" to question 29] Was this person of your own racial or ethnic background? [If served more than once] We are interested in the time last time you served on the staff of an elected public official prior to your first bid for office.
    1 Yes
    0 No

32. [Asked of those who answered "Yes" to question 29] Did you work for someone at the congressional level, or was it a statewide, state legislature, county, city or town, or school board position? [If served more than once] We are interested in the time last time you served on the staff of an elected public official prior to your first bid for office.
    1 Congressional
    2 Statewide
    3 State Legislature
    4 County

5 City
6 Town
7 School Board

33. Elected officials have a variety of reasons for why they first decided to run for a political office. We are interested in the most important factor that influenced your decision to run for public office the very first time. Briefly,

    What was the most important reason influencing your decision to run for public office the very first time?   <<Verbatim>>
    What was the next most important reason?   <<Verbatim>>
    What was the next most important reason?   <<Verbatim>>

34. Using a scale from zero to ten, where zero means not at all likely and ten means extremely likely, how likely is it that you will run for a higher level of office when you leave your current position? [Check:] <<0...10>>

35. The next series of questions pertain to your current elective office. First, in your most recent election for your current office, did you run as an:
    1 Incumbent
    2 Challenger
    3 For an open seat

36. [Asked of those who answered "Challenger" or "For an open seat" to question 35] Was the race for your current office partisan or nonpartisan?
    1 Partisan
    2 Nonpartisan

37. [Asked of those who answered "Challenger" or "For an open seat" to question 35] Are you currently in a district, at-large, or multimember district seat?
    1 District
    2 At-large
    3 Multimember district

38. [Asked of those who answered "Challenger" or "For an open seat" to question 35] What is the name and/or number of your district?
    <<Name and Number: Verbatim>>

39. In your most recent election to your current office, did you provide written materials for voters in languages other than English?

o Does not apply; few voters/ residents don't speak English

1 No

2 Yes

[Asked of those who answered Yes]

What languages? <<Verbatim>>

40. To the best of your recollection, was the approximate margin of victory over your closest opponent in your most recent general election:

4 More than 10%

3 Between 5 and 10%

2 Less than 5%

1 Ran unopposed/No opponent

o Doesn't apply to state/No head-to-head races

41. Some people believe that minority candidates have to overcome special obstacles when they run for elected office. For the next several questions, please tell me whether you strongly disagree, disagree, agree, or strongly agree that you faced any of the following obstacles during your first bid for your current office.

1 Continue

42. How would you rate your level of agreement with the following statement? I received less support from political parties than other candidates.

1 Strongly Disagree

2 Disagree

3 Agree

4 Strongly Agree

43. [Asked of those who answered "Agree" or "Strongly Agree" to question 42] Do you think the biggest factor for this was because of your race or ethnicity; your gender; your race or ethnicity and gender; or some other factor?

1 Race/Ethnicity

2 Gender

3 Race/Ethnicity and Gender

4 Some Other Factor

44. How would you rate your level of agreement with the following statement? I received less support from other political organizations than other candidates.

1 Strongly Disagree

2 Disagree

3 Agree

4 Strongly Agree

45. [Asked of those who answered "Agree" or "Strongly Agree" to question 44] Do you think the biggest factor for this was because of your race or ethnicity; your gender; your race or ethnicity and gender; or some other factor?
   1 Race/Ethnicity
   2 Gender
   3 Race/Ethnicity and Gender
   4 Some Other Factor

46. How would you rate your level of agreement with the following statement? I faced more questions about my qualifications and/or electability than other candidates.
   1 Strongly Disagree
   2 Disagree
   3 Agree
   4 Strongly Agree

47. [Asked of those who answered "Agree" or "Strongly Agree" to question 46] Do you think the biggest factor for this was because of your race or ethnicity; your gender; your race or ethnicity and gender; or some other factor?
   1 Race/Ethnicity
   2 Gender
   3 Race/Ethnicity and Gender
   4 Some Other Factor

48. How would you rate your level of agreement with the following statement? I had a harder time raising money than other candidates.
   1 Strongly Disagree
   2 Disagree
   3 Agree
   4 Strongly Agree

49. [Asked of those who answered "Agree" or "Strongly Agree" to question 48] Do you think the biggest factor for this was because of your race or ethnicity; your gender; your race or ethnicity and gender; or some other factor?
   1 Race/Ethnicity

2 Gender

3 Race/Ethnicity and Gender

4 Some Other Factor

50. How would you rate your level of agreement with the following statement? I received less attention from the mainstream media than other candidates.

1 Strongly Disagree

2 Disagree

3 Agree

4 Strongly Agree

51. [Asked of those who answered "Agree" or "Strongly Agree" to question 50] Do you think the biggest factor for this was because of your race or ethnicity; your gender; your race or ethnicity and gender; or some other factor?

1 Race/Ethnicity

2 Gender

3 Race/Ethnicity and Gender

4 Some Other Factor

52. How would you rate your level of agreement with the following statement? More comments were made about my personal appearance than about my opponents.

1 Strongly Disagree

2 Disagree

3 Agree

4 Strongly Agree

53. [Asked of those who answered "Agree" or "Strongly Agree" to question 52] Do you think the biggest factor for this was because of your race or ethnicity; your gender; your race or ethnicity and gender; or some other factor?

1 Race/Ethnicity

2 Gender

3 Race/Ethnicity and Gender

4 Some Other Factor

54. How would you rate your level of agreement with the following statement? My family's background received greater scrutiny than that of other candidates.

1 Strongly Disagree

2 Disagree

3 Agree

4 Strongly Agree

55. [Asked of those who answered "Agree" or "Strongly Agree" to question 54] Do you think the biggest factor for this was because of your race or ethnicity; your gender; your race or ethnicity and gender; or some other factor?

1 Race/Ethnicity

2 Gender

3 Race/Ethnicity and Gender

4 Some Other Factor

56. Now we want to ask about factors that affect how you view politics in this country. Do you think what happens generally to other minority groups in this country affects what happens in your life and how you view politics?

1 Yes

0 No

57. [Asked of those who answered "Yes" to question 56] Is it a lot, some, or not very much?

3 A lot

2 Some

1 Not very much

58. Do you think what happens to people of your own racial or ethnic background in this country affects what happens in your life and how you view politics?

1 Yes

0 No

59. [Asked of those who answered "Yes" to question 58] Is it a lot, some, or not very much?

3 A lot

2 Some

1 Not very much

60. Do you think what happens to women in this country affects what happens in your life and how you view politics?

1 Yes

0 No

61. [Asked of those who answered "Yes" to question 60] Is it a lot, some, or not very much?
    3 A lot
    2 Some
    1 Not very much

62. [Randomized split sample: Do not read. Click option and move on.]
    0 Women
    1 Minority women

63. [Asked of a randomized split sample of respondents] Shifting the focus slightly, I would like to know whether you think it is easier or harder for women to get a job suitable to their education and training than it is for men.
    1 Easier
    2 About the same
    3 Harder

64. [Asked of a randomized split sample of respondents] Do you think it is easier or harder for women to get ahead in elective politics than it is for men?
    1 Easier
    2 About the same
    3 Harder

65. [Asked of a randomized split sample of respondents] Do you think it is easier or harder for women to be accepted as a member of a profession, such as law or medicine, than it is for men?
    1 Easier
    2 About the same
    3 Harder

66. [Asked of a randomized split sample of respondents] Do you think it is easier or harder for women to get appointed to public office than it is for men?
    1 Easier
    2 About the same
    3 Harder

67. [Asked of a randomized split sample of respondents] Do you think it is easier or harder for minority women to get a job suitable to their education and training than it is for minority men?

1 Easier
2 About the same
3 Harder

68. [Asked of a randomized split sample of respondents] Do you think it is easier or harder for minority women to get ahead in elective politics than it is for minority men?
   1 Easier
   2 About the same
   3 Harder

69. [Asked of a randomized split sample of respondents] Do you think it is easier or harder for minority women to be accepted as a member of a profession, such as law or medicine, than it is for minority men?
   1 Easier
   2 About the same
   3 Harder

70. [Asked of a randomized split sample of respondents] Do you think it is easier or harder for minority women to get appointed to public office than it is for minority men?
   1 Easier
   2 About the same
   3 Harder

71. [Asked of a randomized split sample of respondents] Shifting the focus slightly, I would like to know whether you think it is easier or harder for minority women to get a job suitable to their education and training than it is for minority men.
   1 Easier
   2 About the same
   3 Harder

72. [Asked of a randomized split sample of respondents] Do you think it is easier or harder for minority women to get ahead in elective politics than it is for minority men?
   1 Easier
   2 About the same
   3 Harder

73. [Asked of a randomized split sample of respondents] Do you think it is easier or harder for minority women to be accepted as

a member of a profession, such as law or medicine, than it is for minority men?

1 Easier
2 About the same
3 Harder

74. [Asked of a randomized split sample of respondents] Do you think it is easier or harder for minority women to get appointed to public office than it is for minority men?

1 Easier
2 About the same
3 Harder

75. [Asked of a randomized split sample of respondents] Do you think it is easier or harder for women to get a job suitable to their education and training than it is for men?

1 Easier
2 About the same
3 Harder

76. [Asked of a randomized split sample of respondents] Do you think it is easier or harder for women to get ahead in elective politics than it is for men?

1 Easier
2 About the same
3 Harder

77. [Asked of a randomized split sample of respondents] Do you think it is easier or harder for women to be accepted as a member of a profession, such as law or medicine, than it is for men?

1 Easier
2 About the same
3 Harder

78. [Asked of a randomized split sample of respondents] Do you think it is easier or harder for women to get appointed to public office than it is for men?

1 Easier
2 About the same
3 Harder

79. Now I would like to ask about your views on politics. Generally speaking, do you usually think of yourself as Republican, Democrat, Independent, or of another political affiliation?
    o None – don't think in these terms
    1 Republican
    2 Democrat
    3 Independent
    4 Other <<Verbatim>>

80. [Asked of those who answered "Republican" or "Democrat" to question 79] Would you call yourself a strong [Republican or Democrat]?
    1 Yes
    o No

81. [Asked of those who answered "independent" to question 79] Do you think of yourself as closer to the Republican or Democratic Party?
    o Neither – don't think in these terms
    1 Republican
    2 Democrat

82. How would you describe your views on most matters having to do with politics? Do you generally think of yourself as very liberal, somewhat liberal, middle-of-the road, somewhat conservative, or very conservative?
    1 Very liberal
    2 Somewhat liberal
    3 Middle of the road
    4 Somewhat conservative
    5 Very conservative

83. Now we'd like to ask you a few questions about your constituents – the people who live in the jurisdiction or district that you represent.
    Would you say that more voters in your jurisdiction identify with the Republican Party, the Democratic Party, or are the voters divided about equally between the two parties?
    o Identify with no party
    1 Republican Party
    2 Divided about equally
    3 Democrat Party
    4 Mostly Independent/third-party voters

84. On most political issues, would you characterize the majority of voters in your jurisdiction as:

    1 Very liberal
    2 Somewhat liberal
    3 Middle of the road
    4 Somewhat conservative
    5 Very conservative

85. Would you say that your constituency is mostly:

    1 Poor
    2 Working class
    3 Middle class
    4 Upper middle class
    5 Upper class
    0 Mixed, with no dominant class

86. Would you say that the racial or ethnic makeup of your jurisdiction is mostly:

    1 White, Non-Hispanic
    2 Black
    3 Hispanic or Latino
    4 Asian
    5 American Indian
    6 Other <<Verbatim>> 0 Mixed w/no dominant race

87. To the best of your knowledge, about what percentage of the people who live in your jurisdiction are immigrants?
    <<% Immigrant: Integer>>

88. To better understand the extent of constituent interactions with elected officials, how many constituents contact your office in an average week?
    <<# Contacts: Integer>>

89. To the best of your knowledge, from which racial or ethnic group are the majority of the constituents who contact your office in an average week? [Check list open. Do not read.]

    1 White, Non-Hispanic
    2 Black
    3 Hispanic or Latino
    4 Asian
    5 American Indian
    6 Other <<Verbatim>> 0 Mixed w/no no dominant race

90. Researchers have found that there are many reasons constituents contact their elected officials. I am going to read you a list of some possible reasons. Please tell me which of these would you say is the primary reason why most of your constituents contact you? Is it to:
    1 Influence government policy
    2 Voice a community concern
    3 Get help with a family or personal problem
    4 Get help finding a job
    5 Other <<Verbatim>>

91–92. Next, I'm going to read you a pair of statements. Please tell me which one comes closest to your own view even if neither one is exactly right.
    [Randomized; Check List:]

    1 A
    2 B
    A. In a situation when the views of my constituents conflict with my own, it is more important that my vote reflects the views of my constituents.
    OR
    B. In a situation when the views of my constituents conflict with my own, it is more important that my vote reflects my informed judgment and trust that my constituents will support me.

93. Which of the following statements best describes your voting record in the governing body in which you serve, meaning the decision-making body or governing unit that you are part of or interact with due to your elective position? Are you part of a voting majority on important public policy issues, part of a voting minority, or do you vote with the majority and the minority equally?
    3 Part of a voting majority
    2 Vote with the majority and minority about equally
    1 Part of a voting minority

94. Now I am going to read you a list of types of elected officials. Using a scale from zero to ten, where zero is not at all likely to support your policy initiatives and ten is extremely likely, how likely are each of the following groups to support your policy initiatives? [PROMPT] The scale is from zero to ten, where zero not at all likely to support your policy initiatives and ten is extremely likely to support your policy initiatives?

95. Elected officials from your own party. [Check list:] <<o...10>>
96. Elected officials from your own racial or ethnic background. [Check list:] <<o...10>>
97. Minority elected officials from racial or ethnic backgrounds other than your own. [Check list:] <<o...10>>
98. Female elected officials from nonminority backgrounds. [Check list:] <<o...10>>
99. Elected officials who share your ideology. [Check list:] <<o...10>>
100. Elected officials who are minority women. [Check list:] <<o...10>>
101. Please tell me whether you strongly disagree, disagree, agree, or strongly agree with each of the following statements about possible differences between women and men who serve in elective office.

    [For explanation of skips in randomized set of questions 102–111, see pp. 33–35 of full survey instrument, available at http://gmcl.org/pdf/GMCL_SurveyInstrument.pdf.]

102/107. [Randomized: Female/Male] elected officials are more persuasive than their [male/female] counterparts.
   1 Strongly Disagree
   2 Disagree
   3 Agree
   4 Strongly Agree

103/108. [Randomized: Female/Male] elected officials are better at achieving consensus than their [male/female] counterparts.
   1 Strongly Disagree
   2 Disagree
   3 Agree
   4 Strongly Agree

104/109. [Randomized: Female/Male] elected officials work harder than their [male/female] counterparts.
   1 Strongly Disagree
   2 Disagree
   3 Agree
   4 Strongly Agree

105/110. [Randomized: Female/Male] elected officials are less interested in being in the limelight than in getting the job done compared to their [male/female] counterparts.

1 Strongly Disagree
2 Disagree
3 Agree
4 Strongly Agree

106/111. [Randomized: Female/Male] elected officials are more likely to conduct policymaking behind closed doors compared to their [male/female] counterparts.
1 Strongly Disagree
2 Disagree
3 Agree
4 Strongly Agree

112. [Asked of those who answered "State Legislator" to question 3] Is there a formal women's caucus in your legislative chamber?
1 Yes
0 No

113. [Asked of those who answered "State Legislator" to question 3 and "yes" to question 112] Are men also members of the women's caucus?
1 Yes
0 No

114. [Asked of women who answered "State Legislator" to question 3 and "yes to question 112] Are you a member of the women's caucus?
1 Yes
0 No

115. [Asked of those who answered "State Legislator" to question 3] Is there a formal minority caucus in your legislature?
1 Yes
0 No

116. [Asked of those who answered "State Legislator" to question 3 and "yes" to question 115] Which racial or ethnic group sponsors a minority caucus?
1 Black
2 Hispanic/Latino
3 Asian
4 Native American/American Indian
5 Multiracial
6 Other <<Verbatim >>

117. [Asked of those who answered "State Legislator" to question 3 and 115] Are you a member?
     1 Yes
     0 No

118. [Asked of those who answered "State Legislator" to question 3] Are you a member of a minority Caucus?
     1 Yes
     0 No
     [if YES]: Which one? <<Verbatim>>

119. [Asked of those who answered "State Legislator" to question 3] Is there a formal caucus for minority women in your legislature?
     1 Yes
     0 No

120. [Asked of those who answered "State Legislator" to question 3 and "yes" to question 119] Are you a member?
     1 Yes
     0 No

121. In recent years, the number of women serving in public office has increased across the country. We are interested in whether you think the presence of women has affected the way your particular governing body works. Would you say that women have made a lot of difference, some difference, very little difference, or no difference at all in terms of helping pass policy initiatives to benefit racial or ethnic minorities?
     3 A lot of difference
     2 Some difference
     1 Very little difference
     0 No difference at all

122. In recent years, the number of minorities serving in public office has increased across the country. We are interested in whether you think the presence of minorities has affected the way your particular governing body works. Would you say that minority elected officials have made a lot of difference, some difference, very little difference, or no difference at all in terms of helping pass policy initiatives to benefit women?
     3 A lot of difference
     2 Some difference

1 Very little difference

0 No difference at all

123. Would you say that minority elected officials have made a lot of difference, some difference, very little difference, or no difference at all in terms of helping pass policy initiatives to benefit minority women?

3 A lot of difference

2 Some difference

1 Very little difference

0 No difference at all

124. Would you say that minority elected officials have made a lot of difference, some difference, very little difference, or no difference at all in terms of helping pass policy initiatives to benefit the economically disadvantaged?

3 A lot of difference

2 Some difference

1 Very little difference

0 No difference at all

125. Would you say that minority elected officials have made a lot of difference, some difference, very little difference, or no difference at all in terms of helping pass policy initiatives to benefit racial or ethnic groups?

3 A lot of difference

2 Some difference

1 Very little difference

0 No difference at all

126. Briefly, what do you think is the most important policy issue facing your constituents?

<<Most Important: Verbatim>>

What is the next most important policy issue? <<Next Most Important: Verbatim>>

What is the next most important policy issue? <<Next Important: Verbatim>>

127. Now we're going to ask your opinion on a range of policy proposals currently being debated. Please tell me whether you strongly disagree, disagree, agree, or strongly agree with each of the following policy proposals.

128. The death penalty should be an option as a punishment for those who commit murder.
   1 Strongly Disagree
   2 Disagree
   3 Agree
   4 Strongly Agree

129. The United States Supreme Court should overturn the Roe versus Wade decision, which made abortion legal during the first three months of pregnancy.
   1 Strongly Disagree
   2 Disagree
   3 Agree
   4 Strongly Agree

130. Government should provide childcare services to all parents who desire them with fees charged according to ability to pay.
   1 Strongly Disagree
   2 Disagree
   3 Agree
   4 Strongly Agree

131. Gay and lesbian couples should be allowed to legally form civil unions, giving them some of the legal rights of married couples.
   1 Strongly Disagree
   2 Disagree
   3 Agree
   4 Strongly Agree

132. States no longer need laws prohibiting sexual harassment against women.
   1 Strongly Disagree
   2 Disagree
   3 Agree
   4 Strongly Agree

133. States no longer need laws prohibiting job discrimination against United States Women.
   1 Strongly Disagree
   2 Disagree
   3 Agree
   4 Strongly Agree

134. The US made the right decision in using military force against Iraq.
    1 Strongly Disagree
    2 Disagree
    3 Agree
    4 Strongly Agree

135. The US should bring its troops home from Iraq as soon as possible.
    1 Strongly Disagree
    2 Disagree
    3 Agree
    4 Strongly Agree

136. As a matter of public safety, drivers' licenses should be made available to immigrants, regardless of their legal status in the US.
    1 Strongly Disagree
    2 Disagree
    3 Agree
    4 Strongly Agree

137. Government agencies should provide services in a variety of languages to help non-English speaking clients.
    1 Strongly Disagree
    2 Disagree
    3 Agree
    4 Strongly Agree

138. Noncitizen legal immigrants should be allowed to vote in school board elections if they have children in the public schools.
    1 Strongly Disagree
    2 Disagree
    3 Agree
    4 Strongly Agree

139. Subsidized childcare should be increased for poor working mothers in welfare-to-work programs.
    1 Strongly Disagree
    2 Disagree
    3 Agree
    4 Strongly Agree

140. College education should be allowed to count toward the "work requirement" for women receiving welfare.

1 Strongly Disagree
2 Disagree
3 Agree
4 Strongly Agree

141. Which of the following statements best agrees with your view on abortion:

   A By law, abortion should never be permitted;
   B The law should permit abortion only in cases of rape, incest, or when the life of the woman is in danger; or
   C By law, a woman should always be able to obtain an abortion as a private decision to be made with her physician.

   [Check list:]
   1 A
   2 B
   3 C
   0 None of the above

142. The following questions are specifically about policies concerning education. For each one, please tell me whether you would strongly favor, favor, oppose, or strongly oppose each policy.

143. A constitutional amendment to permit prayer in public schools.
   1 Strongly Favor
   2 Favor
   3 Oppose
   4 Strongly Oppose

144. A law banning preferential school admission on the basis of race or ethnicity.
   1 Strongly Favor
   2 Favor
   3 Oppose
   4 Strongly Oppose

145. A law giving parents government-funded school vouchers to pay for tuition at the public, private, or religious school of their choice.
   1 Strongly Favor
   2 Favor
   3 Oppose
   4 Strongly Oppose

146. A law mandating public schools to provide instruction in other languages for students not proficient in English.
   1 Strongly Favor
   2 Favor
   3 Oppose
   4 Strongly Oppose

147. The No Child Left Behind Act mandating public schools to meet certain testing standards for federal funding.
   1 Strongly Favor
   2 Favor
   3 Oppose
   4 Strongly Oppose

148. A law mandating the teaching of creationism instead of evolution in public schools.
   1 Strongly Favor
   2 Favor
   3 Oppose
   4 Strongly Oppose

149. Another policy we'd like to ask about is affirmative action. Affirmative action refers to any measure, policy, or law used to increase diversity or rectify discrimination so that qualified individuals have equal access to employment, education, business, and contracting opportunities.

150. Using a scale from zero to ten, where zero is not at all important and ten is extremely important, in your opinion, how important are affirmative action programs in terms of helping women achieve equity?
   Check <0...10>>

151. Using a scale from zero to ten, where zero is not at all important and ten is extremely important, in your opinion, how important are affirmative action programs in terms of helping persons of your racial or ethnic background achieve equity?
   Check <0...10>>

152. Have you personally benefited from affirmative action policies in higher education?
   1 Yes
   0 No

153. Have you personally benefited from affirmative action policies in hiring or promotion?
    1 Yes
    o No

154. People have many different views about whether race, gender, or socioeconomic class poses the most important problem facing minority communities today. In your view, which of the following issues poses the most important problem facing minorities in your community today? Is it race, socio-economic class, gender, or a combination of factors?
    [Combination of factors] What are they?
    [Check all that apply– enter other if applicable.]
    1 Race
    2 Socioeconomic class
    3 Gender
    4 Other <<Verbatim>>
    o It has nothing to do with these issues

155. As you may be aware, the Voting Rights Act (or VRA) is scheduled for reauthorization in 2007. We are interested in your views about some of the provisions in the act. Using a scale from zero to ten, where zero is not at all important and ten is extremely important, in your opinion, how important are the protections of equal political access in the current voting rights act for persons of your racial or ethnic background?
    [Check list:] <<0...10>>

156–8. Which of the following voting rights protections would you like to see renewed?

156. Bilingual ballots for speakers of Spanish, Native American, Native Alaskan, and Asian languages.
    1 Yes
    o No

157. The Section 5 (Preclearance) provision that requires federal approval of proposed changes of voting laws or procedures in the covered jurisdictions.
    1 Yes
    o No

158. Federal observers sent to polling places where electoral discrimination based on race or color is suspected.

1 Yes

0 No

159. Finally, I need to ask a few background questions. How old are you?

<<Age: Integer>>

160. How would you describe your primary racial or ethnic background? [Check list open. Do not read.]

1 American Indian

2 Asian/Pacific Islander

3 Black/African American

4 Hispanic/Latino

5 White non-Hispanic

6 Something else <<Verbatim>>

161. How would you describe your ancestry or ethnic origin? [Check list open. Do not read.]

1 American

2 African

3 Caribbean

4 Chinese

5 Japanese

6 Filipino

7 Korean

8 Indian

9 Vietnamese

10 Laotian

11 Hawaiian

12 Samoan

13 Mexican

14 Puerto Rican

15 Cuban

16 Central American

17 South American

18 Something else <<Verbatim>>

162. Other than serving as an elected official, what is your primary occupation?

[Check list open. Do not read.]

1 Attorney

2 Clerical/Secretary

  3 College/University Professor
  4 Elem./Secondary Teacher
  5 Farmer
  6 Insurance Salesperson
  7 Nurse/Health worker
  8 Physician/Dentist
  9 Real Estate Broker/Agent
  10 Self-employed/Business Owner
  11. Social Worker
  12. Homemaker
  13 Minister
  14 Government Employee
  15 Other <<Verbatim>>

163. [Asked of those who self-identified as "American Indian"] Did you serve on any tribal governing bodies prior to running for the state legislature?
  1 Yes
  0 No

164. Are you currently holding any tribal office?
  1 Yes
  0 No

165. Are you a veteran of the US military?
  1 Yes
  0 No

166. Were you born in the United States?
  1 Yes
  0 No

167. [Asked of those who answered "no" to question 166] At what age did you come to the United States?
  <<Age in years: Integer>>

168. [Asked of all but those who answered "DK/NA" to question 166 or 167, or answered "1" to question 167] Were either of your parents born outside of the United States?
  1 Yes
  0 No

169. [Asked of all but those who answered "DK/NA" to question 166 or 167, or answered "1" to question 167] Were either of your grandparents born outside of the United States?
    1 Yes
    0 No

170. What is the highest level of education you have completed? [Check list open. Do not read.]
    1 Less than High School
    2 High School Graduate /GED
    3 Business, Tech., or Vocational School
    4 Some College
    5 College Graduate
    6 Some Graduate School
    7 Master's Degree (MA/ MS)
    8 Law Degree (JD or LLB)
    9 Medical Degree (MD)
    10 Doctorate (PhD)
    11 Other <<Verbatim>>

171. How did you pay for your education? [Do not read. Check all that apply.]
    1 Self/Out-of-pocket
    2 Parents
    3 Grants
    4 Scholarships
    5 Loans
    6 Gov't/G.I. Bill
    7 Work
    8 Other <<Verbatim>> No

172. What is the highest level of education attained by your mother? [Check list open. Do not read.]
    1 Less than High School
    2 High School Graduate / GED
    3 Business, Tech., or Voc. School
    4 Some College
    5 College Graduate
    6 Some Graduate School
    7 Master's Degree (M.A./ M.S.)
    8 Law Degree (J.D. or L.L.B.)

9 Medical Degree (M.D.)
10 Doctorate (Ph.D.)
11 Other <<Verbatim>>

173. What is the highest level of education attained by your father?
[Check list open. Do not read.]
    1 Less than High School
    2 High School Graduate / GED
    3 Business, Tech., or Voc.School
    4 Some College
    5 College Graduate
    6 Some Graduate School
    7 Master's Degree (M.A./ M.S.)
    8 Law Degree (J.D. or L.L.B.)
    9 Medical Degree (M.D.) 10 Doctorate (Ph.D.)
    11 Other <<Verbatim>>

174. [Asked of those who self-identified as Black/African American in question 160 and answered that they had education beyond high school in question 170] On a scale from zero to ten, where zero means not at all involved and ten means extremely involved, how involved were you in black sororities or fraternities before you ran for elected office the very first time?
[Check:] <<0...10>>

175. Did you receive any part of your education outside of the United States?
    1 Yes
    0 No

176. Do you pay attention to the politics of your country of origin or your ancestral homeland?
    1 Yes
    0 No

177. [Asked of those who answered "yes" to question 176] Do you pay a lot, some, or very little attention to the politics of your country of origin or your ancestral homeland?
    3 A lot
    2 Some
    1 Very little

178. What is your marital status? Are you:
    1 Single, never married

2 Married
3 Widowed
4 Separated
5 Divorced
6 Have a domestic partner

179. [Asked of those who answered "Married," "Separated," or "Have a domestic partner" to question 178]
How would you describe the racial or ethnic background of your spouse or partner?
[Check list. Do not read.]
1 American Indian
2 Asian/Pacific Islander
3 Black
4 Hispanic/Latino
5 White non-Hispanic
6 Something else <<Verbatim>>

180. Would you describe yourself as having been raised in a political family?
1 Yes
0 No

181. [Not asked of those who answered "Single, never married" to question 178] Are you currently or have you ever been married to someone who has held public or elective office?
1 Yes
0 No

182. What is your religious preference?
[Check list. Do not read.]
1 Protestant
2 Roman Catholic
3 Jewish
4 Mormon (Church of Jesus Christ latter Day Saints)
5 Orthodox
6 Islam/Muslim
7 Nation of Islam
8 Buddhist
9 Hindu
10 None/Atheist/Agnostic
11 Other <<Verbatim>>

183. [Asked of those who answered "Protestant" to question 182]
     What denomination are you?
     [Check list. Do not read.]
     1 Baptist
     2 Christian
     3 Episcopalian
     4 Jehovah's Witness
     5 Lutheran
     6 Methodist
     7 Presbyterian
     8 Evangelical Christian
     9 Pentecostal
     10 Other <<Verbatim>>

184. Do you speak another language in addition to English?
     1 Yes
     0 No

185. [Asked of those who answered "yes" to question 184] What languages, other than English, do you speak?
     [Check list. Do not read.]
     1 Spanish
     2 Korean
     3 Vietnamese
     4 Chinese
     5 Japanese
     6 French
     7 German
     8 Other <<Verbatim>>

186. Do you receive an annual salary for holding elected office?
     1 Yes
     0 No

187. [Asked of those who answered "Yes" to question 186] What is the annual salary you receive for this office?
     [Round to nearest dollar:] <<Annual salary: Integer>>

188. [Asked of those who answered "No" to question 186] Do you receive any compensation at all?
     1 Yes
     0 No

189. [Asked of those who answered "Yes" to question 188] What is your monthly compensation?
[Round to nearest dollar:] <<Monthly compensation: Integer>>

190. Was the estimated annual income for your household last year:
[Read Options:]
1 Less than $50,000
2 At least $50,000 but less than $100,000
3 At least $100,000 but less than $150,000
4 $150,000 or more?

191–194. I'm going to read you some broad income categories. Please STOP me when I get to the one that includes the estimated annual income for your household in 2005. Was it:
1 Less than $10K
2 $10K to less than $20K
3 $20K to less than $30K
4 $30K to less than $40K
5 $40K to less than $50K
6 $50K to less than $60K
7 $60K to less than $70K
8 $70K to less than $80K
9 $80K to less than $90K
10 $90K to less than $100K
11 $100K to less than $110K
12 $110K to less than $120K
13 $120K to less than $130K
14 $130K to less than $140K
15 $140K to less than $150K
16 $150K to less than $160K
17 $160K to less than $170K
19 $170K to less than $180K
20 $180K to less than $190K
21 $190K to less than $200K
22 $200K or more

195. Growing up, did your family receive any type of US government assistance, including food stamps, public housing, welfare, WIC, unemployment insurance, SSI, or Medicaid?
1 Yes
0 No

196. Your answers have been very helpful to our research. Would it be possible to call back at a later date to ask you some follow-up questions?

    1 Yes
    0 No

197. Thank you for taking the time to complete this interview. If you are interested in learning more about this study, please visit www .gmcl.org or call Professor Christine Sierra in the Political Science Department at the University of New Mexico at _____. I hope you have a nice day/evening. Good Bye.

References

Abdullah, Melina, and Regina Freer. 2008. "Towards a Womanist Leadership Praxis: The History and Promise of Black Grassroots/Electoral Partnerships in California." In *Racial and Ethnic Politics in California: Continuity and Change*, edited by Bruce Cain and Sandra Bass, 95–118. Berkeley: Berkeley Public Policy Press.

Abelman, Nancy, and John Lie. 1995. *Blue Dreams: Korean Americans and the Los Angeles Riots*. Cambridge, MA: Harvard University Press.

ACLU Voting Rights Project. 2009. *Voting Rights in Indian Country: A Special Report of the Voting Rights Project of the American Civil Liberties Union*. (September). Atlanta: ACLU Voting Rights Project.

Acuña, Rodolfo F. 2011. *Occupied America: A History of Chicanos.*,7th ed. Boston: Longman.

Adams, David Wallace. 1995. *Education for Extinction: American Indians and the Boarding School Experience, 1875–1928*. Lawrence: University Press of Kansas.

Adams, John. 1776. "Thoughts on Government." In *The Portable John Adams*, edited and with an introduction by John Patrick Diggins, 233–241. New York: Penguin Books, 2004.

Alexander, Jeffrey C. 2010. *The Performance of Politics: Obama's Victory and the Democratic Struggle for Power*. New York: Oxford University Press.

Allan, Tuzyline Jita. 1995. *Womanist and Feminist Aesthetics: Comparative Review*. Hardcover ed. Athens, OH: Ohio University Press.

Allen, Ann, and David N. Plank. 2005. "School Board Election Structure and Democratic Representation." *Educational Policy* 19(3): 510–527.

Allen, Beverly Lundy. 1997. "A Re-articulation of Black Female Community Leadership: Processes, Networks and a Culture of Resistance." *African American Research Perspectives* 3(2): 61–67.

Alozie, Nicholas O. 1992. "The Election of Asians to City Councils." *Social Science Quarterly* 73(1): 90–100.

Antolini, Denise. 1984. "Women in Local Government: An Overview." In *Political Women: Current Roles in State and Local Government*, edited by Janet A. Flammang, 23–40. Beverly Hills: SAGE.

Arrington, Theodore S., and Thomas Gill Watts. 1991. "The Election of Blacks to School Boards in North Carolina." *Western Political Quarterly* 44(4): 1099–1105.

Ashmore, Richard D., Kay Deaux, and Tracy McLaughlin-Volpe. 2004. "An Organizing Framework for Collective Identity: Articulation and Significance of Multidimensionality." *Psychological Bulletin* 130(1): 80–114.

Assendelft, Laura Van. 2014. "Entry-Level Politics? Women as Candidates and Elected Officials at the Local Level." In *Women and Elective Office: Past, Present, and Future*, 3rd ed., edited by Sue Thomas and Clyde Wilcox, 199–215. New York: Oxford University Press.

Associated Press 2014. "Backers Seek Expansion of Civil Rights Death Law." *Boston Globe*, September 22.

Baca Zinn, Maxine. 1975. "Political Familism: Toward Sex Role Equality in Chicano Families." *Aztlan* 6(1): 13–26.

Baca Zinn, Maxine, and Bonnie Thorton Dill, (eds.) 1994. *Women of Color in US Society*. Philadelphia: Temple University Press.

Badash, David. 2015. "'Hello N*gger': Conservatives Welcome President Obama to Twitter." New Civil Rights Movement, May 19. www.thenewcivilrights-movement.com/davidbadash/1_hello_n_gger_conservatives_welcome_president_obama_to_twitter (Accessed July 5, 2016).

Baer, Denise L., and Heidi Hartmann. 2014. "Building Women's Political Careers: Strengthening the Pipeline to Higher Office." Report. Washington, DC: Institute for Women's Policy Research (IWPR), May.

Banducci, Susan A., Todd Donovan, and Jeffrey A. Karp. 2004. "Minority Representation, Empowerment, and Participation." *Journal of Politics* 66(2): 534–556.

Bandura, Albert. 1982. "Self-Efficacy Mechanism in Human Agency." *American Psychologist* 37(2): 122–147.

Banfield, Edward C., and James Q. Wilson. 1963. *City Politics*. New York: Vintage.

Barker, Lucius J. 1994. "Limits of Political Strategy: A Systemic View of the African American Experience." *American Political Science Review* 88 (1): 1–13.

Barnett, Bernice McNair. 1993. "Invisible Southern Black Women Leaders in the Civil Rights Movement: The Triple Constraints of Gender, Race, and Class." *Gender and Society* 7(2): 162–182.

Barrett, Edith J. 1995. "The Policy Priorities of African American Women in State Legislatures." *Legislative Studies Quarterly* 20(2): 223–247.

Barth, Richard P., Dean F. Duncan, Mary Theresa Hodorowicz, and Hye-Chung Kum. 2010. "Felonious Arrests of Former Foster Care and TANF-Involved Youth." *Journal of the Society for Social Work and Research* 1(2): 104–123.

Barthélémy, Fabrice, Mathieu Martin, and Ashley Piggins. 2014. "Ferguson Shows Us that in Contemporary America, Black Citizenship Is Not Comparable to

That of Others and Life Is Not Secure Or Guaranteed." *USApp–American Politics and Policy Blog*, November 26. http://eprints.lse.ac.uk/60402/ (Accessed July 5, 2016).

Bates, Karen Grigsby. 2015. "African-Americans Question Comparing Gay Rights Movement To Civil Rights." Radio broadcast. National Public Radio, July 2. www.npr.org/2015/07/02/419554758/african-americans-question-comparing-gay-rights-movement-to-civil-rights (Accessed June 30, 2016).

Baumeister Roy F., and Mark R. Leary. 1995. "The Need to Belong: Desire for Interpersonal Attachments as a Fundamental Human Motivation." *Psychological Bulletin* 117(3):497–529.

Baxter, Sandra, and Marjorie Lansing. 1983. *Women in Politics: The Visible Majority*. Rev. ed. Ann Arbor: University of Michigan Press.

Bejarano, Christina E. 2013. *The Latina Advantage: Gender, Race, and Political Success*. Austin: University of Texas Press.

Bell, Chanon. 2011. *History of County Term Limits*. Washington, DC: NACo, National Association of Counties, February. www.naco.org/sites/default/files/documents/County%20Term%20Limits.pdf (Accessed July 5, 2016).

Bennis, Warren. 1999. "The Leadership Advantage." *Leader to Leader* 12(2): 18–23.

Bentele, Keith G., and Erin E. O'Brien. 2013. "Jim Crow 2.0? Why States Consider and Adopt Restrictive Voter Access Policies." *Perspectives on Politics* 11(4): 1088–1116.

Benton, J. Edwin. 2005. "An Assessment of Research on American Counties." *Public Administration Review* 65(4): 462–474.

Berger, Ben. 2009. "Political Theory, Political Science, and the End of Civic Engagement." *Perspectives on Politics* 7(2): 335–350.

Berman, Ari. 2015. *Give Us The Ballot: The Modern Struggle for Voting Rights in America*. New York: Farrar, Straus and Giroux.

Berman, David R., and Tanis J. Salant. 1996. "The Changing Role of Counties in the Intergovernmental System." In *The American County: Frontiers of Knowledge*, edited by Donald C. Menzel, 19–33. Tuscaloosa: University of Alabama Press.

Bers, Trudy Haffron. 1978. "Local Political Elites: Men and Women on Boards of Education." *Political Research Quarterly* 31(3): 381–391.

Black, Jerome H., and Lynda Erickson. 2003. "Women Candidates and Voter Bias: Do Women Politicians Need to Be Better?" *Electoral Studies* 22(1): 81–100.

Black, Maria Julia. 2013. *Making the Personal Political: The Role of Descriptive and Substantive Representation in the "War on Women."* Honors thesis, Wesleyan University.

Blades, Meteor. 2016. "Arizona's primary mess no surprise to American Indians familiar with history of voter suppression." *Daily Kos (online) Newspaper* (March 28). www.dailykos.com/story/2016/3/28/1507226/-Arizona-s-primary-mess-no-surprise-to-American-Indians-familiar-with-history-of-voter-suppression (Accessed June 27, 2016).

Bledsoe, Timothy, and Mary Herring. 1990. "Victims of Circumstances: Women in Pursuit of Political Office." *The American Political Science Review* 84(1): 213–223.

Bligh, Michelle C. 2010. "Personality Theories of Leadership." In *Encyclopedia of Group Processes and Intergroup Relations*, Vol. 2, edited by John M. Levine and Michael A. Hogg, 639–642. Thousand Oaks, CA: SAGE.

Blow, Charles. 2015. "The Obama Years." *New York Times*, February 19. http://nyti.ms/1Fx7Nvm (Accessed July 5, 2016).

Boles, Janet K., and Katherine Scheurer. 2007. "Beyond Women, Children, and Families: Gender, Representation, and Public Funding for the Arts." *Social Science Quarterly* 88(1): 39–50.

Bookman, Ann, and Sandra Morgen, eds. 1987. *Women and the Politics of Empowerment*. Philadelphia: Temple University Press.

Borden, Jeremy. 2015. "KKK Met with Skirmishes at Rally to Protest Confederate Flag Removal." *Washington Post*, July 18. http://wpo.st/gjzvo (Accessed July 5, 2016).

Borreca, Richard. 2005. "Politics Often Runs in Island Families." *Honolulu Star-Bulletin*, March 6. http://archives.starbulletin.com/2005/03/06/news/story6.html (Accessed July 3, 2016).

Bositis, David A. 2002. *Black Elected Officials: A Statistical Summary 2000*. Washington, DC: Joint Center for Political and Economic Studies.

2003a. *Black Elected Officials: A Statistical Summary, 2001*. Washington, DC: Joint Center for Political and Economic Studies.

2003b. "Black Elected Officials Reach Historic Highs: Women Drive the Increase." *FOCUS: The Magazine of the Joint Center for Political and Economic Studies* 31(6): 3–4.

2012. *Blacks and the 2012 Elections: A Preliminary Analysis*. Washington, DC: Joint Center for Political and Economic Studies.

Boston Globe. 2016. "Nation: A Timeline of Same-Sex Marriage in the US." [Online, interactive news report]. Boston: *BostonGlobe.com*, January 9. www.bostonglobe.com/2016/01/09/ same-sex-marriage-over-time/mbVFMQPyxZCpM2eSQMUsZK/story.html (Accessed January 12, 2016).

Boushey, Heather, and Ann O'Leary. 2010. "Our Working Nation: How Working Women Are Reshaping America's Families and Economy and What It Means for Policymakers." Washington, DC: Center for American Progress.

Bowler, Shaun, and Gary M. Segura. 2012. *The Future Is Ours: Minority Politics, Political Behavior, and the Multiracial Era of American Politics*. Thousand Oaks, CA: CQ Press.

Bratton, Kathleen A., Kerry L. Haynie, and Beth Reingold. 2006. "Agenda Setting and African American Women in State Legislatures." *Journal of Women, Politics and Policy* 28 (Summer/Fall): 71–96.

Brewer, Rose. 1993. "Theorizing Race, Class and Gender: The New Scholarship of Black Feminist Intellectuals and Black Women's Labor." In *Theorizing Black Feminisms: The Visionary Pragmatism of Black Women*, edited by S. M. James and A. Busia, 13–30. New York: Routledge.

1999, "Theorizing Race, Class and Gender: The New Scholarship of Black Feminist Intellectuals and Black Women's Labor." *Race, Gender & Class*: 29–47.

Brook, Tom Vanden. 2014. "Army Commanders: White Men Lead a Diverse Force." *USA Today*, September 11. http://usat.ly/1tDkcEU (Accessed July 5, 2016).

Brooks, James. 2015. Director, City Solutions, National League of Cities. Personal communication (email) with Carol Hardy-Fanta, May 26.

Brown, Nadia E. 2014. *Sisters in the Statehouse: Black Women and Legislative Decision Making*. New York: Oxford University Press.

Browning, Rufus P., Dale Rogers Marshall, and David H. Tabb. 1984. *Protest Is Not Enough: The Struggle of Blacks and Hispanics for Equality in Urban Politics*. Berkeley: University of California Press.

eds. 1990. *Racial Politics in American Cities*, 1st ed. White Plains, NY: Longman.

eds. 2003. *Racial Politics in American Cities*, 3rd ed., 366–386. White Plains, NY: Longman.

Burden, Barry C. 2007. *Personal Roots of Representation*. Princeton, NJ: Princeton University Press.

Burnham, Walter Dean. 1965. "The Changing Shape of the American Political Universe." *American Political Science Review* 59(1): 7–28.

Burns, James MacGregor. 1978. *Leadership*. New York: Harper and Row.

Burrell, Barbara. 1992. "Women Candidates in Open-Seat Primaries for the U. S. House: 1968–1990." *Legislative Studies Quarterly* 17(4): 493–508.

2010. "Political Parties and Women's Organizations: Bringing Women into the Electoral Arena." In *Gender and Elections: Shaping the Future of American Politics*., 1st ed., edited by Susan J. Carroll and Richard L. Fox, 211–240. New York: Cambridge University Press.

Burt-Way, Barbara J., and Rita Mae Kelly. 1992. "Gender and Sustaining Political Ambition: A Study of Arizona Elected Officials." *Western Political Quarterly* 45(1): 11–25.

Butterfield, Fox. 2002. "Study Finds Big Increase in Black Men as Inmates since 1980." *New York Times*, August 28. http://nyti.ms/1Xc55Fu (Accessed July 5, 2016).

Button, James, and David Hedge. 1996. "Legislative Life in the 1990s: A Comparison of Black and White State Legislators." *Legislative Studies Quarterly* 21(2): 199–218.

Cannon, Katie G. 1988. *Black Womanist Ethics*, 1st ed. Atlanta: Scholars Press.

Canon, David T. 1990. *Actors, Athletes, and Astronauts: Political Amateurs in the United States Congress*. Chicago: University of Chicago Press.

Canon, David T., Matthew M. Schousen, and Patrick J. Sellers. 1996. "The Supply Side of Congressional Redistricting: Race and Strategic Politicians, 1972–1992." *Journal of Politics* 58(3): 846–862.

Capehart, Jonathan. 2015. "Obama Joins Twitter, Racism Quickly Follows." PostPartisan (blog), *Washington Post*, May 19. http://wpo.st/SvNmo (Accessed July 5, 2016).

Carmichael, Stokely, and Charles V. Hamilton. 1967. *Black Power: The Politics of Liberation in America*. New York: Vintage Books.

Carroll, Susan J. 1984. "Feminist Scholarship on Political Leadership." In *Leadership: Multidisciplinary Perspectives*, edited by Barbara Kellerman, 139–156. Englewood Cliffs, NJ: Prentice-Hall.

1994. *Women as Candidates in American Politics*, 2nd ed. Bloomington: Indiana University Press.

2003. "Have Women State Legislators in the United States Become More Conservative? A Comparison of State Legislators in 2001 and 1988."*Atlantis: Critical Studies in Gender, Culture and Social Justice* 27(2): 128–139.

Carroll, Susan J., Debra L. Dodson, and Ruth B. Mandel. 1991. *The Impact of Women in Public Office: An Overview*. New Brunswick, NJ: Center for American Women and Politics. www.cawp.rutgers.edu/sites/default/files/resources/impactoverview.pdf (Accessed July 5, 2016).

Carroll, Susan J., and Krista Jenkins. 2001a. "Do Term Limits Help Women Get Elected?" *Social Science Quarterly* 82(1): 197–201.

2001b. "Unrealized Opportunity? Term Limits and the Representation of Women in State Legislatures." *Women and Politics* 23(4): 1–30.

2005. "Increasing Diversity or More of the Same? Term Limits and the Representation of Women, Minorities and Minority Women in State Legislatures." *National Political Science Review: Contemporary Patterns of Politics, Praxis, and Culture*, Vol. 10, edited by Georgia A. Persons, 71–84. New Brunswick, NJ: Transaction Publishers.

Carroll, Susan J., and Kira Sanbonmatsu. 2013. *More Women Can Run: Gender and Pathways to the State Legislatures*. New York: Oxford University Press.

Carroll, Susan J., and Wendy S. Strimling. 1983. *Women's Routes to Elective Office: A Comparison with Men's*. Research Report. New Brunswick, NJ: Center for the American Woman and Politics.

Carroll, Tamar. 2008. "Unlikely Allies: Forging a Multiracial, Class-based Women's Movement in 1970s Brooklyn." In *Feminist Coalitions: Historical Perspectives on Second-Wave Feminism in the United States*, edited by Stephanie Gilmore, 196–224. Urbana and Chicago: University of Illinois Press.

Casey, Logan, Patrick O'Mahen, and Marie Puccio. 2011. "Proportions of Women in State Legislatures and Gay-Friendly Partnership Laws." Paper presented at the annual meeting of the Midwest Political Science Association, Chicago, April 1.

CAWP (Center for the American Woman and Politics). 1991. *Gender and Policymaking: Studies of Women in Office*. New Brunswick, NJ: Center for the American Woman and Politics, Eagleton Institute of Politics, Rutgers -The State University of New Jersey.

2001. *Women State Legislators: Past, Present and Future. Highlights and Major Findings*. New Brunswick, NJ: Center for American Women and Politics, Eagleton Institute of Politics, Rutgers University. www.cawp.rutgers.edu/sites/default/files/resources/stlegpastpresentfuture.pdf (Accessed July 5, 2016).

2002. "Women in Elective Office 2002." Fact Sheet. New Brunswick, NJ: Center for American Women and Politics, Eagleton Institute of Politics, Rutgers University. www.cawp.rutgers.edu/sites/default/files/resources/elective2002.pdf (Accessed July 5, 2016).

2007. "Women in Elective Office 2007." Fact Sheet. New Brunswick, NJ: Center for American Women and Politics, Eagleton Institute of Politics, Rutgers University. www.cawp.rutgers.edu/sites/default/files/resources/elective2007.pdf (Accessed July 5, 2016).

2013a. "Women of Color in Elective Office 2013: Congress, Statewide, State Legislature." New Brunswick, NJ: Center for American Women and Politics, Eagleton Institute of Politics, Rutgers University. www.cawp.rutgers.edu/sites/default/files/resources/color2013.pdf (Accessed November 19, 2015).

2013b. "Women State Legislative Committee Chairs 2013." Fact sheet. www.cawp.rutgers.edu/sites/default/files/resources/legleadchairs13.pdf (Accessed July 5, 2016).

2014. "Women in Congress: Leadership Roles and Committee Chairs. Previous Congresses." Fact Sheet. New Brunswick, NJ: Center for American Women and Politics, Eagleton Institute of Politics, Rutgers University. http://cawp.rutgers.edu/sites/default/files/resources/conglead.pdf (Accessed July 5, 2016).

2015. "Women Mayors in U.S. Cities 2015." Fact Sheet. www.cawp.rutgers.edu/fast_facts/levels_of_office/Local-WomenMayors.php (Accessed November 19, 2015).

Celis, Karen. 2012. "On Substantive Representation, Diversity, and Responsiveness." *Politics and Gender* 8(4): 524–529.

Celis, Karen, and Amy G. Mazur. 2012. "Hanna Pitkin's 'Concept of Representation' Revisited: Introduction." *Politics and Gender* 8(4): 508–512.

Chambliss, Theresa.(1992). "The Growth and Significance of African American Elected Officials." In *From Exclusion to Inclusion: The Long Struggle for African American Political Power*, 1st ed., edited by Ralph C. Gomes and Linda Faye Williams, 53–70. Westport, CT: Greenwood Press.

Chang, Edward T., and Jeannette Diaz-Veizades. 1999. *Ethnic Peace in the American City: Building Community in Los Angeles and Beyond*. New York: New York University Press.

Chin, Gabriel J. 1996. "The Civil Rights Revolution Comes to Immigration Law: A New Look at the Immigration and Nationality Act of 1965." *North Carolina Law Review* 75: 273–345.

Cho, Seong-Hoon, JunJie Wu, and William G. Boggess. 2003. "Measuring Interactions among Urbanization, Land Use Regulations, and Public Finance." *American Journal of Agricultural Economics* 85(4): 988–999.

Chow, Esther Ngam-Ling. 1987. "The Development of Feminist Consciousness among Asian American Women." *Gender and Society* 1(3): 284–299.

Chu, Judy. 1989. "Asian Pacific American Women in Mainstream Politics." In *Making Waves: An Anthology of Writings by and about Asian American Women*, edited by Diane Yen-Mei Wong and Asian Women United of California, 405–421. Boston: Beacon Press.

Cillizza, Chris. 2015. "How Rudy Giuliani Marginalized Himself." *Washington Post*, February 19. http://wpo.st/bYXvo (Accessed July 5, 2016).

Clark, Janet. 1998. "Women at the National Level: An Update on Roll Call Voting Behavior." In *Women and Elective Office: Past, Present, and Future*, edited by Sue Thomas and Clyde Wilcox, 118–129. New York: Oxford University Press.

Clark, Meredith D. 2015. "Making the Case for Black with a Capital B. Again," *MediaWire*, August 23, 2015. www.poynter.org/news/mediawire/367611/making-the-case-for-black-with-a-capital-b-again/ (Accessed July 5, 2016).

Clark, Richard L. 2004. "Government by the People: A National Survey of County Elected Officials. Report prepared for the National Association of Counties (July). Athens, GA: Carl Vinson Institute of Government. www.cviog.uga.edu/ncsc/reports/government-by-the-people.pdf (Accessed July 5, 2016).

Clayton, Dewey M., and Angela M. Stallings. 2000. "Black Women in Congress: Striking the Balance." *Journal of Black Studies* 30(4): 574–603.

Clubok, Alfred B., Norman M. Wilensky, and Forrest J. Berghorn. 1969. "Family Relationships, Congressional Recruitment, and Political Modernization." *Journal of Politics* 31(4): 1035–1062.

Coates, Ta-Nehisi. 2015. *Between the World and Me*. New York: Spiegel & Grau.

Cobb, Jelani. 2014. "Voting by Numbers." *New Yorker*, October 27. www.newyorker.com/magazine/2014/10/27/voting-numbers (Accessed July 5, 2016).

Cohen, Cathy. 1999. *The Boundaries of Blackness: AIDS and the Breakdown of Black Politics*. Chicago: University of Chicago Press.

Cohen, Cathy J., Kathleen B. Jones, and Joan C. Tronto, eds. 1997. *Women Transforming Politics: An Alternative Reader*. New York: New York University Press.

Conde, Yvonne M. 1999. *Operation Pedro Pan: The Untold Exodus of 14,048 Cuban Children*. New York: Routledge.

Cooper, Christopher A., and Lilliard E. Richardson, Jr. 2006. "Institutions and Representational Roles in American State Legislatures." *State Politics and Policy Quarterly* 6(2):174–194.

Coughlin, Linda, Ellen Wingard, and Keith Hollihan, eds. 2005. *Enlightened Power: How Women Are Transforming the Practice of Leadership*. San Francisco: Jossey-Bass.

Cox, Oliver Cromwell. 1948. *Caste, Class and Race: A Study in Social Dynamics*. New York: Doubleday.

Coyle, Laurie, Gail Hershatter, and Emily Honig. 1980. "Women at Farah: An Unfinished Story." In *Mexican Women in the United States: Struggles Past and Present*, edited by Magdalena Mora and Adelaida R. Del Castillo, 117–143. Occasional Paper No. 2. Los Angeles: Chicano Studies Research Center Publications, University of California, Los Angeles.

Crawford, Jarret T., and Anuschka Bhatia. 2012. "Birther Nation: Political Conservatism Is Associated with Explicit and Implicit Beliefs that President Barack Obama Is Foreign." *Analyses of Social Issues and Public Policy*, 12(1): 364–376.

Crenshaw, Kimberle. 1989. "Demarginalizing the Intersection of Race and Sex: A Black Feminist Critique of Antidiscrimination Doctrine, Feminist Theory and Antiracist Politics." *University of Chicago Legal Forum* 140: 139–167.

Crenshaw, Kimberle, Neil Gotanda, Gary Peller, and Kendall Thomas. 1995. *Critical Race Theory: The Key Writings that Formed the Movement.* New York: The New Press.

Crowder–Meyer, Melody. 2011. "Candidate Recruitment and Party Networks: How the Characteristics and Choices of Local Party Leaders Affect Women's Representation." Paper presented at Annual Meeting of the American Political Science Association, Seattle, WA, September 1-4.

Cuéllar, Carlos E. 2013. "Patterns of Representation: A Descriptive Analysis of Latino Mayor Cities in the U.S." Paper prepared for the Thomas Anton-Frederick Lippitt Urban Conference on Latino Mayors: Politics and Policy in the City, Brown University, Providence, RI, November 13.

Daffron, Brian. 2013. "Oklahoma's Power Brokers: The 26 Natives Holding State Positions." *Indian Country Today Media Network.* July 18. http://indiancountrytodaymedianetwork.com/2013/07/18/oklahomas-power-brokers-21-natives-holding-state-positions-150479 (Accessed July 5, 2016).

"Power Brokers III: 11 Native State Legislators in Arizona and New Mexico." *Indian Country Today Media Network*, August 15. http://indiancountrytodaymedianetwork.com/2013/08/15/power-brokers-iii-11-native-state-legislators-arizona-new-mexico-150679 (Accessed July 5, 2016).

"Power Brokers IV, Pacific Northwest: The Most Tribes, But Few Legislators." *Indian Country Today Media Network.* August 22. http://indiancountrytodaymedianetwork.com/2013/08/22/power-brokers-iv-northwest-home-most-tribes-less-legislators-150971 (Accessed July 5, 2016).

"Power Brokers V: The Plains States Show the Strength of Native Women." *Indian Country Today Media Network.* September 5. http://indiancountrytodaymedianetwork.com/2013/09/05/power-brokers-v-plains-states-show-strength-native-womeshn-151161 (Accessed July 1, 2016).

"Power Brokers VI: Crossing the Pacific into Hawai'i." *Indian Country Today Media Network*, September 12. http://indiancountrytodaymedianetwork.com/2013/09/12/power-brokers-vi-crossing-pacific-hawaii-151236 (Accessed July 5, 2016).

"Power Brokers VII: Two States See Native Representation in the East." *Indian Country Media Network*, September 26. http://indiancountrytodaymedianetwork.com/2013/09/26/power-brokers-vii-two-states-see-native-representation-east-151455 (Accessed July 5, 2016).

Dahl, Robert A. 1961. *Who Governs? Democracy and Power in an American City*, 1st ed. New Haven, CT: Yale University Press.

Darcy, R., and Charles D. Hadley. 1988. "Black Women in Politics: The Puzzle of Success." *Social Science Quarterly* 69(3): 629–645.

Darcy, Robert, Charles D. Hadley, and Jason F. Kirksey. 1993. "Election Systems and the Representation of Black Women in American State Legislatures." *Women and Politics* 13(2): 73–89.

Darcy, R., Susan Welch, and Janet Clark. 1994. *Women, Elections, and Representation*, 2nd ed. Lincoln: University of Nebraska Press.

Darder, Antonia, Rodolfo D. Torres, and Henry Gutiérrez, eds. 1997. *Latinos and Education: A Critical Reader*. New York: Routledge.

Darling, Marsha J. 1998. "African-American Women in State Elective Office in the South." In *Women and Elective Office: Past, Present, and Future*, 1st ed. edited by Sue Thomas and Clyde Wilcox, 150–162. New York: Oxford University Press.

Davidson, Chandler, and Bernard Grofman, eds. 1994. *Quiet Revolution in the South: The Impact of the Voting Rights Act, 1965–1990*. Princeton, NJ: Princeton University Press.

Davis, Donn G. 2007. "Learning for Leaders: Notes on a Pedagogy for the Praxis of Black Political Leadership." In *Perspectives in Black Politics and Black Leadership*, edited by John Davis, 47–60. Lanham, MD: University Press of America.

Davis, James A., Tom W. Smith, Robert W. Hodge, Keiko Nakao, and Judith Treas. 1991. "Occupational Prestige Ratings from the 1989 General Social Survey." Chicago: National Opinion Research Center [producer]. Ann Arbor, MI: Inter-university Consortium for Political and Social Research [distributor]. doi:10.3886/ICPSR09593.v1.

Dawson, Michael C. 1994. *Behind the Mule: Race and Class in African-American Politics*. Princeton, NJ: Princeton University Press.

    2001. *Black Visions: The Roots of Contemporary African-American Political Ideologies*. Chicago: University of Chicago Press.

Day, Phyllis J. 1979. "Sex-Role Stereotypes and Public Assistance." *Social Service Review* 53(1): 106–115.

Deckman, Mary. 2006. "School Board Candidates and Gender: Ideology, Party, and Policy Concerns." *Journal of Women, Politics and Policy* 28(1): 87–117.

Deloria, Vine, Jr., ed. 1985. *American Indian Policy in the Twentieth Century*. Norman: University of Oklahoma Press.

DeSena, Judith N., ed. 2008. *Gender in an Urban World*. Research in Urban Sociology, Vol.9, 1st ed. Bingley, UK: JAI Press, Emerald Group Publishing.

Dittmar, Kelly. 2013. "What's the Hold-Up? Women's Delayed Entry into Political Office." *Footnote: A Blog of the Center for American Women and Politics*. January 8. www.cawp.rutgers.edu/footnotes/what's-hold-women's-delayed-entry-political-office (Accessed April 20, 2015).

Dodson, Debra L. 2006. *The Impact of Women in Congress*. New York: Oxford University Press.

Dodson, Debra L., and Susan J. Carroll. 1991. *Reshaping the Agenda: Women in State Legislatures*. Report. New Brunswick, NJ: Center for the American Woman and Politics (CAWP), Rutgers University.

Dolan, Julie Anne B., Melissa M. Deckman, and Michele L Swers. 2007. *Women and Politics: Paths to Power and Political Influence*, 1st ed. Upper Saddle River, NJ: Pearson Prentice Hall.

Dolan, Kathleen. 1998. "Voting for Women in the 'Year of the Woman'." *American Journal of Political Science* 42(1): 272–293.

2008. "Women as Candidates in American Politics: The Continuing Impact of Sex and Gender." In *Political Women and American Democracy*, edited by Christina Wolbrecht, Karen Beckwith, and Lisa Baldez, 110–127. New York: Cambridge University Press.

Donovan, Todd, Christopher Z. Mooney, and Daniel A. Smith. 2011. *State and Local Politics: Institutions and Reform*, 2nd ed. Boston: Wadsworth, Cengage Learning.

Dovi, Suzanne. 2002. "Preferable Descriptive Representatives: Will Just Any Woman, Black, or Latino Do?" *American Political Science Review* 96(4): 729–743.

DPIC (Death Penalty Information Center). 2015. "Innocence and the Death Penalty: Assessing the Danger of Mistaken Executions." Last modified July 22. www.deathpenaltyinfo.org/innocence-and-death-penalty-assessing-danger-mistaken-executions (Accessed July 5, 2016).

Draper, Jamie B., and Martha Jiménez. 1992. "A Chronology of the Official English Movement." In *Language Loyalties: A Sourcebook on the Official English Controversy*, edited by James Crawford, 89–94. Chicago: University of Chicago Press.

D'Souza, Dinesh. 2010. *The Roots of Obama's Rage*. Washington, DC: Regnery Publishing.

Du Bois, W. E. B. 1999. *The Souls of Black Folks*. Norton Critical edition, edited by Henry Louis Gates Jr. and Terri Hume Oliver. New York: W. W. Norton.

Duerst-Lahti, Georgia, and Rita Mae Kelly, eds. 1995. *Gender Power, Leadership, and Governance*. Ann Arbor: University of Michigan Press.

Dymally, Mervyn M. 1971. *The Black Politician: His Struggle for Power*. Belmont, CA: Duxbury Press.

Eligon, John. 2015. "Black Mayor Is Voted In and a Small Town's Staff Empties Out." *New York Times*, April 23. http://nyti.ms/1OgMNON (Accessed April 25, 2015).

England, Robert E., Michael W. Hirlinger, and Jason F. Kirksey. 2002. "The New South? Black Representation on Southern School Boards." Paper presented at the annual meeting of the Southern Political Science Association, Savannah, GA, November 7–9.

Epstein, Michael J., Richard G. Niemi, and Lynda W. Powell. 2005. "Do Women and Men State Legislators Differ? In *Women and Elective Office: Past, Present, and Future*, 2nd ed., edited by Sue Thomas and Clyde Wilcox, 94–109. New York: Oxford University Press.

Esgar, Daneya. 2013. "Speak Out: Why We Need More Women and LGBT People in Office." *Outfront* (blog), December 3. http://outfrontonline.com/focus/speak-out-opinion/speak-out-why-we-need-more-women-and-lgbt-people-in-office/#sthash.G1WLRwpt.Y5iVbnzR.dpuf (Accessed July 5, 2016).

Eulau, Heinz, and Paul D. Karps. 1977. "The Puzzle of Representation: Specifying Components of Responsiveness." *Legislative Studies Quarterly* 2(3): 233–254.

Everson, David H. 1992. "The Impact of Term Limitations on States: Cutting the Underbrush or Chopping Down the Tall Timber?" In *Limiting Legislative Terms*, edited by Gerald Benjamin and Michael J. Malbin, 189–204. Washington, DC: CQ Press.

Falcón, Sylvanna M. 2015. "The Globalization of Ferguson: Pedagogical Matters about Racial Violence." *Feminist Studies* 41(1): 218–221.

Fausset, Richard. 2014. "Mostly Black Cities, Mostly White City Halls." *New York Times*, September 28, A1, A12. http://nyti.ms/1sImPJF (Accessed July 6, 2016).

Fenno, Richard F. 1978. *Home Style: House Members in Their Districts*. Boston: Little, Brown.

2003. *Going Home: Black Representatives and Their Constituents*. Chicago: University of Chicago Press.

2007. *Congressional Travels: Places, Connections, and Authenticity*. New York: Pearson/Longman.

Flammang, Janet A. 1984. "Political Women: Current Roles in State and Local Government." *Sage Yearbooks in Women's Policy Studies*, Vol. 8. Beverly Hills: SAGE.

1985. "Female Officials in the Feminist Capital: The Case of Santa Clara County." *The Western Political Quarterly* 38(1): 94–118.

1997. *Women's Political Voice: How Women Are Transforming the Practice and Study of Politics*. Philadelphia: Temple University Press.

Fletcher, Joyce K. 2004. "The Paradox of Postheroic Leadership: An Essay on Gender, Power, and Transformational Change." *The Leadership Quarterly* 15(5): 647–661.

Flora, Cornelia, and Jan Flora. 2008. *Rural Communities: Legacy and Change*, 3rd ed. Boulder, CO: Westview Press.

Flora, Cornelia Butler, Jan L. Flora, and Stephen P. Gasteyer. 2015. *Rural Communities: Legacy and Change*, 4th ed. Boulder, CO: Westview Press.

Flores, Henry. 2015. *Latinos and the Voting Rights Act: The Search for Racial Purpose*. Lanham, MD: Lexington Books.

Ford, Lynne E. 2011. *Women and Politics: The Pursuit of Equality*, 3rd ed. Boston: Wadsworth, Cengage Learning.

Ford, Ramona L. 1990. *Native American Women Activists: Past and Present*. Unpublished master's thesis. Southwest Texas State University.

Fowler, Linda L., and Jennifer L. Lawless. 2009. "Looking for Sex in All the Wrong Places: Press Coverage and the Electoral Fortunes of Gubernatorial Candidates." *Perspectives on Politics* 7(3): 519–536.

Fowlkes, Diane L. 1984. "Ambitious Political Women: Countersocialization and Political Party Context." *Women and Politics* 4(4): 5–32.

Fox, Richard L., and Jennifer L. Lawless. 2004. "Entering the Arena? Gender and the Decision to Run for Office." *American Journal of Political Science* 48(2): 264–280.

2005. "To Run or Not to Run for Office: Explaining Nascent Political Ambition." *American Journal of Political Science* 49(3): 642–659.

2011. "Gaining and Losing Interest in Running for Public Office: The Concept of Dynamic Political Ambition." *Journal of Politics* 73(2): 443–462.

2014. "Uncovering the Origins of the Gender Gap in Political Ambition." *American Political Science Review* 108(3): 499–519.

Fox, Richard L., Jennifer L. Lawless, and Courtney Feeley. 2001. "Gender and the Decision to Run for Office." *Legislative Studies Quarterly* 26(3): 411–435.

Fox, Richard L., and Robert A. Schuhmann. 1999. "Gender and Local Government: A Comparison of Women and Men City Managers." *Public Administration Review* 59(3): 231–242.

Fraga, Luis Ricardo, Linda Lopez, Valerie Martinez-Ebers, and Ricardo Ramírez. 2006. "Gender and Ethnicity: Patterns of Electoral Success and Legislative Advocacy among Latina and Latino State Officials in Four States." In *Intersectionality and Politics: Recent Research on Gender, Race, and Political Representation in the United States*, edited by Carol Hardy-Fanta, 121–140. New York: Routledge.

Fraga, Luis Ricardo, Linda Lopez, Valerie Martinez-Ebers, and Ricardo Ramírez. 2008. "Representing Gender *and* Ethnicity: Strategic Intersectionality" (emphasis in original). In *Legislative Women: Getting Elected, Getting Ahead*, edited by Beth Reingold, 157–174. Boulder, CO: Lynne Rienner.

Fraga, Luis Ricardo, Valerie Martinez-Ebers, Linda Lopez, and Ricardo Ramírez. 2005. "Strategic Intersectionality: Gender, Ethnicity, and Political Incorporation." Paper presented at the annual meeting of the American Political Science Association, Washington, DC, August 31–September 4.

Fraga, Luis Ricardo, Valerie Martinez-Ebers, Ricardo Ramirez, and Linda Lopez. 2003. "Gender and Ethnicity: The Political Incorporation of Latina and Latino State Legislators." Paper presented at the Inequality and Social Policy Seminar, John F. Kennedy School of Government, Cambridge, MA, November 10.

Fraga, Luis R., Kenneth J. Meier, and Robert E. England. 1986. "Hispanic Americans and Educational Policy: Limits to Equal Access." *Journal of Politics* 48(4): 850–876.

Fraga, Luis R., and Sharon A. Navarro. 2007. "Latinas in Latino Politics." In *Latino Politics: Identity, Mobilization, and Representation*, edited by Rodolfo Espino, David L. Leal, and Kenneth J. Meier, 177–194. Charlottesville: University of Virginia Press.

Franzini, Luisa, John Ribble, and William Spears. 2001. "The Effects of Income Inequality and Income Level on Mortality Vary by Population Size in Texas Counties." *Journal of Health and Social Behavior* 42(4): 373–387.

Freeman, Jo. 2008. "How 'Sex' Got Into Title VII: Persistent Opportunism as a Maker of Public Policy." *We Will Be Heard: Women's Struggles for Political Power in the United States*, 171–190. Lanham, MD: Rowman and Littlefield.

Freeman, Marilyn, and Tina Witcher. 1988. "Stepping into Black Power." *Rolling Stone* (March 24): 143–148.

Frost, David M., and Ilan H. Meyer. 2012. "Measuring Community Connectedness among Diverse Sexual Minority Populations." *Journal of Sex Research* 49(1): 36–49.

Fulton, Sarah A., Cherie D. Maestas, L. Sandy Maisel, and Walter J. Stone. 2006. "The Sense of a Woman: Gender, Ambition, and the Decision to Run for Congress." *Political Research Quarterly* 59(2): 235–248.

Gamboa, Suzanne. 2015. "Historic Time for CHC: Two Latinas Lead the Hispanic Group." *NBC News.* January 27. http://nbcnews.to/1H5zrS7 (Accessed July 6, 2016).

Gamson Joshua. 1997. "Messages of Exclusion: Gender, Movements, and Symbolic Boundaries." *Gender and Society* 11(2):178–199.

García Bedolla, Lisa, Katherine Tate, and Janelle Wong. 2005. "Indelible Effects: The Impact of Women of Color in the U.S. Congress." In *Women and Elective Office: Past, Present, and Future*, 2nd ed., edited by Sue Thomas and Clyde Wilcox, 152–175. New York: Oxford University Press.

Garcia, John A. 1986. "The Voting Rights Act and Hispanic Political Representation in the Southwest." *Publius* 16(4): 49–66.

García, Sonia, and Marisela Márquez. 2001. "Motivational and Attitudinal Factors amongst Latinas in U.S. Electoral Politics." *NWSA Journal: A Publication of the National Women's Studies Association* 12(2): 112–122.

García, Sonia R., Valerie Martinez-Ebers, Irasema Coronado, Sharon A. Navarro, and Patricia A. Jaramillo, eds. 2008. *Políticas: Latina Public Officials in Texas.* Austin: University of Texas Press.

Gay, Claudine. 2002. "Spirals of Trust? The Effect of Descriptive Representation on the Relationship between Citizens and Their Government." *American Journal of Political Science* 46(4): 717–732.

2004. "Putting Race in Context: Identifying the Environmental Determinants of Black Racial Attitudes." *American Political Science Review* 98(4): 547–562.

Gay, Claudine, and Katherine Tate. 1998. "Doubly Bound: The Impact of Gender and Race on the Politics of Black Women." *Political Psychology* 19(1): 169–184.

Gellerman, Bruce. 2014. "It Was Like a War Zone: Busing in Boston." Radio broadcast transcript, *WBUR News*, September 5. www.wbur.org/2014/09/05/boston-busing-anniversary (Accessed July 6, 2016).

Gerber, Alan. 1996. "African Americans' Congressional Careers and the Democratic House Delegation." *Journal of Politics* 58(3): 831–845.

Geron, Kim, and James S. Lai. 2002. "Beyond Symbolic Representation: A Comparison of the Electoral Pathways and Policy Priorities of Asian American and Latino Elected Officials." *Asian Law Journal* 9(1): 41–81.

Gertzog, Irwin N. 2004. *Women and Power on Capitol Hill: Reconstructing the Congressional Women's Caucus.* Boulder, CO: Lynne Rienner.

Giddings, Paula. 1984. *When and Where I Enter: The Impact of Black Women on Race and Sex in America.* New York: William Morrow.

1988. *In Search of Sisterhood: Delta Sigma Theta and the Challenge of the Black Sorority Movement.* New York: William Morrow.

Gillespie, Andra. 2010. "Meet the New Class: Theorizing Black Leadership in a 'Postracial' Era." In *Whose Black Politics? Cases in Post-Racial Black Leadership*, edited by Andra Gillespie, 9–42. New York: Routledge.

Gilmore, Stephanie, ed. 2008. *Feminist Coalitions: Historical Perspectives on Second-Wave Feminism in the United States.* Urbana and Chicago: University of Illinois Press.

Gitelson, Alan R., Robert L. Dudley, and Melvin J. Dubnick. 2016. *American Government: Myths and Realities*. New York: Oxford University Press.

Githens, Marianne, and Jewel L. Prestage, eds. 1977. *A Portrait of Marginality: The Political Behavior of the American Woman*. New York: David McKay.

Glynn, Sarah Jane. 2012. "Fact Sheet, Child Care Families Need More Help to Care for Their Children." Washington, DC: Center for American Progress, August 16. https://cdn.americanprogress.org/wp-content/uploads/2012/10/ChildCareFactsheet.pdf (Accessed July 6, 2016).

Gott, Richard. 2005. *Cuba: A New History*. New Haven: Yale Nota Bene Press, Yale University.

Grayson, Deborah R. 1999. "'Necessity was the Midwife of our Politics': Black Women's Health Activism in the 'Post'–Civil Rights Era(1980–1996)." In *Still Lifting, Still Climbing: African American Women's Contemporary Activism*, edited by Kimberly Springer, 131–148. New York: New York University Press.

Griffin, John D. 2014. "When and Why Minority Legislators Matter." *Annual Review of Political Science* 17 (May): 327–336.

Grofman, Bernard, and Lisa Handley. 1989. "Black Representation: Making Sense of Electoral Geography at Different Levels of Government." *Legislative Studies Quarterly* 14(2): 265–279.

Guilford, Gwynn. 2014. "'Offender-Funded': These Seven Charts Explain How Ferguson – and Many Other U.S. Cities – Wring Revenue from Black People and the Poor." *Quartz*, August 28. http://qz.com/257042/these-seven-charts-explain-how-ferguson-and-many-other-us-cities-wring-revenue-from-black-people-and-the-poor/ (Accessed July 6, 2016).

Guinier, Lani. 1994. *The Tyranny of the Majority: Fundamental Fairness in Representative Democracy*. New York: The Free Press.

Guinier, Lani, and Gerald Torres. 2002. *The Miner's Canary: Enlisting Race, Resisting Power, and Transforming Democracy*. 1st (hardcover) ed. Cambridge, MA: Harvard University Press.

Gurin, Patricia, Shirley Hatchett, and James S. Jackson. 1989. *Hope and Independence: Blacks' Response to Electoral and Party Politics*. New York: Russell Sage Foundation.

Gutiérrez, José Angel, Michelle Meléndez, and Sonia Adriana Noyola. 2007. *Chicanas in Charge: Texas Women in the Public Arena*. Lanham, MD: AltaMira Press.

Hall, Richard L. 1996. *Participation in Congress*. New Haven, CT: Yale University Press.

Hamilton, Dona Cooper, and Charles V. Hamilton. 1997. *The Dual Agenda: Race and Social Welfare Policies of Civil Rights Organizations*. New York: Columbia University Press.

Han, Lori Cox. 2010. *Women and U.S. Politics: The Spectrum of Political Leadership*, 2nd ed. Boulder, CO: Lynne Rienner.

Hancock, Ange-Marie. 2004. *The Politics of Disgust: The Public Identity of the Welfare Queen*. New York: New York University Press.

2007. "When Multiplication Doesn't Equal Quick Addition: Examining Intersectionality As A Research Paradigm." *Perspectives on Politics* 5(1): 63–79.

2009. "An Untraditional Intersectional Analysis of the 2008 Election." *Politics and Gender* 5(1): 96–105.

Hanson, Gordon H. 2009. *The Economics and Policy of Illegal Immigration in the United States.* Unpublished report of the Migration Policy Institute (December). www.migrationpolicy.org/research/economics-and-policy-illegal-immigration-united-states (Accessed July 6, 2016).

Hardy-Fanta, Carol. 1993. *Latina Politics, Latino Politics: Gender, Culture, and Political Participation in Boston.* Philadelphia: Temple University Press.

1997. *Latino Electoral Campaigns in Massachusetts: The Impact of Gender.* Boston: Center for Women in Politics and Public Policy, and the Mauricio Gaston Institute for Latino Community Development and Public Policy, University of Massachusetts Boston.

2002. "Latina Women and Political Leadership: Implications for Latino Community Empowerment." In *Latino Politics in Massachusetts: Struggles, Strategies, and Prospects,* edited by Carol Hardy-Fanta and J. Gerson, 193–212. New York: Routledge.

2003. *Women in New England Politics: A Profile and Handbook for Action.* Boston: Center for Women in Politics and Public Policy, John W. McCormack Graduate School of Policy Studies, University of Massachusetts Boston.

2013. "Racial and Ethnic Identity of Elected Officials of Color: A Closer Look at a Complex Matter." Paper presented at the annual meeting of the American Political Science Association, Chicago, August 29–September 1.

Hardy-Fanta, Carol, Pei-te Lien, Dianne M. Pinderhughes, and Christine Marie Sierra. 2006. "Gender, Race, and Descriptive Representation in the United States: Findings from the Gender and Multicultural Leadership Project." *Intersectionality and Politics: Recent Research on Gender, Race, and Political Representation in the United States,* edited by Carol Hardy-Fanta, 7–41. New York: Routledge.

Hardy-Fanta, Carol, Pei-te Lien, Christine M. Sierra, and Dianne M. Pinderhughes. 2007. "A New Look at Paths to Political Office: Moving Women of Color from the Margins to the Center." Paper presented at the annual meeting of the American Political Science Association, Chicago, August 30–September 2.

Hardy-Fanta, Carol, Christine Marie Sierra, Pei-te Lien, Dianne M. Pinderhughes, and Wartyna L. Davis. 2005. "Race, Gender, and Descriptive Representation: An Exploratory View of Multicultural Elected Leadership in the United States." Paper presented at the annual meeting of the American Political Science Association, Washington, DC, September 1–4.

Hart, Richard. 2009. "Estimate of 2009 Total Number of BEOs at All Levels of Office with Gender Breakdown." Personal communication. Washington, DC: Joint Center for Political and Economic Studies.

Harvey, Thomas, John McAnnar, Michael-John Voss, Megan Conn, Sean Janda, and Sophia Keskey. 2014. *Arch City Defenders: Municipal Courts White Paper.* Unpublished manuscript, January 1. https://pdf.yt/d/iyuTY46j7R_fAvpK (Accessed July 6, 2016).

Hawaii Board of Education. 2014. "About the Board." www.hawaiiboe.net/About/Pages/AboutUs.aspx (Accessed July 6, 2016).

Hawkesworth, Mary. 2003. "Congressional Enactments of Race-Gender: Toward a Theory of Raced-Gendered Institutions." *American Political Science Review* 97(4): 529–550.

 2006. "Gender as an Analytic Category." In *Feminist Inquiry: From Political Conviction to Methodological Innovation,* 145–175. New Brunswick, NJ: Rutgers University Press.

Hawkesworth, Mary., and Katherine E. Kleeman. 2001. *Term Limits and the Representation of Women.* Report. New Brunswick, NJ: Center for American Women and Politics, May. www.cawp.rutgers.edu/sites/default/files/resources/termlimitsrepresentationofwomen.pdf (Accessed July 6, 2016).

Haynie, Kerry L. 2001. *African American Legislators in the American States.* New York: Columbia University Press.

Haywoode, Terry L. 1991. *Working Class Feminism: Creating a Politics of Community, Connection, and Concern.* PhD dissertation, City University of New York.

Hedge, David, James Button, and Mary Spear. 1996. "Accounting for the Quality of Black Legislative Life: The View from the States." *American Journal of Political Science* 40(1): 82–98.

Hellwege, Julia Marin, and Christine M. Sierra. 2014. "Profile of the 114th Congress." Unpublished report. University of New Mexico. December 30.

Henderson, Wade. 2005. "The Voting Rights Act of 1965: 40 Years After 'Bloody Sunday,' A Promise Still Unfulfilled." Feature story [online]. The Leadership Conference. March 2. http://www.civilrights.org/voting-rights/vra/2006/the-voting-rights-act-of-1965-40-years-after-bloody-sunday-a-promise-still-unfulfilled.html (Accessed July 4, 2016).

Hero, Rodney. 1992. *Latinos and the U.S. Political System: Two-Tiered Pluralism.* Philadelphia: Temple University Press.

Herrick, Rebekah. 2010. "Legislators' Positions on Gay and Lesbian Rights: The Personal and Political." *Journal of Homosexuality* 57(7): 928–943.

Hess, Frederick M. 2002. *School Boards at the Dawn of the 21st Century: Conditions and Challenges of District Government.* Washington, DC: National School Boards Association.

Hill Collins, Patricia. 1990. *Black Feminist Thought: Knowledge, Consciousness, and the Politics of Empowerment.* Boston: Unwin Hyman.

 1996. "What's in a Name? Womanism, Black Feminism, and Beyond." *The Black Scholar* 26(1): 9–17.

 2000. "Gender, Black Feminism, and Black Political Economy." *Annals of the American Academy of Political and Social Science* 568 (March): 41–53.

Hing, Bill Ong. 1993. *Making and Remaking Asian America through Immigration Policy, 1850–1990.* Stanford, CA: Stanford University Press.

Hochschild, Jennifer, and Vesla Mae Weaver. 2010. "'There's No One as Irish as Barack O'Bama': The Policy and Politics of American Multiculturalism." *Perspectives on Politics* 8(3): 737–759.

Hogue, Carma. 2013. "Government Organization Summary Report: 2012." *Government Division Briefs*, Report G12-CG-ORG. Washington, DC: US Census Bureau, September 26. www2.census.gov/govs/cog/g12_org.pdf (Accessed July 6, 2016).

Holden, Matthew J. 1973. *The Politics of the Black "Nation."* New York: Chandler.

Holzer, Harry, and David Neumark. 2000. "Assessing Affirmative Action." *Journal of Economic Literature* 38(3): 483–568.

Hooghe, Marc, and Dietlind Stolle. 2004. "Good Girls Go to the Polling Booth, Bad Boys Go Everywhere: Gender Differences in Anticipated Political Participation among American Fourteen-Year-Olds." *Women and Politics* 26(3–4): 1–23.

Hooper, Deona. 2015. "Ferguson Proves the United States Justice System Is Not Broken, but Working Perfectly as Designed." *Critical and Radical Social Work* 3(1): 141–147.

Huddy, Leonie, Erin Cassese, and Mary-Kate Lizotte. 2008. "Gender, Public Opinion, and Political Reasoning." In *Political Women and American Democracy*, edited by Christina Wolbrecht, Karen Beckwith, and Lisa Baldez, 31–49. New York: Cambridge University Press.

Hull, Gloria T., Patricia Bell Scott, and Barbara Smith, eds. 1982. *All the Women Are White, All the Blacks Are Men, But Some of Us Are Brave.* New York: Feminist Press.

Humes, Karen R., Nicholas A. Jones, and Roberto R. Ramirez. 2011. "Overview of Race and Hispanic Origin: 2010." 2010 Census Briefs No. C2010BR-02, March. www.census.gov/prod/cen2010/briefs/c2010br-02.pdf (Accessed July 6, 2016).

Jacobs, Cheryl. 2011. "Community Capitals: Political Capital." *Extension Extra*. South Dakota State University (SDSU) Newsletter ExEx16010 (April), South Dakota Cooperative Extension Service. http://pubstorage. sdstate.edu/AgBio_Publications/articles/ExEx16010.pdf (Accessed July 6, 2016).

Jacobson, Gary C., and Samuel Kernell. 1981. *Strategy and Choice in Congressional Elections.* Hardcover edition. New Haven, CT: Yale University Press.

Jaimes, M. Annette. 1997. "American Indian Women at the Center of Indigenous Resistance in Contemporary North America." In *Dangerous Liaisons: Gender, Nation, and Postcolonial Perspectives*, edited by Anne McClintock, Aamir Mufti, and Ella Shohat, 298–329. Minneapolis: University of Minnesota.

Jaimes, M. Annette, with Theresa Halsey. 1992. "American Indian Women at the Center of Indigenous Resistance in Contemporary North America." In *The State of Native America: Genocide, Colonization, and Resistance*, edited by M. Annette Jaimes, 311–343. Race and Resistance Series. Boston: South End Press.

Jaynes, Gerald David, and Robin M. Williams, Jr., eds. 1989. *A Common Destiny: Blacks and American Society*. Washington, DC: National Academies Press.

Jencks, Christopher, and Meredith Phillips. 1998. "The Black-White Test Score Gap: An Introduction." In *The Black-White Test Score Gap*, edited by Christopher Jencks and Meredith Phillips, 1–51. Washington, DC: The Brookings Institution.

Jennings, Jeanette. 1991. "Black Women Mayors: Reflections on Race and Gender." In *Gender and Policymaking: Studies of Women in Office*, edited by Debra L. Dodson, 73–79. New Brunswick, NJ: Center for the American Woman and Politics, Rutgers University.

Johnson, Kevin R. 2012. "Immigration and Civil Rights: Is the 'New' Birmingham the Same as the 'Old' Birmingham?", *William and Mary Bill of Rights Journal* 21(2): 367–397. http://scholarship.law.wm.edu/cgi/viewcontent.cgi?article=1638&context=wmborj (Accessed July 6, 2016).

Johnson, Marilyn, and Susan Carroll. 1978. "Statistical Report: Profile of Women Holding Public Office." In *Women in Public Office*, 2nd ed., edited by Kathy Stanwick and Marilyn Johnson, 1–65. Metuchen, NJ: Scarecrow Press.

Johnson, Paul M. 2013. "A Glossary of Political Economy Terms: Human Capital." www.auburn.edu/~johnspm/gloss/human_capital (Accessed July 6, 2016).

Joint Center for Political and Economic Studies (JCPES). 1991. *Black Elected Officials: A National Roster*. Washington, DC: Joint Center for Political and Economic Studies.

Jones-Correa, Michael. 2011. "Commonalities, Competition and Linked Fate." In *Just Neighbors? Research on African American and Latino Relations in the United States*, edited by Edward Telles, Mark Sawyer, and Gaspar Rivera-Salgado, 63–95. New York: Russell Sage Foundation.

Jordan-Zachery, Julia S. 2009. *Black Women, Cultural Images, and Social Policy*. New York: Routledge.

Joseph, Peniel. 2015. "'Selma' Backlash Misses the Point." *Code Switch: Frontiers of Race, Culture and Ethnicity*. National Public Radio (NPR) radio broadcast. www.npr.org/sections/codeswitch/2015/01/10/376081786/selma-backlash-misses-the-point. (Accessed July 5, 2016).

Junn, Jane, and Nadia Brown. 2008. "What Revolution? Incorporating Intersectionality in Women and Politics." In *Political Women and American Democracy*, edited by Christina Wolbrecht, Karen Beckwith, and Lisa Baldez, 64–78. New York: Cambridge University Press.

Kaba, Amadu Jacky, and Deborah E. Ward. 2009. "African Americans and U.S. Politics: The Gradual Progress of Black Women in Political Representation." *Review of Black Political Economy* 36(1): 29–50.

Kahn, Kim Fridkin. 1993. "Gender Differences in Campaign Messages: The Political Advertisements of Men and Women Candidates for U. S. Senate." *Political Research Quarterly* 46(3): 481–502.

Kaiser Family Foundation. 2001. "Toplines. Race and Ethnicity in 2001: Attitudes, Perceptions, and Experiences." *The Washington Post*/Kaiser

Family Foundation/Harvard University Survey Project. Research report #3143. http://files.kff.org/attachment/race-and-ethnicity-in-2001-attitudes-perceptions-topline (Accessed July 6, 2016).

Kalev, Alexandra, Erin Kelly, and Frank Dobbin. 2006. "Best Practices or Best Guesses? Assessing the Efficacy of Corporate Affirmative Action and Diversity Policies." *American Sociological Review* 71(4): 589–617.

Kallenberger, Kathryn Michele. 2015. "Performing Private Life on the Public Stage: Tracing Narratives of Presidential Family Lives, Leisure and Masculinities in US News Media." Master's thesis, University of Wisconsin Milwaukee. http://dc.uwm.edu/etd/809 (Accessed July 5, 2016).

Kane, Thomas J. 1998. "Racial and Ethnic Preferences in College Admissions." In *The Black-White Test Score Gap*, edited by Christopher Jencks and Meredith Phillips, 431–456. Washington, DC: Brookings Institution Press.

Kathlene, Lyn. 1994. "Power and Influence in State Legislative Policymaking: The Interaction of Gender and Position in Committee Hearing Debates." *American Political Science Review* 88(3): 560–576.

1995. "Position Power versus Gender Power: Who Holds the Floor?" In *Gender Power, Leadership, and Governance*, edited by Georgia Duerst-Lahti and Rita Mae Kelly, 167–193. Ann Arbor: University of Michigan Press.

Katznelson, Ira. 2005. *When Affirmative Action Was White: An Untold History of Racial Inequality in Twentieth-Century America*. New York: W. W. Norton.

Kaufmann, Karen M., and Antonio Rodriguez. 2011. "Political Behavior in the Context of Racial Diversity: The Case for Studying Local Politics." *PS: Political Science and Politics* 44(1): 101–102.

Kawahara, Debra M. 2007. "Making a Difference: Asian American Women Leaders." *Women and Therapy* 30(3–4): 17–33.

Kawahara, Debra M., Edna M. Esnil, and Jeanette Hsu. 2007. "Asian American Women Leaders: The Intersection of Race, Gender, and Leadership." In *Women and Leadership: Transforming Visions and Diverse Voices,* edited by J.L. Chin, B. Lott, J.K. Rice, and J. Sanchez-Hucles, 297–313. Malden, MA, and Oxford: Blackwell Publishing.

Kennedy, Randall. 1986. "Persuasion and Distrust: A Comment on the Affirmative Action Debate." *Harvard Law Review* 99(6): 1327–1346.

2011. *The Persistence of the Color Line: Racial Politics and the Obama Presidency*. New York: Pantheon Books.

Keyssar, Alexander. 2009. *The Right to Vote: The Contested History of Democracy in the United States*. Rev. ed. New York: Basic Books.

Kim, Claire Jean. 2000. *Bitter Fruit: The Politics of Black-Korean Conflict in New York City*. New Haven, CT: Yale University Press.

2001. "The Racial Triangulation of Asian Americans." In *Asian Americans and Politics: Perspectives, Experiences, and Prospects*, edited by Gordon H. Chang, 39–78. Stanford, CA: Stanford University Press.

Kimbrough, Walter M. 1995. "Self-Assessment, Participation, and Value of Leadership Skills, Activities, and Experiences for Black Students Relative to

Their Membership in Historically Black Fraternities and Sororities." *Journal of Negro Education* 64(1): 63–74.

Kimmell, Adrienne. 2014. Email communication with Carol Hardy-Fanta, January 15.

King, Athena, Todd Shaw, and Lester Spence. 2010. "Hype, Hip-Hop, and the Heartbreak: The Rise and Fall of Kwame Kilpatrick." In *Whose Black Politics? Cases in Post-Racial Black Leadership*, edited by Andra Gillespie, 105–129. New York: Routledge.

King, Deborah K. 1988. "Multiple Jeopardy, Multiple Consciousness: The Context of a Black Feminist Ideology." *Signs* 14(1): 42–72.

Klomp, Jeroen, and Jakob de Haan. 2013. "Political Regime and Human Capital: A Cross-Country Analysis." *Social Indicators Research* 111(1): 45–73.

Kluger, Richard. 1975. *Simple Justice: The History of Brown v. Board of Education and Black America's Struggle for Equality*, 1st ed. New York: Knopf Doubleday.

Konigsberg, Eric. 2014. "Who Killed Anna Mae?" *New York Times Magazine*, April 25, MM34. http://nyti.ms/1lNyFim (Accessed July 6, 2016).

Krane, Dale, Carol Ebdon, and John R. Bartle. 2004. "Devolution, Fiscal Federalism, and Changing Patterns of Municipal Revenues: The Mismatch between Theory and Reality." *Journal of Public Administration Research and Theory* 14(4): 513–533.

Kurtz, Donn M. 1989. "The Political Family: A Contemporary View." *Sociological Perspectives* 32(3): 331–352.

Kutner, Jenny. 2015. "Police and City Officials Resign after Missouri Town Elects First Black Female Mayor." *Salon*, April 20. www.salon.com/2015/04/20/police_and_city_officials_resign_after_missouri_town_elects_first_black_female_mayor/ (Accessed July 6, 2016).

Lai, James S., Wendy K. Tam Cho, Thomas P. Kim, and Okiyoshi Takeda. 2001. "Asian Pacific-American Campaigns, Elections, and Elected Officials." *PS: Political Science and Politics* 34(3): 611–617.

Land, Deborah. 2002. "Local School Boards under Review: Their Role and Effectiveness in Relation to Students' Academic Achievement." *Review of Educational Research* 72(2): 229–278.

Landry, Bart. 1987. *The New Black Middle Class*. Berkeley: University of California Press.

Lang, Clarence. 2015. *Black America in the Shadow of the Sixties: Notes on the Civil Rights Movement, Neoliberalism, and Politics*. Ann Arbor: University of Michigan Press.

Lawless, Jennifer L. 2004. "Politics of Presence? Congresswomen and Symbolic Representation." *Political Research Quarterly* 57(1): 81–99.

———. 2012. *Becoming a Candidate: Political Ambition and the Decision to Run for Office*. New York: Cambridge University Press.

Lawless, Jennifer L., and Richard L. Fox. 2005. *It Takes a Candidate: Why Women Don't Run for Office*. New York: Cambridge University Press.

———. 2010. *It Still Takes a Candidate: Why Women Don't Run for Office*. Rev. ed. New York: Cambridge University Press.

Lawless, Jennifer L., and Sean Theriault. 2006. "Women in the U.S. Congress: From Entry to Exit." In *Women in Politics: Outsiders or Insiders?*, 4th ed, edited by Lois Duke Whitaker, 164–181. Upper Saddle River, NJ: Pearson Prentice Hall.

Leal, David L., Valerie Martinez-Ebers, and Kenneth J. Meier. 2004. "The Politics of Latino Education: The Biases of At-Large Elections." *Journal of Politics* 66(4): 1224–1244.

Lee, Barbara. 2012. "Mother Knows Best." *Huffington Post*, May 9. www.huffingtonpost.com/barbara-lee/women-in-politics_b_1502667.html (Accessed July 6, 2016).

Lester Joan Steinau. 2003. *Eleanor Holmes Norton: Fire in My Soul*. First Atria Books hardcover edition. New York: Simon and Schuster.

Lewis, Gregory B., and Charles W. Gossett. 2008. "Changing Public Opinion on Same-Sex Marriage: The Case of California." *Politics and Policy* 36(1): 4–30.

Lien, Pei-te. 2001. *The Making of Asian America through Political Participation*. Philadelphia: Temple University Press.

——— 2006. "The Voting Rights Act and Its Implications for Three Nonblack Minorities." In *The Voting Rights Act: Securing the Ballot*, edited by Richard M. Vallely, 129–144. Landmark Events in U.S. History Series. Washington, DC: CQ Press.

Lien, Pei-te, Carol Hardy-Fanta, Dianne M. Pinderhughes, and Christine M. Sierra. 2007. "Exploring Dimensions of Interracial Connections between Asian and Other Nonwhite Elected Officials." Paper presented at the annual meeting of the Association for Asian American Studies, New York, April 4–7.

——— 2008. "Expanding Categorization at the Intersection of Race and Gender: 'Women of Color' as a Political Category for African American, Latina, Asian American, and American Indian Women." Paper presented at the annual meeting of the American Political Science Association, Boston, August 27–31.

Lien, Pei-te, Dianne M. Pinderhughes, Carol Hardy-Fanta, and Christine M. Sierra, 2007. "The Voting Rights Act and the Election of Nonwhite Officials." *PS: Political Science and Politics* 40(3): 489–494.

Lien, Pei-te, Dianne Pinderhughes, Christine Sierra, and Carol Hardy-Fanta. 2011. "Perceived Constituency Linkages and Dimensions of Representation among Racial Minorities in Subnational Levels of Office." Paper presented at the annual meeting of the American Political Science Association, Seattle, WA, September 1–4.

Lien, Pei-te, and Katie E. O. Swain. 2013. "Local Executive Leaders: At the Intersection of Race and Gender." In *Women and Executive Office: Pathways and Performance*, edited by Melody Rose, 137–156. Boulder, CO: Lynne Rienner.

Lim, Holly Ayesha Raña. 2014. "That's What She Said! Narratives of Asian American Women [*sic*] Political Leadership." Paper presented at the 2014 annual meeting of the Association for Asian American Studies, San Francisco, April 17–19.

Little, Thomas H., Dana Dunn, and Rebecca E. Deen. 2001. "A View from the Top: Gender Differences in Legislative Priorities among State Legislative Leaders." *Women and Politics* 22(4): 29–50.

Locke, Mamie E. 1997. "From Three-Fifths to Zero: Implications of the Constitution for African American Women, 1787–1879." In *Women Transforming Politics: An Alternative Reader*, edited by Cathy J. Cohen, Kathleen B. Jones, and Joan C. Tronto, 377–386. New York: New York University Press.

Lockhart, Emiley. 2013. "When to Discuss the 'I' Word." *EmergeAmerica* (blog), May 3. http://www.emergeamerica.org/blog/when-discuss-%E2%80%9CI%E2%80%9D-word (Accessed July 6, 2016).

Lowndes, Joseph, Julie Novkov, and Dorian T. Warren, eds. 2008. *Race and American Political Development*. New York: Routledge.

Lucas, Tamara, Rosemary Henze, and Ruben Donato. 1997. "Promoting the Success of Latino Language-Minority Students: An Exploratory Study of Six High Schools." In *Latinos and Education: A Critical Reader*, edited by Antonia Darder, Rodolfo D. Torres, and Henry Gutiérrez, 371–397. New York: Routledge.

Maciag, Mike. 2014. "Skyrocketing Court Fines are Major Revenue Generator for Ferguson." *Governing the States and Localities*, August 22. www.governing.com/topics/public-justice-safety/gov-ferguson-missouri-court-fines-budget.html (Accessed July 6, 2016).

MacManus, Susan A. 1996. "County Boards, Partisanship, and Elections." In *The American County: Frontiers of Knowledge*, edited by Donald C. Menzel, 53–79. Tuscaloosa: University of Alabama Press.

MacManus, Susan A., Charles S. Bullock III, Karen Padgett, and Brittany Penberthy. 2006. "Women Winning at the Local Level: Are County and School Board Positions Becoming More Desirable and Plugging the Pipeline to Higher Office?" In *Women in Politics: Outsiders Or Insiders? A Collection of Readings*, 4th ed., edited by Lois Duke Whitaker, 117–136. Upper Saddle River, NJ: Pearson Prentice Hall.

Maestas, Cherie. 2000. "Professional Legislatures and Ambitious Politicians: Policy Responsiveness of State Institutions." *Legislative Studies Quarterly* 25(4):663–690.

Maestas, Cherie D., Sarah Fulton, L. Sandy Maisel, and Walter J. Stone. 2006. "When to Risk it? Institutions, Ambitions, and the Decision to Run for the U.S. House." *American Political Science Review* 100(2): 195–208.

Maestas, Cherie D., and Cynthia R. Rugeley. 2008. "Assessing the 'Experience Bonus' through Examining Strategic Entry, Candidate Quality, and Campaign Receipts in U.S. House Elections." *American Journal of Political Science* 52(3): 520–535.

Mandel, Ruth B., and Katherine E. Kleeman. 2004. *Political Generation Next: America's Young Elected Leaders*. Report. New Brunswick, NJ: Eagleton Institute of Politics, Rutgers University.

Manning, Jennifer E. 2014. *Membership of the 113th Congress*. CRS Report R42964, January 13. Washington, DC: Congressional Research Service.

Manning, Jennifer E., and Ida A. Brudnick. 2014. *Women in the United States Congress, 1917–2014: Biographical and Committee Assignment Information, and Listings by State and Congress*. CRS Report RL30261, October 31. Washington, DC: Congressional Research Service.

Mansbridge, Jane. 1999. "Should Blacks Represent Blacks and Women Represent Women? A Contingent 'Yes'." *Journal of Politics* 61(3): 628–657.

Mansbridge, Jane., and Katherine Tate. 1992. "Race Trumps Gender: The Thomas Nomination in the Black Community." *PS: Political Science and Politics* 25(3): 488–492.

Manuel, Tiffany. 2006. "Envisioning the Possibilities for a Good Life: Exploring the Public Policy Implications of Intersectionality Theory." In *Intersectionality and Politics: Recent Research on Gender, Race, and Political Representation in the United States*, edited by Carol Hardy-Fanta, 173–203. New York: Routledge.

Mariani, Mack D. 2008. "A Gendered Pipeline? The Advancement of State Legislators to Congress in Five States." *Politics and Gender* 4(2): 285–308.

Márquez, Benjamin. 2003. *Constructing Identities in Mexican American Political Organizations: Choosing Issues, Taking Sides.* Austin: University of Texas Press.

Marschall, Melissa, and Paru Shah. 2015. "Dialogue: Local Elections in American Politics. Introduction." *Politics, Groups, and Identities* 3(2): 274–277.

Marschall, Melissa, Paru Shah, and Anirudh Ruhil. 2011. "Symposium: The Study of Local Elections." *PS: Political Science and Politics* 44(1): 97–100.

Masud-Piloto, Felix Roberto. 1996. *From Welcomed Exiles to Illegal Immigrants: Cuban Migration to The U.S., 1959–1995.* Lanham, MD: Rowman and Littlefield.

Masuoka, Natalie. 2008. "Political Attitudes and Ideologies of Multiracial Americans: The Implications of Mixed Race in the United States." *Political Research Quarterly* 61(2): 253–267.

Mayhew, David R. 1974. *Congress: The Electoral Connection.* New Haven, CT: Yale University Press.

McClain, Paula D., and Joseph Stewart Jr. 2002. *"Can We All Get Along?" Racial and Ethnic Minorities in American Politics*, 2nd ed. Boulder, CO: Westview Press.

McCool, Daniel, Susan M. Olson, and Jennifer L. Robinson. 2007. *Native Vote: American Indians, the Voting Rights Act, and the Right to Vote.* New York: Cambridge University Press.

McCrary, Peyton. 2003. "Bringing Equality to Power: How the Federal Courts Transformed the Electoral Structure of Southern Politics, 1960–1990." *University of Pennsylvania Journal of Constitutional Law* 5: 665–708.

McDonagh, Eileen. 2009. *The Motherless State: Women's Political Leadership and American Democracy.* Chicago: University of Chicago Press.

McGee, Jennifer. 2011. "Conspiracy Theory in the Age of the Internet: The Case of the 'Birthers'." Unpublished manuscript. http://aska-r.aasa.ac.jp/dspace/bit-stream/10638/1155/1/0041-001-201103-053-066.pdf (Accessed July 6, 2016).

Meier, Kenneth J. and Robert E. England. 1984. "Black Representation and Educational Policy: Are They Related?" *American Political Science Review* 78(2): 329–403.

Merl, Jean. 2012. "Obituaries: Mervyn Dymally 1926–2012. Groundbreaker in California Politics." *Los Angeles Times.* http://articles.latimes.com/2012/oct/08/local/la-me-mervyn-dymally-20121008 (Accessed July 6, 2016).

Mettler, Suzanne. 2005. "'The Only Good Thing Was the GI Bill': Effects of the Education and Training Provisions on African-American Veterans' Political Participation." *Studies in American Political Development* 19(1): 31–52.

Mezey, Susan Gluck. 1980. "Perceptions of Women's Roles on Local Councils in Connecticut." In *Women in Local Politics*, edited by D. W. Stewart, 177–197. Metuchen, NJ: Scarecrow Press.

Michelson, Melissa R. 2010. "Majority-Latino Districts and Latino Political Power." *Duke Journal of Constitutional Law & Public Policy* 5: 159–175.

Miler, Kristina C. 2007. "The View from the Hill: Legislative Perceptions of the District." *Legislative Studies Quarterly* 32(4): 597–628.

    2010. *Constituency Representation in Congress: The View from Capitol Hill.* New York: Cambridge University Press.

Miller, Kevin. 2015. "Tribal Representatives Withdraw from Maine Legislature as Rift with State Grows." *Portland Press Herald*, May 26.

Miller, Lisa. 2014. "Racialized State Failure and the Violent Death of Michael Brown." *Theory and Event* 17(3). http://muse.jhu.edu/journals/theory_and_event/vo17/17.3S.miller.html (Accessed July 6, 2016).

Mills, David. 1990. "The Wrongs of the Rites of Brotherhood." *Washington Post*, June 18: B1, B6. http://wpo.st/Fvuto (Accessed July 6, 2016).

Minta, Michael D. 2011. *Oversight: Representing the Interests of Blacks and Latinos in Congress.* Princeton, NJ: Princeton University Press.

    2012. "Gender, Race, Ethnicity, and Political Representation in the United States." *Politics and Gender* 8(4): 541–547.

Mohanty, Chandra Talpade. 1984. "Under Western Eyes: Feminist Scholarship and Colonial Discourses." *Boundary* 2(12/13): 333–358.

Moncrief, Gary F., Peverill Squire, and Malcolm E. Jewell. 2001. *Who Runs for the Legislature?* Upper Saddle River, NJ: Prentice Hall.

Moncrief, Gary F., and Joel A. Thompson. 1992. "Electoral Structure and State Legislative Representation: A Research Note." *Journal of Politics* 54(1): 246–256.

Moncrief, Gary, Joel Thompson, and Robert Schuhmann. 1991. "Gender, Race, and the State Legislature: A Research Note on the Double Disadvantage Hypothesis." *The Social Science Journal* 28(4): 481–487.

Montejano, David. 1987. *Anglos and Mexicans in the Making of Texas, 1836–1986.* Austin: University of Texas Press.

Montoya, Lisa J., Carol Hardy-Fanta, and Sonia Garcia. 2000. "Latina Politics: Gender, Participation, and Leadership." *PS: Political Science and Politics* 33(3): 555–562.

Moore, Robert G. 2005. "Religion, Race, and Gender Differences in Political Ambition." *Politics and Gender* 1(4): 577–596.

Mora, Magdalena, and Adelaida R. Del Castillo, eds. 1980. *Mexican Women in the United States: Struggles Past and Present.* Occasional Paper No. 2. Los Angeles: Chicano Studies Research Center Publications, University of California, Los Angeles.

Moraga, Cherríe, and Gloria Anzaldúa, eds. 2015. *This Bridge Called My Back: Writings by Radical Women of Color*. 4th ed. Albany: State University of New York Press.

Moran, Rachel F. 2005. "Undone by Law: The Uncertain Legacy of Lau v. Nichols." *Berkeley La Raza Law Journal* 16(1): 1–10.

Muñoz, Carlos, Jr., and Charles P. Henry. 1990. "Coalition Politics in San Antonio and Denver: The Cisneros and Peña Mayoral Campaigns." In *Racial Politics in American Cities*, edited by Rufus P. Browning, Dale Rogers Marshall, and David H. Tabb, 179–190. New York: Longman.

Myers, Ardie. 1997. "Review: *National Association of Colored Women's Clubs, 1895–1992. Part 1: Minutes of the National Conventions, Publications, and President's Office Correspondence. Part 2: President's Office Files, 1958–1968*, by Lillian Serece Williams, Randolph Boehm; *A Guide to the Records of the Microfilm Edition of the National Association of Colored Women's Clubs, 1895–1992. Part 1: Minutes of the National Conventions, Publications, and President's Office Files, 1958–1968*, by Lillian Serece Williams, Randolph Boehm." *Journal of American History* 84(1): 260–261.

NACo (National Association of Counties). 2015. "Learn About [*sic*] What Counties Do: County Characteristics," www.naco.org/counties/learn-about-what-counties-do (Accessed July 6, 2016).

Nakanishi, Don, and James S. Lai, eds. 2003. *Asian American Politics: Law, Participation, and Policy*. Lanham, MD: Rowman and Littlefield.

NALEO (National Association of Latino Elected and Appointed Officials). 2007. "A Profile of Latino Elected Officials in the United States and their Progress since 1996." Los Angeles: National Association of Latino Elected Officials (NALEO) Educational Fund.

2011. "Directory of Latino Elected Officials: Hispanic Political Leadership Facts." Unpublished fact sheet.

2012. National Directory of Latino Elected Officials. Los Angeles: National Association of Latino Elected Officials (NALEO) Educational Fund.

2014. "At-A-Glance: Latino Elected Officials." *National Directory of Latino Elected Officials: NALEO Educational Fund*. www.naleo.org/at_a_glance (Accessed July 6, 2016).

National Center for Education Statistics. 2011–2012. "State Education Data Profiles: Hawaii." http://nces.ed.gov/programs/stateprofiles/sresult.asp?mode=short&s1=15 (Accessed July 6, 2016).

National League of Cities. 2013a. "Characteristics. Race and Ethnicity." City Councils. www.nlc.org/build-skills-and-networks/resources/cities-101/city-officials/city-councils (Accessed July 6, 2016).

2013b. "Number of Municipal Governments and Population Distribution." www.nlc.org/build-skills-and-networks/resources/cities-101/city-structures/number-of-municipal-governments-and-population-distribution (Accessed July 6, 2016).

Navarro, Sharon A. 2008. *Latina Legislator: Leticia Van De Putte and the Road to Leadership*. College Station: Texas A&M University Press.

Nelson, Albert J. 1991. *Emerging Influentials in State Legislatures: Women, Blacks, and Hispanics*. Westport, CT: Praeger.

Nelson, William E. 2000. *Black Atlantic Politics: Dilemmas of Political Empowerment in Boston and Liverpool.* SUNY Series in Afro-American Studies. Paperback edition. Albany: State University of New York Press.

Nepstad, Sharon Erickson, and Clifford Bob. 2006. "When Do Leaders Matter? Hypotheses on Leadership Dynamics in Social Movements." *Mobilization: An International Journal* 11(1): 1–22.

NHLA (National Hispanic Leadership Agenda). 2014. "National Hispanic Leadership Agenda 113th Congressional Scorecard." Report. http://national-hispanicleadership.org/images/Scorecards/NHLA_2014scorecard_090915_forweb_2.pdf (Accessed July 6, 2016).

Nir, David. 2015. "Just How Many Elected Officials Are There in the United States? The Answer Is Mind-Blowing." *Daily Kos.* March 29. www.dailykos.com/story/2015/03/29/1372225/-Just-how-many-elected-officials-are-there-in-the-United-States-The-answer-is-mind-blowing# (Accessed July 6, 2016).

Niven, David. 1998. "Party Elites and Women Candidates: The Shape of Bias." *Journal of Women and Politics* 19(2): 57–80.

Nnamaeka, Obioma. 2015. "Womanism – Bibliography: Black. Women. Feminism. Womanist." *Science Encyclopedia* [free online]. http://science.jrank.org/pages/8159/Womanism.html (Accessed July 6, 2016).

Nobles, Melissa. 2000. *Shades of Citizenship: Race and the Census in Modern Politics.* Stanford, CA: Stanford University Press.

NORC. 2013. "1989 Prestige Scores. Appendix F: Occupational Classification Distributions." *General Social Surveys, 1972–2012: Cumulative Codebook,* 2,993-3000. https://study.sagepub.com/sites/default/files/gss_codebook.pdf (Accessed July 6, 2016).

O'Connor, Karen. 2003. "Do Women in Local, State, and National Legislative Bodies Matter? A Definitive Yes Proves Three Decades of Research by Political Scientists." *Why Women Matter Summit,* 24–26. Washington, DC: The White House Project.

O'Lear, Casey. 2012. "Women Win When Women Work Together." *EmergeAmerica* (blog). www.emergeamerica.org/news/women-win-when-women-work-together (Accessed July 6, 2016).

Oliver, Melvin, and Thomas M. Shapiro. 2006. *Black Wealth, White Wealth: A New Perspective on Racial Inequality.* Tenth anniversary edition. New York: Routledge.

Omi, Michael, and Howard Winant. 2015. *Racial Formation in the United States,* 3rd ed. New York: Routledge.

Ong, Elena. 2003. "Transcending the Bamboo and Class Ceilings: Defining the Trajectory to Empower Asian Pacific Islander American Women in Politics." In *Asian American Politics: Law, Participation, and Policy,* edited by Don T. Nakanishi and James S. Lai, 331–354. Lanham, MD: Rowman and Littlefield.

Orey, Byron D., L. Marvin Overby, and Christopher W. Larimer. 2007. "African-American Committee Chairs in U.S. State Legislatures." *Social Science Quarterly* 88(3): 619–639.

Pachon, Harry, and Louis DeSipio. 1992. "Latino Elected Officials in the 1990s." *PS: Political Science and Politics* 25(2): 212–217.

Palmer, Barbara, and Dennis Simon. 2008. *Breaking the Political Glass Ceiling: Women and Congressional Elections*, 2nd ed. New York: Routledge.

Palus, Christine Kelleher. 2011. "Tribulations, Triumphs, and Tentative Trajectories in the Study of Local Political Participation." *PS: Political Science and Politics* 44(1): 113–114.

Park, Edward J.W., and John S.W. Park. 2001. "Korean Americans and the Crisis of the Liberal Coalition: Immigrants and Politics in Los Angeles." In *Governing American Cities: Interethnic Coalitions, Competition, and Conflict*, edited by Michael Jones-Correa, 91–108. New York: Russell Sage Foundation.

Parker, Brenda. 2008. "Beyond the Class Act: Gender and Race in the 'Creative City' Discourse." In *Gender in an Urban World*, edited by Judith N. DeSena, 201–232. Research in Urban Sociology, Vol. 9, 1st ed. Bingley, UK: JAI Press, Emerald Publishing.

Parker, Christopher S. 2009. *Fighting for Democracy: Black Veterans and the Struggle against White Supremacy in the Postwar South*. Princeton Studies in American Politics Series, edited by Ira Katznelson, Martin Shefter, and Theda Skocpol. Princeton, NJ: Princeton University Press.

Parker, Frank R. 1990. *Black Votes Count: Political Empowerment in Mississippi after 1965*. Chapel Hill: University of North Carolina Press.

Patterson, Orlando. 2009. "Race and Diversity in the Age of Obama." *Sunday Book Review, New York Times*, August 14, BR23.

Paxton, Pamela, Matthew A. Painter II, and Melanie M. Hughes. 2009. "Year of the Woman, Decade of Man: Trajectories of Growth in Women's State Legislative Representation." *Social Science Research* 38(1): 86–102.

Payne, Charles. 1995. *I've Got the Light of Freedom: The Organizing Tradition and the Mississippi Freedom Struggle*. Berkeley and Los Angeles: University of California Press.

Perea, Juan F. 1992. "Demography and Distrust: An Essay on American Languages, Cultural Pluralism, and Official English." *Minnesota Law Review* 77: 269–373.

Perry, Huey L., and Wayne Parent, eds. 1995. *Blacks and the American Political System*, 1st ed. Gainesville: University Press of Florida.

Persily, Nathaniel. 2007. "The Promise and Pitfalls of the New Voting Rights Act." *Yale Law Journal* 117(2): 174–254.

Pettit, Becky, and Bruce Western. 2004. "Mass Imprisonment and the Life Course: Race and Class Inequality in U.S. Incarceration." *American Sociological Review* 69(2): 151–169.

Pew Research Center. 2015a. "Support for Same-Sex Marriage at Record High, but Key Segments Remain Opposed." Research report. Washington, DC: Pew Research Center, June 8. www.people-press.org/2015/06/08/support-for-same-sex-marriage-at-record-high-but-key-segments-remain-opposed/ (Accessed July 6, 2016).

2015b. "Changing Attitudes on Gay Marriage." Graphics and Slideshow, July 29. www.pewforum.org/2015/07/29/graphics-slideshow-changing-attitudes-on-gay-marriage/ (Accessed July 6, 2016).

Philips, Anne. 1995. *Politics of Presence*. New York: Clarenden Press, Oxford University Press.

ed. 1998. *Feminism and Politics*. New York: Oxford University Press.

1999.*Which Inequalities Matter?* Malden, MA: Polity Press.

Philpot, Tasha S., and Hanes Walton Jr. 2007. "One of Our Own: Black Female Candidates and the Voters Who Support Them." *American Journal of Political Science* 51(1): 49–62.

Pieper, Mary. 2013. "Emily's List Works to Get Democratic Women Elected to Public Office." *Globe Gazette*, August 10. http://globegazette.com/news/local/emily-s-list-works-to-get-democratic-women-elected-to/article_43dd1doc-0170-11e3-89ff-0019bb2963f4.html (Accessed July 6, 2016).

Pinderhughes, Dianne M. 1987. *Race and Ethnicity in Chicago Politics: A Reexamination of Pluralist Theory*. Urbana and Chicago: University of Illinois Press.

1992. "Divisions in the Civil Rights Community," in Politics, Values, and the Thomas Nomination, PS: Political Science and Politics, 25(3): 485–487.

1993. "The Civil Rights Movement." In *Black Women in America: An Historical Encyclopedia*, Vol. 2, edited by Darlene Clark Hine, Elsa Barkley Brown, and Rosalyn Terborg-Penn, 239–241. Brooklyn, NY: Carlson Publishing.

1995. "Black Interest Groups and the 1982 Extension of the Voting Rights Act." In *Blacks and the American Political System*, edited by Huey Perry and Wayne Parent, 203–224. Gainesville: University Press of Florida.

2003. "Urban Racial and Ethnic Politics." In *Cities, Politics, and Policy: A Comparative Analysis*, ed. John P. Pelissero. Washington, DC: Congressional Quarterly Press, 97–125.

2011. "What's Left of the Obama Presidency and Change Politics." Paper presented at the 43rd Meeting of the National Conference of Black Political Scientists, Las Vegas, NV, December 15.

Pinderhughes, Dianne, Pei-te Lien, Christine Sierra, and Carol Hardy-Fanta. 2009. "How *Do* We Get Along? Linked Fate, Political Allies, and Issue Coalitions." Paper presented at the annual meeting of the American Political Science Association, Toronto, Canada, September 2–6.

Pitkin, Hanna Fenichel. 1967. *The Concept of Representation*. Berkeley: University of California Press.

Pittinsky, Todd L., Laura M. Bacon, and Brian Welle. 2007. "The Great Women Theory of Leadership? Perils of Positive Stereotypes and Precarious Pedestals." In *Women and Leadership: The State of Play and Strategies for Change*, edited by Barbara Kellerman and Deborah L. Rhode, 93–116. San Francisco: John Wiley & Sons.

Polinard, Jerry L., Robert D. Wrinkle, and Tomas Longoria. 1990. "Education and Governance: Representational Links to Second Generation Discrimination." *Political Research Quarterly* 43(3): 631–646.

Press, Bill. 2012. *The Obama Hate Machine: The Lies, Distortions, and Personal Attacks on the President – and Who Is Behind Them*. Hardcover edition. New York: Thomas Dunne Books (St. Martin's Press).

Prindeville, Diane-Michele. 2002. "A Comparative Study of Native American and Hispanic Women in Grassroots and Electoral Politics." *Frontiers: A Journal of Women Studies* 23(1), 67–89.

———. 2003. "'I've seen Changes': The Political Efficacy of American Indian and Hispanic Women Leaders." *Women and Politics* 25(1/2): 89–113.

———. 2004a. "The Role of Gender, Race/Ethnicity, and Class in Activists' Perceptions of Environmental Justice." In *New Perspectives on Environmental Justice: Gender, Sexuality, and Activism*, edited by Rachel Stein, 93–108. New Brunswick, NJ: Rutgers University Press.

———. 2004b. "Feminist Nations? A Study of Native American Women in Southwestern Tribal Politics." *Political Research Quarterly* 57(1): 101–112.

Prindeville, Diane-Michele, and John G. Bretting. 1998. "Indigenous Women Activists and Political Participation: The Case of Environmental Justice." *Women and Politics* 19(1): 39–58.

Prinz, Timothy S. 1993. "The Career Paths of Elected Politicians: A Review and Prospectus." In *Ambition and Beyond: Career Paths of American Politicians*, edited by Shirley Williams and Edward L. Lasher, 11–63. Berkeley: Institute of Governmental Studies.

Pritchard, Anita. 1992. "Changes in Electoral Structures and the Success of Women Candidates: The Case of Florida." *Social Science Quarterly* 73(1): 62–70.

Pulido, Laura. 2006. *Black, Brown, Yellow, and Left: Radical Activism in Los Angeles*. Berkeley: University of California Press.

Ransford, Paige, and Meryl Thomson. 2011. "Moving through the Pipeline: Women's Representation in Municipal Government in the New England Region of the United States." In *Women and Representation in Local Government: International Case Studies*, edited by Barbara Pini and Paula McDonald, 21–36. New York: Routledge.

Reed, Adolph L., Jr. 1986. *The Jesse Jackson Phenomenon: The Crisis of Purpose in Afro-American Politics*. New Haven, CT: Yale University Press.

Reed, Adolph L. 2000. *Class Notes: Posing as Politics and Other Thoughts on the American Scene*. New York: New Press.

Rehfeld, Andrew. 2009. "Representation Rethought: On Trustees, Delegates, and Gyroscopes in the Study of Political Representation and Democracy." *American Political Science Review* 103(2): 214–230.

Reingold, Beth. 1996. "Conflict and Cooperation: Legislative Strategies and Concepts of Power among Female and Male State Legislators." *Journal of Politics* 58(2): 464–485.

———. 2000. *Representing Women: Sex, Gender, and Legislative Behavior in Arizona and California*. Chapel Hill: University of North Carolina Press.

———. 2008a. "Understanding the Complex World of Women in US Politics." In *Legislative Women: Getting Elected, Getting Ahead*, edited by Beth Reingold, 1–17. Boulder, CO: Lynne Rienner.

———. 2008b. "Women as Officeholders: Linking Descriptive and Substantive Representation." In *Political Women and American Democracy*, edited by Christina Wolbrecht, Karen Beckwith, and Lisa Baldez, 128–147. New York: Cambridge University Press.

Reingold, Beth, and Jessica Harrell. 2010. "The Impact of Descriptive Representation on Women's Political Engagement: Does Party Matter?" *Political Research Quarterly* 63(2): 280–294.

Reingold, Beth, and Kerry L. Haynie. 2014. "Representing Women's Interests and Intersections of Gender, Race, and Ethnicity in U.S. State Legislatures." In *Representation: The Case of Women*, edited by Maria C. Escobar-Lemmon and Michelle M. Taylor-Robinson, 183–204. New York: Oxford University Press.

Reingold, Beth, and Adrienne R. Smith. 2012. "Welfare Policymaking and Intersections of Race, Ethnicity, and Gender in U.S. State Legislatures." *American Journal of Political Science* 56(1): 131–147.

2014. "Legislative Leadership and Intersections of Gender, Race, and Ethnicity in the American States." Paper prepared for presentation at the Annual Meetings of the American Political Science Association, Washington, DC, August 28–31.

Reynolds, Glenn Harlan. 2014. "Asians Get the Ivy League's Jewish Treatment." *USA Today*, November 24. http://usat.ly/1zPOolf (Accessed July 6, 2016).

Riley, Jason L. 2015. "The New Jews of Harvard Admissions: Asian-Americans are Rebelling over Evidence that They Are Held to a Much Higher Standard, but Elite Colleges Deny Using Quotas." *Wall Street Journal*, May 19. http://on.wsj.com/1AqQ1Jr (Accessed July 6, 2016).

Rinehart, Sue Tolleson. 1991. "Do Women Leaders Make a Difference? Substance, Style and Perceptions." In *Gender and Policymaking: Studies of Women in Office*, edited by Debra L. Dodson, 93-102. New Brunswick, NJ: Center for the American Woman and Politics (CAWP), Eagleton Institute of Politics, Rutgers University.

Robinson, Ted, and Robert E. England. 1981. "Black Representation on Central City School Boards Revisited." *Social Science Quarterly* 62(3): 495–502.

Robinson, Toni, and Greg Robinson. 2006. "The Limits of Interracial Coalitions: Mendez v. Westminster Reexamined." In *Racial Transformations: Latinos and Asians Remaking the United States*, edited by Nicholas De Genova, 93–119. Durham, NC: Duke University Press.

Robson, Deborah Carol. 2000. "Stereotypes and the Female Politician: A Case Study of Senator Barbara Mikulski." *Communication Quarterly* 48(3): 205–222.

Rocca, Michael S., Gabriel R. Sanchez, and Jason L. Morin. 2011. "The Institutional Mobility of Minority Members of Congress." *Political Research Quarterly* 64: 897–909.

Rogers, Melvin L. 2014. "Introduction: Disposable Lives." *Theory and Event* 17(3). [Online]. http://muse.jhu.edu/journals/theory_and_event/vo17/17.3S.rogers.html (Accessed July 6, 2016).

Rosenthal, Cindy Simon. 1998a. *When Women Lead: Integrative Leadership in State Legislatures*. New York: Oxford University Press.

1998b. "Getting Things Done: Women Committee Chairpersons in State Legislatures." In *Women and Elective Office: Past, Present, and Future*, edited by Sue Thomas and Clyde Wilcox, 175–187. New York: Oxford University Press.

Ross, Janell. 2015. "Are Race Relations Really Worse under President Obama?"

Online news analysis. Washington Post. Online news analysis. https://www
.washingtonpost.com/news/the-fix/wp/2015/08/04/are-race-relations-really-
worse-under-president-obama/ (Accessed July 4, 2016).

Rosser-Mims, Dionne M. 2005. "An Exploration of Black Women's Political
Leadership Development." PhD dissertation, University of Georgia.

2010. "Black Feminism: An Epistemological Framework for Exploring
how Race and Gender Impact Black Women's Leadership Development."
Advancing Women in Leadership Journal 30(15): 1–17. http://awljournal.
org/Vol30_2010/Rosser-Mims_black%20feminism_vol_30_No_15_9_21_
10.pdf (Accessed July 6, 2016).

Rucker, Mary L. 2013. *Obama's Political Saga: From Battling History,
Racialized Rhetoric, and GOP Obstructionism to Re-Election.* Lanham,
MD: Lexington Books.

Rudolph, Thomas J., Amy Gangl, and Dan Stevens. 2000. "The Effects of
Efficacy and Emotions on Campaign Involvement." *Journal of Politics*
62(4): 1189–1197.

Rule, Wilma. 1992. "Multimember Legislative Districts: Minority and Anglo
Women's and Men's Recruitment Opportunity." In *United States Electoral
Systems: Their Impact on Women and Minorities,* edited by Wilma Rule and
Joseph F. Zimmerman, 57–72. Contributions in Political Science, Number
294.New York: Greenwood Press.

Rusin, Sylvia, Jie Zong, and Jeanne Batalova. 2015. "Cuban Immigrants in the
United States." *Migration Information Source: The Online Journal of the
Migration Policy Institute,* April 7. www.migrationpolicy.org/article/cuban-
immigrants-united-states (Accessed July 6, 2016).

Ryan, William. 2002. "The Unz Initiatives and the Abolition of Bilingual
Education." *Boston College Law Review* 43(2): 487–519. http://lawdigitalc-
ommons.bc.edu/bclr/vol43/iss2/4 (Accessed July 6, 2016).

Saint-Germain, Michelle A. 1992. "Patterns of Legislative Opportunity in
Arizona: Sex, Race, and Ethnicity." In *United States Electoral Systems: Their
Impact on Women and Minorities,* edited by Wilma Rule and Joseph
F. Zimmerman, 119–128. Contributions in Political Science, No. 294.
New York: Greenwood Press.

Saito, Leland T. 1998. *Race and Politics: Asian Americans, Latinos, and
Whites in a Los Angeles Suburb.* Urbana and Chicago: University of
Illinois Press.

2009. *The Politics of Exclusion: The Failure of Race-Neutral Policies in Urban
America.* Stanford, CA: Stanford University Press.

Salomone, Rosemary C. 2010. *True American: Language, Identity, and the
Education of Immigrant Children.* Cambridge, MA: Harvard University
Press.

Salter, Jim, and Jim Suhr. 2015. "Ferguson Election Triples Number of Blacks
on City Council." *Associated Press,* April 8. www.voanews.com/content/ap-
ferguson-election-triples-number-of-blacks-on-city-council/2710984.html
(Accessed July 6, 2016).

Samuelsohn, Darren. 2015. "Rudy Giuliani: President Obama Doesn't Love
America: The Former New York Mayor Makes His Remarks at a Scott Walker

Event." *Politico*, February 18. www.politico.com/story/2015/02/rudy-giuliani-president-obama-doesnt-love-america-115309 (Accessed July 6, 2016).

Samuelson, Donald L. 2009. "Black Enough for Me." In *Family Affair: What It Means to be African American Today*, edited by Gil L. Robertson, 367–370. Chicago: Bolden Books, Agate Publishing.

Sanbonmatsu, Kira. 2002. "Political Parties and the Recruitment of Women to State Legislatures." *Journal of Politics* 64(3): 791–809.

——— 2003. "Candidate Recruitment and Women's Election to the State Legislatures." Report. New Brunswick, NJ: Center for American Women and Politics, Rutgers University. www.cawp.rutgers.edu/sites/default/files/resources/candrecruitment_0.pdf (Accessed July 6, 2016).

——— 2006a. *Where Women Run: Gender and Party in the American States*. Ann Arbor: University of Michigan Press.

——— 2006b. "Gender Pools and Puzzles: Charting a 'Women's Path' to the Legislature." *Politics and Gender* 2(3): 387–400.

Sanbonmatsu, Kira, Susan J. Carroll, and Debbie Walsh. 2009. *Poised to Run: Women's Pathways to the State Legislatures*. New Brunswick, NJ: Center for American Women and Politics, Rutgers University.

Sandberg, Sheryl, with Nell Scovell. 2013. *Lean in: Women, Work and the Will to Lead*. New York: Alfred A. Knopf.

Schenken, Suzanne O'Dea. 1999. *From Suffrage to the Senate: An Encyclopedia of American Women in Politics*, Vol. 1: A–M. Santa Barbara: ABC-CLIO.

Schiffer, Molly A. 2014. "Women of Color and Crime: A Critical Race Theory Perspective to Address Disparate Prosecution." *Arizona Law Review* 56: 1203–1225.

Schlesinger, Joseph A. 1966. *Ambition and Politics: Political Careers in the United States*. Chicago: Rand McNally.

Schmidt, Ronald Sr., Edwina Barvosa-Carter, and Rodolfo D. Torres. 2000. "Latina/o Identities: Social Diversity and U. S. Politics." *PS: Political Science and Politics* 33(3): 563–567.

Schneider, Judy. 2015. "House Standing Committee Chairs and Ranking Minority Members: Rules Governing Selection Procedures." CRS Report RS21165, November 23. Washington, DC: Congressional Research Service. www.fas.org/sgp/crs/misc/RS21165.pdf (Accessed July 6, 2016).

Schroedel, Jean Reith, and Marcia L. Godwin. 2005. "Prospects for Cracking the Political Glass Ceiling: The Future of Women Officeholders in the Twenty-First Century." In *Women and Elective Office: Past, Present, and Future*, 2nd ed., edited by Sue Thomas and Clyde Wilcox, 264–280. New York: Oxford University Press.

Schwindt-Bayer, Leslie A., and William Mishler. 2005. "An Integrated Model of Women's Representation." *Journal of Politics* 67(2): 407–428.

Scola, Becki. 2006. "Women of Color in State Legislatures: Gender, Race, Ethnicity and Legislative Office Holding." In *Intersectionality and Politics: Recent Research on Gender, Race, and Political Representation in the United States*, edited by Carol Hardy-Fanta, 43–70. New York: Routledge.

——— 2014. *Gender, Race, and Office Holding in the United States: Representation at the Intersections*, 1st ed. New York: Routledge.

Shah, Paru. 2015. "Dialogue: Local Elections in American Politics. Stepping Up: Black Political Ambition and Success." *Politics, Groups, and Identities* 3(2): 278–294.

Shaw, Todd, Louis DeSipio, Dianne Pinderhughes, and Toni-Michelle C. Travis. 2015. *Uneven Roads: An Introduction to U.S. Racial and Ethnic Politics.* Thousand Oaks, CA: SAGE CQ Press.

Shrestha, Laura B. 2006. *The Changing Demographic Profile of the United States.* CRS Report for Congress RL32701, May 5. Washington, DC: Congressional Research Service.

Sierra, Christine Marie. 1993. "Chicano Political Development: Historical Considerations." In *Beyond 1848: Readings in the Modern Chicano Historical Experience*, edited by Michael R. Ornelas, 159–177. Dubuque, IA: Kendall/Hunt Publishing.

———. 2010. "Latinas and Electoral Politics: Movin' on Up." In *Gender and Elections: Shaping the Future of American Politics*, 2nd ed., edited by Susan J. Carroll and Richard L. Fox, 144–164. New York: Cambridge University Press.

Sierra, Christine Marie., and Adaljiza Sosa-Riddell. 1994. "Chicanas as Political Actors: Rare Literature, Complex Practice." *National Political Science Review* 4: 297–317.

Silver, Larry B., Barbara J. Silver, Morton M. Silverman, William Prescott, and Luisa del Pollard. 1985. "The Cuban Immigration of 1980: A Special Mental Health Challenge." *Public Health Reports(1974–) Association of Schools of Public Health* 100(1): 40–48.

Simien, Evelyn M. 2006. *Black Feminist Voices in Politics.* Albany: State University of New York Press.

Sjoberg, Laura. 2014. "Feminism." In *The Oxford Handbook of Political Leadership*, edited by R.A.W. Rhodes and Paul 'T Hart, 72–86. New York: Oxford University Press.

Skocpol, Theda, and Vanessa Williamson. 2012. *The Tea Party and the Remaking of Republican Conservatism.* New York: Oxford University Press.

Skowronek, Stephen. 2003. *The Politics Presidents Make: Leadership from John Adams to Bill Clinton*, 6th ed. Cambridge, MA: Harvard University Press.

Smith, Adrienne R., Beth Reingold, and Michael Leo Owens. 2012. "The Political Determinants of Women's Descriptive Representation in Cities." *Political Research Quarterly* 65(2): 315–329.

Smith, Heather A., and Owen J. Furuseth, eds. 2006. *Latinos in the New South: Transformations of Place.* Burlington, VT: Ashgate.

Smith, Jennifer E. 1999. "ONAMOVE: African American Women Confronting the Prison Crisis." In *Still Lifting, Still Climbing: Contemporary African American Women's Activism*, edited by Kimberly Springer, 219–240. New York: New York University Press.

Smith, Michael A. 2003. *Bringing Representation Home: State Legislators among Their Constituencies.* Columbia: University of Missouri Press.

Smith, Robert. 1996. *We Have No Leaders: African Americans in the Post-Civil Rights Era.* Albany: State University of New York Press.

Smooth, Wendy G. 2001. *African American Women State Legislators: The Impact of Gender and Race on Legislative Influence*. PhD dissertation, University of Maryland College Park.

———. 2006. "Intersectionality in Electoral Politics: A Mess Worth Making." *Politics and Gender* 2(3): 400–414.

———. 2008. "Gender, Race, and the Exercise of Power and Influence." *Legislative Women: Getting Elected, Getting Ahead*, edited by Beth Reingold, 175–196. Boulder, CO: Lynne Rienner.

———. 2010. "African American Women and Electoral Politics: A Challenge to the Post-Race Rhetoric of the Obama Moment." In *Gender and Elections: Shaping the Future of American Politics*, 2nd ed., edited by Susan J. Carroll and Richard L. Fox, 165–186. New York: Cambridge University Press.

Sonenshein, Raphael J. 1993. *Politics in Black and White: Race and Power in Los Angeles*. Princeton, NJ: Princeton University Press.

Soss, Joe, Richard C. Fording, and Sanford F. Schram. 2008. "The Color of Devolution: Race, Federalism, and the Politics of Social Control." *American Journal of Political Science* 52(3): 536–553.

Sourcebook of Criminal Justice Statistics. 2011. "Table 6.1.2011. Adults on Probation, in Jail or Prison, and on Parole, United States 1980–2011." *Persons under Correctional Supervision, National Estimates*, June 1. University at Albany, Hindelang Criminal Justice Research Center. www.albany.edu/sourcebook/pdf/t612011.pdf (Accessed July 6, 2016).

Springer, Kimberly, ed. 1999. *Still Lifting, Still Climbing: Contemporary African American Women's Activism*. New York: New York University Press.

Stewart, Joseph, Jr., Robert E. England, and Kenneth J. Meier. 1989. "Black Representation in Urban School Districts: From School Board to Office to Classroom." *The Western Political Quarterly* 42(2): 287–305.

Stofferahn, Curtis W. 2009. "Cooperative Community Development: A Comparative Case Study of Locality-Based Impacts of new Generation Cooperatives." *Community Development* 40(2): 177–198.

Stokes-Brown, Atiya Kai. 2012. *The Politics of Race in Latino Communities: Walking the Colorline*. New York: Routledge.

Sue, Stanley, and Sumie Okazaki. 1990. "Asian-American Educational Achievements: A Phenomenon in Search of an Explanation." *American Psychologist* 45(8): 913–920.

Sullivan, Patricia. 2010. *Lift Every Voice: The NAACP and the Making of the Civil Rights Movement*. New York: The New Press.

Svara, James H. 2003. "Two Decades of Continuity and Change in American City Councils." Unpublished report. Washington, DC: National League of Cities. www.skidmore.edu/~bturner/Svara%20citycouncilrpt.pdf (Accessed July 6, 2016).

Takash, Paule Cruz. 1993. "Breaking Barriers to Representation: Chicana/Latina Elected Officials in California." *Urban Anthropology and Studies of Cultural Systems and World Development* 22(3/4): 325–360.

Tarr-Whelan, Linda. 2009. *Women Lead the Way: Your Guide to Stepping Up to Leadership and Changing the World*. San Francisco: Berrett-Koehler.

Tate, Katherine. 2003. *Black Faces in the Mirror: African Americans and Their Representation in Congress*. Princeton, NJ: Princeton University Press.

　2004. "Political Incorporation and Critical Transformations of Black Public Opinion." *Du Bois Review* 1(02): 345–359.

Tate, Katherine, and Sarah Harsh. 2005. "'A Portrait of the People': Descriptive Representation and Its Impact on U.S. House Members' Ratings." In *Diversity in Democracy: Minority Representation in the United States*, edited by Gary M. Segura and Shaun Bowler, 216–231. Charlottesville: University of Virginia Press.

Taylor, Paul. 2012. "The Growing Electoral Clout of Blacks Is Driven by Turnout, Not Demographics." *Pew Research Center*, December 26. http://pewrsr.ch/RikdPs (Accessed July 6, 2016).

Taylor, Paul., and D'Vera Cohn. 2012. "A Milestone En Route to a Majority Minority Nation." *Pew Research Center Social and Demographic Trends*, November 7. http://pewrsr.ch/UkWWOA (Accessed July 6, 2016).

Teixeira, Ruy, and John Halpin. 2012. "The Obama Coalition in the 2012 Election and Beyond." Report. Washington, DC: Center for American Progress, December.

Telles, Edward, Mark Sawyer, and Gaspar Rivera-Salgado. 2011. *Just Neighbors? Research on African American and Latino Relations in the United States*. New York: Russell Sage Foundation.

Terchek, Ronald J. 1980. "Political Participation and Political Structures: The Voting Rights Act of 1965." *Phylon* 41(1): 25–35.

Tharps, Lori L. 2014. "The Case for Black with a Capital B." *New York Times*, November 18. www.nytimes.com/2014/11/19/opinion/the-case-for-black-with-a-capital-b.html (Accessed July 6, 2016).

Thomas, Sue. 1991. "The Impact of Women on State Legislative Policies." *Journal of Politics* 53(4): 958–976.

　1992. "The Effects of Race and Gender on Constituency Service." *Western Political Quarterly* 45(1): 169–180.

　1994. *How Women Legislate*. New York: Oxford University Press.

　1998. "Introduction." In *Women and Elective Office: Past, Present, and Future*, 1st ed., edited by Sue Thomas and Clyde Wilcox, 1–14. New York: Oxford University Press.

　2003. "The Impact of Women in Political Leadership Positions." In *Women and American Politics: New Questions, New Directions*, edited by Susan J. Carroll, 89–110. New York: Oxford University Press.

　2005. "Introduction." In *Women and Elective Office: Past, Present, and Future*, 2nd ed., edited by Sue Thomas and Clyde Wilcox, 3–25. New York: Oxford University Press.

　2014. "Introduction." In *Women and Elective Office: Past, Present, and Future*, 3rd ed., edited by Sue Thomas and Clyde Wilcox, 1–26. New York: Oxford University Press.

Thomas, Sue, and Susan Welch. 2001. "The Impact of Women in State Legislatures: Numerical and Organizational Strength." In *The Impact of Women in Public Office*, edited by Susan J. Carroll, 166–184. Bloomington: Indiana University Press.

Tichenor, Daniel J. 2002. *Dividing Lines: The Politics of Immigration Control in America*. Princeton, NJ: Princeton University Press.

Tirado, Miguel David. 1970. "Mexican American Community Political Organization: The Key to Chicano Political Power." *Aztlán* 1(1): 53–78.

Tolleson–Rinehart, Sue. 1991. "Do Women Leaders make a Difference? Substance, Style and Perceptions." In *Gender and Policymaking*, edited by Debra L. Dodson, 93–102. Report. New Brunswick, NJ: Center for the American Woman and Politics, Rutgers University.

2001. "Do Women Leaders Make a Difference? Substance, Style and Perceptions." In *The Impact of Women in Public Office*, edited by Susan J. Carroll, 149–165. Bloomington: Indiana University Press.

Torres, María de los Angeles. 2003. *The Lost Apple: Operation Pedro Pan, Cuban Children in the US, and the Promise of a Better Future*. Boston: Beacon Press.

Trounstine, Jessica. 2009. "All Politics Is Local: The Reemergence of the Study of City Politics." *Perspectives on Politics* 7(3): 611–618.

Trounstine, Jessica, and Melody E. Valdini. 2008. "The Context Matters: The Effects of Single-Member versus At-Large Districts on City Council Diversity." *American Journal of Political Science* 52(3): 554–569.

Tucker, M. Belinda, and Claudia Mitchell-Kernan, eds. 1995. *The Decline in Marriage Among African Americans: Causes, Consequences, and Policy Implications*. New York: Russell Sage Foundation.

US Census Bureau. 1995. "1992 Census of Governments, Vol. 1: Government Organization, Number 2: Popularly Elected Officials." Report GC92(1)-2. www.census.gov/prod/2/gov/gc/gc92_1_2.pdf (Accessed July 6, 2016).

2011. "2010 Census Shows America's Diversity." www.census.gov/newsroom/releases/archives/2010_census/cb11-cn125.html. Last modified September 9, 2014. (Accessed July 6, 2016).

2012. "Table 421. Hispanic Public Elected Officials, by Office, and State." *Statistical Abstract of the United States*. Washington, DC: United States Census Bureau.

US Senate. 2015. "About the Senate Committee System." www.senate.gov/general/common/generic/about_committees.htm (Accessed July 6, 2016).

Vagins, Deborah J., and Laughlin McDonald. 2013. "Supreme Court Put a Dagger in the Heart of the Voting Rights Act." *ACLU Blog*, July 2. www.aclu.org/blog/supreme-court-put-dagger-heart-voting-rights-act (Accessed July 6, 2016).

Vengroff, Richard, Zsolt Nyiri, and Melissa Fugiero. 2003. "Electoral System and Gender Representation in Sub-National Legislatures: Is There a National–Sub-National Gender Gap?" *Political Research Quarterly* 56(2): 163–173.

Vesterby, Marlow, and Ralph E. Heimlich. 1991. "Land Use and Demographic Change: Results from Fast-Growth Counties." *Land Economics* 67(3): 279–291.

Vigil, Maurilio E. 1987. *Hispanics in American Politics: The Search for Political Power*. Lanham, MD: University Press of America.

Volden, Craig, Alan E. Wiseman, and Dana E. Wittmer. 2013. "When Are Women More Effective Lawmakers Than Men?" *American Journal of Political Science* 57(2): 326–341.

Wahlke, John C. 1971. "Policy Demands and System Support: The Role of the Represented." *British Journal of Political Science* 1(3): 271–290.

Wahlke, John C., Heinz Eulau, William Buchanan, and Leroy C. Ferguson. 1962. *The Legislative System*. New York: John Wiley & Sons.

Walker, Alice. 1983. *In Search of Our Mothers' Gardens: Womanist Prose*. San Diego: Harcourt Brace Jovanovich.

Walker, Samuel, Cassia Spohn, and Miriam DeLone. 2012. "The Color of Death: Race and the Death Penalty." In *The Color of Justice: Race, Ethnicity, and Crime in America*, 5th ed., 345–402. Belmont, CA: Wadsworth, Cengage Learning.

Walker-Moffat, Wendy. 1995. *The Other Side of the Asian American Success Story*, 1st ed. San Francisco: Jossey-Bass.

Walters, Ronald, and Robert Smith. 2007. "Black Leadership: Toward a Twenty-First Century Perspective." In *Perspectives in Black Politics and Black Leadership*, edited by John Davis, 61–69. Lanham, MD: University Press of America.

Walton, Hanes Jr., Sherman C. Puckett, and Donald R. Deskins. 2012. *The African American Electorate: A Statistical History*. Thousand Oaks, CA: CQ Press.

Wang, Tova Andrea. 2012. *The Politics of Voter Suppression: Defending and Expanding Americans' Right to Vote*. A Century Foundation Book. Ithaca: Cornell University Press.

Wasem, Ruth Ellen. 2012. *U.S. Immigration Policy on Permanent Admissions*. CRS Report for Congress, RL32235, March 13. Washington, DC: Congressional Research Service.

Wei, William. 1993. *The Asian American Movement*. Philadelphia: Temple University Press.

Weisman, Jonathan, and Jennifer Steinhauer. 2013. Senate Women Lead in Effort to Find Accord. *New York Times*. October 15, A1.

Welch, Susan. 2008. "Commentary on 'Recruitment of Women to Public Office: A Discriminant Analysis,' 1978. *Political Research Quarterly* 61(1): 29–31.

Welch, Susan, and Albert Karnig. 1978. "Representation of Blacks on Big City School Boards." *Social Science Quarterly* 59 (1): 162–172.

Welch, Susan, and Lee Sigelman. 1982. "Changes in Public Attitudes toward Women in Politics." *Social Science Quarterly* 63(2): 312–322.

Western, Bruce, Vincent Schiraldi, and Jason Ziedenberg. 2003. "Education and Incarceration." Policy Report. Washington, DC: Justice Policy Institute. www.justicepolicy.org/images/upload/03-08_REP_EducationIncarceration_AC-BB.pdf (Accessed July 6, 2016).

Whicker, Marcia Lynn, and Malcolm Jewell. 1998. "The Feminization of Leadership in State Legislatures." In *Women and Elective Office: Past, Present, and Future*, edited by Sue Thomas and Clyde Wilcox, 163–174. 1st ed. New York: Oxford University Press.

Whitby, Kenny J. 1997. *The Color of Representation: Congressional Behavior and Black Interests*. Ann Arbor: University of Michigan Press.

2007. "Dimension of Representation and the Congressional Black Caucus." In *African American Perspectives on Political Science*, edited by Wilbur C. Rich, 195–211. Philadelphia: Temple University Press.

Who Leads US? 2014. "Overview, Top Lines and Methodology." Washington, DC: New Organizing Institute and Women's Donor Network.

http://wholeads.us/wp-content/uploads/2015/01/NOI-WDN-Two-Pager-FINAL.pdf (Accessed April 10, 2014).

Wilkins, David E., and Heidi Kiiwetinepinesiik Stark. 2011. *American Indian Politics and the American Political System*, 3rd ed. Lanham, MD: Rowman and Littlefield.

Williams, Linda Faye. 2001. "The Civil Rights–Black Power Legacy: Black Women Elected Officials at the Local, State, and National Levels." In *Sisters in the Struggle: African–American Women in the Civil Rights–Black Power Movement*, edited by Bettye Collier-Thomas and V. P. Franklin, 306–331. New York: New York University Press.

2003. *The Constraint of Race: Legacies of White Skin Privilege in America*. University Park: Pennsylvania State University Press.

Williams, Margaret S. 2008. "Ambition, Gender, and the Judiciary." *Political Research Quarterly* 61(1): 68–78.

Williams, Melissa S. 1998. *Voice, Trust, and Memory: Marginalized Groups and the Failings of Liberal Representation*. Princeton, NJ: Princeton University Press.

Wilson, Carter. 2015. *Metaracism: Explaining the Persistence of Racial Inequality*. Boulder, CO: Lynne Reinner.

Wilson, Marie C. 2004. *Closing the Leadership Gap: Why Women Can and Must Help Run the World*. New York: Viking.

2007. *Closing the Leadership Gap: Add Women, Change Everything*. Rev. ed. New York: Penguin.

Winders, Jamie. 2005. "Changing Politics of Race and Region: Latino Migration to the US South." *Progress in Human Geography* 29(6): 683–699.

Wirt, Frederick. 2008. *Politics of Southern Equality: Law and Social Change in a Mississippi County*. Piscataway, NJ: Aldine Transaction.

Wolfers, Justin, David Leonhardt, and Kevin Quealy. 2015. "1.5 Million Missing Black Men." *New York Times*, April 20. http://nyti.ms/1P5Gpa7 (Accessed July 6, 2016).

Wolfley, Jeanette. 1991. "Jim Crow, Indian Style: The Disenfranchisement of Native Americans." *American Indian Law Review* 16(1): 167–202.

Wong, Cara J. 2010. *Boundaries of Obligation in American Politics: Geographic, National, and Racial Communities*. New York: Cambridge University Press.

Wong, Carolyn. 2006. *Lobbying for Inclusion: Rights Politics and the Making of Immigration Policy*. Stanford, CA: Stanford University Press.

Wong, Janelle, S. Karthick Ramakrishnan, Taeku Lee, and Jane Junn. 2011. *Asian American Political Participation: Emerging Constituents and Their Political Identities*. New York: Russell Sage Foundation.

Woodhall, Maureen. 1987. "Human Capital Concepts." In *Economics of Education Research and Studies*, edited by George Psacharopoulos, 21–24. Oxford: Pergamon.

Wright, Gerald C. 2008. "Charles Adrian and the Study of Nonpartisan Elections." *Political Research Quarterly* 61(1): 13–16.

Young, Iris Marion. 1990. *Justice and the Politics of Difference*, 1st ed. Princeton, NJ: Princeton University Press.

2000. *Inclusion and Democracy*. Oxford Political Theory, Series editors: Will Kymlicka, David Miller, and Alan Ryan. New York: Oxford University Press.

Zerilli, Linda. 2008. "Feminist Theory and the Canon of Political Thought." *In The Oxford Handbook of Political Theory*, edited by John S. Dryzek, Bonnie Honig, and Anne Phillips, 106–124. New York: Oxford University Press.

Zhang, Stacey Wenjun. 2009. "Organization Prepares Veterans to Run for Office." News article. *The Daily Princetonian*, September 17.

Zimmerman, Jonathan. 2012. "Asian-Americans, the New Jews on Campus." *The Chronicle of Higher Education*, April 29. http://chronicle.com/article/Asian-Americans-the-New-Jews/131729/ (Accessed July 6, 2016).

Index

In this index, "officials" are considered to be elected officials. First-time candidates are indicated as such under specific groups of officials. The main demographic groups – American Indians, Asian Americans, Blacks, Latinos/as, and Whites – are divided into sections corresponding to officials (men and women) and to general populations of men and women. There are also sections dedicated to men of color and women of color, both as officials and as general populations.

"Latinos/as" is used when Hispanic/Latino men and women are combined in discussions of specific topics. This corresponds to a generic classification "Latino" in the text. Otherwise, specific gender is indicated by "Latinos," "Latina" or "Latinas," "Latino officials," and "Latina officials." There is a separate heading for Hispanics. Although African American is often used interchangeably with Black, for the sake of consistency, we use Black (rather than black or African American).

Figures, tables, boxes, and maps are indicated in *italics* by *f*, *t*, *b*, and *m*, respectively.

Index